AQA Physical Education

A2

Exclusively endorsed by AQA

ACC. No: GCS O19332

GOWER COLLEGE SWANSEA
LEARNING RESOURCE CENTRE

CLASS No: 796·07 BEV

GOWER COLLEGE SWANSEA
LEARNING RESOURCE CENTRE
GORSEINON
SWANSEA SA4 6RD

Paul Bevis
Mike Murray

 Nelson Thornes

Gower College Swansea
Library
Coleg Gŵyr Abertawe
Llyrfgell

Text © Paul Bevis and Mike Murray 2009
Original illustrations © Nelson Thornes Ltd 2009

The right of Paul Bevis and Mike Murray to be identified as authors of this work has
been asserted by them in accordance with the Copyright, Designs and Patents Act
1988.

All rights reserved. No part of this publication may be reproduced or transmitted in
any form or by any means, electronic or mechanical, including photocopy, recording
or any information storage and retrieval system, without permission in writing from the
publisher or under licence from the Copyright Licensing Agency Limited, of Saffron
House, 6–10 Kirby Street, London, EC1N 8TS.

Any person who commits any unauthorised act in relation to this publication may be
liable to criminal prosecution and civil claims for damages.

Published in 2009 by:
Nelson Thornes Ltd
Delta Place
27 Bath Road
CHELTENHAM
GL53 7TH
United Kingdom

12 13 / 10 9 8 7 6 5 4

A catalogue record for this book is available from the British Library

ISBN 978 1 4085 0016 3

Cover photograph by Photolibrary
Illustrations by Peters and Zabransky UK Ltd and Fakenham Photosetting Ltd
Page make-up by Fakenham Photosetting Ltd
Printed and bound in China by 1010 Printing International Ltd

Acknowledgements
The authors and publishers wish to thank the following for permission to use copyright material:

p47 www.mountainz.co.nz; p49 United States Tennis Association, www.playerdevelopment.usta.com; p51(l) Corbis/Chris Rogers,(r)
Science Photo Library/Scott Camazine, Chilibeck, P D et al., Effect of in-season creatine supplementation on body composition
and performance in rugby union football players. Journal of Applied Physiology, Nutrition, and Metabolism, 2007 and W.D. Katch &
F. I. McArdle, Exercise Physiology; Energy Nutrition and Human Performance, Lippincott Williams & Wilkins 1996; p57 Science Photo
Library/P Marazzi; p59 Reuters/Denis Balibouse; p66 Getty/Stu Forster; p69 Getty/Tom Dulat; p75 www.lactae.com; p76 British
Rowing Association; p77 Getty/Evelyn Steinweg; p80 Getty/AFP/Indranil Mukherjee; p81 Action Plus; p86 Getty/Norbert Schmidt; p89
www.kriokomory.pl; p91 Alamy/IML Image Group Ltd; p93 Hypoxico Inc; p104 Corbis/Xinhua Press/Li Ga; p106 Reuters/Phil Noble;
p107 Action Plus; p109 Getty/AFP/William West; p114 Corbis/Xinhua Press/Cheng Min; p116 Corbis/Xinhua Press; p131 Corbis/
Nice One Productions; p137 Corbis/Andrew Gombert; p139 Getty/ Adam Pretty; p142, T. Orlick, Psyching for Sport: Mental training
for Athletes, Leisure Press 1986, reprinted by kind permission of Terry Orlick www.zoneofexcellence.ca; p143 C. D. Spielberger,
Theory and research in anxiety. In Charles D. Spielberger (Ed.), Anxiety and behaviour. New York: Academic Press 1966; p175 M. Lee,
Coaching Children in Sport: Principles & Practice, published by Routledge, 1993, p156 PA/Nick Potts; p157 Getty/ Stu Forster; p163
Corbis/Reuters/Ian Hodgson; p165 Getty/ Al Bello; p166(tl) Action Images/Carl Recine,(r) Corbis/Ben Radford; p170 Reuters/Djordje
Kojadinovic; p171(bl) Corbis/Nic Bothma,(br) Corbis/Kim Ludbrook; p187 Alamy/Richard Wareham Fotografie; p188 Getty/Mike
Finn-Kelcey; p191 (m) Getty/Jack Atley,(r) Getty/Sandra Behne; p192, A. V. Carron et al., The measurement of cohesiveness in sport
groups. in J.L. Duda (ed.), Advances in Sport and Exercise Psychology Measurement, Fitness Information Technology 1998; p193
Getty/Ross Kinnaird; p193 Sven-Goran Eriksson, Inside Football, Carlton Books Ltd, reprinted with permission; p195 Reuters; p196
Getty/Cameron Spencer; p198 Corbis/Christian Liewig; p211 Getty/Vladimir Rys; p212 Action Images/Paul Harding; p213 Getty/Alex
Livesey; p215 Corbis/Richard Baker; p216 Getty/Ian Walton; p217 Getty/Michael Steele; p221 Reuters/Glyn Kirk; p222 Corbis/Xinhua
Press/Liu Dawei ; p225 Alamy/Polka Dot; p227, Department of Culture, Media and Sport (DCMS), Game Plan: A Strategy for Delivering
Government's Sport and Physical Activity Objectives, 2002. Reprinted under Crown Copyright PSI License C2008000256; p229 I.
Balyi quote, www.cwsportspartnership.org; p230 I. Stafford, Coaching for Long-term Athlete Development: Improving Participation
& Performance in Sport, Coachwise Business Solutions on behalf of Sports Coach UK, 2005; p242 Mary Evans/ Illustrated London
News Ltd; p244(t) Bridgeman Art Library/Illustrated London News Ltd, (b)Topfoto/Fotomas; p245 Getty/Bob Thomas; p247 Getty/
Hulton Archive; p249 Getty/Jamie McDonald; p251 Getty/Popperfoto; p254 Action Images/Jason O'Brien, p254, The distribution
of behaviour diagram from Sport in Society by Jay Coakley, McGraw Hill, 2006; p258 (tl) PA Photos, (bl) Corbis/Ben Radford; p260
Reuters/Mykhaylo Markiv; p262 Getty/Phil Cole; p264 Reuters/Denis Balibouse; p265 Corbis/Dominic Favre; p268 Reuters/Regis
Duvignau; p270 Getty/Shaun Botterill; p273 Corbis/Aidan Crawley; p274 Getty/David Cannon; p277 (t) Bskyb; p278 PA Photos/Adam
Davy; p282 Getty/Clive Mason; p288 John Walmsley; p289(t) Alamy/Darek Miszkiel, (br) John Walmsley.

Every effort has been made to contact the copyright holders and we apologise if any have been overlooked. Should copyright have
been unwittingly infringed in this book, the owners should contact the publishers, who will make the corrections at reprint.

Contents

AQA introduction

Nelson Thornes has worked in partnership with AQA to ensure this book and the accompanying online resources offer you the best support for your A Level course.

All resources have been approved by senior AQA examiners so you can feel assured that they closely match the specification for this subject and provide you with everything you need to prepare successfully for your exams.

These print and online resources together **unlock blended learning**; this means that the links between the activities in the book and the activities online blend together to maximise your understanding of a topic and help you achieve your potential.

These online resources are available on **kerboodle!** which can be accessed via the internet at **www.kerboodle.com/live**, anytime, anywhere. If your school or college subscribes to this service you will be provided with your own personal login details. Once logged in, access your course and locate the required activity.

For more information and help visit **www.kerboodle.com**

Icons in this book indicate where there is material online related to that topic. The following icons are used:

💡 Learning activity

These resources include a variety of interactive and non-interactive activities to support your learning:

- animations
- presentations
- simple interactive activities
- simulations.

✔ Progress tracking

These resources include a variety of tests that you can use to check your knowledge on particular topics (Test yourself) and a range of resources that enable you to analyse and understand examination questions (On your marks…).

🔍 Research support

These resources include WebQuests, in which you are assigned a task and provided with a range of web links to use as source material for research. These are designed as extension resources to stretch you and broaden your learning, in order for you to attain the highest possible marks in your exams.

How to use this book

This book covers the specification for your course and is arranged in a sequence approved by AQA.

The book is divided up into sections which cover the entirety of Unit 3 of your specification (Chapters 1–19) and Chapter 20, which covers what is required for your practical coursework.

The features in this book include:

In this chapter you will

At the beginning of each section you will find a list of learning objectives that contain targets linked to the requirements of the specification. The relevant specification reference is also provided.

■ Key terms

Terms that you will need to be able to define and understand.

■ Activities

Suggestions for practical activities that you can carry out.

■ Links

Highlighting any areas where topics relate to one another.

AQA Examiner's tip

Hints from AQA examiners to help you with your studies and to prepare you for your exam.

AQA Examination-style questions

Questions in the style that you can expect in your exam. These occur at the end of each unit to give practice in examination-style questions for a particular section.

AQA examination questions are reproduced by permission of the Assessment and Qualifications Alliance.

You should now be able to:

A bulleted list of learning outcomes at the end of each chapter, summarising core points of knowledge.

■ Web links for this book

Because Nelson Thornes is not responsible for third party content online, there may be some changes to this material that are beyond our control. In order for us to ensure that the links referred to are as up-to-date and stable as possible, the websites provided are usually homepages with supporting instructions on how to reach the relevant pages if necessary.

Please let us know at **kerboodle@nelsonthornes.com** if you find a link that doesn't work and we will do our best to redirect the link, or to find an alternative site.

Introduction to this book

In much the same way as in our corresponding AS Level student book, this A2 book is divided into four sections and mirrors both the order and the content of the AQA specification. Section 3.1 is concerned with exercise physiology, and is concerned with several difficult topics about energy systems, muscle function and control, elite-training supplements, methods and rehabilitation, and biomechanics. Section 3.2 is about the psychological aspects of elite performance and involves the study of arousal, anxiety, aggression and confidence, which affect how individuals behave. In this section, we shall also look at the effects of others on performance and at groups and leadership. Section 3.3 studies some contemporary issues in the world of sport, such as the impact of elite sports championships, the production of elite sports performers, the development of Olympism, and the positive and negative effects of commercialisation on sport. Sixty per cent of the A2 course is examined in a single PHED3 examination. This leaves the remaining 40 per cent for the PHED4 coursework. But it should be noted early in the course that there is also a large theoretical component in the PHED4 coursework.

Unit 4 of the specification involves the coursework, and this too is divided into three sections. Section A involves the assessment of your ability to perform a single role in a competitive situation. This section is worth half of the coursework marks. Section B asks you to analyse your own performance (or that of another performer if you choose the coaching option) to identify weaknesses as compared to an elite performer. Section C then asks you to suggest theoretical reasons for the weaknesses that you identified and appropriate corrective practices to improve those weaknesses. Sections B and C can be produced in a written form and/or may involve an oral presentation.

There is no doubt that the A2 theoretical content is conceptually more difficult to understand than the materials found in the AS Level course, and the examination questions tend to be in a more difficult format. The coursework is also more complex, although it only involves a single role, rather than two. However, you are a year older, a year wiser and a year more mature, so don't become disheartened before you start, but be prepared to work!

UNIT 3.1

Applied physiology to optimise performance

Introduction

When studying physiology at AS Level you looked at health, fitness and diet; the oxygen delivery system of the heart, blood and lungs; and the way that the body moves in certain actions. The physiology that you need to study for A2 is more concerned with how your body uses its food and oxygen to supply energy to its contracting muscles when you are exercising. It is also concerned with how your body generates and uses forces when you are performing, and the preparation that an elite performer may need to undertake in order to optimise their performance.

In order to give you a better understanding of how the body moves, Chapter 1 outlines how you use various sources of chemicals, coming originally from the food that you eat, to generate the energy you need using oxygen (aerobically). This chapter also looks at how your need for oxygen becomes a limiting factor in producing energy and how there is a need for extra oxygen even after you have finished exercising. Chapter 2 investigates how, when there is a demand, you are able to produce energy anaerobically (however, these systems are restrictive in terms of what the body can achieve because there are limits on how long you can exercise with a lack of oxygen as well as on your body's ability to deal with the by-products of the chemical reactions).

In Chapter 3 you will study the structure of muscle and how it contracts; this will enable you to gain a better understanding of how you control movement. Chapter 4 shows you how many different supplements have been used to try and improve an elite athlete's performance, while from Chapter 5 you will develop a clearer understanding of some of the methods that elite performers use for their training in order to optimise performance. In Chapter 6 you look at the downside of training, the potential for injury that every elite performer must face up to, but you also study the more recently developed methods used to speed up recovery.

Finally, in Chapters 7 and 8, you will gain a clearer understanding of how the body moves and uses its muscles to generate forces, enabling a performer to run, jump or throw.

1 Aerobic energy systems

Key terms

Adenosine triphosphate (ATP): our energy currency, found in all cells; when broken down it releases its stored energy.

Resynthesise: to rebuild/remake/make again.

In order that we can move, our muscles need to contract; and, in order to contract, our muscles need a supply of energy. The energy we need for muscle contractions is supplied to us in the form of food, which is broken down within cells to release energy that is used to form chemicals. These chemicals can then be broken down to release the energy stored within them; therefore, we tend to talk about the body using chemical energy. Muscles use the chemical energy stored in specific compounds to move. The body then converts the energy found into a form that it can handle. You eat food for energy. The body is not particular what food you eat: it is able to convert the majority of it into a form that can be used to make energy. The body is, however, fairly picky about what it will and won't use as a chemical from which it can manufacture energy, and it is very exact about the chemical that it produces as its energy supply.

Adenosine triphosphate (ATP)

The immediately (directly) usable form of chemical energy for muscular activity is a compound called **adenosine triphosphate (ATP)**.

ATP = Adenosine — Energy — P_i — Energy — P_i — Energy — P_i

a

Adenosine — P_i - P_i - P_i $\xrightarrow{\text{ATPase}}$ Adenosine — P_i - P_i + P_i + Energy

b (ATP) (ADP)

Fig. 1.1 *Structure of adenosine triphosphate*

It is the body's job to transfer the chemical energy stored in the food we eat into the usable energy found in ATP. Energy is released when ATP is broken down, and energy is required to **resynthesise** it.

The breakdown of ATP releases adenosine diphosphate (ADP) and phosphate (P).

Fig. 1.2 *The breakdown of ATP*

The body then rebuilds (resynthesises) ATP from the breakdown products:

ADP + P + energy = ATP

Whenever we use ATP to supply the energy we need, we have to make that molecule of ATP immediately. We do not have a store of ATP.

Hence, when a muscle fibre needs ATP to supply the energy for the fibre to contract, that ATP has to be produced or resynthesised right away.

We are able to resynthesise ATP from three different types of chemical reactions that take place within muscle cells. Two depend on the food we eat, whilst the third relies on a chemical called phosphocreatine, which is found in muscles.

Most of the time, we tend to be resting, sleeping or performing everyday tasks like sitting and standing. The energy that we need to perform these tasks and keep us alive involves chemical reactions that use oxygen. Using oxygen in order to produce the ATP that we need is said to involve **aerobic** processes. Just occasionally, we need to supply our muscles with energy much more rapidly than normal. Under these circumstances, we are able to do so without the need for oxygen.

Energy sources

We obtain our energy from the food we eat. Remember from AS Level that there are six classes of food, three of which can be used as energy sources: namely, carbohydrates, fats and proteins. Whatever form these foods take in our diet, following digestion carbohydrates become **glucose**; fats are broken down into fatty acids and glycerol; and proteins are digested into amino acids. These **energy sources** then enter the blood system and become available for the body.

All the carbohydrate we eat eventually becomes glucose that dissolves in the blood plasma and circulates around the body in the blood system. This glucose may be used by all cells and tissues, including working muscles, as an energy source for the resynthesis of ATP. Any excess glucose that enters the blood following digestion of a meal may be stored in muscles and the liver as **glycogen**. Glycogen may also be used as a source of ATP by muscles, as it is easily and quickly broken down into glucose. When our muscle and liver glycogen stores are full, any excess glucose from digestion is converted into fat droplets and stored in **adipose tissue**. Adipose tissue is found surrounding various organs, but much of it lies just under the skin.

The glycerol and fatty acids (called free fatty acids when present in the blood) that are formed during the digestion of fat, may be used directly from the blood, but most are converted back into fats and stored as **triglycerides** in adipose tissue. Glycerol may be converted into glucose, which is what happens when the diet is lacking in carbohydrate, or when glycogen stores have been depleted as may happen during long-duration exercise that demands continuous energy supplies (e.g. during a marathon).

Amino acids, the breakdown products of protein digestion, are usually used by the body for growth and repair; but, unlike carbohydrates and fats, excess amino acids cannot be stored. Instead they are broken down by the liver, and the nitrogen-containing part of the molecule is excreted as urea. When we exercise, the part of the amino acid left after the urea has been removed may be converted into glucose or used in some stage of the energy production system. Up to 10 per cent of our energy demands may be met through protein breakdown.

To a certain extent, the food sources that we take in as part of our diet are interconvertible, in that the various energy sources may be changed from one form to another. These interconversions are mainly a function of the

Link

For more information on phosphocreatine, see Chapter 2 – Anaerobic energy systems (page 16).

Key terms

Aerobic: with oxygen.

Glucose: the main form of carbohydrate found in the body; dissolves in blood plasma; used as an energy source.

Energy sources: the substrates (starting chemicals) used to provide the ATP that is used for muscle contractions.

Glycogen: a stored form of carbohydrate found in muscle and liver; used as an energy source.

Adipose tissue: special tissue made up of cells in which fats are stored; mainly found under the skin and surrounding major organs.

Triglycerides: main form of stored fat; used as an energy source.

Link

For more information on energy production in the absence of oxygen, see Chapter 2 – Anaerobic energy systems (page 15).

AQA Examiner's tip

Be aware that examination questions may ask about energy systems or energy sources – these terms are different and should not be confused.

Link

For more information on energy supplies during a marathon, see Chapter 5 – Specialised training (page 67).

liver. In practice, some conversions are easier than others. Thus the liver readily converts excess glucose into fat, but less readily into glycogen. With the reverse reactions, the conversion of glycogen into glucose is easily done in the liver but less readily accomplished in muscles, whilst very little glucose can be produced from fat.

When we are resting, approximately a half to two-thirds of our energy comes from fats, whilst the remainder comes from carbohydrate. This ratio alters when we exercise, but the exact proportions depend on many factors such as the type of exercise, the type of diet the performer has had, the performer's level of fitness and the type of muscle fibres involved in the exercise. It is therefore difficult to say with any conviction how much fat a performer is using in any particular exercise.

Aerobic energy from glucose

Muscles are able to use their stored glycogen or glucose available from blood as an immediate source of energy during exercise. During exercise, the complete breakdown of glycogen and glucose to provide energy for ATP resynthesis is possible, provided that the supply of oxygen to the muscles can be maintained. The breakdown of glycogen and glucose using oxygen is therefore said to be an aerobic process.

Exercising muscles can obtain carbohydrate from glycogen stored in the liver and in the muscles themselves, from glucose circulating in the blood and from fat that is either circulating in the blood or is stored in adipose tissue. The brain, however, is only able to use blood glucose for energy, and so levels of glucose in the blood must be maintained; otherwise the brain would shut down (you faint!) owing to lack of glucose for its energy needs. This is what most of the glycogen stored in the liver is used for, an emergency supply for the brain. The use of protein as an energy source is fairly complex but also happens to be small enough to be negligible and will not be considered further.

Using muscle glycogen as an energy source presents a problem for the body in that such stores are limited, and muscle fatigue occurs rapidly when glycogen stores become depleted. We have a limited supply of muscle glycogen, and any exercise lasting longer than two hours will tend to fully deplete these stores. This is why the use of fat as an energy source is so important during such exercise as a marathon run.

During recovery from exercise, there is an initial rapid replacement of used glycogen, but complete recovery, in terms of building glycogen stores back up to normal levels, may take more than 24 hours. So the longer an exercise lasts (i.e. the more endurance based it is), the more we tend to use fats as an energy source.

Fat may only be used as an energy source if oxygen is present. In other words, fat breakdown is an aerobic process. The use of fat as an energy source therefore depends on the supply of oxygen to the muscles. In slow-twitch muscle fibres especially, fat is the main energy source during most activities that last longer than an hour. Because training increases the body's capacity to supply oxygen to the working muscles, it also increases the muscle fibres' ability to use fats as an energy source.

Very little fat is stored in muscles, and therefore the glycerol and fatty acids needed as energy sources must be supplied by the blood. Glycerol released from fat stores may enter the energy pathways (see later) or be converted into glucose for use in the normal way. Adipose tissue releases free fatty acids, which are transported around the blood, bound to proteins.

■ Link

For more information on slow-twitch muscle fibres, see Chapter 3 – Muscles (page 36).

Activities

1 Make a list of six sporting activities where you think fat might be the major energy source.

2 Produce a flow chart, poster or a presentation that shows the interconversion of glucose, glycogen, fatty acids and glycerol within the body.

In the presence of oxygen, molecules of glycogen, glucose and fats may be completely broken down. Remember from AS Level that carbohydrates and fats are made up from the elements carbon, hydrogen and oxygen. Complete breakdown of these chemicals using oxygen will produce carbon and oxygen (carbon dioxide) and hydrogen and oxygen (water), whilst at the same time releasing energy for ATP resynthesis. The majority of ATP production is confined to specialised organelles, the **mitochondria**. (These are sausage-shaped bodies, often called the 'powerhouses' of cells, because they are the site of the aerobic manufacture of ATP.) The breakdown is through a series of chemical reactions that take place within these mitochondria. As might be expected, muscle cells tend to have large numbers of mitochondria.

The aerobic production of ATP has several advantages over other systems:

- There are no fatiguing by-products.
- The starting chemicals are in abundant supply and are rarely exhausted.
- Far more ATP is produced from aerobic metabolism than can be produced from **anaerobic** metabolism.

Glucose that is derived from carbohydrates in the diet is stored in muscle (and liver) as glycogen. The glycogen is then broken down to glucose as needed. The initial stage in the breakdown of glucose or glycogen is called **glycolysis** and produces a chemical called **pyruvic acid (pyruvate)**. During this process, some ATP (four molecules of ATP for each molecule of glucose) is produced. Glycolysis takes place in the sarcoplasm (equivalent to cytoplasm) of muscle cells.

Key terms

Mitochondria: organelles (within the cell) where chemical reactions of aerobic production take place.

Anaerobic: a process that takes place without oxygen.

Glycolysis: the process of breaking down glycogen into pyruvic acid, producing some (four molecules) ATP.

Pyruvic acid/pyruvate: the end product of glycolysis.

AQA Examiner's tip

Both terms – 'pyruvic acid' and 'pyruvate' – are correct: acids dissociate to release H^+. Pyruvic acid dissociates to release H^+ and leaves pyruvate – either term is accepted by examiners. The same is true of 'lactic acid' and 'lactate'.

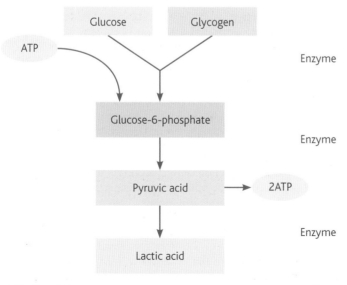

Fig. 1.3 *Glycolysis*

The pyruvic acid formed during glycolysis is added to an enzyme called coenzyme A (CoA) to become acetyl CoA to allow it to enter the next stage in aerobic breakdown, which occurs within the mitochondria and is called the **Krebs cycle**.

■ **Key terms**

Krebs cycle: a series of chemical reactions in the mitochondria that oxidises acetyl CoA to carbon dioxide and combines hydrogen with hydrogen carriers.

Electron transport chain: series of chemical reactions where hydrogen is oxidised to water and large amounts (34 molecules) of ATP are generated.

Beta-oxidation: breakdown of fats into acetyl CoA within sarcoplasm.

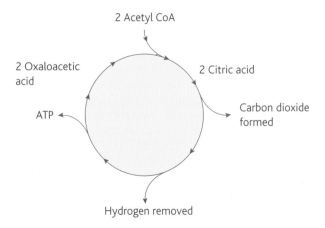

Fig. 1.4 *The Krebs cycle*

The Krebs cycle consists of a series of eight enzyme-driven reactions that oxidise acetyl CoA to carbon dioxide. The hydrogen atoms that are part of acetyl CoA are transferred to chemicals called hydrogen carriers, which eventually enter the next stage of aerobic metabolism, the **electron transport chain**. In the electron transport chain, a series of carrier molecules are involved in the oxidising of the hydrogen contained within the hydrogen carriers, producing water as a by-product and generating large quantities of ATP (34 molecules of ATP for each molecule of glucose, plus 4 from glycolysis, giving a total yield of 38 molecules of ATP).

In summary, the pyruvic acid produced from glycolysis eventually becomes converted into carbon dioxide and water, and large amounts of energy are released in the form of ATP. This process requires large amounts of oxygen for its completion.

Aerobic energy from fat

The Krebs cycle is not only the pathway for the oxidation of carbohydrate but also necessary for the complete oxidation of fats. The fatty acids formed from the breakdown of triglycerides are themselves broken down within the sarcoplasm, by a process called **beta-oxidation**, to acetyl CoA which can then enter the Krebs cycle, and eventually the electron transport chain, for ATP production.

At rest, approximately a half to two-thirds of our energy requirements comes from fat metabolism, and only a half to one-third from carbohydrates. During exercise, the reliance on fats diminishes dramatically in explosive sports, but in endurance events the mixed use of fats and carbohydrates becomes important. The 'mix' of these energy sources depends on the intensity and the duration of the exercise, the athlete's level of fitness, and the athlete's diet and nutritional status.

All the fat in our diet is primarily carried in the blood as 'free' fatty acids. The first stage of fat breakdown is the beta-oxidation of these fatty acids into acetyl CoA. This 'prepares' the fatty acid for entry into the

■ **Link**

For more information on the electron transport chain, see Chapter 2 – Anaerobic energy systems (page 17).

■ **Activity**

Produce a poster or overhead projector (OHP) or PowerPoint presentation that summarises the aerobic resynthesis of ATP from carbohydrates.

AQA **Examiner's tip**

It is important, and becomes more important later, that you are able to draw a diagram that summarises the aerobic resynthesis of ATP from glucose. In the exam, diagrams, if annotated, will be marked.

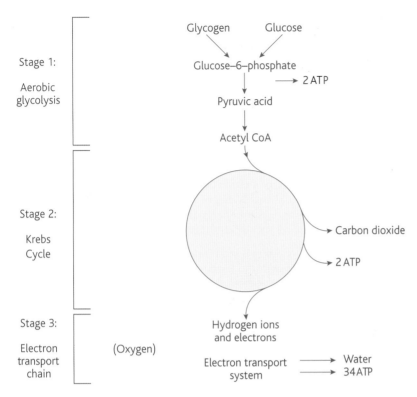

Fig. 1.5 *Summary of production of ATP by aerobic processes*

mitochondria. Once the fatty acid is in the mitochondria, the final result of fat breakdown is the same as for glycogen: water and carbon dioxide are produced and energy is liberated for the resynthesis of ATP.

The use of fats for energy is dependent on adequate supplies of oxygen – it is an aerobic process. Fats cannot be broken down without oxygen being present. The use of fats by the body thus ultimately depends on the body's ability to supply oxygen to the working muscles. If the exercise primarily involves slow, continuous activity (lasting at least an hour), fat can be the main substrate used; the majority of our energy is derived from fats.

However, fat breakdown requires more oxygen than glucose breakdown because fat has more carbon atoms in its structure, and aerobic processes convert those carbon atoms into carbon dioxide – more carbon is present in fat therefore more oxygen is needed. So, when it begins to become difficult to take in oxygen in sufficient amounts and sufficiently quickly, oxygen supply becomes a limiting factor for the Krebs cycle and the electron transfer chain. This occurs during intensive exercise, when there is not enough oxygen available to oxidise the carbon in fat and glucose becomes the preferred fuel. Exercise at close to maximum intensity therefore uses glucose as the main fuel source. Appropriate training increases the body's ability to take in oxygen to the muscles, and thus increases the ability to use fat for energy.

Fat would appear to be an ideal substrate for aerobic metabolism because it contains more carbon atoms and therefore produces more carbon dioxide and therefore more ATP. However, it should be remembered that fat is not available for exercise where oxygen supplies become limited and so cannot be used for fast, explosive exercise. Also, fat stores might have value as an energy source, but they also need to be carried around as excess non-functional weight. This extra weight means that there will be a corresponding increase in the amount of energy required for the completion of a given task. That is why extra fat is of little use to most activities: it restricts the amount of energy that can be provided for efficient movement.

Only a relatively small amount of fat is stored in muscles as triglycerides; hence it is the free fatty acids that are circulating in the blood that are the main reservoirs for fat supplies for energy in muscles. When these are being used, triglyceride stores in the adipose tissue are mobilised to release free fatty acids into the blood plasma, and these are then transported to the working muscles.

Endurance training increases the body's ability to release free fatty acids from their fat stores, and this is one of the reasons why the trained performer can use more fats for energy than the less fit. If not used, the free fatty acids can be resynthesised into fats and stored in adipose tissue.

Remember that the breakdown of fats requires the presence of carbohydrates, because, without carbohydrates, the Krebs cycle within the mitochondria will not operate. Therefore, if the demand for energy remains high during prolonged, continuous exercise, carbohydrate (glycogen) stores become depleted, and the breakdown of fats will slow because of the lack of carbohydrates. This may occur in long-duration exercise, where lack of glycogen means that the Krebs cycle slows and so does ATP resynthesis. Marathon runners describe a symptom of 'hitting the wall' when this occurs.

> ■ Activity
>
> Paula Radcliffe, who holds the world record for the fastest marathon run by a woman, hit the wall in the 2004 Olympics in Athens. She faded, then stopped, slumping down on the pavement next to the spectators, crying. Hitting that wall is not a pretty sight.
>
> Describe in your own words what is happening in terms of energy sources, to a marathon runner who 'hits the wall'.

Fat reserves also constitute an insulating layer beneath the skin, which acts as a barrier to heat loss and can thus prevent the heat, which is generated through exercise, being dissipated. Similarly, excess fat can be restrictive to joint movement.

Training effects

When we train, our bodies adapt. If the training is of a type that stresses the aerobic energy systems, the adaptations are those that make these systems more efficient:

- cardiac hypertrophy and increased resting stroke volume
- decreased resting heart rate and reduced exercising and maximal heart rate
- increased blood volume and haemoglobin
- increased muscle stores of glycogen and triglycerides and increased myoglobin content of muscle
- increased capilliarisation of muscle, increased number and size of mitochondria and increased concentrations of oxidative enzymes.

Maximal oxygen consumption ($\dot{V}O_2$ max) increases as a result of the above.

> ■ Key terms
>
> **Maximal oxygen consumption ($\dot{V}O_2$ max):** the maximum amount of oxygen taken in, transported and used by the body per minute. Also known as aerobic capacity and measured in millilitres of oxygen, for each kilogram body weight each minute (ml/kg/min).

Activities

1. Choose four of the bulleted points and explain how each benefits the performer.

2. Review the poster or OHP or PowerPoint presentation that summarised the role and the circumstances of the aerobic system in providing energy to muscles, and add fat metabolism to the poster or presentation.

Oxygen consumption

When we exercise, or even when we are at rest, our bodies are using oxygen to resynthesise ATP. This ATP is needed for the heart, for the muscles of respiration to contract and to keep the brain functioning. The amount of oxygen used by our bodies to produce ATP is called our oxygen uptake or **oxygen consumption**.

When we begin to exercise, we need more ATP and therefore use more oxygen; our oxygen consumption increases. (The abbreviation '$\dot{V}O_2$' is usually used when referring to oxygen consumption.) Invariably, when we begin exercising there is insufficient oxygen available to produce all the ATP we require aerobically. It takes time for the heart and circulatory systems to adjust to the needs of the body in terms of oxygen supply. The mitochondria also take time to adjust to the demands being made of them. During this time, some of the ATP you require is produced without oxygen and so oxygen consumption is actually less than the intensity of the exercise demands. When the amount of oxygen consumed is lower than the amount actually required, there is an **oxygen deficit**.

Key terms

Oxygen consumption: the amount of oxygen used by the body.

Oxygen deficit: when insufficient oxygen is available at the start of exercise to provide all the ATP needed aerobically.

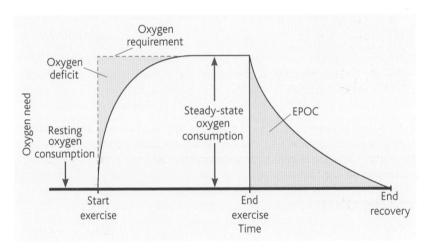

Fig. 1.6 *Oxygen consumption during rest and exercise*

$\dot{V}O_2$ varies with levels of exercise because the amount of ATP required for muscles to contract varies. When we exercise, we take in more oxygen than when at rest in order to supply mitochondria in muscle fibres so that they can manufacture ATP aerobically. If the level of exercise intensity increases, so does the level of oxygen uptake. This relationship continues until, during extreme exercise, we reach a level of maximal oxygen consumption.

The term 'maximal oxygen consumption ($\dot{V}O_2$ max)' is used to refer to the maximum amount of oxygen that an individual can consume during strenuous exercise. $\dot{V}O_2$ max varies considerably between individuals, ranging from 2 to 3 dm^3 each minute of oxygen in sedentary unfit women

AQA Examiner's tip

Maximum oxygen consumption is not the amount of oxygen taken in. A considerable amount of oxygen 'goes out' as well. It's the amount used.

Link

For more information on lactate threshold and OBLA, see Chapter 2 – Anaerobic energy systems (page 17).

Key terms

Steady state: the period of exercise when oxygen consumption matches the energy being used.

Aerobic capacity: the maximum rate at which a person can consume oxygen.

to values in excess of $10\,dm^3$ each minute of oxygen in endurance-trained male athletes. Because oxygen consumption depends on so many factors, including fitness, weight, percentage body fat, etc., it is quite common to see $\dot{V}O_2$ max measured in millilitres per kilogram per minute (ml/kg/min).

It is the level of this $\dot{V}O_2$ max that mainly determines our ability to maintain high levels of intense exercise for more than a few minutes. When we exercise, we need to resynthesise more ATP; energy production requires the use of oxygen. $\dot{V}O_2$ max is usually regarded as an accurate indication of the athlete's aerobic fitness or stamina, since it estimates directly how much oxygen the athlete has available for ATP resynthesis. $\dot{V}O_2$ max therefore varies with training and fitness. The fitter you are in terms of aerobic fitness, the higher your $\dot{V}O_2$ max.

When you exercise, you tend to work at a level of oxygen consumption that is some percentage of your $\dot{V}O_2$ max, the value being dependent on your level of fitness and the intensity of the exercise. You do not work at your $\dot{V}O_2$ max; you cannot maintain this level of intensity for more than a few seconds. In fact, the majority of people cannot achieve their $\dot{V}O_2$ max when exercising; they lack the necessary motivation and/or fitness to do so.

Linked to this is the concept of lactate threshold or OBLA.

The harder you exercise, the more likely you are to generate lactic acid as a waste product within your muscles and eventually within your blood. Athletes must therefore balance the intensity of their exercise so as not to accumulate too much lactic acid within their blood, whilst at the same time working at a level close to their $\dot{V}O_2$ max. The fitter the athlete, the higher is their $\dot{V}O_2$ max, and the closer to their $\dot{V}O_2$ max that their lactic acid threshold occurs.

You consume oxygen whilst at rest, in order to supply the body's need for some ATP to maintain life and actions such as the heart beating, breathing, and contraction of the muscles to hold your body position. This resting oxygen consumption is approximately 3.5 ml/kg/min. Once you begin to perform exercise, oxygen consumption rises. If the level of exercise is submaximal, the oxygen consumption reaches a '**steady state**', where it levels out. At this level, the amount of oxygen being used by the body matches the amount needed by the body to produce the ATP required for that level of exercise.

In practice, oxygen consumption is measured by subtracting the volume of oxygen expired during a period of time from the volume of oxygen inspired during the same time period. During a treadmill run or a cycle ergometer ride or any other static aerobic activity where it is possible to increase the workload every 2 or 3 min, oxygen consumption will rise during each stage of the test, until the runner is unable to continue owing to exhaustion. At this time, the runner is said to have reached their work or **aerobic capacity**. The amount of oxygen being consumed in these final few seconds of exercise is then measured, to give a value for $\dot{V}O_2$ max; this is an example of a direct method of measurement.

Activity

Draw a graph that shows how oxygen consumption (*y*-axis) varies during submaximal exercise.

- Use time for the *x*-axis and include a resting period prior to exercise and a recovery period after exercise.
- Label the steady state and oxygen deficit on your graph.

Training effects

Training has little effect on $\dot{V}O_2$ max. The extent of the effect largely depends on the genetic disposition of the performer to become adapted to training, the intensity of the training workload and the length of time that the training programme is undertaken. Training can increase $\dot{V}O_2$ max by between 5 and 10 per cent. The main causes of these increases are changes to the blood, heart and muscles. The major benefit of training, the idea of becoming 'fitter', is much more concerned with delaying lactate threshold.

The volume of the circulating blood and the levels of haemoglobin increase within days of the commencement of training. This will cause an increase in the stroke volume of the heart because of increased venous return (Starling's law of the heart). There is a longer-term effect on the heart. A training programme that lasts months or even years will result in cardiac hypertrophy.

This hypertrophy also increases the stroke volume of the heart, and, as resting cardiac output would remain relatively constant, this results in a reduction in the resting heart rate (bradycardia). Remember from AS Level that:

$$Q = SV \times HR$$

and that as training causes an increase in stroke volume (SV) and Q (cardiac output) remains the same, the heart rate must decrease.

Training also causes biochemical and structural changes to skeletal muscles, each of which enables the muscle fibres to use oxygen to resynthesise ATP at a more efficient rate. Thus training causes an increase in the size and numbers of mitochondria within muscle fibres, together with a corresponding increase in oxidative enzyme concentrations. Training also causes an increase in myoglobin content of muscle fibres, and an increase in the capilliarisation of muscle fibres. In addition, training causes a decrease in lactic acid accumulation in muscles, which is usually described as an increase in lactic acid tolerance.

After exercise

As can be seen from Figure 1.6 on page 9, bodily processes do not immediately return to their resting levels after exercise, especially if the exercise has been stressful. Recovery from exercise is largely associated with restoring the status quo as far as energy systems are concerned. During recovery, our energy demand is much lower than whilst we are exercising, but our oxygen demand is still quite high for a period of time, the length of which depends on the intensity of exercise.

This higher-than-resting level of oxygen consumption used to be called our oxygen debt but is now more properly called our **excess post-exercise oxygen consumption (EPOC)**.

There are two components to EPOC, an initial **fast (alactacid) component** and a longer-lasting **slow (lactacid) component**.

The fast component is concerned with quickly using extra oxygen in aerobic ATP production so that levels of phosphocreatine can be resynthesised, so getting the ATP-PC energy system back to normal. At the same time, extra oxygen is rapidly used up, re-saturating the myoglobin that transports oxygen from the blood to the muscle fibres with oxygen. The fast component is replaced very quickly if exercise is highly aerobic.

Link

For more information on lactate threshold, see Chapter 2 – Anaerobic energy systems (page 20).

For more information on lactic acid tolerance, see Chapter 2 – Anaerobic energy systems (page 23).

AQA Examiner's tip

You should be able to draw Figure 1.6 on page 9 from memory, labelling all the parts.

Key terms

Excess post-exercise oxygen consumption (EPOC): the volume of oxygen consumed above resting levels following exercise/during recovery.

Fast (alactacid, i.e. without lactic acid) component: oxygen used for rapid resynthesis of phosphocreatine and resaturation of myoglobin.

Slow (lactacid, i.e. with lactic acid) component: oxygen used to remove lactic acid and maintain high heart rate, breathing rate and body temperature.

Link

For more information on the ATP-PC energy system, see Chapter 2 – Anaerobic energy systems (page 16).

During strenuous exercise, we produce lactic acid. Returning the body systems to normal following strenuous exercise may take several hours – the slow component. This slower phase of the recovery process is also used for other processes apart from removing lactic acid (e.g. when there is a demand for extra oxygen to supply the breathing and the heart muscles that continue to work hard once exercise has finished, and to maintain the increase in temperature that occurs).

Activity

Draw a graph that shows how oxygen consumption (*y*-axis) varies as exercise intensity increases (*x*-axis). Include on your graph a period prior to exercise when the subject is resting and a period after exercise when the subject is recovering. On your graph, label:

- $\dot{V}O_2$ max
- oxygen deficit
- EPOC.

Link

EPOC is studied in greater depth in Chapter 2 – Anaerobic energy systems (page 25).

The size and duration of EPOC varies with the intensity of the exercise from which you are recovering. Intense exercise requires more oxygen for recovery than a lighter exercise regime would do, and recovery will take longer. For similar reasons, the longer the duration of the exercise, the longer recovery will take. Lastly, your level of fitness affects the duration of EPOC, with fitter performers able to recover quicker.

Activity

Produce a poster or a presentation that shows the fast and slow components of EPOC, together with their specific roles.

 You should now be able to:

- describe how the body uses ATP as an 'energy currency'
- name and describe the location of the various aerobic energy sources
- describe the aerobic breakdown of carbohydrates and fats, relating to intensity and duration of exercise
- suggest how oxygen consumption is a limiting factor to performance
- define and explain maximum oxygen consumption and oxygen deficit
- explain excess post-exercise oxygen consumption (EPOC).

1   The triathlon is an athletic event that involves performers undertaking a long-distance swim, immediately followed by a cycle race and then finally a run of several kilometres.

   (a)   Identify two of the major energy sources used by a triathlete.   *(2 marks)*

   (b)   Briefly explain how these energy sources are used for the resynthesis of ATP.   *(5 marks)*

AQA, June 2006

2   Research has been conducted into 'activity cycles' of intermittent sports such as soccer, hockey and rugby, which are reliant on efficient energy systems.

   (a)   Identify the principal energy source for each of the following activity cycles in these types of physical activities:

      (i)   walking

      (ii) sprinting

      (iii) jogging.   *(4 marks)*

   (b)   What are the disadvantages of using fat as an energy source during exercise?   *(3 marks)*

AQA, January 2003

3   Figure 1.7 shows the levels of muscle glycogen in an elite performer who takes part in a two-hour period of intensive exercise followed by a recovery period.

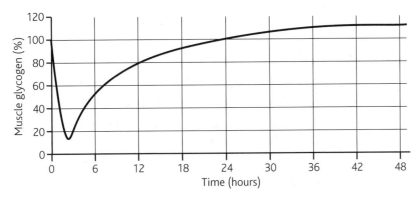

Fig. 1.7

   (a)   Describe and explain the effects of the exercise and recovery periods on the levels of glycogen in the elite performer.   *(5 marks)*

   (b)   The fitness levels of elite performers will vary. One measure of fitness is $\dot{V}O_2$ max. What do you understand by the term '$\dot{V}O_2$ max'?   *(2 marks)*

AQA, January 2007

4   Figure 1.8 shows how the oxygen uptake of a footballer undertaking
         exercise is followed by a recovery period.

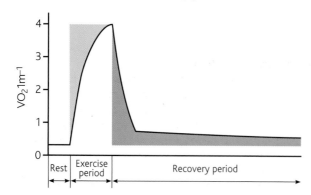

Fig. 1.8

(a)   Why does the footballer incur an oxygen deficit during exercise?   *(3 marks)*

(b)   Excess Post-exercise oxygen consumption (EPOC) is considered
         to have two components. State two aims of the first component
         and explain how it is achieved in the body.   *(4 marks)*

AQA, June 2003

2 Anaerobic energy systems

Key terms

Anaerobic energy system: a process that provides energy for the resynthesis of ATP without the use of oxygen.

Coupled reaction: a chemical reaction in which energy is transferred from one side of the reaction to the other.

Links

- For more information on how ATP is used in muscle contraction, see Chapter 3 – Muscles (page 34).

- For more information on aerobic exercise, see Chapter 1 – Aerobic energy systems (page 2).

The **anaerobic energy systems** are a vital part of the body's way of getting energy to resynthesise adenosine triphosphate (ATP). In Chapter 1 – Aerobic energy systems (page 2), you learned how important ATP is to the body – it is the only energy source that cells, including muscle cells, can use. You learned that we have limited supplies of ATP within the body and that we must therefore constantly resynthesise ATP to ensure that we can continue to work or live. You will also have learned how the body transfers chemical energy from stored forms of glucose (glycogen) and uses that energy to resynthesise ATP. Chapter 1 discussed how that process works when the body has sufficient oxygen available to ensure that there is a complete breakdown of glucose, thereby making the whole process an aerobic one. This works well when the body is at rest or only working at a moderate level of intensity. However, sport performers are frequently working at much higher levels of intensity and more ATP is being used to provide energy for muscle contraction. Under these conditions, it becomes impossible for the body to provide the energy required to resynthesise ATP from the aerobic energy systems, and other energy systems come into play.

This chapter explains the energy systems that are used during exercise levels that stretch from moderately intense to maximal work. It also explains the points at which the switch from the aerobic system occurs, how this relates to a performer's level of fitness and physiological efficiency, and how the body deals with the unwanted products that are produced. Finally, the chapter concludes with an examination of how different energy systems come into play in a variety of sporting situations and how the contributions of the aerobic and anaerobic energy systems to ATP resynthesis work as a continuum rather than there being a direct switch from one to another. In Chapter 3 – Muscles, you will see how ATP is actually used in muscle contraction.

Activity

Draw a diagram to show the reversible reactions of ATP breakdown and resynthesis.

ATP resynthesis – which energy system?

The energy system that the body uses to resynthesise ATP is dependent on the intensity of work being carried out. You will recall that ATP breakdown and resynthesis is a **coupled reaction**.

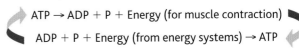

$$\text{ATP} \rightarrow \text{ADP} + \text{P} + \text{Energy (for muscle contraction)}$$
$$\text{ADP} + \text{P} + \text{Energy (from energy systems)} \rightarrow \text{ATP}$$

The ATP breakdown and then resynthesis is also known as a reversible reaction.

In the previous chapter, we saw that, when we are at rest or engaged in low to moderate levels of exercise, resynthesis of ATP is done aerobically. The more intense the exercise, the more ATP is used to provide energy for muscle fibre contraction, and therefore the more ATP we need to resynthesise. At some point, as you exercise or work at higher levels, the body becomes unable to provide the oxygen for the complete breakdown of glucose either quickly enough or in sufficient quantities to ensure that enough energy is available for ATP resynthesis.

The muscles have sufficient ATP available for very short bursts of high-intensity activity (less than 2 s). For anything longer than that, it is necessary to resynthesise the ATP during the activity to ensure that it can be sustained. If the body is working at an intensity that is above a fast jog (for most people) it cannot do this aerobically and the body must provide the energy for ATP resynthesis by using the anaerobic energy systems.

There are two anaerobic energy systems:

- the **phosphocreatine** (PC) energy system or ATP-PC system
- the **lactate anaerobic energy system**.

The phosphocreatine or ATP-PC energy system

Phosphocreatine is an energy-rich compound that when broken down releases energy to resynthesise ATP.

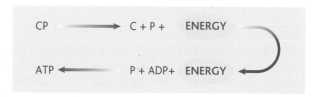

Fig. 2.1 *The PC energy system and ATP resynthesis*

As you can see from Figure 2.1, no oxygen is involved and so the process is entirely anaerobic. For every molecule of PC that is broken down, sufficient energy is released to resynthesise one molecule of ATP. The great benefit of the PC system is that the energy is released rapidly and allows for the rapid resynthesis of ATP that is necessary if the body is undertaking short bursts of maximal work, for example when sprinting. Another benefit is that there are no waste products from the process.

The disadvantage of the PC system is that stores of phosphocreatine are limited, only sufficient for approximately 5 to 8 s of high-intensity or maximal flat-out work. The PC stores are replenished but it can take up to 3 min to fully refuel – not much use when you need to sprint to the next tackle. The replenishment of phosphocreatine is covered in much more depth later in this chapter (page 24).

So although the PC system is excellent for providing energy rapidly, its effects last only for a short period of time. So if we wish to work at a high level for longer, we need another source of energy to resynthesise ATP. That system would be the lactate anaerobic energy system or lactic acid system.

Lactate anaerobic energy system

The lactate anaerobic energy system involves the partial breakdown of glucose. A full breakdown of glucose can only occur in the presence of oxygen.

In Figure 2.2 you can see that hydrogen is released both during glycolysis, the breakdown of glucose to pyruvate, and during the complex chemical equations occurring during the Krebs cycle. These hydrogen ions are

Key terms

Phosphocreatine: an energy-rich compound of creatine and phosphoric acid, found in muscle cells.

Lactate anaerobic energy system: the system that produces energy for ATP resynthesis by breaking down glucose without oxygen and producing lactate as a by-product.

AQA Examiner's tip

- The terms 'phosphocreatine', 'PC', 'creatine phosphate' or 'CP' systems are interchangeable; all are acceptable within an examination answer.
- The terms 'lactate' or 'lactic acid' are interchangeable; both are acceptable in an examination answer.

Activity

List five instances in sport (with at least two from your own sport) which are likely to make use of the PC energy system.

Link

Information about how some performers attempt to improve their PC system by using nutritional supplements is to be found in Chapter 4 – The elite performer: food, supplements and performance-enhancing drugs (pages 50–9).

For more information on the aerobic breakdown of glucose, see Chapter 1 – Aerobic energy systems (page 4).

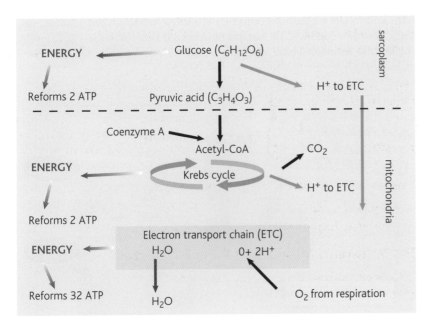

Fig. 2.2 *The aerobic breakdown of glucose*

combined with oxygen from respiration in the electron chain to form water. This process works well for low-intensity exercise, but more ATP must be resynthesised as the level of work increases and therefore more glucose is broken down and more hydrogen is transferred to the electron transport chain.

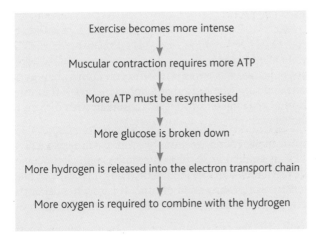

Fig. 2.3 *Exercise intensity, hydrogen, oxygen relationship*

More oxygen becomes available as the ventilation rate and cardiac output increase. The amount of oxygen that can be made available to and used by muscle cells is finite; it is known as the $\dot{V}O_2$ max.

The lactate threshold

If the body continues to work hard, more hydrogen, which is released as a result of the glycolysis of glucose and the Krebs cycle, enters the electron transport chain (ETC) to be combined with oxygen. At some point (dependent on $\dot{V}O_2$ max) so much hydrogen enters the ETC that it exceeds the amount of oxygen available. The excess hydrogen ions cannot

> **Link**
>
> For more information on the Krebs cycle, see Chapter 1 – Aerobic energy systems (page 6).
>
> For more information on $\dot{V}O_2$ max, see Chapter 1 – Aerobic energy systems (page 8).

remain unattached and so combine with the pyruvate to form lactate or lactic acid (see Figure 2.3). The point at which this occurs is known as the **lactate threshold** (see page 28).

Key terms

Lactate threshold: the level of exercise intensity at which you are producing more lactate than can be removed or resynthesised; lactic acid starts to accumulate in the bloodstream and muscle, owing to excess hydrogen combining with pyruvate to form lactate.

Muscle fatigue: the decline in muscle function as muscles are used intensively and repeatedly.

Link

For more information on the electron transport chain, see Chapter 1 – Aerobic energy systems (page 2).

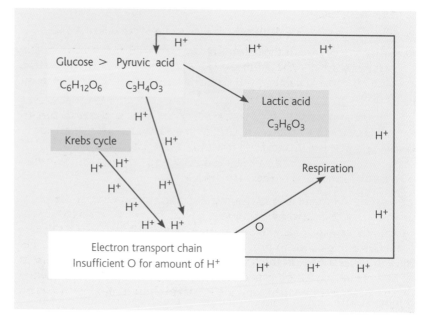

Fig. 2.4 *Pyruvate to lactate – lactate anaerobic energy system*

AQA Examiner's tip

You are not expected to learn, nor will you be asked to give, chemical formulae in an examination answer.

The chemical formulae of glucose, pyruvate and lactate show clearly what is happening during this anaerobic energy system process:

■ glucose $C_6H_{12}O_6$
■ pyruvate $C_3H_4O_3$
■ lactate $C_3H_6O_3$.

As you can see, lactate has two more hydrogen atoms than pyruvate. This is because, during the lactate anaerobic energy system process, excess hydrogen (that which cannot be combined with oxygen in the ETC) combines with pyruvate to form lactate.

The lactate anaerobic energy system does not resynthesise ATP as rapidly as the ATP-PC system because there are more chemical processes involved but it is still very quick and can enable the body to engage in maximal or high-intensity work for a period of time. It is much quicker than the aerobic energy systems discussed in Chapter 1 – Aerobic energy systems.

The drawback with the lactate anaerobic system is the production of lactic acid and its accumulation in the muscle cells and the blood. Conventionally, it was thought that the accumulation of lactic acid affects muscle contraction and that this is what causes fatigue.

Activity

Using information from Chapter 1 (see page 5), construct a simple flowchart to show the complete breakdown of glucose, including the production of lactate from pyruvate and the reverse during excess post-exercise oxygen consumption (EPOC).

■ Fatigue, lactate threshold and $\dot{V}O_2$ max

We have all experienced fatigue, which can be described as being unable to sustain a level of work. However, here we are more concerned with muscles, and a more physiologically accurate definition of **muscle fatigue** would refer to the inability of a muscle to maintain contractile force as a result of repeated contractions.

The following three factors are believed to contribute to muscle fatigue:

An increasingly acidic environment (acidosis) causes a breakdown in the chemical reactions that produce muscle fibre contractions (acidosis is caused by the build-up of lactic acid and the release of hydrogen ions). This is most likely to occur during high to intense levels of exercise.

Glucose reserves are depleted during sustained periods of work.

There is a change in the balance of the chemicals that propagate the nervous stimulus (the action potential) within the muscle fibre. This decreases the excitability of the muscle fibre and therefore reduces its ability to contract; it fatigues.

The currently accepted view that high levels of lactic acid cause muscle fatigue is now being challenged. Intriguingly, some researchers are now claiming that, instead of being a fatiguing agent, lactic acid may in fact prolong high levels of work by counteracting the chemical changes referred to in the third of these factors (above).

The cause of fatigue also varies depending on the nature of the physical activity in which you are engaged. If you are running a marathon, you are likely to be running aerobically and using the breakdown of glucose to provide the energy for ATP reformation. The fatiguing factor here is the level of glycogen; it can be reduced almost to zero, resulting in the experience of 'hitting the wall' – that sudden onset of extreme tiredness and a significant drop in pace even down to a walk.

For other activities such as the 100 m sprint it may not be evident that fatigue is even setting in but an analysis of 10 m splits of a 100 m runner shows that over the last 20 to 25 m they are indeed slowing down. If you look at the graph in Figure 2.5, you can see that it is the runner who slows down the least in the latter part of the race who wins – Maurice Greene.

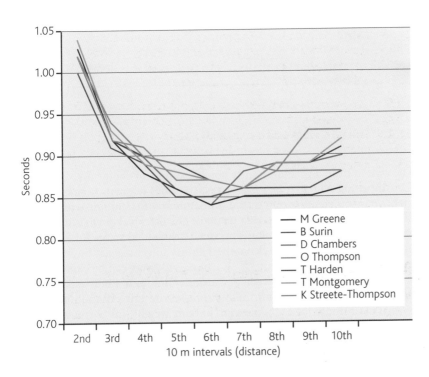

Fig. 2.5 *10 m split times for the 1999 100 m World Championships*

■ **Activity**

For your own activity, identify the likely causes of fatigue and when during the activity these are most likely to occur.

AQA Examiner's tip

Physiological research continues to give us a better understanding of how the body works. The causes of fatigue are becoming a hotly debated topic. For the purposes of the current AQA specification, it is quite acceptable to state that an accumulation of lactic acid causes muscle fatigue. Should you have gained a deeper understanding of the causes of muscle fatigue and be able to express them accurately, you will be credited within an examination answer.

■ **Key terms**

Onset of blood lactacid accumulation (OBLA): the point at which lactic acid (lactate) starts to accumulate within the blood; normally a rapid increase follows.

In this case, the reason for the decrease in speed is the performers' inability to acquire sufficient energy to resynthesise ATP so that their ATP level is declining. This is because the phosphocreatine stores are running out (remember that they only provide sufficient energy for 5 to 8 s of maximal work). Although the aerobic and lactic acid systems are available, they cannot provide the energy quickly enough to sustain ATP levels at this level of work. The runner will not, however, experience any effects from lactic acid as it has not yet started to accumulate. This is not true of performers who work hard for longer periods of time.

Fatigue and the lactate threshold

One of the major causes of fatigue is the build-up of lactic acid in the muscles. As a performer increases their level of work they cross a point known as the lactate threshold; this is when the amount of lactate in the blood starts to increase. We are constantly producing small amounts of lactate, even when working at a low level, but it has no effect on us because we are able to deal with it as quickly as it is produced; the normal amount of lactic acid in the blood is 1 to 2 mmol. As we begin to exercise more intensely, a point is reached at which lactate starts to accumulate; this is known as the **onset of blood lactacid accumulation (OBLA)** (see Figure 2.6). Lactic acid accumulation is generally considered to occur when blood lactate levels exceed 4 mmol for each litre of blood. This is happening because the anaerobic lactate energy system produces more lactic acid than can be dealt with and the acid starts to accumulate in the muscles and the blood.

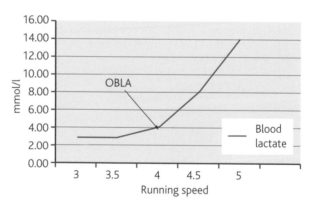

Fig. 2.6 *Onset of blood lactacid accumulation (OBLA)*

The switch from a predominantly aerobic supply of energy for resynthesising ATP to anaerobic lactate methods happens because we have insufficient oxygen in the mitochondria to combine with the hydrogen being released as a result of glucose breakdown (during glycolysis and the Krebs cycle). The lactate threshold varies for each individual performer and reflects their ability to get oxygen into the mitochondria or the performer's $\dot{V}O_2$ max. $\dot{V}O_2$ max can be expressed in terms of cubic metres of oxygen per minute ($dm^3 min^{-1}$) but, as $\dot{V}O_2$ max varies with body size, it is normally expressed in terms of millilitres of oxygen per minute for each kilogram of body weight ($ml^{-1} kg^{-1} min^{-1}$). Table 2.1 shows the variations in $\dot{V}O_2$ max values for a range of performers and non-performers.

Table 2.1 indicates that as exercise intensity increases, oxygen consumption increases until a maximum level is reached – the $\dot{V}O_2$ max.

■ **Link**

For more information on mitochondria, see Chapter 1 – Aerobic energy systems (page 5).

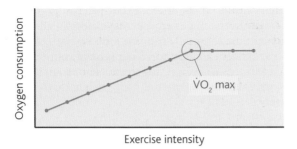

Fig. 2.7 *Oxygen consumption relative to exercise intensity*

If you continue to work at or above this level of intensity, you cross the lactate threshold.

Table 2.1 $\dot{V}O_2$ *max levels for different types of athletes*

Individual	Female $\dot{V}O_2$ max (ml/kg/min)	Male $\dot{V}O_2$ max (ml/kg/min)
Untrained		
Untrained aged 20–29	33–42	43–52
Untrained aged 40–49	26–35	36–44
Untrained aged 60–69	22–23	31–38
Elite		
Marathon runner	70–80	80–90
Rower	58–65	60–72
Basketball player	43–60	40–60
Nordic skier	60–75	65–94
Greg Lemond – Tour de France cyclist, 3-time winner		93
Michael Indurain – Tour de France cyclist, 5-time winner		94
Bjorn Daehlie – cross-country skier, 12 Olympic golds		96

Activity

Using the data from Table 2.1, draw some conclusions about the differences in $\dot{V}O_2$ max for the different groups shown.

$\dot{V}O_2$ max differences

From Table 2.1, it can be seen that there are huge differences between the $\dot{V}O_2$ max values for untrained as opposed to elite performers, between men and women, between different age groups and between elite performers in different sports.

What may account for these differences? There are three factors at play:

- A person's age – as you get older, your $\dot{V}O_2$ max decreases. Although this decrease can be slowed by continuing to exercise, it cannot be prevented.
- Whether they are male or female (a genetic differentiation) – on average, women have a 20 per cent lower $\dot{V}O_2$ max than men, although for trained performers (men and women) the gap can reduce to approximately 10 per cent.
- The amount of training they have undertaken (also related to genetic inheritance) – you can improve your $\dot{V}O_2$ max by appropriate training.

However, there is a limit to the amount that you can improve and that is set by your genetic make-up. The physiological adaptations or improvements that are caused by training are also limited by your genetic inheritance. It is thought that up to 75 per cent of your $\dot{V}O_2$ max may be genetically determined. So even if you were able to train as hard as Greg Lemond or Bjorn Daehlie, you are not going to be able to achieve their $\dot{V}O_2$ max levels.

$\dot{V}O_2$ max is a function of the body's ability to get oxygen into the lungs, transfer it to the blood, transport it to the muscle cells and into the mitochondria and then make use of that oxygen in energy processes. From the work you undertook for AS Level Physical Education Unit 2 and in the previous chapter of this book, you should recall that the factors that affect the efficiency of that process are:

- the surface area of the alveoli (genetically determined)
- red blood cell and haemoglobin levels
- the capillary density in the lungs
- the efficiency of the heart and circulatory system
- the capillary density in the muscles' cells
- transfer of oxygen to mitochondria via the myoglobin
- take-up and use of oxygen by mitochondria.

All the factors listed above, except for alveoli surface area, can be improved through aerobic training, but every individual has a genetic limitation on how much improvement can be made. Research generally indicates that it is the improvements in delivery to the muscle cells, rather than utilisation by the mitochondria, that have the greatest effects on $\dot{V}O_2$ max.

Activity

1. If you have not already done so, undertake the multi-stage fitness test (under the direction of a member of staff) to estimate your $\dot{V}O_2$ max.

2. Compare the scores of all members of the group and relate them to their specialist physical activity.

3. If all members of the group were to undergo a period of aerobic training, which individual would be likely to make the most progress?

Why does a high $\dot{V}O_2$ max help sustain performance?

The more oxygen that can be brought and used within the mitochondria, the longer a performer can work without accumulating lactic acid. Lactic acid accumulates when we have insufficient oxygen to combine with the hydrogen released during the breakdown of glucose. The excess hydrogen combines with the pyruvic acid produced during glycolysis to form lactic acid.

Figure 2.8 shows levels of lactic acid in the blood in relation to the speed being swum by an elite female swimmer. The swimmer has to decide how fast she should swim. Swimming at 1.33 m a second she would complete a 200 m swim in 2 min 30 s; at 1.36 m a second, she would take 2 min 27 s – the difference between gold and nowhere. But, as you can see from the graph, lactic acid is accumulating in the body when she is swimming at the faster pace and this will eventually cause fatigue. If the fatigue hits the swimmer too early, she will need to slow her pace, and this could lose her the race. Pace judgement in relation to the lactate threshold and the maximal lactate steady state is critical.

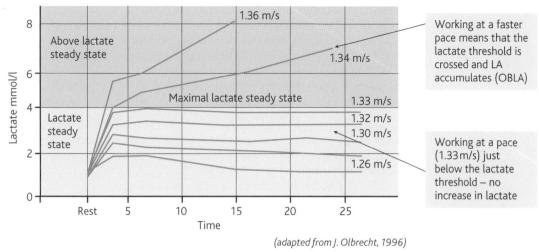

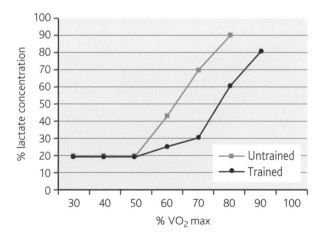

(adapted from J. Olbrecht, 1996)

Fig. 2.8 *Lactate production and work levels for an elite swimmer*

Is $\dot{V}O_2$ max the only determining factor?

No, another major factor is the percentage of your $\dot{V}O_2$ max that is used before you cross the lactate or aerobic/anaerobic threshold. This is more technically known as the '%$\dot{V}O_2$ max' (or, even more technically, the 'fractional percentage of oxygen consumption') and refers to the highest rate of work that can be sustained for 20 to 40 minutes without becoming fatigued.

An untrained person is able to use between 50 and 70 per cent of their $\dot{V}O_2$ max. Training can improve this to 75 to 90 per cent of $\dot{V}O_2$ max. However, each person will have a genetically set limit to the percentage of their $\dot{V}O_2$ max that they can use, and training will not take them beyond that level. Clearly, being able to use a higher percentage of your $\dot{V}O_2$ max will raise the aerobic/anaerobic threshold. In Figure 2.9 you can see that the untrained performer will be accumulating lactic acid at a much lower percentage of $\dot{V}O_2$ max.

Fig. 2.9 *Percentage of $\dot{V}O_2$ max at which OBLA occurs*

Fatigue and lactate tolerance

Performers vary in their ability to tolerate lactate. **Lactate tolerance** refers to how well the body can withstand the effects of the accumulation of lactic acid in the muscles and bloodstream. Some researchers consider that this

---

AQA Examiner's tip

The terms 'anaerobic threshold', 'aerobic threshold' and 'lactate threshold' are all equally correct and may be used interchangeably within an examination answer.

Key terms

Lactate tolerance: the ability to withstand the effects of lactic acid accumulation.

is related to the amounts of bicarbonates (e.g. sodium bicarbonate) within the blood and other body fluids. The hydrogen ions that are not combined with oxygen and lactic acid can be combined with bicarbonates which render them less acidic – this is because bicarbonates are alkalising agents. These alkalising agents draw the hydrogen ions and the lactic acid from the muscle cells into the blood, possibly reducing the effects of fatigue. Blood flow away from the muscles also contributes to this process and can be improved through training by increasing capillary density at the muscle site.

There is also evidence to suggest that increased lactate tolerance is a psychological factor, with elite performers being more highly motivated than non-elite performers and therefore more willing to ignore for longer the fatiguing effects of acidosis. In an attempt to increase the level of bicarbonates within the body, some performers take them as nutritional supplements.

What happens after intense exercise?

To recover from intense exercise and to prepare for the next bout of work, the body needs to:

■ restore the levels of ATP

■ restore the levels of phosphocreatine

■ reduce the level of lactic acid to the normal level of approximately 1.6 mmol/l

■ reload myoglobin with oxygen

■ restore the levels of muscle glycogen.

These processes are known as 'recovery' (often 'oxygen recovery'). As you will see, all except the fifth require oxygen to be available. Remember that, when the body is recovering from intense exercise, more oxygen is required above the level normally used at that workload: i.e. there is what is known as 'excess post-exercise oxygen consumption (EPOC)'.

Restoring ATP levels

The body is constantly restoring ATP by resynthesis. After intense exercise, levels will take 48 to 72 hours to restore to normal. This requires energy from the breakdown of glucose, which of course requires oxygen.

Restoring phosphocreatine

When energy for ATP synthesis is required very rapidly (during periods of intense work such as sprinting), it is provided by the breakdown of phosphocreatine. This is a reversible reaction.

PC → Phosphate + **Creatine** and releasing energy (used for ATP resynthesis)

To restore levels of phosphocreatine the process must be reversed:

Phosphate + Creatine → PC but requires energy (from glucose breakdown)

The energy that is provided for the PC resynthesis comes from the breakdown of glucose, therefore making an oxygen demand.

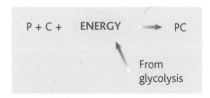

Fig. 2.10 *Phosphocreatine resynthesis*

■ Link

For more information on nutritional supplements, see Chapter 4 – The elite performer: food, supplements and performance-enhancing drugs (page 50).

■ Link

For more information on EPOC, see Chapter 1 – Aerobic energy systems (page 11).

AQA Examiner's tip

It is quite acceptable to use abbreviations such as EPOC and OBLA when writing an examination answer – as long as you know what they mean!

■ Key terms

Creatine: substance formed by the body that stores energy and is used as an energy source for ATP resynthesis.

AQA Examiner's tip

Phosphocreatine breakdown and resynthesis is an example of a coupled and reversible reaction.

Dealing with excess lactic acid

As we have seen, during intense exercise the body moves from working aerobically to working anaerobically. As a result, the aerobic–anaerobic threshold is crossed (also known as the lactate threshold) and the point of OBLA is reached. The amount of lactic acid accumulating in the blood is determined by how long you work above the lactate threshold. It is important to deal with this accumulation of lactic acid because:

◼ it is likely to play a role in muscle fatigue

◼ lactic acid is a useful source of energy.

There are two methods by which the body deals with an excess of lactic acid.

◼ One is by converting the lactic acid to pyruvate (oxidation). The pyruvate can then go through the usual aerobic process in the Krebs cycle to produce energy for ATP reformation. This process requires oxygen and occurs in the mitochondria.

◼ The other is by transporting the lactic acid to the liver via the bloodstream where it can be reconverted to glucose via a process known as the Cori cycle. This also indirectly involves the use of oxygen.

Reloading myoglobin with oxygen

Myoglobin transports oxygen (as oxymyoglobin) through the muscle cell into the mitochondria. During normal levels of work, the myoglobin is fully loaded with oxygen and can be considered as an oxygen store. After intense work much of this oxygen has been used and has to be replenished, which makes an oxygen demand.

Restoring the levels of muscle glycogen

During sustained levels of exercise the body uses a large amount of glucose. As of part of the recovery process, glucose levels are restored from glycogen stores within the body and from carbohydrate dietary intake.

Activity

Prepare a recovery plan that you could use after an intense and sustained period of activity. Your recovery plan should include the time immediately following the end of the activity and continue until you will have reached full recovery, i.e. when the body will have returned to its pre-exercise state.

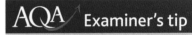

Examiner's tip

The replenishment of phosphocreatine, reloading of myoglobin and the oxidation of lactic acid can all occur during the performance – as long as the athlete is working below their lactate threshold. Do not make the mistake of thinking that these processes only occur during recovery.

Link

For more information on glucose, see Chapter 1 – Aerobic energy systems (page 4).

Recovery and EPOC

From Chapter 1 – Aerobic energy systems (page 2), you learned that there are fast and slow components of recovery involving EPOC. We will now look at these in more detail.

In Figure 2.11 you can see that heart and breathing rates are raised during exercise but do not immediately return to resting levels when exercise ceases. This indicates that the body needs more oxygen than is required by the body during rest or **active recovery**.

Figure 2.12 shows the amount of oxygen required aerobically to meet the demands of high-level, intense exercise. The flat line of the graph shows that the performer is working at or beyond the lactate threshold – they are getting as much oxygen to the muscle cells as possible. On

Key terms

Active recovery: the use of light energy to aid recovery.

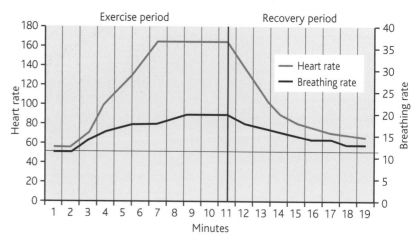

Fig. 2.11 *Heart and breathing rates during intense exercise and recovery*

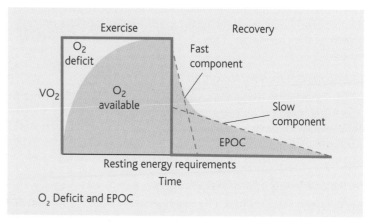

Fig. 2.12 *Oxygen deficit, recovery and EPOC*

the left-hand side of the graph we can see the area marked 'O$_2$ deficit', indicating that they are working beyond what can be met aerobically and have crossed the aerobic–anaerobic, or lactate, threshold. The line at the bottom of the chart indicates the oxygen requirement for the resting performer, or the low level of activity when recovering. Above that level and after the cessation of exercise, we can see the excess post-exercise oxygen consumption. Some of that oxygen is required for the fast component of recovery and some for the slow.

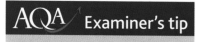

Examiner's tip

Do not refer to 'oxygen debt'. You are only concerned with oxygen deficit.

Activity

Collect heart rate data to show the changes in your own heart rate (and the heart rate of other members of your learning group) that occur prior to exercise, during sustained exercise and for 10 minutes after recovery. Prepare a chart showing:

■ your personal data

■ data from the whole group

■ average data.

The fast or alactacid component

The fast component is also known as the alactacid component because no lactic acid is involved. During the fast component of recovery, ATP and PC levels are restored, along with the reloading of myoglobin with oxygen. Figure 2.13 shows the speed at which PC stores are replenished. Within one minute, some 75 per cent of PC has been restored, and within four minutes virtually 100 per cent levels have been achieved. It also takes approximately one to two minutes to reload the myoglobin with oxygen. Given that oxygen is required for both processes, they will be more efficient if the performer has a high $\dot{V}O_2$ max and is able to effectively supply oxygen to the muscles – something that improves with aerobic fitness.

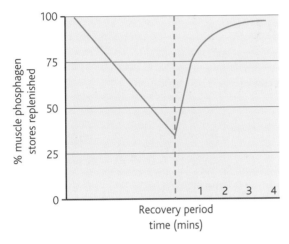

Fig. 2.13 *Phosphocreatine recovery rates*

The slow or lactacid component

During this process, the excess lactic acid is removed from the muscle cells or the blood. The lactic acid is actually used during this process and should not be thought of as a waste product. Table 2.2 shows the approximate usage of the lactic acid. The process of oxidation to carbon dioxide and water involves reconversion to pyruvate and then continues through the aerobic processes of the Krebs cycle and the electron transport chain. All through this process, energy is being released for ATP resynthesis. The conversion of the remaining lactic acid to glucose, glycogen and protein shows that lactic acid should not be seen as a waste product.

Table 2.2 *What happens to lactic acid during recovery*

Destination	Approximate percentage of lactic acid involved
Oxidation into carbon dioxide and water	65
Conversion into glycogen and then stored in muscle liver	20
Converted into protein	10
Converted into glucose	5

AQA Examiner's tip

Although lactic acid has been referred to as a 'waste product' because it can cause fatigue, in another sense it is an energy source providing energy for ATP reformation via glycolysis. You will be expected to understand this dual function of lactic acid.

Activity

On the chart that you prepared in the last learning activity, draw the slow and fast components of recovery.

Which energy system will I use during my sport?

You should already be able to answer that question. You should know that the answer will depend on three factors:

■ the intensity of the workload during your sport activity

■ the duration of the workload

■ your level of fitness.

For some activities, the answer is very clear. If you are a 100 m runner, your event is going to be all over in 10 to 12 s, albeit of maximal exercise. As well as your stores of ATP, you will also predominantly use your ATP-PC system, also known as the alactic anaerobic system.

As you increase the distance from 100 to 400 m, your phosphocreatine supplies will be exhausted and you will be unable to resynthesise them whilst running, and so the predominant energy system will be the lactic acid system.

Table 2.3 *Exercise time and energy systems*

Duration (seconds)	Classification	Energy supplied by
1–2	Anaerobic	ATP
2–5	Anaerobic	mix of ATP and PC
5–8	Anaerobic	PC predominating
8–45	Anaerobic, lactic	PC + glycogen (anaerobic)
45–240	Aerobic + anaerobic	glycogen (anaerobic) + lactic production
240+	Aerobic	glycogen and fatty acids

AQA Examiner's tip

■ It is common for an exam question to give you a sporting or performance scenario and ask you to identify which energy system is being used. You should practise analysing the use of energy systems as often as you can.

■ Do not fall into the trap of thinking that energy systems suddenly switch from one to another. They all work together and often simultaneously. The level of intensity or duration of work determines which is predominant.

Activity

Watch a video of an elite 800 m race. On the first viewing, try and identify the phases of the race and the level of intensity of work on a scale of 1 to 10, with 10 being a flat-out sprint and 1 being walking pace.

For the marathon, the predominant energy system will be the aerobic system. It is possible that you will be able to raise your running speed and therefore the intensity of the work towards the end and you may cross the lactate threshold.

All these athletic events may be steady state, and it is clear that one energy system or another will be the predominant one used to supply the energy for ATP resynthesis. It is unlikely, however, that you will be working at a constant and steady level of intensity. If you are a racket player, or engaged in a team invasion game like rugby or netball, your level of intensity will vary greatly throughout the activity. This may also be true of athletes involved in races where there is the opportunity to vary their pace.

Take an 800 m race as an example: the athlete completes the race in a time of approximately 1 min 55 s, but it is unlikely that this runner will have run at exactly an even pace throughout the race. You can see from Table 2.4 that the change in the runner's pace, and therefore intensity of work, results in changes to the predominant energy system that is being used. The important thing to note is that all energy systems, unless chemically exhausted, can be brought into play. During Stages 2, 6 and 7, the lactate system has been brought into play because the runner's work intensity (running speed) has caused them to cross the lactate threshold.

During Stages 3 and 5, because the runner has reduced their running speed they have fallen back below the lactate threshold and are running aerobically. During that time, it is possible that the body is also reducing the lactate levels by utilising any spare oxygen from the aerobic energy systems.

Table 2.4 *The energy system use during an 800 m race*

Stage	Stage description	Stage distance (metres)	Stage time (seconds)	Total time (seconds)	Predominant energy system?	Commentary
1	Rapid acceleration, preparing for Stage 2	10	2.4	2.4	ATP ATP-PC	Aerobic system getting started
2	To the end of the first bend, getting near the front	100	12.5	14.9	ATP–PC Lactic acid (LA)	ATP-PC becoming exhausted. LA system for short period. Some accumulation of LA
3	Steady pace to end of the first lap	290	44.0	58.9	Aerobic	Possibly sufficient aerobic capacity to reduce LA accumulation
4	Accelerating, responding to overtaking runner on bend	70	10.0	68.9	LA	Crossed lactate threshold. LA accumulation
5	Back straight – decelerate then steady pace	130	21.0	89.9	Aerobic	Possibly sufficient aerobic capacity to reduce LA accumulation
6	Gradual increase in pace round final bend and entering straight	120	16.0	105.9	Aerobic → LA	Crossing lactate threshold again
7	Running at maximal pace	80	9.5	115.4	LA	Has the runner gone too early – will acidosis-induced fatigue set in?
Total		**800**	**115.4**			

Activity

Observe a high-level sport performance (either individual or team; either live or on video). Prepare a table similar to Table 2.4, breaking the performance down into stages, and then identify the energy systems being used. You may find this useful to do for your own specialist activity.

The understanding of the different energy systems, how they contribute to performance and how the body restores and replenishes those energy systems (recovery), is fundamental to your understanding of the physiology of human performance.

Links

Information about how the energy systems can be supported through nutritional support and specialised training systems is covered in Chapter 4 – The elite performer: food, supplements and performance-enhancing drugs, and Chapter 5 – Specialised training.

☑ *You should now be able to:*

- describe the role that ATP plays during high-intensity exercise
- discuss how the body provides the energy to resynthesise ATP when we are working very hard
- relate how hard a performer is working to the predominant energy system being used
- describe the causes of fatigue and relate them to the intensity of work being undertaken and the energy systems being used
- describe what happens to the waste products that are being produced during periods of high intensity and how they are used to provide more energy
- relate levels of aerobic fitness to fatigue and to intensity of work.

AQA Examination-style questions

1   It has been said that the winner of a 100 m race is the runner who slows
     the least. Explain, using your knowledge of energy systems, why this might
     be the case.   *(7 marks)*

2   During a game of hockey, a performer accumulates a lactic acid
     concentration of 8 mmol. Two minutes later in the game their lactate
     concentration is 4.8 mmol.

     (a)   Suggest reasons why the performer's level of lactic acid had
            risen to 8 mmol.   *(4 marks)*

     (b)   Give an explanation as to why their lactate concentration had
            fallen two minutes later.   *(3 marks)*

3   An 800 m runner undertakes aerobic training to improve their $\dot{V}O_2$ max.
     Why might this improve their 800 m personal best?   *(7 marks)*

4   After a period of intense exercise a performer shows evidence of
     heightened ventilation rate and heart rate two minutes after the end of
     exercise.

     (a)   In terms of recovery, why does the performer exhibit these
            raised heart and ventilation rates?   *(4 marks)*

     (b)   Why should the organisers of world championship athletics
            meetings allow at least three days between 1500 m races? Use
            your knowledge of recovery in your answer.   *(3 marks)*

3 Muscles

In this chapter you will:

- understand the detailed structure of a muscle
- understand how muscle fibres contract
- understand how muscle fibres work together
- understand how muscles adjust their force of contraction
- understand how we use motor units with different characteristics in sport performance
- understand how we get the energy for muscle.

Key terms

Skeletal muscle: the muscle that causes our bodies to move, also called striated muscle.

Myofibril: part of a muscle fibre, contains sarcomeres and the contractile proteins actin and myosin.

Link

For information on the role that muscles play in lever systems, see *AQA Physical Education AS*, Chapter 6 – Analysis of movements (pages 59 to 74).

Muscles cause movement. You learned at AS Level that muscles pull on bones and that, because these bones form lever systems with other bones, movement occurs. In Chapter 1 – Aerobic energy systems (page 2) we learned that we use our muscles to convert the chemical energy of ATP into mechanical work. The resynthesis of ATP takes place within all cells of the body, but we are especially concerned with ATP resynthesis within muscle fibres. There are different types of muscle within our body. The heart has a particular type of muscle called cardiac muscle. Many of our internal organs move through the action of involuntary muscle. We are only concerned with the muscle that causes movement. **Skeletal muscle**, as its name implies, is the muscle attached to the skeleton. It is also called striated muscle. The contraction of skeletal muscle fibres is under voluntary control. We need to study the structure of muscle and how it contracts. Muscle fibre contraction is a complex topic area, involving the learning of many new (and long) terms, and there is a considerable amount of biochemistry involved. We are also required to understand how muscle fibres work to produce a variety of different strengths of contraction and how different muscle fibres are used in different sporting actions.

Muscle structure

Skeletal muscle is made up of thousands of cylindrical muscle fibres, often running the full length of a muscle. The fibres are bound together by connective tissue through which run blood vessels and nerves. Each muscle fibre contains:

- numerous thin, thread-like **myofibrils** that are arranged like a telephone cable and run the entire length of the fibre
- many mitochondria
- an extensive network of interconnecting tubes called the sarcoplasmic reticulum
- many nuclei.

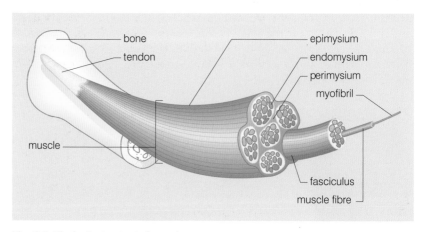

Fig. 3.1 *The basic structure of muscle*

The number of muscle fibres within a muscle is probably fixed early in life, and training does not usually increase the number. In adults, increased strength and muscle mass come about through increases in the thickness of the individual fibres and in the amount of connective tissue.

Because a muscle fibre is not a single cell, its parts are often given special names such as:

- sarcolemma (for plasma membrane)
- **sarcoplasmic reticulum** (for endoplasmic reticulum)
- **sarcoplasm** (for cytoplasm).

The nucleus and mitochondria in a muscle fibre are located just beneath the sarcolemma, and the sarcoplasmic reticulum extends between the myofibrils. When viewed under a microscope, skeletal muscle fibres show a pattern of banding across their length that gives rise to their other name, striated muscle.

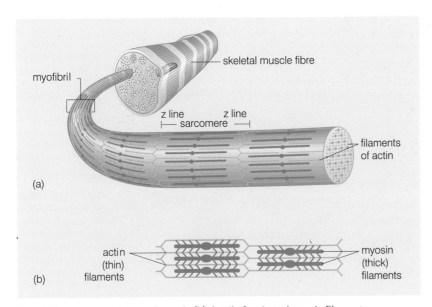

Fig. 3.2 *(a) Microstructure of muscle (b) detail of actin and myosin filaments*

The striated appearance of the muscle fibre is created by a pattern of alternating dark and light bands. The dark bands are called the **A bands**, and the light bands are the **I bands**. The centre of the A bands is divided by another region, the **H zone**. The I bands are bisected by the **Z line**. The reoccurring unit in a myofibril is the **sarcomere**, which extends from one Z line to the next.

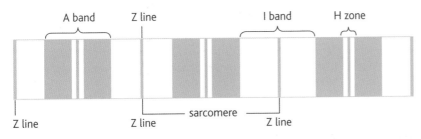

Fig. 3.3 *Sarcomeres and myofibril bands*

> ### Key terms
>
> **Sarcoplasmic reticulum:** equivalent to the endoplasmic reticulum of cells. It forms a network of channels that spread out over the surface of the myofibrils and acts as a store of calcium ions that when released initiate muscle contraction.
>
> **Sarcoplasm:** the equivalent of cytoplasm – the liquid interior of a muscle fibre.
>
> **A band:** the dark band in a myofibril.
>
> **I band:** the light band in a myofibril.
>
> **H zone:** the lighter region in the centre of the A band.
>
> **Z line:** the darker region in the centre of the I band.
>
> **Sarcomere:** the repeating unit of a myofibril, goes from one Z line to another.

Key terms

Myosin: thick protein filament.

Actin: thin protein filament.

Troponin: globular protein on actin.

Tropomyosin: thread-like protein that winds around the surface of actin.

AQA Examiner's tip

You must be able to label a diagram showing the different bands and zones within a myofibril, and then be able to explain how the regions change size during a muscle contraction.

Each myofibril is made up of arrays of parallel protein filaments. The thick filaments are composed of the protein **myosin**. The thin filaments are composed chiefly of the protein **actin** along with smaller amounts of two other proteins, **troponin** and **tropomyosin**.

The thick filaments of myosin produce the dark A band. The thin filaments of actin extend in each direction from the Z line. Where they do not overlap the thick filaments, they create the light I band. The H zone is that portion of the A band where the thick and thin filaments do not overlap.

Shortening of the sarcomeres in a myofibril produces the shortening of the myofibril and, in turn, of the muscle fibre of which it is a part.

The sliding-filament hypothesis

At the end of each molecule of myosin in the thick filaments there is a round part called the myosin head (it is a bit like the head of a golf club). The myosin heads have binding sites for the actin molecules in the thin filaments and ATP.

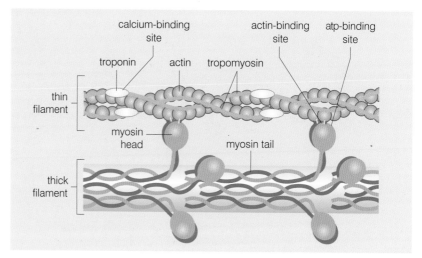

Fig. 3.4 *The arrangement of the protein filaments in a myofibril*

Activation of the muscle fibre by a nerve impulse causes the myosin heads to bind to actin. Once this has happened, the myosin head changes shape and this draws the thin filament a short distance past the thick filament. Then the binding breaks (for which ATP is needed) and re-forms farther along the thin filament to repeat the process. As a result, the filaments are pulled past each other in a ratchet-like action. There is no shortening, thickening, or folding of the individual filaments. The process works in much the same way as using your arms to pull on a length of rope. Your arm is the myosin with your hand being the myosin head; the rope is the thin actin filament. First, you grip the rope with one hand (myosin binds to actin); then you pull the rope (myosin head changes shape and draws the actin a short distance); then you let go of the rope (the binding breaks); then you grab the rope further along with your other hand before pulling again (repeat the process).

Images from electron microscopy support this model. As a muscle contracts:

- the Z lines come closer together
- the width of the I bands decreases

- the width of the H zones decreases
- but there is no change in the width of the A bands.

Conversely, as a muscle is stretched:

- the width of the I bands and H zones increases
- but there is still no change in the width of the A bands.

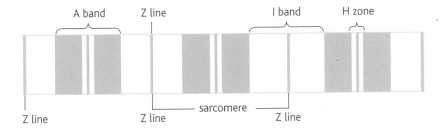

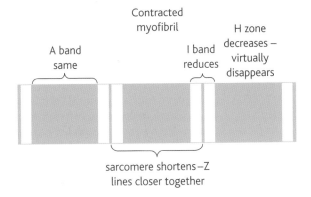

Fig. 3.5 *Changes to width of bands and zones*

Activity

Produce a poster or PowerPoint presentation that shows the changes that occur in the bandings and zones within a sarcomere between resting and contracting.

The cause of these changes is the arrival of a nerve impulse at the junction between a motor neurone and the muscle fibre. In resting muscle fibres, the thick myosin heads are prevented from attaching to the thin actin filaments by the presence of tropomyosin (see Table 3.1). Also when resting, the myofibrils have large stores of calcium ions in the sarcoplasmic reticulum. Spaced along the sarcolemma of the muscle fibre are extensive in-foldings of the membrane that form **transverse tubules** (t-tubules) that spread repeatedly into the interior of the myofibril. These transverse tubules end near the calcium-filled sacs of the sarcoplasmic reticulum.

The arrival of a nerve impulse initiates a wave of electrical activity that spreads over the surface membrane of the myofibril and eventually reaches the ends of the transverse tubules and hence the sarcoplasmic reticulum. This wave of electrical activity triggers the release of the calcium ions from the sarcoplasmic reticulum. The calcium ions diffuse out of the sarcoplasmic reticulum and go among the thick and thin filaments in the sarcomeres.

Some of the calcium ions that have been released from the sarcoplasmic reticulum attach themselves to the troponin molecules on the thin actin filaments. When the calcium ions bind to the troponin, it causes a change in the shape of the troponin molecule; this in turn causes the tropomyosin molecule to move. The tropomyosin normally winds around the actin molecule, covering the myosin-binding site of the actin

Key terms

Transverse tubules: a network of folds/tubes from the membrane of a myofibril that provide access for electrical activity to the inside of the myofibril.

molecule, thus preventing myosin from attaching to actin. When the tropomyosin moves because of the change in shape of the troponin, the myosin-binding site on the thin actin filament for the myosin head is exposed and the myosin binds to the actin.

When the myosin binds to the actin, it activates an enzyme called myosin-ATPase. Myosin-ATPase causes ATP to breakdown and energy to be released. This energy is used to cause the change in shape of the myosin head, which in turn moves the actin filament. Once the myosin head has changed shape and moved the actin, it detaches from the actin and relocates on another active site further along the actin molecule. This reattachment activates more myosin-ATPase to breakdown ATP and release energy, and the myosin head changes shape pulling the actin filament along.

This change in the myosin head's shape and the accompanying pulling of the actin filament are repeated for hundreds of different myosin heads and actin-binding sites. It is these interactions between the actin filament and myosin heads, linked to the release of energy through the action of myosin-ATPase and the breakdown of ATP, that causes the actin to slide over the myosin and is how the sarcomere contracts.

Because of the speed of the wave of electrical activity, it arrives virtually simultaneously at the ends of all the transverse tubules, ensuring that all sarcomeres contract together. Once nerve stimulation stops, the wave of electrical activity ceases; the calcium ions are pumped back into the sarcoplasmic reticulum; and the protein molecules return to their resting shape, with the tropomyosin covering the active site on the actin filament. This means that the myosin heads cannot bind to the actin. Myosin-ATPase is no longer formed and therefore no ATP is broken down and energy is not released. There is no tension generated in the muscle and it relaxes.

■ Activity

Draw a table with three columns headed 'Structure', 'Resting' and 'Contracting'. Under the heading 'Structure', list all the structures involved in muscle contraction. Under the headings 'Resting' and 'Contracting', write in the function of each structure during the resting and contracting phase of a muscle.

■ Different types of muscle fibres

There are two major types of muscle fibre within a single skeletal muscle: **slow-twitch** (ST) and fast-twitch (FT).

Slow-twitch fibres

Slow-twitch fibres are sometimes called type I fibres and fast-twitch are called type II. They are named according to how quickly they can reach peak tension (contract). Slow-twitch fibres are relatively slow in generating peak force; fast-twitch fibres are about 10 times faster at generating peak force. Most muscles in your body contain a mixture of fast- and slow-twitch muscle fibres. Slow-twitch fibres are adapted for slow rhythmical contractions, although they can still contract quickly enough for all essential sporting activities. Slow-twitch fibres tend to be smaller in size and produce less overall force than fast-twitch fibres, and they are more energy efficient, producing more force for the same energy input, and are therefore well adapted for prolonged exercise, where

■ Key terms

Slow-twitch muscle fibres: contract up 10 times as slowly as fast-twitch fibres but have greater endurance.

the supply of energy might become a factor that limits performance. By comparison, fast-twitch fibres are easily fatigued.

Activity

Complete the table to show the differences between fast- and slow-twitch muscle fibres.

	Fast-twitch	Slow-twitch
Type of contractions		
Size		
Amount of force produced		
Energy efficiency		
Adapted for		
Fatigability		

Most muscles contain different proportions of slow-twitch and fast-twitch fibres as shown in Table 3.1.

Table 3.1 *The proportions of muscle fibre types in different muscles*

Athlete	Gender	Muscle	Percentage of slow-twitch muscle	Percentage of fast-twitch muscle
Sprint runner	Male	Gastrocnemius	24	76
	Female	Gastrocnemius	27	73
Distance runner	Male	Gastrocnemius	79	21
	Female	Gastrocnemius	69	31
Swimmer	Male	Posterior deltoid	67	33
Shot-putter	Male	Gastrocnemius	38	62
Non-athlete	Male	Vastus lateralis	47	53

In general, slow-twitch (type I) fibres have a high level of endurance; they are suited to aerobic exercise. They produce their ATP primarily from aerobic energy pathways.

Because of this, they are recruited most often during low-intensity endurance events. As should be expected, this type of muscle fibre has a high aerobic capacity, which is linked to a greater number of blood capillaries for the delivery of oxygen per fibre than the fast-twitch type. Slow-twitch fibres contain more myoglobin (the red pigment that combines with oxygen) than fast-twitch fibres. For this reason, they are sometimes called red fibres. Slow-twitch fibres contain many more mitochondria and their associated oxidative enzymes than fast-twitch fibres.

Fast-twitch fibres

Fast-twitch (type II) muscle fibres have relatively poor aerobic endurance. They are better suited to anaerobic activity, as they produce their ATP primarily from anaerobic energy pathways.

Link

For more information on aerobic energy pathways, see Chapter 1 – Aerobic energy systems (pages 2–12).

■ Link

For more information on anaerobic energy pathways, see Chapter 2 – Anaerobic energy systems (pages 15–30).

■ Key terms

Fast-twitch type IIa (FOG): characteristics are fast contraction, large force, fatigues easily.

Fast-twitch type IIb (FG): characteristics are very rapid contractions, very large forces, fatigues very easily.

Fast-twitch muscle fibres are well adapted to short, intense bursts of effort. They have a larger diameter than slow-twitch fibres, because there are more myosin filaments in them, and the myosin is thicker than the type found in slow-twitch fibres. Because of the type of myosin involved and its arrangement in the myofibrils, fast-twitch fibres are able to produce more force than slow-twitch fibres. This greater force of contraction in fast-twitch fibres is helped by having a more complex arrangement of sarcoplasmic reticulum and that means that calcium ions can be released and returned to storage more quickly than in slow-twitch fibres. Fast-twitch fibres also possess a different type of myosin-ATPase that releases energy from ATP quicker than the type found in slow-twitch fibres. As should be expected from your reading of Chapter 2 – Anaerobic energy systems, fast-twitch fibres have larger stores of phosphocreatine than slow-twitch fibres.

■ Activity

Fast- and slow-twitch muscle fibres differ in terms of the predominant energy systems they use. Make a list of the major characteristics that this gives each type of fibre.

Different types of fast-twitch fibre

Although talking about differences between fast- and slow-twitch fibres is convenient, there are in fact at least two types of fast-twitch fibres: a **fast-twitch type IIa (FOG)** or fast oxidative glycolytic, and a **fast-twitch type IIb (FG)** or fast-twitch glycolytic.

Fast-twitch type IIa (FOG) fibres fatigue easily because of their limited endurance. Thus, IIa fibres appear to be used mainly during short, high-intensity endurance events such as a 1-mile run, or 400 m swim. Although the significance of fast-twitch type IIb (FG) fibres is not fully understood, the fibres appear to be used infrequently in normal low-intensity exercise and are the predominant fibre that is recruited in highly explosive events, such as 100 m sprints, or 50 m swims. The maximum contraction velocity of a single slow-twitch fibre is approximately one-tenth that of a type IIb fibre. Type I fibres also produce less maximum force than type IIb fibres. Type IIa fibres lie somewhere between type I and type IIb in their maximum contraction velocity and maximum force production. Because of the high velocity of contraction and the large forces they produce, type IIb fibres are probably one of the key elements required for successful performances in speed-dependent activities like sprinting. It is therefore not surprising to find that successful sprint athletes possess more of these IIb fibres than the average person. Table 3.2 summarises the differences between these muscle fibre types.

It would appear from early research that the percentage of fibre types that any one muscle and/or any one person has is due to heredity. Distribution at birth varies, although the average proportions through the whole body would appear to be 50 per cent slow-twitch and 50 per cent fast-twitch.

Recent research suggests that classifying muscle fibre types as slow-twitch, fast-twitch type IIa and fast-twitch type IIb is in fact too simplistic: it may be better to think about there being two extremes of muscle fibre, slow-twitch and fast-twitch type IIb, each having widely different characteristics in terms of predominant energy metabolism and speed and force of contraction. Accordingly, fast-twitch type IIa fibres would fall into a middle band, with some slow-twitch characteristics and some type IIb characteristics.

Table 3.2 *Characteristics of muscle fibres*

Characteristics of muscle fibres	Slow oxidative fibres (type I)	Fast oxidative glycolytic fibres (type IIa)	Fast glycolytic fibres (type IIb)
Structural			
Fibres per motor neurone	10–180	300–800	300–800
Motor neurone size	Small	Large	Large
Type of myosin ATPase	Slow	Fast	Fast
Sarcoplasmic reticulum development	Low	High	High
Functional			
Aerobic capacity	High	Moderate	Low
Anaerobic capacity	Low	High	Very high
Contractile speed	Slow	Fast	Fast
Fatigue resistance	High	Moderate	Low
Motor unit strength	Low	High	High

Effects of training

Further research, however, has shown that certain characteristics of muscle fibres can be altered by training. One part of the myosin filament determines how the entire muscle fibre functions. This component of myosin exists in three forms: I, IIa and IIb. Slow-twitch fibres contain mainly the type I component, while fast-twitch types IIa and IIb contain a predominance of the type IIa and IIb components, respectively.

Studies on paralysed muscle have found that when activity is absent, so are type IIa fibre-types. This supports the idea that the type IIb component, and therefore IIb fibres, constitutes the only fibre-type setting in humans. It has also been known for some time that increases in such activities as strength or power training can lead to conversion of muscle fibres. But, unfortunately, this conversion operates in one direction only, changing fast type IIb fibres into slower type IIa fibres. Not only that, but, if the heavy training continues for a month or more, virtually all type IIb fibres will change into type IIa, thereby reducing the sprinting potential of the performer.

The interesting thing here is what happens when the heavy strength training stops: the newly formed type IIa fibres revert back to type IIb. In fact, the body overcompensates and converts more type IIa to type IIb than originally existed. As yet, it is not clear how long an athlete needs to train heavily for and how long they need to rest to produce maximum overcompensation of fast-twitch type IIb fibres, but the potential to develop a regimen is there.

Characteristics of different muscle fibre types in relation to sporting performance

Just as you might expect elite sprinters to have more fast-twitch type IIb fibres than the average person, it would be likely that, on average, marathon runners have a greater proportion of slow-twitch fibres than the rest of the population. However, mere possession of the correct proportions of fast-twitch or slow-twitch muscle fibres is no guarantee of sporting success in a particular activity.

Research into the ratios of slow-twitch to fast-twitch muscle fibres involving muscle biopsy of elite male athletes has found different percentages of slow-twitch fibres in sprinters and marathon runners and some overlap between the two types of athlete. As shown in Table 3.3, some sprinters have a higher percentage of slow-twitch fibres than marathon runners.

Table 3.3 *The percentage of slow-twitch fibres for different types of elite male athlete*

	Range of percentage of slow-twitch fibres	Average percentage of slow-twitch fibres
Male marathon runners	50–95	85
Male 800 m runners	50–80	55
Male sprinters	20–55	35

This suggests that, for some elite marathon runners and sprinters at least, the presence of a high proportion of slow-twitch and fast-twitch muscle fibres, respectively, is not the sole determinant of good performance. It is likely that other factors must influence performance at these events. These factors could be physical, such as length of lever, $\dot{V}O_2$ max, physique, etc., or psychological, such as motivation, commitment, confidence, etc.

Activity

Refer to Table 3.3. What would be the perfect proportion of fast- and slow-twitch muscle fibres for an athlete for each event? Hence which of the three groups of elite athletes is best suited to their event?

Motor units and spatial summation

All the motor neurones leading to skeletal muscles have branches, each of which ends in a junction with a single muscle fibre. The place where a motor neurone meets a muscle fibre is the neuromuscular junction. Nerve impulses passing down a single motor neurone will thus trigger contraction in all the muscle fibres at which the branches of that neurone terminate. This minimum unit of contraction is called a **motor unit**.

Each muscle fibre within a motor unit either contracts or does not contract. There is no such thing as a partial contraction. This is the **all or nothing law**. When the motor neurone of a motor unit activates the muscle fibres within that motor unit, all the fibres in that unit will contract, and they will contract maximally.

Motor units vary in size. The motor unit is small in muscles over which we have precise control:

- A single motor neurone triggers fewer than 10 fibres in the muscles controlling eye movement.
- The motor units of the muscles controlling the larynx are as small as two to three fibres for each motor neurone.

In contrast, a single motor unit for a muscle like the gastrocnemius muscle may include 1,000 to 2,000 fibres.

Key terms

Motor unit: a motor neurone and its muscle fibres.

All or nothing law: muscles fibres either contract or do not contract; there is no such thing as a partial contraction.

All fibres within a motor unit are the same type, either fast-twitch or slow-twitch. There are no mixed motor units containing a mixture of fibres. In nearly all activities, it is the motor units with slow-twitch fibres that are first recruited by the brain to cause movements. Only if the intensity of the activity is very great, or the slow-twitch fibres become fatigued, are fast-twitch motor units recruited. This is why fatigue appears to arrive suddenly. Initially, when a muscle is contracting, the slow-twitch motor units are working; as they tire, they are replaced by motor units that are primarily fast-twitch in nature and produce lactic acid, and therefore fatigue follows quickly.

It is the motor neurone that supplies a motor unit which largely determines the type of fibre within that motor unit, and thus it is probably more accurate to talk of fast- and slow-twitch motor units. The motor neurone in slow-twitch motor units is smaller in diameter than that in a fast-twitch motor unit, and activates 10 to 180 slow-twitch muscle fibres, rather than the 300 to 800 muscle fibres activated by a fast-twitch motor neurone.

Hence, when a slow-twitch motor neurone stimulates its fibres, far fewer muscle fibres contract than when a single fast-twitch motor neurone stimulates its fibres. This is one of the reasons why fast-twitch motor units develop more force than slow-twitch motor units: more individual muscle fibres are involved.

It should be obvious to everybody that different activities require muscle contractions involving differing amounts of strength. The strength required to throw a dart is much less than that required to throw a javelin. There are two main ways of varying the strength of contraction of a muscle, both of which require an understanding of the idea of motor units.

Although the response of a motor unit is all or nothing, the strength of the response of the entire muscle is determined by the number of motor units activated, and the size of the motor units involved. This is **spatial summation**. In order to achieve a greater force of contraction, the brain recruits more and/or bigger motor units.

Even at rest, most of our skeletal muscles are in a state of partial contraction called tonus. Tonus is maintained by the activation of a few motor units at all times, even in resting muscle. As one set of motor units relaxes, another set takes over.

☑ *You should now be able to:*

- describe the microscopic structure of skeletal muscle
- describe the sliding-filament hypothesis of muscle contraction
- describe the main differences between fast- and slow-twitch muscle fibres
- discuss whether the distribution of muscle-fibre types is a good predictor of performance
- explain the role of motor units
- explain spatial summation.

Link

For more information on lactic acid, see Chapter 2 – Anaerobic energy systems (page 16).

AQA Examiner's tip

Questions concerning motor units require detailed answers – a motor unit consists of a motor neurone and its accompanying muscle fibres. Each motor unit is made up of only one type of muscle fibre and all the fibres contract fully at the same time – the all or nothing law.

Key terms

Spatial summation: changes in strength of contraction are brought about by altering the number and size of motor units involved.

AQA Examiner's tip

There are other forms of muscle summation, but you need only know spatial summation.

1 (a) Identify the position of myosin and actin in Figure 3.6, a diagram of skeletal muscle.

(2 marks)

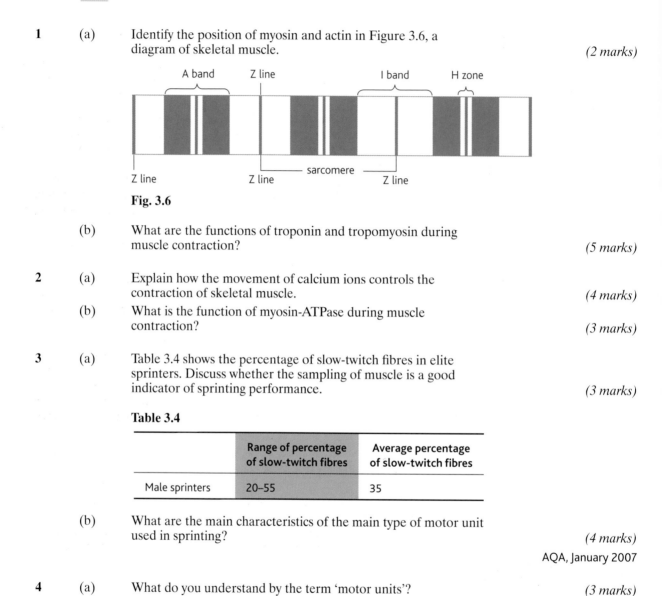

Fig. 3.6

(b) What are the functions of troponin and tropomyosin during muscle contraction?

(5 marks)

2 (a) Explain how the movement of calcium ions controls the contraction of skeletal muscle.

(4 marks)

(b) What is the function of myosin-ATPase during muscle contraction?

(3 marks)

3 (a) Table 3.4 shows the percentage of slow-twitch fibres in elite sprinters. Discuss whether the sampling of muscle is a good indicator of sprinting performance.

(3 marks)

Table 3.4

	Range of percentage of slow-twitch fibres	Average percentage of slow-twitch fibres
Male sprinters	20–55	35

(b) What are the main characteristics of the main type of motor unit used in sprinting?

(4 marks)

AQA, January 2007

4 (a) What do you understand by the term 'motor units'?

(3 marks)

(b) How are motor units involved in spatial summation?

(4 marks)

AQA, June 2005

4 The elite performer: food, supplements and performance-enhancing drugs

In this chapter you will:

- understand the importance of water in a performer's diet and how a performer can maintain their water–salt balance

- understand why athletes take food supplements, such as creatine, protein drinks, and bicarbonate of soda, and the use of herbal remedies

- examine the evidence for the effectiveness of food and health supplements

- understand the physiological reasons for the use of performance-enhancing drugs

- understand the consequences to the health of a performer from the use of performance-enhancing drugs.

AQA Examiner's tip

For questions on water, candidates will be expected to know the claimed or actual benefit and any adverse effects of taking or not taking on water.

Key terms

Dehydration: the condition that occurs when the amount of water in the body falls below normal, disrupting the balance of sugars and salts (electrolytes) in the body.

The substances that are taken into the body play a vital role in the preparation of a sport performer. As you learned in Chapter 1 – Aerobic energy systems, and Chapter 2 – Anaerobic energy systems, digested food substances provide the sources of the energy required to resynthesise ATP, without which we could not live let alone perform at an elite level.

In this chapter, we shall look at other elements of the modern-day performer's diet, both legal and illegal. Elite performers are, of course, different from the average person. The amount and intensity of work undertaken by elite performers necessitates that that their diet should always be carefully planned. Whilst having the right amounts of a range of foodstuffs will provide all the necessary nutrition for many performers, elite performers are always seeking that tiny advantage that puts them on the podium.

We shall investigate why players are handed water or electrolytic drinks at almost every pause in an elite-level team game and why marathon organisers provide water stops every few kilometres. There are now a large number of food supplements sold in health shops, supermarkets and across the internet, and sport performers may spend a great deal of money seeking that extra edge – are they wise to do so, i.e. do the supplements work? Food supplements are usually legal and do not contravene international sports' drug guidelines yet elite performers are constantly tempted to seek and use illegal performance-enhancing drugs. In this chapter, we shall consider the physiological benefits of performance-enhancing drugs and their effect upon the performer. Later in the book, the legal and ethical implications of using these substances will be examined.

Sport performers face many decisions about what they put into their body. This chapter will provide you with the factual information necessary to make informed choices and, of course, to answer questions on this important and developing topic. It is important to understand that a textbook can only give you a basic understanding. Any performer should ensure that they are fully informed, taking advice from expert nutritionists and coaches, before making decisions about diet and supplements to their diet.

Water

Water is the most basic, but vital, part of our diet. In this section we look at the role that water plays in the maintenance of normal body functions, the effects of **dehydration** and when and how fluids should be taken.

Water and the body's electrolytic balance

Water makes up between 50 and 60 per cent of an adult's body mass, and a third of this is found within the blood plasma. Without water, death can occur in days. Water is important because it:

- regulates body temperature
- carries nutrients and oxygen to all cells in the body via the blood plasma
- helps to convert food into energy and absorb nutrients

- is required for expiration
- removes waste
- protects and cushions vital organs and joints.

In addition, the body's wide range of **electrolytes** are vital for the proper functioning of cells, particularly muscle cells, and for ensuring that nutrients and waste products are exchanged and that the body's pH level (the body's acidity or alkalinity) is maintained.

The most important electrolytes in the body are sodium, potassium and chlorine. Sodium and potassium (positively charged ions) and chlorine (negatively charged ions) are vital for the electrical transmission of nerve impulses that amongst other things control muscle contraction. Electrolytes readily dissolve in water and therefore the water and electrolytes in the body are closely linked; a deficiency in one can alter the overall concentrations within the body, adversely affecting performance.

The problem of dehydration and electrolyte loss

Water is lost from the body through the expulsion of waste products (urine and faeces) and when exhaling and sweating. The amount of water lost through exhaling and sweating varies in relation to environmental conditions, such as temperature, humidity and altitude, and the amount of exercise you are undertaking.

The amount of water lost from exhaling can vary between a quarter to a third of a litre per day; water loss is greatest in cold temperatures, as the inhaled air is dry, or when at altitude. On the other hand, water loss when sweating is greatest under conditions of high temperature. Environmentally, most water is lost when conditions are hot and humid. With high humidity, the sweat forming on the skin does not evaporate and the body cannot cool itself.

Under all environmental conditions, exercise causes more fluid loss. When we exercise, we produce heat as a by-product and the body must lose that heat to maintain its internal temperature within the normal range. Exercise also raises our breathing rate and we lose more water vapour by exhaling. We also lose electrolytes through sweating.

The loss of water from the body (dehydration) has a number of detrimental effects. Blood plasma has a high proportion of the body's water and if water losses are high the blood thickens. This causes a reduction of blood flow and a rise in cardiac activity to maintain flow to the organs and the muscles. As blood volume decreases, blood flow to the skin reduces and the body cannot cool itself effectively, so body temperature rises. Rises in core body temperature are serious, leading to heat stress, collapse and even death (see Table 4.1 on page 47). Fluid loss which exceeds 3 to 5 per cent of our body weight reduces aerobic exercise performance and impairs reaction time, judgement, concentration and decision making.

A change in the **electrolytic balance** of the body also has detrimental effects. The electrolytic balance is affected by electrolyte loss through sweating and by an unbalanced diet. The liver functions to filter out excess electrolytes that can be caused by such diet imbalances as too much salt (sodium chloride). Loss of electrolytes can cause impairments to performance by causing:

- drowsiness and impaired decision making
- muscle weakness and fatigue
- muscle cramps
- interference in the neural control of the heart causing an abnormal heart rhythm.

■ **Key terms**

Electrolytes: the scientific term for the ions of salts such as sodium. Ions are electrically charged particles.

■ **Key terms**

Electrolytic balance: the proportion or concentration of electrolytes within the fluids of the body.

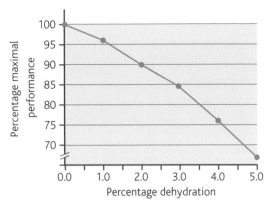

Fig. 4.1 *The effect of dehydration on performance*

As electrolytes are dissolved in water, any change to the amount of water in the body will also change the electrolytic balance. They must be seen as being inter-related and must both be regulated, particularly when exercising and in environmentally abnormal conditions.

Temperature regulation

The body strives to maintain its core temperature between 36 °C and 37 °C. The body is constantly monitoring the internal core temperature and skin temperature. When the skin or core temperature exceeds 37 °C, the body takes steps to lose the excess heat. Equally importantly, the body must prevent itself from becoming too cool as this will also impair performance and normal functioning.

AQA Examiner's tip

In answer to an examination question on water balance, the examiner will expect a discussion of electrolytes.

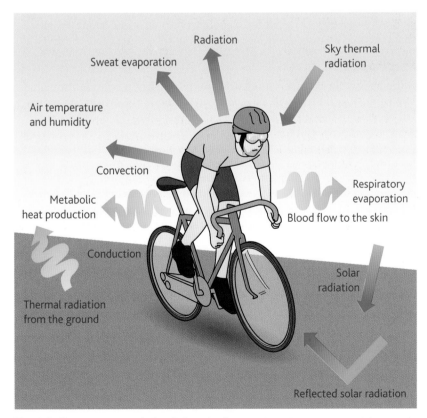

Fig. 4.2 *Temperature regulation during exercise*

■ Activity

Using a thermometer, take your temperature at various times during the day – waking up, after a meal, after exercise, after rest, just before bed, etc.

1 Does your temperature vary?

2 What may have caused any variation?

Cooling

The body loses heat by radiation, conduction, convection and evaporation. The body radiates heat because it is normally warmer than its surroundings. When exercising in conditions of high temperature, the body can actually acquire heat from the environment. Heat loss from convection is greater when we have air circulating around us. If the air is still, air next to the skin is warmed and insulates us, decreasing heat loss. Conduction is the movement of heat from a warm surface to a cool surface. If the surrounding air is warm, heat loss via conduction is reduced.

Heat loss by evaporation is the major way in which the body guards against overheating. When we sweat, water is deposited on the skin from the sweat glands. This water then evaporates and has a cooling effect. As body temperature rises as a result of exercise, we react in two main ways. Blood circulation to the surface of the body is increased by arterio- and vasodilation (the widening of the blood vessels) resulting in a reddening of the skin, particularly the face. Heat is then lost through increased radiation and conduction.

Sweating, the main process in which heat is lost, occurs when the sweat glands in the skin are innervated (stimulated) by the nervous system, causing more sweat (water and sodium chloride) to be secreted on to the skin. As sweat evaporates, it has a cooling effect. It is important to note that it is not sweating that causes cooling but the evaporation of the sweat.

Keeping warm

If the body's core temperature falls to 35 °C, we begin to suffer from **hypothermia** and this will cause impaired function. Core temperatures fall because of the effect of the environment cooling the body (through low temperatures and high winds) and/or the body's inability to generate heat, owing to fatigue. Performers who operate in cold conditions (skiers, mountain climbers, etc.) maintain core temperatures by ensuring that they take on board sufficient energy through their food intake (they can be using 6,000 to 8,000 calories a day) and by preventing heat loss by wearing warm and windproof clothing. The body also generates heat by shivering – involuntary muscle contractions that produce heat.

■ **Key terms**

Hypothermia: a potentially fatal condition occurring when the core body temperature falls below 35 °C.

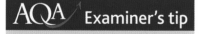 Examiner's tip

Don't assume that questions about temperature regulation will always focus on controlling a rise in body temperature – keeping warm is also an important area.

■ Activity

Keep a food diary for three days, listing everything that you eat and how much energy it contains.

1 Calculate the amount of energy that you have ingested.

2 Calculate how much exercise you would have to do to use that energy.

The body has a very narrow temperature range within which it works. If temperatures fall outside that range, the body's functioning can be impaired severely enough to cause death (see Table 4.1).

Table 4.1 *The effects of variations in body temperature*

44 °C	Almost certainly death will occur; however, people have been known to survive up to 46.5 °C	Over-heating
43 °C	Possibly death, or serious brain damage, continuous convulsions and shock. Cardio-respiratory collapse will occur	
42 °C	May become comatose, severe delirium, vomiting, and convulsions can occur. Blood pressure may be high or low and heart rate will be very fast	
41 °C	Fainting, vomiting, severe headache, dizziness, confusion, hallucinations, delirium and drowsiness, possibly palpitations and breathlessness	
40 °C	Profuse sweating, fainting, dehydration, weakness, vomiting, headache and dizziness	
39 °C	Severe sweating, flushed and very red. Fast heart rate and breathlessness	
38 °C	Sweating, feeling very uncomfortable	
37 °C	Normal body temperature	
36 °C	Mild to moderate shivering (it drops this low during sleep). May be a normal body temperature	
35 °C	Intense shivering, numbness and bluish/grayness of the skin	
34 °C	Hypothermia. Severe shivering, loss of movement of fingers, blueness and confusion	
33 °C	Moderate to severe confusion, sleepiness, depressed reflexes, progressive loss of shivering, slow heart beat, shallow breathing. Shivering may stop	
32 °C	Hallucinations, delirium, complete confusion, extreme sleepiness becoming comatose, shivering stopped	
31 °C	Comatose, rarely conscious. Very shallow breathing and slow heart rate	
28 °C	Severe heart rhythm disturbances are likely and breathing may stop at any time. Patient may appear to be dead	
24–26 °C	Death usually occurs due to irregular heart beat or respiratory arrest. However, some people have been known to survive with body temperatures as low as 14.2 °C	Over-cooling

Maintaining the water and electrolytic balance

Any attempt to maintain water and electrolytic balances must be in relation to:

- the intensity and duration of exercise
- the environmental conditions
- the convenience of ingesting fluids and electrolytes.

Sport events can of course be varied. A performer should therefore consider what they can do prior to the event, during the event and after the event.

Fig. 4.3 *Keeping warm*

Activity

Consider your own sport event or one where you act as a coach. Be as specific as you can in your planning.

1. What are the effects of the event likely to be on the water and electrolytic balances of the body of an elite performer competing under their normal environmental conditions?

2 Do the characteristics of your sport or level of competition mean that you could be performing under different environmental conditions – if so, what would they be?

3 What can you do before the event to prepare for any disturbance to the water or electrolytic balance?

4 What can you do during the event?

5 What should you do after the event?

What should you take on board?

Drinking plain water causes bloating, suppresses thirst (and thus further drinking), stimulates more water loss through urine output and affects the body's level of sodium. It is better therefore to use drinks that also contain electrolytes and carbohydrates. The addition of a carbohydrate allows the drink to be more palatable (electrolytes and water taste a bit like the sea!) and also add a valuable, easily absorbed energy supply. This is true not only for endurance performers like cyclists and marathon runners but also for games players (there is now some evidence that ingestion of carbohydrates during an event can maintain alertness and judgement). Isotonic CHO-electrolyte drinks generally contain 4 to 8 per cent carbohydrate and 10 to 25 mmol/l of sodium.

The various concentrations of carbohydrates, electrolytes and water are dependent on a number of factors: body weight, intensity and duration of exercise, temperature, humidity and level of fitness. A performer considering using isotonic drinks must first seek the advice of a knowledgeable coach or sport nutritionist.

Prior to an event

Ensure that you do not become dehydrated on the way to the event or prior to the event. It is not necessary to use specialist electrolytic drinks at this stage. Performers are generally advised to:

* drink 400 to 600 ml of fluid 2 to 3 hours prior, and then 150 to 350 ml fluid about 15 min before exercise
* eat a meal or snack, high in carbohydrate, 2 to 4 hours prior (ideal carbohydrate foods include whole grains, vegetables, fruit, juices, milk, yogurt, soy drinks).

During the event

Performers should ingest water, carbohydrate and electrolytes whenever possible, even if they do not feel thirsty – exercise can prevent you 'feeling thirsty' even though you are beginning to dehydrate. How much and how often will depend on convenience: marathon runners have regular opportunities, but opportunities for team game players are less frequent.

Performers must be aware of how quickly carbohydrates become available as glucose in the bloodstream – 'blood sugar'. Carbohydrates with a higher **glycaemic index** are absorbed more quickly into the bloodstream, so the performer's choice of carbohydrate depends on whether they want rapid restoration of blood sugar levels after prolonged work or a slower release of glucose into the bloodstream. Current thinking is that, by ingesting small amounts of a range of carbohydrates with different glycaemic index ratings, you are using all the body's digestive and transport mechanisms to get glucose into the bloodstream and will help maintain a sustained level of blood sugar, avoiding peaks and troughs.

■ Key terms

Glycaemic index: a system for ranking carbohydrates according to how quickly they are converted to glucose and enter the bloodstream, raising blood sugar levels.

Activity

In a playground or sports field, set up some tables or drinking stations with some isotonic drinks and then run around the course at a submaximal pace and ingest some fluid at each station. Consider the problems of a marathon runner:

- timing the run to the table with others
- getting hold of the drink
- ingesting the fluid
- the problem with used drink containers on the floor.

After the event

Performers, particularly endurance performers or those competing in conditions of high heat and humidity, are rarely able to keep themselves completely hydrated. There are several reasons:

- Exercise represses thirst and performers underestimate their level of dehydration.
- There are limited opportunities to drink during an event.
- There is an intolerance to taking on too much fluid; feelings of sickness are likely (dehydration will exacerbate those feelings).
- There may be an underestimate of how much the performer is sweating.

It is estimated that, during competition, endurance runners and canoeists generally drink about 500 ml/h and dehydrate at a rate of 500 to 1,000 ml/h. Triathletes have been shown to lose an average of 1.7 per cent of body weight for a 3 h event and 3.7 per cent for a 12 h event.

Given this fact, rehydration after an event is vital, particularly if the performer is going to be competing again later on in the day or the next day.

The essential need is to restore the water and electrolytic balance and to replenish carbohydrates. Immediately after the event an electrolytic drink will help, but then the performer should revert to their normal diet, but with plenty of fluids, carbohydrates, etc.

The United States Tennis Association offers the following advice to tennis players on post match nutrition

Eat carbohydrates as soon as possible, preferably within 30 minutes of a match. Begin by drinking a sports drink as you walk off the court.

Replace 150 percent of body fluids lost or at least 20 oz. per pound of weight loss within 2 hours of a match.

Eat a high-carbohydrate meal that also contains a lean protein source within 2 hours after play to maximize muscle glycogen recovery (rebuild energy stores) and to support protein synthesis in muscle.

During tournament play, be sure to include carbohydrates, protein, fluid and sodium in the evening meal to quicken recovery from play.

Normally no need to salt foods if consuming foods and beverages that are natural sodium sources.

Avoid high-protein and high-fat foods as these will contribute to dehydration.

www.playerdevelopment.usta.com

AQA Examiner's tip

When answering questions about fluid intake and dehydration, you will be expected to discuss more than fluid intake during an event. To get high marks you should discuss pre- and post-event strategies.

■ Food supplements – why?

There has been a growth in the use of food supplements in the general population and by sport performers. The range of supplements includes vitamins, minerals, protein supplements and herbal remedies alongside specific products such as creatine.

■ Activity

Visit a health food shop or use a website and see the how many of the products on sale claim to help physical or sport performance. Do you think the claims made are justified?

■ Key terms

UK Sport: the UK-wide organisation responsible for delivering world-class sporting success in conjunction with a range of partner organisations.

Ergogenic aid: a performance-enhancing aid or substance, legal or illegal.

In general, if performers follow a well-balanced diet it should not be necessary to take food supplements. By taking food supplements, performers run the risk of taking something that is on **UK Sport**'s list of banned substances. In May 2003 an International Olympic Committee (IOC) study tested 640 supplements available in the UK and found that nearly 20 per cent contained banned substances.

UK Sport states that:

> UK athletes are advised to be cautious and vigilant in their choice to use any supplement. No guarantee can be given that any particular supplement, including vitamins and minerals, **ergogenic aids** and herbal remedies, is free from Prohibited Substances.

uksport.gov.uk

The range of supplements available is very wide but the AQA specification only requires a working knowledge of the ones discussed in this section.

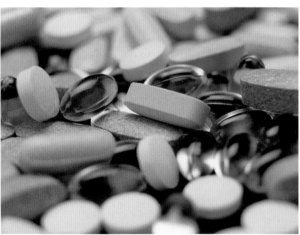

Fig. 4.4 *Food supplements or natural food?*

Creatine

Phosphocreatine plays an important role in providing the energy for rapid muscular contractions and for maximal work over a short period.

It has been known since the 1920s that it is possible to raise the body's level of creatine (a substance formed by the body and used as an energy source for ATP resynthesis) by taking dietary supplements. Studies show that high-dose creatine supplements (approximately 20 g/day) can increase the amount of creatine in muscles. But the evidence to date on the effect on performance is mixed, with nearly as many studies showing negative results as positive ones. There is some evidence to show that there may be some benefit to high-intensity, short-burst athletes.

From a study of rugby players in 2007, it was concluded that:

> Creatine supplementation may enhance muscular performance, but it is unclear if it would interfere with aerobic endurance during running because of increased body mass.

P. D. Chilibeck, C. Magnus and M. Anderson, Effect of in-season creatine supplementation on body composition and performance in rugby union football players. Journal of Applied Physiology, Nutrition and Metabolism, *2007*

On the other hand, its long-term effects are unknown and, since creatine is excreted by the kidneys, there may be long-term effects on that organ although none has yet been found. Some studies reported that those taking creatine supplements were more liable to muscle cramping; others that takers suffered from diarrhoea. More research work is being undertaken.

Creatine is not on UK Sport's list of banned substances but the NCAA (the US body responsible for school, college and university sport) prohibits schools and colleges from providing young performers with creatine supplements.

Protein supplements

There is no evidence to suggest that sport performers, even elite performers, need to take any more protein than is available from a normal balanced diet, particularly as diets in most Western countries often contain more protein than is required. Excess amounts of protein are dealt with by the liver and kidneys and over many years the taking of protein supplements may have a detrimental effect on those two organs.

Performers who take **protein drink** supplements do so in the hope that it will allow them to build more muscle mass, but Katch and McArdle state that:

> Amino acid supplementation in any form has not been shown by adequate experimental design and methodology to increase muscle mass or significantly improve muscular strength, power, or endurance.

W. D. Katch and F. I. McArdle, Exercise Physiology; Energy Nutrition and Human Performance, *1996*

Herbal remedies

The use of herbal remedies stems from the practice of herbalism, which is a traditional medicinal therapy based on the use of plants and plant extracts. Herbal remedies are used alongside or instead of modern medicines, therapies and treatments. Herbal remedies are administered via oils, tinctures and infusions. If linked to the practice of homeopathy, only minute quantities of the extracts are used; scientists who have researched the use of homeopathic remedies conclude that the trace amounts involved are so small that they could not have any effect within the body. The outcome of research into the use of herbal remedies is also unclear; some studies report that use of products such as arnica can reduce muscle soreness, whilst others have found no benefit whatsoever.

AQA Examiner's tip

You will be expected to gain sufficient knowledge and understanding to be able to evaluate critically the claims made by the manufacturers about the value of food supplements.

Link

For more information on the role of phosphocreatine in muscular contraction see Chapter 2 – Anaerobic energy systems (page 16).

Activity

Consider the demands of your activity – would the claimed benefits of creatine supplement help improve your performance?

AQA Examiner's tip

Full examination questions will ask you to connect your knowledge of nutrition with your knowledge of the physiology of energy systems.

Key terms

Protein drink: a drink that is approximately 70 per cent protein; it is made from powdered substances mixed with milk, orange juice, etc.

During the 1990s, Chinese female athletes achieved a high degree of success, and claims were made for the use of traditional Chinese supplements and remedies. A number of these athletes were subsequently found to have taken banned performance-enhancing drugs. In China the line between traditional herbal remedies and drugs is a blurred one and the issue is proving difficult for the Chinese sport authorities to resolve. UK Sport's warnings over the use of supplements would certainly extend to herbal remedies bought over the counter as in many cases the ingredients are not listed.

Nevertheless, despite the doubts and scientific uncertainty there are many performers who are convinced that a herbal or homeopathic treatment has helped them where conventional medicine could not.

Caffeine

Caffeine is a natural **stimulant** found in coffee, tea, cola, chocolate and some prescription medicines. Research has shown that the taking in of caffeine can extend prolonged aerobic exercise by increasing the use of lipids (fats) to provide the energy for ATP resynthesis, thereby saving the body's glycogen stores. However, this effect was less evident for habitual users of caffeine or those who had a high-carbohydrate diet.

The evidence for sprint and high-intensity performers is much less clear as studies have produced contradictory findings. There is limited evidence that there may be a benefit to neuromuscular function: small amounts of caffeine, for example a mug of coffee, have been shown to have a favourable impact on decision making and reaction time.

There can be disadvantages to the use of caffeine. Those who do not normally ingest caffeine may experience **anxiety**, stomach upsets, restlessness, insomnia, tremors and heart rate abnormalities. In addition, caffeine can act as a **diuretic**, which could lead to unnecessary pre-exercise loss of fluid, with problems for temperature regulation.

Bicarbonate of soda

Bicarbonate of soda has been used for many years in the practice of bicarbonate or **soda loading** to delay the onset of fatigue when a performer is engaged in prolonged anaerobic exercise. Your natural bicarbonate supply is part of the body's **buffering** system against the effects of the increased acidity caused by the diffusing of lactate and hydrogen ions from the muscle cells. It would therefore follow that, if you can increase the amount of bicarbonate in the system, fatigue during anaerobic exercise will be delayed because it will allow the hydrogen ions to leave the muscle cells at a faster rate, allowing anaerobic energy systems to be used for longer.

The evidence suggests that soda loading may be of benefit in events conducted at near-maximum intensity for a duration of 1 to 7 min or in sports that are dependent on repeated anaerobic bursts. It may also help high-intensity aerobic exercise (but not low-intensity).

Soda loading is undertaken by first calculating the amount to be taken and then dividing that into five equal doses to be taken at 30 min intervals starting 3 h before competition.

There are few known side effects to the use of soda loading. Some performers have reported stomach cramps and diarrhoea. As with all supplements, bicarbonate of soda should only be taken with the advice

■ **Key terms**

Caffeine: a naturally occurring stimulant. It is no longer listed as a banned substance by WADA or UK Sport.

Stimulant: a drug that temporarily quickens some vital process such as in the central nervous system.

Anxiety: a negative aspect of feeling stress; worries over the possibility of failure.

Diuretic: a drug used to increase urine formation and output.

Bicarbonate of soda: a white soluble compound ($NaHCO_3$) used in effervescent drinks and as an antacid.

Soda loading: ingesting sodium bicarbonate to improve the buffering of hydrogen ions during anaerobic exercise.

Buffering: the ability of the blood to compensate for additions of lactic acid or hydrogen ions and maintain the pH level.

■ Activity

Review the activity characteristics of your own sport. Do you think that performers in your sport would benefit from soda loading?

of a nutritionist or an experienced coach. As individuals react differently to supplements, supplements should never be used for the first time in a competition environment.

Activity

In groups, research the effectiveness of supplements. Each member of the group should research one of the supplements discussed above and prepare a presentation, containing evidence for or against their chosen supplement based on the latest research.

⬛ The athlete's diet

Sport performers have for well over 2,000 years attempted to gain a competitive advantage by manipulating their diet. Many beliefs about diet were based on ill-founded science; however, it is true to say that there were times when an effective process was stumbled upon. Over the last 50 years or so, much more research has been conducted into the best nutritional approach for high-level sport performers.

Sports vary widely in the demands made upon the body. **Elite sport** performers often have to compete in countries where the climatic environment is widely different from what they are used to in their own country. The standard of elite performers and the narrow margins between victory and defeat mean that no avenue has been left untouched in the search for improvement in performance.

So have the researchers been able to come up with an athlete's diet? If you read the advertisements from the sports nutrition companies, you may be led to believe that the use of high-tech food supplements and drinks will be the answer to your prayers. Not so.

It is generally true that any performer who is competing and training hard can meet all their nutritional needs from a normal diet as long as that diet meets all their carbohydrate energy needs. But this is only true if:

- the performer is aware of what constitutes a balanced diet
- the basic quality of the diet is nutritionally balanced, supplying sufficient amounts of key nutrients
- the 'extra' calories consumed to fuel training are derived from nutritious foods and not from 'empty calories' (e.g. sugary foods such as confectionary, junk food and fizzy drinks)
- the performer has no special needs (e.g. it is now believed that female athletes undertaking high levels of training may require more iron in their diet).

Research in the UK, Europe, South America and the USA indicates that few elite performers are very knowledgeable and findings showed that many, when tested, were lacking in a range of vitamins, minerals and trace elements. Although the need for good nutrition is recognised by sport performers, few seem have gone as far as changing their dietary habits.

So what is to be done? Sport performers serious about an appropriate dietary regime should undertake a proper nutritional assessment with the guidance of a qualified nutritionist. The assessment should consist of:

⬛ Examiner's tip

The inclusion of any food supplement in this text should not be taken as an endorsement of the supplement's use. Research evidence is often contradictory and individuals react differently to any food or food supplement. As has been repeatedly said, performers should seek the advice of experts before engaging in any dietary or food supplement regime.

⬛ Key terms

Elite sport: sport participated in by international performers and/or professionals or by teams performing at national or international level.

■ a detailed food diary containing details of all foods/portion sizes consumed (this diary should be kept for at least three days and preferably longer)

■ a questionnaire about general dietary habits

■ analysis of the competition and training demands made on the body.

Undertaking such an assessment will identify any specific dietary requirements that cannot be met within the following nutritional guidelines:

■ Take on board sufficient carbohydrates, of a range of glycaemic scores, to meet your energy demands.

■ Drink enough fluids to remain hydrated or to rehydrate.

■ Eat a healthy and balanced diet comprising whole and unprocessed foods – e.g. wholegrain breads and cereals, fresh fruits and vegetables, high-quality proteins such as lean meats, fish and low-fat dairy produce, beans and lentils, nuts and seeds.

■ Can a performer have an optimal weight?

A sport performer does not wish to be carrying more weight than is necessary because energy is required to move it: hence the concept of an optimal weight.

Our bodies are made up of many tissues and our body weight is an amalgam of all these. The ones that we can most easily manipulate are our muscle mass and fat. However, it is not a simple matter of reducing the fat percentage to as little as possible. Fat is not necessarily undesirable: it is vital for providing energy for low-intensity endurance events, as well as for insulation against the cold and the protection of internal organs.

As you will recall from your AS Level Physical Education studies, too much fat or obesity leads to ill health, related to coronary heart disease and diabetes, and a reduced power-to-weight ratio for the performer. A simple measure of a healthy body weight is the **body mass index (BMI)** which is calculated by dividing body weight in kilograms by the square of the person's height in metres.

Below is the process for calculating the BMI of an athlete who weighs 90 kg and is 1.89 m tall:

$$BMI = \frac{weight\ (kg)}{height^2\ (m^2)}$$

$$BMI = \frac{90}{1.89^2}$$

$$BMI = \frac{90}{3.57}$$

$$BMI = 25.2$$

Individuals with a BMI over 27 are considered to be at a significantly greater risk of health problems than those with a BMI under 27.

Body fat percentage

From the performer's point of view, it is important to have the correct amount of fat in the body in relation to their age, sex and chosen sport. For example, marathon runners would prefer to have a lower percentage of fat than say rugby players or sumo wrestlers. The BMI is not a good method for determining your optimal level of fat as it is based upon a

---

Link

The use of carbohydrates in the practice of glycogen loading is discussed in detail in Chapter 5 – Specialised training (from page 67) and also in Chapter 6 – Sports injuries (from page 85).

Key terms

Body mass index (BMI): a statistical comparison of weight and height.

weight and height ratio. Resistance-trained performers will have a high fat-free muscle mass but can have the same BMI as an untrained adult.

Activity

For the range of positions and roles in your own sport activity:

1. Research the range of body types that may represent the ideal. In particular, look at the body weights and the percentage of body fat for males and females.

2. Compare those to the average for males and females in the population.

3. Compare your finding with those of others in the group and note how performers in different sports will have different values for weight, muscle mass and body fat percentage.

Measuring body fat percentage

There are two usual methods of gaining an accurate measure of body fat percentage:

■ Bioelectrical impedance – an electrical current is put through the body. Muscle has a lower electrical impedance than fat, and measurement of the impedance gives an estimate of body fat percentage. Although this is an accurate measure, it is affected by the body's level of hydration.

■ Skin-fold callipers – the callipers are used to measure the levels of subcutaneous fat at different sites around the body (commonly the triceps, biceps, subscapular, suprailiac and the thigh). The measurements are added together then entered into an equation and a body fat percentage is obtained.

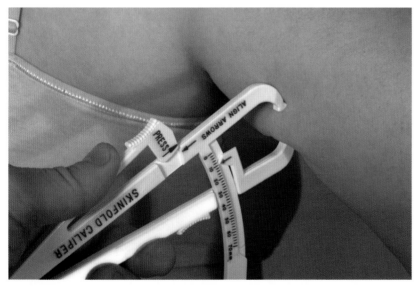

Fig. 4.5 *Measuring body fat with skin-fold callipers*

Manipulating body fat percentage

Having gained a reasonably accurate measure of your body fat percentage, you are now able to manipulate your body composition by either changing your energy input (eating) or your energy output (training). Whilst for most performers it is a question of the power-to-weight ratio, for performers who compete within weight categories (martial arts, boxing, etc.), weight management as well as body fat percentage is important.

■ Performance-enhancing drugs and their effects

Having taken an extensive look at what performers can put into their bodies legally, we now move on to looking at the ergogenic aids that fall into the banned category, i.e. performance-enhancing drugs.

Performers have been experimenting with the use of drugs to improve their performance since the Ancient Olympics. Since the 1950s, the use of drugs in sport has become more regular and systematic; this has involved large amounts of research, accompanied by the development of sophisticated testing and screening regimes to try and catch those who break the rules that govern sport. In this section, we are concerned with the physiological effects of a range of substances, and their long-term side effects. The performance-enhancing drugs included within the specification are:

- **erythropoietin** (EPO)
- **anabolic steroids – testosterone**
- human growth hormone (**HGH**)
- **beta blockers**
- diuretics
- stimulants.

Erythropoietin

Erythropoietin is a naturally occurring hormone within the body that is responsible for the regulation of red blood cell production. You will recall from your AS Level studies that red blood cells carry oxygen, combining the haemoglobin within the cell with oxygen to form oxyhaemoglobin. A performer with a higher density of red blood cells within the blood is potentially able to carry more oxygen, improving their $\dot{V}O_2$ max. The artificial form of the hormone was developed in the 1980s using genetic manipulation and was developed to help patients with anaemia.

Various studies have found that EPO is effective in raising the red blood cell count and that the effect lasts for approximately six weeks. Altitude training can have a similar effect, as can the use of high-altitude houses.

Adverse side effects occur if a performer keeps on using EPO. The increase in the haemocrit (the proportion of the blood that is red blood cells) causes the blood to become more viscous, which places a greater strain on the heart. Some performers who have died of heart failure have shown high levels of red blood cells.

In recent years, genetic scientists have isolated the gene that turns naturally occurring EPO on and off. Tests on mice showed that the effect lasted for over 20 to 30 weeks. It is not known if such tests have been done on humans.

Anabolic steroids – testosterone

Anabolic steroids are a class of chemicals related to the hormone testosterone. They increase the synthesis of protein within cells, particularly muscle cells which results in the build-up of muscle tissue. Use of anabolic steroids also produces a decline in the breakdown rate of these muscle-building proteins and decreases the amount of fat in muscle

■ Link

The ethics of drug use, the methods of testing and the policies that have been put in place to eradicate drug use in sport are covered in Chapter 18 – Deviance in sport (pages 264–70).

■ Key terms

Erythropoietin: a hormone that controls red blood cell production.

Anabolic steroid: a hormone that increases protein use and muscle cell production.

Testosterone: a steroid hormone that develops muscle mass and is responsible for the development of male secondary sexual characteristics.

HGH: artificial human growth hormone; when produced using recombinant DNA, this looks identical to the natural hormone.

Beta blocker: a drug that blocks the release of chemicals, such as adrenaline, thereby causing the heart rate to stay low and helping the performer to stay calm.

■ Links

For more information on high-altitude houses, see Chapter 5 – Specialised training (page 67).

and overall fat levels. Anabolic steroids reduce recovery time by inhibiting the action of other steroid hormones that promote the breakdown of muscles by blocking the effects of cortisol; this prevents muscle breakdown and enhances recovery.

The resultant increase in muscle tissue enhances the strength of the performer and their ability to recover quickly after sustained performances or training. The more rapid recovery allows for heavier training regimes.

Anabolic steroid use can lead to a number of dangerous side effects, including liver and kidney tumours, jaundice, fluid retention, high blood pressure, increases in cholesterol, greater danger of blood clotting, pre-disposition to tendon injuries, damage to the peripheral nerves in the body, and severe acne. In females, adverse effects of anabolic steroids include menstrual abnormalities, deepening of voice, shrinkage of breasts, male-pattern baldness and an increase in sex drive, acne and body hair. In males, there is damage to the testes and development of breasts. Some of these effects appear to be permanent even when drug use is stopped.

Younger steroid users risk permanently halting their growth, which could result in shorter stature.

Human growth hormone

Human growth hormone (HGH, hGH, rhGH) is a naturally occurring hormone that regulates growth but is also found to control the turnover of muscle, bone and collagen and the regulation of fat metabolism. These effects continue even after puberty. It is thought that exercise acts as a major stimulus for the production of HGH, which is also connected to diet and sleep patterns. It is possible that athletes may be able to manipulate their HGH levels without resorting to illegal drug use.

The use of artificial HGH was first noted when a phial of the substance was found in a changing room at the 1992 Barcelona Olympics. Today, recombinant human growth hormone (rhGH) may well be the drug of choice across a range of sprinting and other explosive activities. Growth hormone produced using gene technology is identical to the naturally occurring form. The use of HGH and rhGH can enhance the performance of explosive activities by increasing muscle mass and repairing bones, ligaments and tendons.

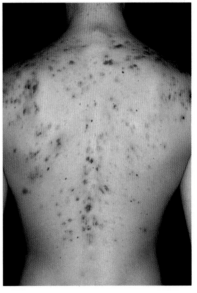

Fig. 4.6 *The adverse effect of steroids*

The adverse side effects of using HGH in any of its forms vary depending on dosage and length of use. The effects can include all or some of the following: minor to chronic joint pain, joint swelling, fluid retention and, more seriously, high blood pressure and abnormal bone and cartilage growth, irregular heart rhythms, increased risk of diabetes, joint and facial deformities, and a shut down of the pituitary gland.

Beta blockers

Beta blockers have a calming effect and reduce tension; they are used in sports where accuracy and a steady hand are required, such as archery and shooting. Beta blockers work by blocking the action of adrenaline and noradrenaline in particular, part of the sympathetic nervous system which mediates the 'fight or flight' response. Beta blockers cause arteries to widen, slow the action of the heart and decrease its force of contraction, thereby lowering blood pressure and resulting in a reduced workload for the heart.

The adverse side effects of beta blockers include cold hands and feet, tiredness and sleep disturbance. Less common side effects include impotence, dizziness, wheezing, digestive tract problems, skin rashes and dry eyes.

Diuretics

Diuretics may change your body's natural balance of fluids and salts (electrolytes) by increasing urine production and output. This loss of water may allow an athlete to compete in a lighter weight class, which may give them an advantage. By diluting the urine, diuretics also help athletes pass drug tests. When taken at the higher doses by athletes, adverse effects may be significant and include:

- dehydration
- decreased ability to regulate body temperature
- potassium deficiency
- heart arrhythmias
- muscle cramps
- exhaustion.

Stimulants

Stimulants have been used in sport since the Ancient Olympics. Most well known are the group known as amphetamines, but caffeine, at certain levels, is also on the banned list from the **World Anti-Doping Agency (WADA)**. Stimulants enhance performance by increasing the activity of the central and sympathetic nervous systems; this can:

- increase mental alertness and sometimes aggressiveness
- decrease fatigue and allow people to improve performance in endurance events
- increase heart rate and metabolic rate
- raise blood pressure and body temperature.

Stimulants can also have detrimental side effects that can diminish performance. Nervousness and irritability make it hard to concentrate during a match and lack of sleep can cause tiredness. Performers who take stimulants may become psychologically addicted to them, or develop a tolerance so that they need greater amounts to achieve the same effect.

A note of warning

The use of performance-enhancing drugs is widespread in a number of sports. Disregarding the moral and ethical questions, it is clear that many elite performers use such drugs without considering or researching the possible side effects of taking many of the substances on offer. They take the word of the drug company or the person selling them the drug. Many of the drugs have not been the subject of research over time – we do not know all the side effects.

> ■ **Key terms**
>
> **World Anti-Doping Agency (WADA):** established in 1999, the agency is responsible for promoting, coordinating, and monitoring at international level the fight against the use of drugs in sport.

> ■ Activity
>
> Research examples of and stories about the long-term side effects of performance-enhancing drugs. As a starting point, research the experiences of the East German athletes of the 1970s.

Fig. 4.7 *World Anti-Doping Agency*

☑ *You should now be able to:*

- explain why it is important to maintain your water and electrolyte balance and the best way of doing this

- know why post-event rehydration is important

- evaluate the claims made for food supplements and make informed decisions about their use

- devise your own diet to meet your needs and the needs of others when engaged in high-level training or competition

- describe the physiological effects of a range of performance-enhancing drugs and discuss why performers are tempted to take them in terms of their physiological benefits

- understand the adverse side effects of performance-enhancing drugs and use this knowledge in a debate about the wisdom of using such illegal ergogenic aids.

1 Marathon runners often run in high temperatures or humid conditions.

    (a)   What problems in terms of temperature regulation will this bring? *(2 marks)*

    (b)   State two problems that a dehydrated marathon runner might suffer from. *(2 marks)*

    (c)   How can the athlete overcome these problems? *(3 marks)*

2 Creatine supplements have become popular with performers trying to improve their performance.

    (a)   What performance improvements do they expect to receive? *(2 marks)*

    (b)   How does this relate to the role of creatine phosphate as an energy system? *(3 marks)*

    (c)   What side effects might a regular user of a creatine supplement experience? *(2 marks)*

3   (a)   Describe the dietary preparations that you would make in the run-up to an extended sport competition – a football or tennis tournament. You should consider a time period from one month before to the morning of the first match. *(4 marks)*

    (b)   Some endurance athletes engage in carbo loading. How do they do this? *(3 marks)*

4 EPO is a drug taken by some endurance athletes.

    (a)   What is EPO? *(2 mark)*

    (b)   How does it benefit an endurance athlete? *(3 marks)*

    (c)   What dangers might there be in making use of the gene that regulates natural erythropoietin? *(2 marks)*

5 Specialised training

In this chapter you will:

- understand how we develop increased power

- describe how elite performers may improve flexibility

- explain the benefits and drawbacks of training at altitude

- understand how endurance performers increase their energy supplies

- describe how elite performers structure their training programmes

- understand how to maintain performance in extreme environments

- explain how elite performers measure how hard they are training.

Key terms

Plyometrics: a type of training designed to improve power. Plyometric exercises involve bounding, jumping or hopping to make muscle groups work eccentrically before a powerful concentric contraction.

Glycogen loading: a technique used by long-distance athletes to alter the body's stores of glycogen to above normal levels through changes in diet and exercise, thereby artificially increasing the amount of glycogen available during an event; also known as carbo-loading.

Periodisation: dividing the overall training programme into parts or periods that are designed to achieve different goals.

This chapter is concerned with several specialised training methods that are popular with elite performers. When you studied AS Level Physical Education, the principles of training were part of Unit 2 – Practical aspects of physical education. Those general principles are used by elite performers and their coaches, but their training needs to be far more scientific in order to maximise their performance. Training for elite athletes is concerned with maximising performance for specific occasions and has two goals, improving fitness and improving technique.

To improve fitness, coaches apply the training principles, in that they identify the major energy system being used by the performer (see Chapter 1 – Aerobic energy systems, and Chapter 2 – Anaerobic energy systems), and then use the overload principle to develop that energy system. Many activities use different energy systems at different times during performance. In which case, the principle of specificity needs to be applied and training programmes designed to suit the energy demands. Use of the principle of overload will improve fitness. Improving technique is more than simply a matter of practice: practice must involve the correct technique. Using these principles will result in faster and more forceful movements or improved endurance, all of which improve performance. Different techniques have been developed to improve power (**plyometrics**), flexibility (proprioceptive neuromuscular facilitation (PNF) stretching) and endurance (altitude training, **glycogen loading** and thermoregulation in differing environments). Further specialisation of training methods involves using knowledge of exercise and recovery to structure a training programme (**periodisation**) and using technology to make sure that the elite performer's efforts are being accurately measured to achieve the ideal intensity for improvement (lactate sampling and respiratory exchange ratio).

Plyometrics

In AS Level Physical Education, you looked at the components of fitness. One of the most important components for sport performers is power. Power is strength multiplied by speed and is required to move the body quickly. The need for power is especially high in performers who have to lift their bodies, such as high jumpers and basketball players, but power is also necessary in performers who have to move their bodies quickly, for example sprinters and long jumpers.

Plyometrics is a type of training designed to produce fast, powerful movements, generally for the purpose of improving performance in a particular activity. Plyometric exercises are specialised, high-intensity training techniques used by elite athletes specifically to develop their power. Plyometric training involves high-intensity, explosive muscular contractions that engage the stretch reflex (stretching the muscle before it contracts so that it contracts with greater force). The stretch reflex is a protective mechanism that prohibits overstretching of muscle fibres. Any tendency to overstretch is detected by specialised receptors in muscles called **muscle spindles**. When these are suddenly activated, a nerve impulse is sent to the spinal chord which results in the immediate contraction of the muscle being overstretched.

Key terms

Muscle spindles: receptors in muscle that supply information about the changes in length of muscle and also about the rate of change in muscle length.

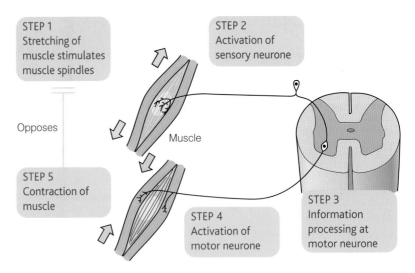

STEP 1
Stretching of muscle stimulates muscle spindles

STEP 2
Activation of sensory neurone

Opposes

Muscle

STEP 5
Contraction of muscle

STEP 4
Activation of motor neurone

STEP 3
Information processing at motor neurone

Fig. 5.1 *Diagram of stretch reflex*

You should be able to remember from AS Level that there are two types of isotonic muscle contractions, eccentric and concentric. Eccentric contractions occur when the muscle lengthens as it develops tension. These contractions occur during downward movements, because the muscle controls descent against the force of gravity. When muscles shorten while contracting, this involves concentric contractions which occur during upward movements. A plyometric contraction involves an initial rapid eccentric movement, followed by an explosive concentric movement. A muscle that is eccentrically stretched before a concentric contraction will contract more forcefully and more rapidly. A classic example is the squat just prior to a vertical jump: when the performer lowers the body quickly, the muscles involved in the jump are momentarily stretched producing a more powerful movement.

Plyometrics works as a form of power training because, when a quick stretch is detected in the muscles, an involuntary, protective stretch reflex occurs to prevent overstretching and injury. The stretch reflex increases the activity in the muscle undergoing the stretch or eccentric muscle action, allowing it to act much more forcefully. The result is a powerful braking effect and the potential for a powerful concentric muscle action. If the concentric muscle action does not occur immediately after the pre-stretch, the potential energy produced by the stretch reflex response is lost. In other words, if there is a delay between dipping down and then jumping up, the effect of the counter-dip is lost.

All plyometric movements involve three phases:

■ The first phase is the pre-stretch or eccentric muscle action, when elastic energy is generated and stored.

■ The second phase is the short time between the end of the pre-stretch and the start of the concentric muscle action; this brief period where you change from stretching to contracting the muscle is known as the amortisation phase. The shorter this phase, the more powerful the subsequent muscle contraction will be.

■ The final phase is the actual muscle contraction. In practice, this is the movement that the performer wants to develop – the powerful jump or throw.

This sequence of three phases is called the stretch-shortening cycle.

Fig. 5.2 *Typical plyometric exercises*

■ Activity

One very quick and simple way to demonstrate the effect of the stretch-shortening cycle is to perform two vertical jumps following a thorough warm up.

1 During the first vertical jump, bend your knees and hips (an eccentric muscle action or pre-stretch) and hold the semi-squat position for 3 to 5s before jumping up vertically (concentric contraction) as high as possible. The brief delay increases the amortisation phase.

2 On the second jump bend your knees and hips to the same degree but jump up immediately without any delay. This keeps the amortisation phase to a minimum and makes best use of the stored energy. The second jump will be higher.

By utilising the stretch-shortening cycle, movements can be made more powerful and explosive. Plyometrics is simply a set of drills designed to stimulate the stretch reflex and the corresponding additional forceful

Questions on this area are concerned with the theory of how plyometrics works as well the practicalities of how to do it in practice.

contraction over and over again – preferably during movements that mimic those in the performer's sport.

Some coaches have questioned the suitability of plyometrics because there is a risk of injury, owing to the forceful nature of the muscle contractions and the loading that occurs in the joints involved. As a precaution, it is suggested that performers attempting to introduce plyometric training do so with a substantial strength-training background. Injuries are more likely to occur with this form of training if there are depth jumps from too great a height, improper landing or an inappropriate landing surface. The landing surface is very important: it should possess adequate shock-absorbing properties (e.g. grass, rubber mats or a suspended floor). Concrete, tiles, hardwood and crash mats are not suitable for plyometrics.

A wide variety of research has shown that plyometrics can improve performance in vertical jumping, long jumping, sprinting and sprint cycling. It appears also that a relatively small amount of plyometric training is required to improve performance in these tasks. Using a variety of plyometric exercises, such as depth jumps, counter-movement jumps, leg bounding and hopping, etc., can improve performance where leg power is an important contributing factor.

■ PNF stretching

You should remember from AS Level that flexibility is an important component of fitness. Stretching as a means of increasing flexibility is overwhelmingly recommended by coaches and is widely practised by athletes in almost every sport. It seems to be one of those common-sense things to do. Stretching should not simply be used as part of a warm-up: there should be a long-term programme to increase flexibility. Increasing your flexibility will also improve your performance because of the greater range of motion available to your joints. Stretching is also thought to reduce the risk of injury.

Static stretching requires that the muscle be stretched to a point of resistance and held for a period of time. Dynamic or ballistic stretching involves repetitive bouncing, rebounding or rhythmic motions and is generally thought to be more dangerous and less effective than static stretching. Proprioceptive neuromuscular facilitation uses alternating contraction and relaxation movements for flexibility. PNF stretching is one of the most effective forms of flexibility training for increasing the range of motion of a joint. PNF techniques can be both passive (no associated muscular contraction) and active (voluntary muscle contraction). While there are several variations of PNF stretching, they all have one thing in common: they facilitate or help the body's muscular inhibition. This is the reason why PNF is superior to other forms of flexibility training. A couple of PNF styles are practised today. For the fitness professional, the most practical style of PNF is the contract–relax, antagonist–contract (CRAC) technique, which uses isometric muscle contractions as its basis. Remember from AS Level that isometric contractions are those involving no movement.

Isometric muscle contractions completed immediately before a passive stretch help to achieve autogenic inhibition, where the muscles gradually relax. Muscle spindles are highly specialised receptors, located within muscle cells, which protect the muscle from injury. They sense how far and how fast a muscle is being stretched and, when activated, produce the stretch reflex. This reflex action (see Figure 5.2) causes the muscle to contract and prevents overstretching of the joint. For example, if you are lying on your back performing a hamstring stretch, and take the stretch to the limit of your range of movement, your leg starts to jump and twitch. At this point, the muscle spindles have been activated and are telling the muscle to contract to prevent any further stretching.

Also located within the muscle's tendon is another sensor (see Figure 5.3); called the Golgi tendon organ (GTO), this senses how much tension is being placed on the tendon.

However, the GTO differs from the muscle spindle in that, when activated, it relaxes the muscle. Autogenic inhibition is reflex relaxation that occurs in the same muscle where the Golgi tendon organ is stimulated. Often the isometric contraction is referred to as 'hold' and the concentric muscle contraction is referred to as 'contract'.

PNF stretching is best performed with a partner, but most stretches can be performed alone. When working with a partner, it is very important that the partner remains attentive and focused on the performer so as not to cause overstretching.

Here are some other general guidelines for PNF stretching:

■ Avoid PNF immediately before, or on the morning of, a competition and leave 48 h between PNF stretching routines.

■ Perform only one exercise per muscle group in a session, but attempt two to five sets of the chosen exercise.

■ Each set should consist of one stretch held for up to 30 s after the contracting phase.

■ PNF stretching is not recommended for anyone under the age of 18.

■ If PNF stretching is to be performed as a separate exercise session, a thorough warm-up consisting of 5 to 10 min of light aerobic exercise and some dynamic stretches must precede it.

■ Altitude training

Altitude training has been used for many years as a means to improve performance in endurance athletes. The popular belief that altitude training enhances endurance has probably developed from the success of a number of Kenyan and Ethiopian middle- to long-distance runners who lived at altitude.

The scientific theory behind altitude training was based on the assumption that aerobic performance may be enhanced because of increases in the number of red blood cells produced by being at altitude. At high altitude (usually over 2,500 m (8,000 feet) above sea level), the partial pressure of oxygen is reduced even though the air still contains approximately 21 per cent oxygen. The body adapts to this relative lack of oxygen by increasing the concentration of red blood cells and haemoglobin. A larger concentration of red blood cells means that more oxygen can be carried by the blood to the muscles, thus allowing higher performance in aerobic or endurance-based activities that depend on aerobic energy production. These increases in red blood cell numbers are stimulated by an increase in the secretion of the hormone erythropoietin (EPO). The body naturally produces EPO to regulate red blood cell production and it should not be confused with synthetic EPO, which can be used to artificially increase red blood cell numbers.

People who suggest that altitude training has benefits for the endurance performer claim that, when such athletes return to sea level (where they are competing), they will – for 10 to 14 days – still have a higher

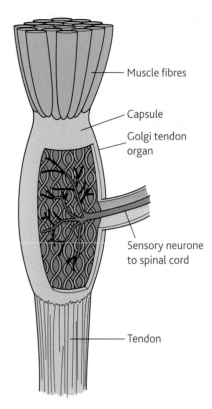

Muscle fibres

Capsule

Golgi tendon organ

Sensory neurone to spinal cord

Tendon

Fig. 5.3 *Golgi tendon organ*

AQA Examiner's tip

Questions on this area are concerned with the theory of how PNF stretching works as well as the practicalities of how to do it.

Activity

Devise and produce an instruction leaflet for a PNF stretch for the hamstrings, pectorals and quadriceps. (You could research using the internet and/or use your own ideas.)

Link

For more information on erythropoietin (EPO), see Chapter 4 – The elite performer: food, supplements and performance-enhancing drugs (page 56).

Fig. 5.4 *Kenyan athletes finished first, second and third in the 3,000 m steeplechase at the 2000 Athens Olympics*

concentration of red blood cells and this will improve their aerobic capacity. Altitude training also produces changes in muscle tissue by increasing the myoglobin levels in muscle, and exposure to altitude also seems to increase the muscles' ability to buffer the lactate that builds up in muscles during and after exercise.

Traditionally, athletes have lived and trained at moderate altitude (1,800–2,500 m) for several weeks at a time, two to three times a year. However, although the athlete can focus solely on training, these specialised training camps demand a lot of time, money and sacrifices, such as leaving the home, job and family. Training at these camps involves several phases:

■ **Acclimatisation** – this starts immediately on arrival at altitude. During this phase the athlete will get used to the reduced pO_2 and must not overdo exhaustive training; the athlete also needs to take more time for recovery between workouts compared with when at sea level. The duration of this phase ranges from 3 to 10 days, depending on the total duration of the camp and the training frequency.

■ **Primary training** – this lasts between one to three weeks but can be longer depending on the athlete's goals. The aim is to progressively increase the training volume until the athlete reaches the volume and intensity of training that were occurring at sea level.

■ **Recovery** –this phase can last for two to five days and is designed to prepare for the return to sea level and to allow the athlete to recover completely from the fatigue produced by high-altitude training. The training volume and intensity is gradually reduced.

Upon return to sea level, there are three more phases:

■ A positive phase – seen during the first one to four days, this is when there is an increase in the oxygen-carrying capacity of the blood.

■ Then there is progressive return to sea-level training volume and intensity, during which the probability of good performance is reduced; this may be due to the altered fitness levels and

■ Link

For more information on meeting goals, see Chapter 13 – Confidence (page 178).

coordination losses while training at altitude. However, after several days of sea-level training, there will be improvements in fitness and coordination.

▓ Finally, there is a fitness peak 15 to 20 days after return to sea level. The optimal time for competition is during this phase. A combination of positive factors (increased oxygen transport, improved economy and maintenance of breathing adaptations) explains the better performance during this third phase.

Some athletes live permanently at high altitude, only returning to sea level to compete.

Another method of altitude training attempts to maintain training intensity, while gaining the benefits of altitude: athletes live at moderate altitude but train at sea level or closer to sea level.

As there are only a few places around the world where high altitude is within commuting distance of sea level, coaches have developed a variety of techniques to simulate at sea level the experience of living or training high: for example, hypoxic (reduced oxygen) rooms or chambers.

In Finland, a scientist designed a 'high-altitude house'. The air inside the house, which is situated at sea level, is at normal pressure but modified to a concentration of oxygen that is about the same as the concentration at the altitudes often used for altitude training. Athletes live and sleep inside the house but perform their training outside (at normal oxygen concentrations). Using this method results in improvements in EPO and red blood cell levels. This technology has been commercialised and is being used by thousands of competitive athletes in cycling, triathlon, Olympic endurance sports, American football, basketball, hockey, soccer, and many other sports that can take advantage of the improvements in strength, speed, endurance, and recovery.

Opponents of altitude training argue that an athlete's red blood cell concentration goes back to normal within a few days of returning to sea level and that, while at altitude, the reduced levels of oxygen make it impossible to train at the same intensity that the performer could at sea level, reducing the training effect and leading to a drop in fitness. There is also the problem of wasting training time on travel from the high-altitude camp to the training area, the threat of altitude sickness and the psychological problem of spending considerable parts of the year away from home. Repeated travel to and from altitude is stressful for athletes, not to mention having to adapt to the weather changes between altitude and sea level, increased fatigue due to the travel, the financial costs, etc. There are also limits to the amount of EPO that the body will produce.

To summarise, it appears that all the hypoxic methods can induce favourable adaptations. However, the optimal method of altitude training is still unknown; consequently, some experimentation may be required and, while that continues, not all altitude training will produce positive outcomes for the performer; in fact there will be many performers for whom altitude training is actually detrimental to performance.

▓ Glycogen loading

You learned in Chapter 1 – Aerobic energy systems (page 2) that glycogen is the predominant energy source used during athletic events lasting longer than about an hour. Fat could be used during such

> **AQA Examiner's tip**
>
> You may have to comment on the effectiveness of altitude training; such training may help the performance of endurance athletes but may also cause problems.

exertions but, as you saw in that chapter, fat supports a lower intensity of exercise, because it uses more oxygen to resynthesise ATP, and thus speed drops when fat becomes the main provider of energy for ATP resynthesis. The main problem for the endurance athlete is that, unlike fat, stores of glycogen in your body are fairly limited. In addition, the glycogen in your muscles is quite rapidly depleted during fairly intense exercise, so that muscles will begin to suffer a shortage of glycogen after 60 to 90 min of activity and will have to resort to the slower fat metabolism. Marathon runners have a term for this phenomenon; they talk about 'hitting the wall' which accurately describes the sensation felt as a predominantly glycogen-based metabolism suddenly switches to a fat-based system.

What elite endurance athletes have realised is that they need to boost their muscle glycogen stores to more than normal, so that they do not have to resort to fat metabolism for ATP resynthesis during their event. This technique is called glycogen loading.

The original research concerning glycogen loading suggested that it is necessary to deplete glycogen stores through heavy exertion before ingesting a high carbohydrate diet; this allows the body to store more glycogen than normal (**supercompensation**). The methods used to increase glycogen stores, however, had the drawback of leaving the athletes heavy-legged, owing to the intensive exercise programme that was needed to deplete the glycogen stores. In practice, most athletes prefer to reduce their training load prior to a major competition rather than increase it (see page 71). A further problem was that supercompensation makes the performer feel bloated and lethargic because of the extra glycogen and because glycogen storage also involves storage of water.

Owing to the above, most athletes now tend to avoid training very hard to produce supercompensation; instead they simply increase their carbohydrate intake as a method of glycogen loading. Simply increasing carbohydrate intake in the days approaching a competition, while maintaining the usual tapering-down of training, routinely leads to high levels of muscle glycogen being stored. Scientists have suggested that a carbohydrate intake of 6 to 8 g of carbohydrate per kilogram of body mass was sufficient to permit glycogen loading. However, many endurance athletes follow a reduced carbohydrate diet to maintain low body weight, and the suggested intake proved to be too high for these athletes. So simply eating carbohydrates for a few days prior to an endurance event as a means of glycogen loading worked sometimes, but not for everybody, and its success was mainly a hit-or-miss affair.

Most recent research has come up with a plan for glycogen loading that only takes one day and produces incredibly high levels of muscle glycogen. The plan works around one key concept: very high intensities of exercise actually stimulate higher rates of muscle glycogen storage than moderate intensities of exercise carried out for prolonged periods. Most athletes try to avoid high-intensity exercise just prior to a competition, but the research found that it only required a 3 min burst of intense exercise, immediately followed by a 24 h high-carbohydrate eating regime involving 9 g of carbohydrate per kilogram of body weight. 'Immediately' in this case meant that the high-carbohydrate diet started less than 20 min after the exercise. This appears to open a 'carbo window' in the muscles when glycogen stores can be increased dramatically. This 'window' appears to close about 2 h after the intense exercise.

Key terms

Supercompensation: storing more glycogen than normal.

AQA Examiner's tip

Most A2 questions are scenario based, and, as glycogen loading is only suitable for endurance athletes, a question could easily be linked to other endurance-based training aspects, such as altitude training or thermoregulation.

Link

More information on the practice of glycogen loading can be found in Chapter 6 – Sports injuries (page 85).

Fig. 5.5 *Marathon running*

Marathon runners (or other endurance athletes getting ready for a competition lasting longer than an hour) could follow their normal diet during the week leading up to the race, with no risk of bloating, lethargy, heaviness or gastric discomfort, and training could be tapered appropriately. The day before the big race, the athletes could warm up, go hard for 3 min and then begin consuming large quantities of carbohydrate. They should feel great and have extra glycogen in their leg muscles at the starting line the following morning.

Periodisation

If you want to improve your performances, you can't train in the same way all the time. If you did, your body would simply adapt to the training you were doing; your fitness would settle in at a fixed level; and you could train far into the next century without making one bit of improvement. Hoping to perform better with an unchanging training programme is like expecting to become a maths wizard while working on only the simple equations encountered in first-year algebra.

Owing to the body's tendency to merely maintain the norm, if you want to get better your workouts must progress to a higher level of difficulty. This is the training principle of progression. To progress, you could simply increase your intensity, volume and/or frequency of training over time. As long as you weren't exceeding your body's ability to adapt, you would steadily get better.

Such progression does produce performance gains, but by itself it can never help you to reach your full potential, because it ignores the fact that your training must also be goal oriented.

An athlete needs to do a number of specific things in order to optimise performance, and these goals aren't always reached merely by adjusting the workload in your training programme. For example, the endurance performer needs to increase their $\dot{V}O_2$ max and their lactate threshold. They also need to increase the strength of their muscles and connective tissues and in doing so increase their power. By developing their

> ### Link
>
> For more information on goal setting, see Chapter 11 – The effect of anxiety on performance (page 142).

Links

■ For more information on lactate threshold, see Chapter 2 – Anaerobic energy systems (page 17).

■ For information on recovery during training, see *AQA Physical Education AS*, Chapter 15 – Practical exercise physiology (page 226).

Key terms

Macrocycle: a long-term training plan with a long-term goal, often a single competition.

Mesocycle: a goal-based block of training sessions.

Microcycle: a repeating group/ pattern of training sessions.

technique they will increase their efficiency and not waste energy. Remember from the AS Level course that you also need to allow time to recover fully from training.

It would also be foolish to expect to optimise your lactate threshold at the same time that you were making large gains in power, since the training required is different. It's also not a good idea to throw yourself into power training without first building a broad base of strength to protect you from injury during the high-intensity power workouts; also, maximal gains in power simply can't be achieved unless muscles first develop the ability to generate greater force. What all this means is that you must do things in step-by-step fashion when you train, rather than attempt to improve everything at once.

For all these reasons, the periodisation of your training is critically important. There are some complicated definitions of periodisation training, but, put simply, the term means dividing your overall training programme into parts or periods that are designed to achieve different goals. Since you cannot do everything at once, you must divide your training time up into discrete blocks and tackle one or two goals at a time.

Macrocycles, mesocycles and microcycles

Proper periodisation means coordinating training correctly over extended periods of time, long enough to make large gains in fitness and prepare properly for major competitions. In theory, your training programme should be divided up into units called **macrocycles**, **mesocycles**, and **microcycles**. A microcycle is a number of training sessions which form a repeating unit. For example, if your training consists of a hard day, an easy day, and then a rest day, followed again by the hard–easy–rest pattern, these three days represent your basic training unit, or microcycle. If you're a rugby player and your typical training week consists of a weights workout, an interval session on the track, an evening squad session, and a rest day before the match on Saturday, that repetitive weekly pattern is your microcycle.

In contrast, a mesocycle is a block of training, consisting of some number of microcycles, which emphasises the reaching of a particular goal. This block of training could, for example, be the time that a shot-putter spends concentrating on their overall strength training as a prelude to working on another mesocycle that would emphasise improving their speed across the circle. The rugby player may spend several weeks working on their line-out techniques. A macrocycle is a long stretch of training which is intended to accomplish an extremely significant overall goal, such as the preparation for and completion of a very important competition. A macrocycle is made up of a number of different mesocycles and covers a period of many months.

Typically, a microcycle lasts for 5 to 10 days (for many athletes, a microcycle is simply one week of training in a predictable way); a mesocycle usually covers 4 to 12 weeks, and a macrocycle lasts for 10 to 12 months. Many athletes who periodise their training don't alter their macrocycles very much; one year is very similar to the next, and thus the year is the largest unit of periodisation. However, some athletes think longer term and may use 'large macrocycles' which consist of two to four 'small macrocycles,' each of which lasts about a year. These small macrocycles may differ from each other considerably. For example, a high jumper preparing for the 2012 Olympics might spend most of 2010 (the first small macrocycle) working on agility, flexibility, strength, and power, devoting little time to actual jumping or competition, and then shift over in 2011 (the second small macrocycle) to a much greater emphasis on technique and an increase in the number of competitive efforts. In this case, the 32-month period from the beginning of 2010 to the summer Olympic Games in 2012 could be considered the large macrocycle.

Tapering and peaking

Performers involved in certain activities, such as swimming and athletics, will be competing regularly but often with a single competition in mind. In order to maintain fitness, but avoid **overtraining**, these performers will attempt to maintain a high level of fitness throughout the season, attending lesser competitions but trying to make sure that they perform at their best in the big competition. So that they can be at an optimal state of readiness for a competition, these performers will begin reducing their daily training loads a few days prior to a big event; this is called **tapering**. Athletes will also want to make sure that they are mentally and physically ready for the big event, fully ready for the rigours of the big competition; this is called **peaking**.

Wave-like periodisation

There is not one best periodisation plan; what works for one athlete may have an adverse effect on the performance of another. This is because different athletes can have dramatically different needs. For example, a runner with relatively poor muscular strength might need to spend several mesocycles focusing on developing their strength by carrying out a variety of resistance-training routines. In contrast, a very strong runner would spend considerably less time on such activities and might need to spend more time on remedying a specific weakness, such as a poor lactate threshold or a low $\dot{V}O_2$ max. So periodisation is specific.

The commonest form of periodisation is the so-called wave-like periodisation pattern. Athletes first build up their volume (total quantity of training) to a high level (creating a big 'wave' of miles), while intensity (speed) of training remains fairly modest. This initial period of training is supposed to establish basic strength and endurance. The mileage wave then gradually reduces, being replaced by a steadily increasing wave of intensity (less long-distance, more speed work). The theory is that the athlete is ready for major competitions once the intensity wave has peaked. After the competitive season is over, the individual rests for a while before starting another mileage wave and beginning a new season of training. In these circumstances, the regular weekly training pattern would be the microcycle, each wave is the mesocycle and the build-up to major competitions is the macrocycle.

■ Thermoregulation in differing environments

During exercise, the body generates heat as a waste product of muscle contraction. Humans are homeothermic, that is they keep their internal body temperature constant. During exercise, heat is produced; and it is therefore necessary to lose that heat to keep body temperature constant. In order for heat to be lost from the body, it must have access to the outside. For this to occur, blood is moved from the core of the body to close to the surface of the skin; from here heat can be lost to the surrounding environment by any of four mechanisms:

- ■ Conduction involves the transfer of heat through direct contact, from warm skin to clothes and air.
- ■ Convection involves transfer of heat by gases. Air passing over our skin takes away air molecules that have been warmed by the skin.

■ Key terms

Overtraining: the physical and mental state that is due to excessive training without adequate recovery.

Tapering: reducing the amount of training and/or the training intensity prior to competition day.

Peaking: making sure that both mind and body are at their best for a competition.

AQA Examiner's tip

You will need not only to be able to state but also to define the terms 'microcycle', 'mesocycle' and 'macrocycle', and you must do so in more detail than simply giving a timescale. Saying that a macrocycle is a year-long set of training is not enough.

■ Activity

Describe how the energy systems involved in wave-like periodisation will differ from one type of wave to another.

■ Link

To find out more about temperature regulation, see Chapter 4. The elite performer: food, supplements and performance enhancing drugs (pages 45–47).

■ Radiation is the main way we lose heat when we are resting. Your body loses about 60 per cent of its heat through radiating infrared rays to its surroundings, because the surroundings are cooler than your body. You also receive radiated heat from the sun.

■ Evaporation is the main way that we lose heat during exercise. As fluid evaporates from the skin, heat is lost. As your internal body temperature increases because of exercise, you produce more sweat, which evaporates, losing heat from the body.

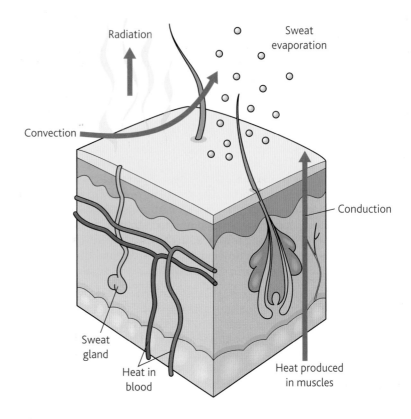

Fig. 5.6 *Mechanisms for the removal of heat*

Sweating

In order for sweating to work as a cooling system, the sweat must evaporate from the skin's surface. Sweat that stays on the skin's surface or that drips off provides little or no cooling effect. When the humidity of the surrounding air is high, sweat evaporation is limited. When you sweat in high humidity, little evaporation takes place, and you become very wet and feel uncomfortable. If the humidity is low, sweating becomes easier; you don't get covered with sweat and you feel OK. In fact, sweat appearing on the skin's surface is a sign of exercise in warm or humid conditions and of the evaporation system not working efficiently.

Internal body temperature

The internal body temperature is kept at about 37 °C. Regulating that temperature is a function of the thermoregulatory centre in the hypothalamus of the brain. Changes in body temperature, such as those caused by exercise, are detected by receptors and information is sent to the hypothalamus, which starts mechanisms such as sweating to cool the body. Another way of controlling heat is through the action of rings of smooth muscle around arterioles. Under the control of the hypothalamus, these are able to dilate, which increases blood flow to the skin so that warm blood from the body's core dissipates its heat by conduction, convection and radiation. In cold conditions, it is necessary to generate heat; this is done by shivering, a rapid involuntary cycle of contraction and relaxation of the skeletal muscles.

The blood

During exercise, the blood has to perform two main functions: it has to supply the muscles with the nutrients and oxygen they require, and it has to supply the skin to allow heat to be lost. Therefore, during exercise in a warm environment a large proportion of the cardiac output must be shared by the skin and the working muscles. Remember from AS Level that when exercising there is a redistribution of blood with extra being supplied to the skin and muscles. This in turn reduces the volume of blood returning to the heart and so reduces the stroke volume.

The heart

In order to maintain the cardiac output required, there has to be a gradual increase in heart rate (a phenomenon known as cardiovascular drift). But these changes are limited in their effectiveness in terms of performance. The combination of a high rate of heat production from the exercise and a restricted capacity for heat loss can lead to **hyperthermia** (high body temperature), which may progress to heat illness, inevitably impairing exercise performance.

The ability to cycle or run for long periods is known to be lower at 21 °C than at 11 °C and is even further reduced at 31 °C, when $\dot{V}O_2$ max becomes markedly reduced, heart rate increases and internal temperature is raised. The heart rate rises in an attempt to meet the need to increase blood flow to the skin for cooling and to maintain oxygen supply to the working muscles.

Fluid intake

Heat exposure combined with exercise results not just in hyperthermia but also in **hypohydration** (low fluid levels) if fluid losses are not replaced, and this combination will dramatically reduce exercise capacity.

Water is essential for numerous functions in the body. When the body's fluid levels become depleted, through increased sweating and/or inadequate fluid intake, dehydration can occur. Almost all levels of dehydration are associated with a reduction in sport performance. High temperatures, humidity and strenuous exercise all increase the amount of fluid lost as sweat. Under extreme conditions of temperature and humidity, water can be lost at a rate of 2 to 3 l per hour. Replacing these fluid losses is particularly important to prevent dehydration and its associated dangers. Symptoms of dehydration include lethargy, nausea, loss of appetite, anxiety, inability to concentrate and, in later stages, dizziness, vomiting, mental confusion and increasing weakness. This can lead eventually to exhaustion, heat stroke and, in some cases, can be fatal. Thirst is not a reliable indicator of fluid needs. Dehydration limits performance, although the exact mechanisms for this are still unclear. It may be that dehydration decreases the blood plasma volume, which results in less oxygen being delivered to the exercising muscles and increases breathing and heart rates.

In order to prevent dehydration, attention to fluid intake before, during and after exercise is important. Suitable fluids should be consumed in the

Link

For information on the redistribution of blood during exercise, see *AQA Physical Education AS*, Chapter 4 – Blood transport system (pages 43–5).

Key terms

Hyperthermia: a condition in which body temperature is elevated to a very high level.

Hypohydration: a condition in which there are very low levels of fluid in the body.

Link

For information on cardiovascular drift, see *AQA Physical Education AS*, Chapter 5 – Heart function (page 57).

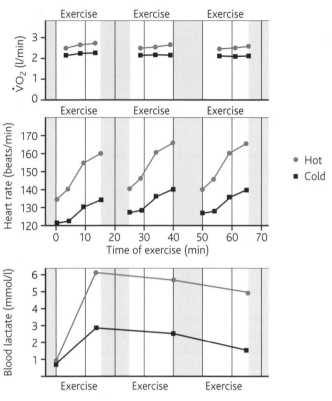

Fig. 5.7 *Effects of temperature on exercise*

hours before exercise. For most people, between approximately 500 and 1,000 ml of fluid during the two hours prior to exercise will be suitable. It is also important to drink early and at regular intervals during exercise, ideally at a rate that matches sweat loss. Since thirst does not provide a guide to fluid needs, fluid intake should be planned for each activity, depending on factors such as duration of the event and conditions. To encourage regular consumption, it is important to find a fluid that is pleasant to drink. Beverages containing carbohydrate are particularly useful during moderate- to high-intensity exercise of greater than 60 to 90 min duration. It is also recommended that sodium be included in rehydration fluids consumed during exercise lasting more than one hour. Sodium will enhance the taste of the drink and promote the retention of fluids consumed. A deliberate effort needs to be made to replace fluids lost during exercising. Drinks containing carbohydrate and electrolytes (sodium and potassium) are useful for recovery, providing carbohydrate for glycogen storage and promoting fluid retention.

Preparation for exercise in extreme temperatures involves planning for fluid intakes before, during and after competition.

Exercise in extreme conditions

Little can be done about the environmental conditions when performing. So if the conditions are threatening, athletes must reduce their efforts otherwise there is a risk of hyperthermia. The body can acclimatise to environmental conditions, and research suggests that several weeks of training in high temperatures and/or high humidity improves the efficiency of the body in removing excess heat.

Even elite athletes are likely to find that performance deteriorates when they exercise in the cold. In cold environments, the body attempts to gain

■ Link

For more information on dehydration, see Chapter 4 – The elite performer: food, supplements and performance-enhancing drugs (pages 43–5).

heat by shivering and by vasoconstriction of arterioles near the skin's surface. Heat loss is increased by wind, which increases convection. This effect is known as wind chill. Cold reduces the strength of muscles. They can generate less force (see Figure 5.7) and produce more lactate. During continued exercise in the cold, energy supplies quickly reduce and exercise intensity declines, and the performer becomes increasingly likely to suffer from hypothermia (a potentially fatal condition that occurs when the core body temperature falls below 35 °C).

Measuring the intensity of training

Lactate sampling

Elite athletes are capable of training at intensities close to their $\dot{V}O_2$ max and therefore close to a point where exhaustion may occur. It is therefore essential for them to achieve the right intensity of training. There needs to be sufficient intensity for the training to be beneficial without the training being so intense as to cause long-lasting damage. If we wish to be scientific about training, how can we measure how hard athletes are working or how close they are to their $\dot{V}O_2$ max without resorting to the use of complicated laboratory equipment? In other words, how do we measure intensity? We could use the Borg scale or measure the athlete's heart rate, as mentioned at AS Level. However, these are not sufficiently accurate for the elite performer. Measurements on the Borg scale are subjective, as they depend on the participant's perception of how hard they think they are working, and are therefore likely to be influenced by other variables such as psychological state. Heart rate may be slightly more reliable, but it too could be affected by other influences such as arousal, body condition, etc.

The development of suitable devices for lactate sampling has enabled this to be used by many athletes and coaches as a tool for measuring intensity. Lactate sampling involves taking a minute sample of the performer's blood; within a few seconds, the hand-held machine (see Figure 5.8) analyses the sample and produces a read-out of the amount of lactate present.

Fig. 5.8 *A lactate sampler*

Lactate threshold is usually taken to be a 2 mmol increase in lactate per litre of blood above resting levels. Lactate threshold is also sometimes referred to as OBLA, but OBLA is taken to be a level of 4 mmol of

AQA Examiner's tip

Questions on this topic may be concerned with the effect that high temperatures have on performance and/or on how the body regulates temperature.

Link

For more information on temperature regulation, see Chapter 4 – The elite performer: food, supplements and performance-enhancing drugs (pages 45–7).

Link

For more information on the effects of arousal, see Chapter 10 – Arousal (from page 131).

lactate per litre of blood. If lactate levels rise during training it is because anaerobic glycolysis is occurring in the exercising muscles and this is becoming the main method of resynthesising ATP. Performers need to train at levels of oxygen consumption and therefore intensity that are above their lactate threshold. The higher the reading of lactate in the blood, the higher the intensity of the workout being taken. Through experience and knowledge of their lactate levels, a coach will know how hard a performer is working. You can imagine a scene in a training camp where the coach is telling the athlete that they must keep repeating an exercise until their lactate level reaches some (presumably high) figure. Lactate threshold is linked to $\dot{V}O_2$ max. Specifically, the higher the percentage of $\dot{V}O_2$ max, or the higher the pace at which the lactate threshold occurs, the fitter the athlete. Lactate sampling can therefore also be used to measure potential – it can be used as a fitness test. Blood sampling is not easily used for games players. The test requires the performer or at least part of their body to be relatively stationary. That is why blood sampling tends to used with rowers or cyclists who are working on rowing machines or stationary bicycles. Physiologists call these specialised machines that are designed to measure workload, ergometers. Lactate sampling has also been used with swimmers who can be sampled as they take very short breaks between sets of exercises.

Fig. 5.9 *Elite rower in training*

The respiratory exchange ratio

The **respiratory exchange ratio (RER)** is the ratio of the carbon dioxide released by the body to the volume of oxygen consumed, ($\dot{V}CO_2/\dot{V}O_2$); it can be used to estimate the relative contributions of fat and carbohydrate to the provision of energy for ATP resynthesis. RER works as an indicator of fat and carbohydrate breakdown, because fat and carbohydrate differ in terms of the amount of oxygen used and carbon dioxide produced during oxidation.

Remember that fat oxidation requires much more oxygen than carbohydrate metabolism.

Thus, when fat is the major fuel, the amount of oxygen being consumed will tend to be a big number, which will make $\dot{V}CO_2/\dot{V}O_2$ and hence RER a small number. Correspondingly, the amount of oxygen being consumed will be a more modest number when carbohydrate is the key fuel, and therefore $\dot{V}CO_2/\dot{V}O_2$ and RER will be bigger since less oxygen is required to break down carbohydrates than is needed to break down fat.

Link

For more information on OBLA and $\dot{V}O_2$ max, see Chapter 2 – Anaerobic energy systems (pages 20 and 8 respectively).

Key terms

Respiratory exchange ratio (RER): the ratio of carbon dioxide released to oxygen used by the body.

Links

For more information on fat metabolism, see Chapter 1 – Aerobic energy systems (pages 6–9).

The measurement of $\dot{V}CO_2/\dot{V}O_2$ is completed using a cycle ergometer or treadmill, with the athlete attached to a gas analyser, so that the volumes of carbon dioxide being produced and oxygen being consumed are measured directly.

In fact, when physiologists measure RER at about 0.70, they estimate that 100 per cent of the energy for exercise is coming from fat; when RER settles at 1.00, carbohydrate is almost the sole source of fuel. And when RER is at 0.85, metabolism is equally divided between fat and carbohydrates. As you can see, RER measured during exercise can tell physiologists where an athlete is with regard to fuel usage.

Endurance-type training improves the ability of muscles to use fat as an energy source, but using fat is also a sign of aerobic work. Many elite performers depend on anaerobic processes to provide energy for their event. Fat is not used as an anaerobic energy source. By knowing the RER at which the performer is exercising, coaches can see whether they are working anaerobically or aerobically. A RER of less than 1.00 shows that some fat is being used and therefore some of the exercise is involving fat metabolism and aerobic work. It is only when the RER reaches 1.00 that the coach can be sure that the energy is being provided solely by anaerobic means. In other words, the RER becomes another means of measuring intensity. Because of the need for the athlete to be linked to expensive laboratory equipment, using RER as a means of measuring intensity is limited to those performers who are able to train while using ergometers (e.g. rowers, cyclists and runners).

Fig. 5.10 *Direct measurement of oxygen uptake*

✔️ *You should now be able to:*

- describe the method and principles behind plyometric training
- describe the method and principles behind PNF stretching
- describe the main advantages and disadvantages of altitude training
- discuss the needs of the endurance athlete in terms of glycogen loading and temperature regulation
- explain the principles of periodisation
- explain the use of lactate sampling and the respiratory exchange ratio as ways of measuring intensity of training.

1   (a)   In terms of the physical preparation of a team, what do you
            understand by the term 'periodisation'?   *(4 marks)*

    (b)   How does knowledge of the respiratory exchange ratio provide
            a coach with information about exercise intensity?   *(3 marks)*

2   Elite performers may attend altitude training sessions in order to improve
    their performance.

    (a)   What are the supposed benefits of altitude training?   *(4 marks)*

    (b)   Why is altitude training not always as effective as it should be?   *(3 marks)*

3   The training that elite performers undertake may include plyometrics and
    proprioceptive neuromuscular facilitation (PNF) stretching.

    Explain the methods and mechanisms involved in one of these methods
    of training.   *(7 marks)*

4   Marathon runners carefully plan their training to deal with the demands
    they may encounter during a race.

    (a)   Some runners may supercompensate by using glycogen loading
            as part of their preparation. What do you understand by the
            terms 'supercompensate' and 'glycogen loading'?   *(3 marks)*

    (b)   Effective temperature regulation is vital to the marathon
            runner. How is body temperature regulated?   *(4 marks)*

6 Sports injuries

Key terms

Rehabilitation: treatments designed to support the process of recovery from injury or illness, enabling the performer to regain maximum self-sufficiency and function as soon as possible.

Activity

1. Research the protective equipment for your activity, including the NGB regulations relating to the use of protective equipment.

2. Prepare a presentation about the protective equipment for your activity.

Elite performers spend a great deal of time and resources preparing themselves so that they can compete at the highest level. Being prevented from competing or performing because of injury is something all performers experience; it is frustrating and can affect future progression or income and reward for professional performers. Many injuries are due to inadequate preparation, poor equipment or incorrectly learned skills, and the knowledgeable performer can prevent many injuries from occurring. It has been suggested that injury rates could be cut by up to 25 per cent if performers took the proper preventive steps. Nevertheless, there are times when an injury is unavoidable and the performer must know how to return to full fitness as quickly as possible.

Our knowledge of how to prevent injury is now far more advanced and, increasingly, elite performers and their coaches are resorting to high-tech methods of preparation to prevent and recover from injury. There are certain misconceptions about sports injuries, for example that males have a higher rate of injuries than females and that speed training is a significant cause of sport injuries (the research shows that neither of these statements is true).

Given the need for elite performers to return to match fitness as soon as possible, many new high-tech **rehabilitation** methods are being introduced. As we shall see, the effectiveness of these new rehabilitation methods has been fully researched and the methods may not be as effective as claims suggest. It is true, however, that much can be done to prevent injury and to get the performer back into training or competition as soon as possible.

How proper preparation can reduce injuries

Proper preparation could reduce sports injuries by up to 25 per cent. Many of the recommended strategies are simple to put into practice and do not require greater resources, except perhaps when investing in high-quality equipment.

The importance of using the right equipment

Using the wrong equipment is responsible for a wide variety of sport injuries. Performers must have correctly fitting and appropriate footwear, protective equipment, clothing and the means to support weak joints.

Taping and bracing

Often, players have their ankles taped to prevent ligament injuries, or they wear a knee or elbow brace to provide extra stability to the joint. Taping must be done expertly if it is to provide support without limiting mobility, and braces must be fully adjustable so that they can limit movement in joints where ligaments have been stretched as a result of an earlier injury. Taping and bracing are also used during the recovery period after an injury.

Protective equipment

Players use a wide variety of equipment to protect themselves from impact injuries or penetrative injuries. Helmets, mouth guards, body armour, knee pads, fencing masks and eye protectors (for squash) are examples of such

Helmet

Gloves

Forearm guard

Box

Thigh guard

Pads

Fig. 6.1 *The right protective equipment can be vital for potentially dangerous sports such as cricket*

Key terms

National governing body (NGB): an organisation responsible for the promotion, development and regulation of a sport in the UK.

Friction: a force that opposes movement between two surfaces.

AQA Examiner's tip

Examination questions will not focus on a specific sport, but it would enhance your answer if you could give examples of protective equipment.

Link

For more information on hypothermia, see Chapter 4 – The elite performer: food, supplements and performance-enhancing drugs (page 46).

Activities

1 Get somebody to video you whilst you run at something like middle-distance pace, then whilst you are sprinting. Does your running style change in terms of your foot action?

2 If you have the opportunity, visit a specialist shop selling running shoes and see if they can do an analysis of your running style.

equipment. For the equipment to be effective, it must be an accurate fit for the performer and meet **national governing body (NGB)** regulations.

Shoes and boots

Ill-fitting sports shoes cause a whole variety of problems (e.g. shin splints, hip injuries, inflammation of the Achilles tendon, lower back pain, runner's knee, calluses and blisters on feet, etc.). Footwear must also give sufficient **friction** or traction against the ground, without gripping so excessively that performers suffer from ankle or knee injuries due to rotational forces.

To ensure that sports footwear allows for optimal performance and also protection from injury, it must be the correct size and suit the foot of the individual. This means considering the shape of the arch of the foot, undertaking a gait analysis (an analysis of stride length and the angles of the knee, hip and ankle joints during locomotion) and having an understanding of the way in which the individual runs – neutral, pronated or supinated:

■ Neutral – the heel of the runner makes contact with the ground and the foot travels in a straight line as it moves forward.

■ Pronated – the heel hits the ground but this time the foot moves to the side as it travels forward (pronation refers to the inward roll of the foot).

■ Supinated – the heel hits the ground and the foot rolls outward.

If you are a regular runner it is worth having your style of running analysed and purchasing the shoe that suits that style. Football boots are produced for different ground conditions and a range of high-tech materials is used to give support, cushioning, stability and protection (e.g. Kevlar, blown polystyrene, glass fibre and compression-moulded foam).

An example of poor design in sports shoes is the 'killer tab', which sticks up at the top of the heel and is the commonest cause of injury to the Achilles tendon. The top of the shoe's heel should be cut away, unless full ankle support is required.

Clothing: keeping cool, staying warm, dealing with sweat

Appropriate clothing can go some way to help avoid sport-related injuries or environmentally related dangers. When taking part in outdoor adventure activities, it is important to stay warm and dry. The risk of hypothermia is significantly increased if you get wet and cold, especially if there is the associated danger of wind chill.

When competing in high temperatures, it is important to decrease your chances of suffering from heat cramps, heat exhaustion and heat stroke. It is possible for the onset of these conditions to begin within 12 to 15 min when undertaking strenuous exercise in high temperatures. Sweating is one of the body's cooling mechanisms, and wearing synthetic, microfibre-type clothing that allows the sweat to 'wick' away from the body quickly will help the performer avoid problems with overheating and discomfort. In addition, avoid overheating by ingesting plenty of fluids; warm up in the shade; and acclimatise the body by training in the same temperature and humidity conditions.

Injury prevention and training

In sport, all performers train so that they can perform better – be it to improve strength, aerobic capacity, flexibility or power. Appropriate training can also reduce a performer's susceptibility to injury. Performers in a wide range of sports now include **core strength/core stability** training as part of their regular workouts.

Strength training and conditioning

As part of a **conditioning** programme, strength training will improve performance and help minimise the risk of injury. The conditioning work that is undertaken must relate specifically to the physical demands of the activity and should include a focus on common injuries. For example, players of racket games are prone to shoulder injuries, particularly injuries to the rotator cuff.

Strength training requires resistance work and can involve body-weight exercises, isometric work and the use of weights and resistance devices such as rubber bands.

A very wide range of performers can benefit from improvements in core strength and stability. Core strength training involves developing the deep trunk muscles, paraspinal muscles and the pelvic floor muscles which then help to stabilise the spine, particularly in the lower lumbar region. Before any movement takes place, these muscles contract to give trunk stability, which helps control movement and transfer energy. Conditioning that improves core strength can help improve performance and posture and makes the performer less prone to lower-back injuries and pain. Core strength training can be undertaken using body-weight exercises, balance boards or isometric exercises. Exercise systems such as Pilates also focus on core strength and stability.

Link

For more information on dehydration and water balance, see Chapter 4 – The elite performer: food, supplements and performance-enhancing drugs (pages 43–5).

AQA Examiner's tip

Ensure that you have understood the temperature-control mechanisms covered in Chapter 4 – The elite performer: food, supplements and performance-enhancing drugs. This will allow you to give a full answer to questions relating to this part of the specification.

Key terms

Core strength/core stability: the ability of the core muscles to maintain correct alignment of the spine and pelvis while the limbs are moving.

Conditioning: physical activities that prepare the body for intense exercise.

Fig. 6.2 *Conditioning – vital for injury prevention and recovery*

■ Activity

1 Review your own training regime. Does it include any core strength and stability conditioning?

2 If not, devise a core strength development programme for yourself, or with your coach.

AQA Examiner's tip

Questions will focus on the importance of core stability and general conditioning, and the problems that a lack of core stability and conditioning could cause, and will ask you to give some examples of the exercises that you could use to improve core stability.

Fig. 6.3 *Core stability – vital in injury prevention*

Strong, well-conditioned muscles act as important balancing agents for the forces that are generated throughout the body when we engage in physical activity. When muscles are strong they help to reduce the repetitive strain that occurs during running or playing football, rugby or basketball. Middle- and long-distance runners can have knee and hip problems if they neglect their strength training and there are imbalances between the forces generated by quadriceps, hamstrings, hip flexors and calves.

The effects of strength exercise are similar for muscle tissue and bone tissue. The same training stimulus that increases muscle density also increases bone density and mineral content.

The dangers of overtraining

Overtraining is a cause of many injuries. Overtraining can be caused in two ways: by overstressing the body during training sessions and by not allowing sufficient time for recovery after an intense training session or performance. The characteristics of an overtrained performer include long-lasting fatigue and worsening of performance under competitive conditions; the performer may be tempted to work harder to improve their physical condition. Overtraining is also described as staleness, overwork, over-reaching, burn-out and chronic fatigue. Fatigued and tired muscles provide inadequate support for tendons, ligaments, and bones; thereby increasing the risk of strains, sprains, and stress fractures.

A number of conditions may be symptomatic of the overtrained performer:

■ deep muscle soreness

■ a nagging injury that will not go away

- difficulty in working hard enough to raise the heart rate to the desired training level
- loss of appetite
- recurrent sore throats and flu-like symptoms, inability to shake off a cold – this may be as a result of a depressed **immune system** (known as immuno-suppression)
- not sleeping properly and associated feelings of tiredness.

To avoid injury caused as a result of training too hard, performers should:

- allow sufficient time for recovery (include one or two days of rest/recovery within the training programme)
- restore glycogen stores after hard sessions or performances (monitor physical condition and if the symptoms of overtraining are becoming evident then reduce the training load)
- not train when ill
- build up training loads gradually after illness
- try and use meditation or relaxation techniques to improve sleep
- ensure that diet is nutritionally balanced.

It is also important to recognise when the body is damaged and when further exercise will do short-term, or even long-term, damage. Do not train through pain. A temporary loss of training time and fitness is far better than long-term damage to the body. If something starts to hurt during training – stop. By continuing to train when hurt, performers can cause chronic deterioration of a knee joint or other anatomical region and experience problems in later life.

> ### Key terms
>
> **Immune system:** the integrated system of organs, tissues, cells, and antibodies that protects us from illness and disease.

> ### Link
>
> For more information on diet, see Chapter 4 – The elite performer: food, supplements and performance-enhancing drugs (pages 53–6).

> ### Activities
>
> 1. Review your training and playing programme. Does it allow sufficient time for recovery?
> 2. Do you suffer from any of the symptoms of overtraining?

Training hard is necessary to help the body to supercompensate (achieve the improved levels of performance noticeable after hard training followed by proper rest). The repairs that the body makes to muscle tissue and muscle glycogen stores and the replenishing of testosterone and cortisol levels all allow the performer to take a significant step forward. The necessity of balancing that against overtraining and the impact of what is known as the 'unexplained underperformance syndrome' are critical reasons why elite performers require elite coaches and medical and nutritional advice and support.

Young children and overtraining

Children are different physiologically – they are not miniature adults – and great care must be taken when devising training regimes and competition programmes for them. To train children as if they are small adults risks causing damage to developing joints and musculature as well as putting them off sport for life. Overtraining or overplaying or using inappropriate training regimes for strength or speed development can lead to inflammation of tendons, mild tendonitis (swelling of a tendon) and stress fractures. Overdevelopment or imbalanced development of musculature can cause strong muscle pulls at the tendon–bone junction and at the attachment to the growth plate, which can cause inflammation and stress fractures. However, recent evidence dispels the myths that weightlifting in children is both dangerous, owing to a risk of growth plate injury, and ineffective, because children are unable to increase strength. Resistance training that is supervised and properly planned in relation to the child's developmental age and physique is recognised to be safe and effective and may also reduce injury risk in young performers.

Youth and adolescent performers are most at risk from overuse injuries during times of rapid growth. One common overuse injury seen in adolescents is Osgood–Schlatter's disease. Repetitive running or jumping can cause the patella tendon, which attaches to the tibia, to become inflamed and can cause a painful bump. Tight hamstrings also seem to be a feature of this injury. Server's disease is a growth plate inflammation of the calcaneaus (heel bone) and is found in young football players.

The Long Term Athlete Development Programme

Increasing numbers of young performers are becoming prone to overuse injury. The **Long Term Athlete Development Programme (LTAD)**, developed by Dr Istvan Balyi and adopted by bodies such as **Sport England** and **sport coach UK**, is a strategy for developing performers from childhood through to adulthood. Although the programme's focus is on performer development, it has valuable advice for preventing inappropriate training and coaching programmes for children. The LTAD identifies two overlapping stages relating to children's sport:

- the FUNdamental Stage (ages 5–11)
- the Learning to Train Stage (ages 8–12).

Fig. 6.4 *Long Term Athlete Development Programme (LTAD)*

The FUNdamental stage (5–11)

At this stage there should be:

- fun for every child at every session
- quality participation in a wide range of sports
- development of FUNdamental motor skills – running, jumping, throwing, kicking, striking, catching, gliding, skipping
- development of the child's ABC – agility, balance and coordination
- low-volume training to develop speed and endurance using FUN games
- introduction to the simple rules and ethics of sports
- strength training with exercises that use the child's own body weight, e.g. medicine ball and Swiss ball exercises.

Key terms

Long Term Athlete Development Programme (LTAD): a generic strategy for the development of performers from the nursery to the podium. Sport NGBs adapt it to their specific needs.

Sport England: the non-governmental body responsible for developing participation and the standards of sport in England.

sport coach UK: the body responsible for developing a national coaching framework and for overseeing coach education and development in the UK.

The Learning to Train stage (8–12)

This second stage, which begins to help children to understand how and why to train, involves:

- further development of fundamental movement skills
- learning general overall sports skills
- continuing to develop strength with medicine ball, Swiss ball and own-body-weight exercises as well as hopping and bounding exercises
- continuing to develop endurance with games and relays
- introducing basic flexibility exercises
- continuing to develop speed with specific activities during the warm-up, such as agility, quickness and change of direction
- developing knowledge of warming up, cooling down, stretching, hydration, nutrition, recovery, relaxation and focusing
- structuring of any competition (a 70:30 training/practice-to-competition ratio is recommended).

The LTAD has been taken up by many sports and developed into sport-specific models.

Carbohydrate intake and glycogen loading

Endurance athletes are now advised to have a diet high in carbohydrates (1.5 to 3 g of carbohydrate for each kilogram of body weight). Regular hard training or competition tends to reduce muscle glycogen levels, which can lead to fatigue and injury.

To further reduce the risk of being injured through being overtired, some performers increase their carbohydrate intake when engaged in heavy training or high-level competition. Each time you exercise, muscle glycogen becomes depleted to some extent. With a high carbohydrate intake every day, it is more likely that you will restore the carbohydrate that has been used, thereby enabling the body to cope with another hard bout of training the following day.

To delay fatigue during exercise, take carbohydrates in drink form with a concentration of 6 to 8 per cent to ensure easier and quicker absorption. To avoid hypoglycaemia or low blood sugar during exercise, carbohydrate should not be consumed within one hour of the start of exercise. The best pre-game strategy is to eat a light meal which contains around 100 g of carbohydrate three to four hours prior to exercise.

Endurance performers also use a technique known as glycogen loading; this causes a temporary increase in the levels of glycogen in the body just prior to competition by convincing the body to store more glycogen than normal.

■ The importance of the warm-up and the warm-down

Preparing the body for exercise, be it in training or competition, and undertaking post-exercise warm-downs, have a beneficial effect on performance, injury prevention and recovery.

■ Link

For a more detailed discussion of the LTAD model, see Chapter 16 – Elite performers and World Games (pages 229–32.)

AQA Examiner's tip

Exam questions will focus on the principles behind the LTAD and the specific recommendations for the two levels in this section. Examples from your own sport will help persuade the examiner that you understand what you are talking about.

■ Links

- For more information on glycogen, see Chapter 1 – Aerobic energy systems (pages 2–6).
- More details on the practice of glycogen loading can be found in Chapter 5 – Specialised training (pages 67–9).

AQA Examiner's tip

Be sure to take advice from an experienced coach or nutritionist before undertaking anything other than a normal balanced diet as part of an exercise or recovery plan.

The warm-up

Modern thinking on the warm-up is that it should be active and dynamic. There is thought to be less benefit in doing static stretches after some gentle pulse raising. The following are likely features of an active warm-up routine:

- There is a general cardiovascular warm-up lasting 5–10 min (light jogging, skipping or footwork patterns in a speed ladder), raising the body's core temperature to enhance the elasticity of muscles, tendons, ligaments and other joint structures.

- At the same time, the performer should begin focusing and concentrating their mind for the coming training session or performance.

- The cardiovascular warm-up is followed by a range of 8 to 10 dynamic exercises that address all the major muscle groups (hamstrings, quadriceps, calves/Achilles and hip flexors) on an equal basis.

- Each exercise is completed over 20–30 m and is followed by a light jog back to the starting point to maintain the warm-up effect.

- The exercises are specific to the sport, mimicking the actions involved in the activity.

- The exercises are undertaken with an increasing level of intensity or dynamic range of movement.

- The post-cardiovascular portion should take 10–20 min, depending on the age of the performer.

Fig. 6.5 *Using the speed ladder: an active warm-up*

The benefits of the active warm-up are:

- maintenance of warmth in the body and muscles (core temperatures may decrease after sitting and stretching for 10–15 min)

- preparation of the muscles and joints in a more sport-specific manner than is achieved by static stretching

- improvement of coordination and motor ability as well as energising the nervous system (this may particularly benefit the younger performer who is still in a stage of skill development) better mental preparation (proper mental preparation for any sport is vital and active warm-up forces performers to focus and concentrate on the task at hand).

There is much debate over the value of warm-up both in terms of enhanced performance and injury prevention. Research evidence is not clear but on several factors there is agreement:

- High-intensity warm-ups (80 per cent $\dot{V}O_2$ max plus) may be detrimental to performance.
- Lower-intensity (60 per cent $\dot{V}O_2$ max) warm-ups do no harm and will probably be beneficial.
- Warm-ups that are dynamic and take joints through a greater range of motion than is used in the activity seem to help in injury prevention and performance.
- Warm-up should be activity specific and not just consist of generalised jogging and static stretching.

The warm-down

The warm-down has a number of beneficial effects and should be designed to decrease any injurious effects of the performance or training session, and to prepare the performer for the next session. It can do this by preventing blood from pooling in the limbs and lactic acid from building up in the muscles. It will help muscles and tendons to relax and loosen, stopping them from becoming stiff and tight.

The warm- or cool-down should be active but, in contrast to the warm-up, static stretching is advised for the warm- or cool-down accompanied by light cardiorespiratory work.

Pain, stiffness and soreness are experienced after intense work. This post-exercise condition, which is known as **delayed onset of muscle soreness (DOMS)**, is caused by damage to the muscle fibres and connective tissue, resulting in inflammation and increased local muscle temperature. DOMS seems to be caused by intense muscular activity and eccentric muscle contractions. It was thought that lactic acid may also be a cause, but recent research indicates that this may not be the case.

To avoid DOMS or to recover from it:

- undertake an active dynamic warm-up (see above)
- when starting an exercise programme, avoid movements that entail strenuous eccentric muscle action (downhill running, plyometrics, etc.)
- gradually increase the intensity and duration of exercise
- after the initial stages of training, do extra amounts of any eccentric exercise that may have caused DOMS
- undertake an active warm-down, including passive stretching
- consider the use of therapeutic massage.

Ensuring proper recovery after injury

Proper recovery after injury is vital, both to ensure that the athlete returns to their pre-injury level of performance and also to prevent the injury from occurring again. If the injury was the result of muscular or joint imbalances, or poor biomechanical 'form', and nothing is done to correct that imbalance, the injury will reoccur almost as soon as the athlete starts to increase their training load.

Activity

Devise an active warm-up routine that would be appropriate to your own sport activity.

AQA Examiner's tip

You will be expected to be quite specific about the activities and strategies that you would use in a warm-up or warm-down, and to be able to justify their inclusion.

Key terms

Delayed onset of muscle soreness (DOMS): the pain felt in the muscles the day after intense exercise.

Activity

Devise an active warm-down routine that would be appropriate to your own sport activity.

So how does an athlete recover from injury? Clearly, the kind of injury that the performer has suffered is a factor. If it is a soft-tissue injury, or just general fatigue, the following may be included:

- light aerobic activity – less than 50 per cent of $\dot{V}O_2$ max
- stretching
- therapeutic massage
- contrast showers (alternating hot with cold)
- sleeping or lying down still
- cold/ice baths
- food (especially carbohydrates)
- hydration
- whirlpool baths.

A number of these strategies may be appropriate after injuries involving damage to bones.

Immediate treatment of a soft-tissue injury is vital if the performer is to be able to compete as soon as possible.

RICE

Rest, Ice, Compression, Elevation (RICE): the acronym RICE represents the elements in the proper treatment regime for soft-tissue injuries; this regime can help to reduce pain and speed up the healing process and is a well-known way of giving immediate treatment. The RICE treatment (see below) should be continued for up to 48 hours. Gentle mobility exercises can begin once the swelling has gone down, when gentle heat and contrast showers (warm and cold) will be beneficial.

Rest

The performer should rest as soon as the injury occurs, if the injury cannot be 'shaken off', or as soon as the performer leaves the field and also during the recovery period.

Ice

The injured area should be iced for 10 to 15 min; then the ice should be taken off for 20 min and so on. This reduces internal bleeding (due to vasoconstriction) and the flow of fluids from damaged cells and controls inflammation and swelling. Ice should not be used for longer periods of time and should always be wrapped in a towel or something similar to avoid damage to the skin or frostbite.

Compression

Compression reduces or helps control swelling, and swelling delays healing.

Elevation

Elevation also helps reduce swelling and inflammation; it is most effective if the injured area is elevated above the level of the heart.

Recovering from intense exercise

Over recent years, recovery from intense exercise has been the focus of much attention. So far we have mentioned the use of warm-down, replenishment of energy stores and rehydration. Those suffering from DOMS can also make use of therapeutic massage.

■ **Key terms**

Rest, Ice, Compression, Elevation (RICE): an immediate treatment plan for acute soft-tissue injury; it limits inflammation and swelling.

AQA Examiner's tip

As well as knowing the RICE procedure, you will be expected to explain the benefits of each of its component parts.

■ Link

For more information on rehydration, see Chapter 4 – The elite performer: food, supplements and performance-enhancing drugs (pages 47–9).

Cryotherapy

In general terms, **cryotherapy** is the use of cooling measures to treat chronic or acute injuries. As part of the RICE procedure, ice is used for an acute injury. Ice baths are often used as part of post-match recovery in contact sports such as rugby, for much the same reason that ice is used on sprains and strains.

A **cryogenic** chamber is cooled with liquid nitrogen to a temperature of −110 °C. Cryogenic-chamber therapy is a treatment for muscle and joint pain, in which the patient is placed in the chamber for a few minutes. The performer is protected from frostbite with socks, gloves and mouth and ear protection but otherwise wears nothing but a bathing suit! Pain relief can last for up to 6 to 8 hours after treatment.

Fig. 6.6 *Cryogenic-chamber therapy*

Replenishing the energy stores

It is important to replenish the carbohydrate and the glycogen stores after exercise. Performers may take a drink 20 to 30 min after exercise or eat a high-carbohydrate food, such as bread, bagels, pretzels or fruit. The goal is to consume at least 50 g shortly after exercise. After the initial recovery phase, those performers engaging in high levels of training or competition should have a high-carbohydrate diet. This will vary from performer to performer but should be in the region of 1.5 to 3 g of carbohydrate per kilogram of body weight.

> ### Activity
>
> Devise a personal post-match/heavy-training session, carbohydrate-replenishment diet. Include details of amounts and sources of carbohydrates. Make sure that the foods are ones that you like to eat!

Specialised support following sports injuries

We have looked at how we might recover immediately after a training session or a competition. After a long-term injury, the performer is keen to get back into training so that they can return to the competitive arena. This raises the question as to whether an athlete should train when injured.

> ### Key terms
>
> **Cryotherapy:** the general or local use of cold temperatures in the treatment of injury.
>
> **Cryogenic:** any process carried out at very low temperature, below −50 °C.

> ### AQA Examiner's tip
>
> Remember to seek the advice of an experienced coach or nutritionist before changing your normal balanced diet.

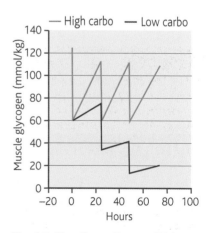

Fig. 6.7 *The effects of low- and high-carbohydrate diets on glycogen levels during daily bouts of exercise*

Should a performer train when injured?

The answer used to be no – rest and treatment were the order of the day. Nowadays, the expectation is that, once the rehabilitation period has begun, a performer is likely to get off the physiotherapist's couch and get working on specific strengthening and flexibility exercises. These exercises will be designed not only to ensure that the part that has been injured returns to its fully functioning state but also to try and eliminate the cause of the injury or make sure that there is no permanent weakness. Flexibility work will be important, as will resistance training. The kinds of strength training required will obviously depend on the injury and the sport activity. It could also be focused on strengthening other areas of the body.

The performer will also want, if possible, to maintain aerobic fitness. If running is not possible then water-based training (see below) will be used. Performers will also use alternatives to their usual training methods, to avoid stressing the injured area.

Core strength training

Core strength training (see page 81) can often be carried out during the rehabilitation period. Injuries are frequently caused by explosive limb movements undertaken when the body is in a state of imbalance or there is some other biomechanical inefficiency due to lack of core strength and stability. If core strength training is undertaken during rehabilitation, the injury is less likely to reoccur in the future. During the rehabilitation phase, the performer should focus on the whole movement or what is known as the **kinetic chain**. The kinetic chain approach recognises that the body is a coordinated structure, with each part linked as in a chain. A deficiency in one part of the chain can cause a problem or an injury in another part. Trying to rehabilitate a muscle or a joint in isolation from the other connected joints or muscles, including the core stabilising muscles, will make the performer far more likely to suffer from similar injuries in the future.

Activity

For your own sport, consider some common injuries. Devise a post-injury alternative exercise programme that will avoid overstressing the injured area, maintain flexibility and also enable some aerobic work to be done.

Key terms

Kinetic chain: a system consisting of muscles, joints, and neural components that must work together to enable optimal movement.

Activity

Select one of the core skills or techniques from your sport. Using the kinetic-chain approach, try to identify all the joints and muscles that are involved in the production of that movement.

Water-based training

Water-based training or aquatic therapy is any activity performed in water to help in rehabilitation and recovery from hard training or serious injury. Water training is often used when athletes need to maintain cardiovascular fitness while continuing their sport-specific training patterns (e.g. running) but without exposing the damaged tissues to further trauma.

The great benefit of aquatic therapy is that, when in the water, the body weighs about 10 per cent of its land weight. With the addition of a buoyancy belt or a flotation vest, there is virtually no impact or jarring on any of the body's joints, muscles, ligament, tendons or bones; this is highly beneficial to someone recovering from injury. Water also creates resistance to movement in all directions through a full range of motion or motor skills. The performer can increase or decrease the resistance and therefore the intensity by changing the speed of the movements in the water.

AQA Examiner's tip

Too often, candidates discuss recovery only in terms of injury treatment; they forget the active part that the performer has to play through conditioning activities, proprioceptive retraining, etc.

To undertake aquatic therapy the performer adopts a running posture – head up, shoulders back, torso relatively straight, leaning very slightly forward. The standard motion is a straight running action, using long, smooth strides and arm action. From that basic technique, almost any sport-related movement can be developed and replicated (e.g. cross-country skiing, hurdling, basketball defensive crouch).

It is also possible to make use of underwater fitness equipment such as treadmills, cross-trainers and bikes.

  Activity

If you have the opportunity to use a pool at school or college (or use your local pool if you don't mind others watching) try some aqua therapy. Use basic running actions and then try actions that are more specific to your sport. Don't worry if you do not have a flotation belt or vest – a T shirt with a normal float inside is a cheap alternative.

Fig. 6.8 *Aquatic-therapy conditioning gym*

Physiotherapy and sports massage

Sports massage (sometimes known as therapeutic massage) is the application of massage techniques to the muscle and connective tissues of the body to enhance and maximise sport performance. It is used to increase the range of movement and flexibility and to relieve muscle soreness. It may help injury prevention and promote faster recovery from high-intensity training and injury. There is no doubt that therapeutic massage after heavy exercise may relieve the symptoms of delayed onset of muscle soreness, but claims that it can improve muscle strength or function are less certain and some research shows that performance can be impeded by overuse of massage other than for pain management or recovery after injury.

Proprioceptive retraining

Proprioception is the coordination of balance and joint-positioning sense. For smooth and coordinated movements to be produced, the brain must know accurately the position of the limbs and joints and also the rate of movement of the limbs. This information comes from the proprioceptors in the joints, tendons, and muscles (Golgi tendon organs, muscle spindles) and from our visual and auditory senses as well as our sense of touch.

After a period of injury, the performer's proprioceptive sense may be impaired and, unless retrained, is likely to cause a recurrence of the

  Key terms

Proprioception: the body's awareness of position, posture, movement and changes in state of balance.

Fig. 6.9 *Balance board*

injury. The performer should undertake exercises such as hopping on a trampette, unilateral balance drills, balance-board exercises and hopping and jumping drills to restore the lost proprioception. The performer may also use taping or bracing to aid joint alignment and increase sensory input.

Technology and injury recovery

As elite sport is an important part of our economy and provides many people with the means of earning a living, it has become vital that performers return to a competitive state as quickly as possible. Sports science and technological research have essential roles in the provision of better rehabilitative processes. Among the resources available to elite performers are cryogenic chambers and computerised axial tomography (CAT or CT), a scanning technique enabling a series of detailed pictures of areas inside the body to be taken from different angles (the pictures are created by a computer linked to an X-ray machine). Also available are magnetic resonance imaging (MRI), which uses magnetic fields to produce two- or three-dimensional images of joints and tissues inside the body without using X-rays, and electrotherapy, ultrasound and even alternative medical procedures such as acupuncture.

Hyperbaric chambers

Hyperbaric chambers are a recent innovation. Hyperbaric oxygen therapy (HBO$_3$) involves the inhalation of oxygen under high pressure and is undertaken in hyperbaric chambers or pressure chambers. It was initially used 20 years ago to treat gangrene, carbon-monoxide poisoning and radiation sickness and in the treatment of divers suffering from decompression sickness.

Hyperbaric oxygen treatment boosts white blood cell activity in damaged parts of the body, thereby controlling infections, and constricts blood vessels and diminishes blood flow to the injured region, helping to reduce pressure and swelling. Whilst this would be helpful, it should not be assumed that HBO$_3$ is a cure-all. Although several football clubs and elite athletes use the treatment, there is little research to indicate that it is effective in all sport injuries. In fact, a recent research paper in the *International Journal of Sports Medicine* reported that HBO$_3$ treatment had no effect on soft tissue rehabilitation.

Oxygen tents

An oxygen tent, which consists of a canopy placed over the head and shoulders or over the entire body, provides an oxygen-rich environment. Some endurance athletes have been using oxygen tents to try and improve $\dot{V}O_2$ max or to recover from injury more quickly. However, once again, research so far shows little benefit

Hypoxic tents

On the other hand, using a **hypoxic tent**, an enclosed living space that simulates high altitude by maintaining a lower oxygen concentration, has been shown to have real benefits. The tent is used to stimulate the body's natural adaptations to altitude by facilitating the production of more oxygen-carrying red blood cells and haemoglobin. This improves the athlete's ability to perform work, because more oxygen is available to the working muscles, and is of benefit to endurance performers.

One of the problems with altitude training is that, because of the lower oxygen concentration, the performer cannot work at their normal training loads. Sleeping in a simulated altitude environment allows the

■ **Key terms**

Hyperbaric chamber: an air-tight chamber that can simulate air pressure at altitude or at depth.

Hypoxic tent: a form of hyperbaric chamber that simulates low-pressure or altitude conditions.

AQA **Examiner's tip**

You will need to discuss the various treatments and why some are being used even though their effectiveness has been called into question by research findings. The commercial pressures of the sports rehabilitation business should not be ignored.

body to achieve some of the positive adaptations to altitude while still permitting the athlete to perform workouts at oxygen-rich sea level, where their muscles can perform at their normal work level. Most athletes use altitudes between 2,500 and 3,500m and, rather than tents, have specially constructed rooms or dormitories.

A note of warning

The prevention and treatment of sports injuries is now a multi-disciplinary, high-tech business. Elite performers can afford the best support and treatment and they can train harder and recover more quickly than ever before. It is important, however, that new treatment is thoroughly researched and validated before we can assume that it brings any benefits. As with sport nutrition, there are commercial providers offering treatments that, although not harmful, are yet to be fully researched.

Fig. 6.10 *Hypoxic tent – train at sea level, sleep at 3,000m!*

☑ *You should now be able to:*

- plan pre-match or competition training regimes so as to reduce chances of injury
- devise an effective warm-up and warm-down
- know how pre-match nutrition can help performance
- know what to do immediately after intense exercise to speed up recovery
- know what specialised treatments are available to treat sports injuries.

AQA Examination-style questions

1   A basketball player twists their ankle in a game and has to leave the court.
    (a)   Describe the immediate treatment that they should use.   *(4 marks)*
    (b)   The injury does not respond to the treatment. Describe two
          other treatments that could be used to help recovery.   *(3 marks)*

2   Warm-up and warm-down are useful in preventing injury and in aiding
    the recovery process after intense exercise.
    (a)   What activities would you include in the warm-up and why?   *(4 marks)*
    (b)   What would you include in the warm-down and why?   *(3 marks)*

3   Rapid recovery from injury is vital for elite performers and they now use
    a wide range of injury recovery techniques. For each of the following
    methods describe the treatment and its purpose.
    (a)   Cryotherapy   *(2 marks)*
    (b)   Proprioceptive retraining   *(3 marks)*
    (b)   Therapeutic massage   *(2 marks)*

4   For a named sport, describe the steps that a performer could take to
    reduce their chances of injury, prior to competition.   *(7 marks)*

7 Mechanical concepts

Key terms

Force: something that tends to cause a change in motion, measured in metres per second squared (kg/ms^{-2}).

Impulse: the effect of a force acting over a period of time.

Velocity (m s^{-1}): the rate of change of displacement or displacement divided by time, measured in metres per second.

Displacement: the shortest straight-line measurement between two points.

AQA Examiner's tip

Virtually all mechanical quantities that are covered in this specification include the idea of direction as well as magnitude (size).

Mechanics is the study of the conditions under which objects move or stay at rest. For our purposes, an object is anything that has mass, and this can include a performer, a ball, a javelin, etc. The key concepts in the study of the movement of objects are **force** and Newton's laws of motion. These are studied within the subject of physics; however, no previous knowledge of physics and no great mathematical knowledge are required to understand the mechanics that you need to know.

Like every object on the earth, all your performances in sport are affected by forces. Forces cause movement; forces change the way in which you move and forces stop movement. The way in which an object moves is called its motion. The way in which you move depends on the size and direction of the forces acting on you. There are two basic types of motion, linear and angular; this chapter is concerned with linear motion, i.e. motion in a straight line. First, we will look at the terms used to describe linear motion. We will achieve a better understanding of forces and of how Newton's laws govern our motion and the motion of all objects, and finally we will look at one particular aspect of linear motion, **impulse**.

The physics of sprinting

Consider a man who is running in a straight line. If the man runs 100m in 15s, we can calculate his average speed, because:

$$\text{Average speed in metres per second (m s}^{-1}\text{)} = \frac{\text{Distance covered}}{\text{Time taken}}$$

In the case described above:

$$\text{Average speed} = \frac{100}{15} = 6.67 \text{ (m s}^{-1}\text{)}$$

The units are metres per second; this means that the performer is running 6.67 m every second. When describing linear motion, however, we use the word **velocity** to describe how fast a body moves. Velocity is a similar concept to speed but includes the idea of 'direction'.

In other words, all velocities take place in a certain direction, and the concept of distance is replaced with that of **displacement**. Displacement is the shortest straight line between the starting point and the finishing point. Therefore:

$$\text{Average velocity} = \frac{\text{Displacement}}{\text{Time}}$$

So, the average velocity for an athlete who runs 100m in 12s is:

$$\text{Average velocity} = \frac{100}{12} = 8.33 \text{ m s}^{-1}.$$

The average velocity for a 100m race can be a useful measure. However, taking velocities for separate parts of an event is more accurate and provides more information. For example, we can measure the average velocity of a performer at different stages of a 100m sprint on a track. Timekeepers can be placed at 10m intervals down the track, and they can time how long it takes the athlete to reach the point opposite where they are standing (timed from the starting point).

Activity

Make arrangements to complete this experiment. You will need a participant who is willing to run, a starter and at least 10 timekeepers, each supplied with a stopwatch.

1 When the starter gives the 'go' command, all the timekeepers start their watches.

2 Each timekeeper waits until the athlete passes their timing point before stopping their watch.

   ■ If you have sufficient timekeepers and stopwatches, have more than one timekeeper at each timing point and calculate the average time recorded for the runner to reach that timing point.

   ■ This experiment can also be done using a video camera and a suitably marked track, with the times for each section calculated after the run.

3 Present the results of the experiment as a table (such as Table 7.1), showing the time taken, and hence the average velocity, for each 10 m section of the race.

4 Draw a graph of the results that you obtained, plotting total displacement on the x-axis against average velocity on the y-axis.

Table 7.1 *Table of average velocities during a 100 m sprint*

Timing point (displacement in metres)	Distance covered (metres)	Time to reach this point (seconds)	Time taken for this 10 m section (seconds)	Average velocity for each 10 m section = displacement ÷ time (m s^{-1})
Start	0	0	0	0 ÷ 0 = 0
10	10	1.7	1.7 – 0.0 = 1.7	10 ÷ 1.7 = 5.88
20	10	2.9	2.9 – 1.7 = 1.2	10 ÷ 1.2 = 8.33
30	10	4.0	4.0 – 2.9 = 1.1	10 ÷ 1.1 = 9.09
40	10	5.0	5.0 – 4.0 = 1.0	10 ÷ 1.0 = 10.00
50	10	6.0	6.0 – 5.0 = 1.0	10 ÷ 1.0 = 10.00
60	10	7.1	7.1 – 6.0 = 1.1	10 ÷ 1.1 = 9.09
70	10	8.3	8.3 – 7.1 = 1.2	10 ÷ 1.2 = 8.33
80	10	9.6	9.6 – 8.3 = 1.3	10 ÷ 1.3 = 7.69
90	10	11.0	11.0 – 9.6 = 1.4	10 ÷ 1.4 = 7.14
100	10	12.6	12.6 – 11.0 = 1.6	10 ÷ 1.6 = 6.25

The important thing to see from these results is that the velocity of the performer should change during the different stages of the race. The performer's velocity should gradually increase as they go through the 10, 20, 30 and 40 m points; their velocity should remain the same through the 50 m point and should decrease through the 60, 70, 80, 90 and 100 m points. As Figure 7.1 shows, first the trend of the graph is upward, indicating that velocity is increasing; then the graphed line remains horizontal, showing that velocity is unchanging; and then the trend of the graph is downward, showing where velocity is decreasing. The highest point on the graph is where velocity remains constant.

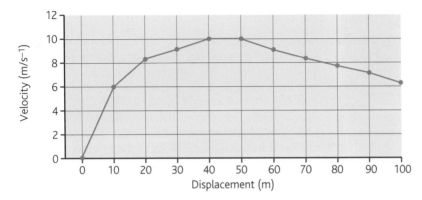

Fig. 7.1 *Displacement time graph for a 100 m sprint*

These changes in velocity can be partly related to the differing energy sources used during a 60 m sprint. Remember that performers have rather limited stores of phosphocreatine (PC): enough to last for 5–8 s of maximal exertion.

What we can see from these results is the consequence of these limited stores. During maximal exertion (sprinting), PC is used as an energy source to provide for the resynthesising of adenosine triphosphate (ATP). The results show that after 6 s the performer's velocity decreases because they have begun to run out of PC and have predominantly to use the lactate anaerobic system to resynthesise ATP. Because the lactate anaerobic system involves many more chemical reactions than the PC system and is therefore slower at resynthesising ATP, not as much force can be exerted by the muscles and the performer slows down.

Look back at Figure 7.1; the graph shows that the performer's velocity changes during the race. We call a change in velocity **acceleration**. Acceleration can be defined as the rate of change of velocity.

It is possible to calculate acceleration:

$$\text{Average acceleration (m s}^{-2}) = \frac{\text{Final velocity} - \text{Initial velocity}}{\text{Time}}$$

$$Acceleration = \frac{v_f - v_i}{t}$$

Hence, we can use the results from Table 7.1 to find our sprinter's change in velocity over the 20 to 30 m section, i.e. their acceleration:

■ Their initial velocity (after 20 m) is $8.33 \, \text{m s}^{-1}$.

■ Their final velocity (after 30 m) is $9.09 \, \text{m s}^{-1}$.

■ The time taken to run between the 20 and 30 m points is 1.1 s.

Therefore, the sprinter's acceleration = $(9.09 - 8.33) \div 1.1 = 0.69 \, \text{m s}^{-2}$.

The units are metres per second per second. In other words, for every metre that this athlete covers, their velocity increases by $0.69 \, \text{m s}^{-1}$.

You can also see acceleration on the graph in Figure 7.1: acceleration is represented by the steepness or gradient of the graph. In Figure 7.1, the steepest part of the graph is the slope between 0 and 10 m. This is the part of the race where acceleration was greatest. Between 40 and 50 m the velocity remained the same, and therefore there was no acceleration. On the graph, the plot line shows this by being horizontal and parallel to the x-axis. From 50 m on to the finish of the race, the graph slopes down. This is because the runner's velocity was decreasing. This reduction in velocity is called **deceleration**.

Link

For more information on phosphocreatine and energy systems, see Chapter 2 – Anaerobic energy systems (from page 16).

Key terms

Acceleration (m s^{-2}): the rate of change of velocity or the difference between final and initial velocities divided by the time taken, measured in metres per second squared.

Deceleration: a negative change in velocity over time or negative acceleration.

AQA Examiner's tip

■ You might be asked to explain the reasons for the deceleration experienced by a performer during a 100 m sprint. You might also be asked to explain the difference between velocity and acceleration.

■ Although we are using mathematics to help our understanding of the concepts involved, no mathematics is required for the mechanical aspects of the AQA exam.

■ Key terms

Vector: a quantity that has two dimensions, magnitude and direction.

Scalar: a quantity that has a single dimension, magnitude.

■ Vectors and scalars

Mathematics and science allow us to describe and understand the world around us. We live in a world governed by the passing of time and three dimensions in space (up and down, left and right, back and forth). We observe that there are some quantities and processes in our world that depend on the direction in which they occur, and there are some quantities that do not depend on direction. For example, the volume of an object, the three-dimensional space that an object occupies, does not depend on direction. If we have a $1\,m^3$ block of iron and we move it up and down and then left and right, we still have a $1\,m^3$ block of iron. On the other hand, the location of an object does depend on direction. If we move the $1\,m^3$ block $8\,km$ to the north, the resulting location is very different from if we moved it $8\,km$ to the east. Mathematicians and scientists call a quantity that depends on direction a **vector** quantity. A quantity that does not depend on direction is called a **scalar** quantity.

Vector quantities have two characteristics, magnitude (size) and a direction. Scalar quantities have only magnitude or the quantity (or amount) of whatever you are measuring. When comparing two vector quantities of the same type, you have to compare both the magnitude and the direction. Vectors, because they have direction, also have a line of application and a point where they are having an effect; this is called the point of application. For these reasons, vectors are usually represented by arrows, which can also show direction, line of application, point of application and, if drawn to scale, magnitude.

For scalars, you only have to compare the magnitude. When doing any mathematical calculation on a vector quantity (like adding, subtracting and multiplying), you have to consider both the magnitude and the direction. This makes dealing with vector quantities a little more complicated than scalars, but fortunately we can limit our knowledge to knowing just that they have both magnitude and direction. Velocity, acceleration and displacement are vectors, and all have direction as well as magnitude (size). Measurements such as speed, distance and temperature, which only have magnitude, are scalars.

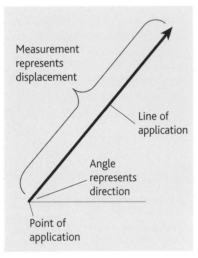

Fig. 7.2 *A vector represented by an arrow*

■ Activity

Provide definitions for each of the parameters listed in this table and identify which are vectors and which are scalars.

Term	Definition	Vector or scalar
Displacement		
Velocity		
Acceleration		
Vector		
Scalar		
Deceleration		
Speed		

Newton's laws

Basic concepts

Forces

Forces are what change a body's state of motion. If a performer or ball changes its state of motion from being at rest to moving, then this involves a force. Similarly, if a performer or ball changes its direction, or slows, or even stops, then a force caused that change in motion. Forces are the 'push' or 'pull' that one body applies to another body, to affect its state of motion. But not all forces are large enough to have these effects.

Imagine a set of weights lying on the gym floor. Two weightlifters are taking turns, trying to lift the barbell. The stronger lifter manages to lift it off the floor; but the weaker fails, even though he was still applying a force to the barbell, trying to move it.

This gives us a better definition of a force: a force is that which alters or tends to alter a body's state of rest or of uniform motion in a straight line.

> ### Activity
>
> Think of a sport with which you are familiar and imagine that sport taking place.
>
> **1** Can you think of examples from that sport of a body's state of motion being changed from rest to moving (quickening) or from moving to rest (slowing) or the body's direction being changed?
>
> **2** Having identified these examples, can you further identify what causes these changes in speed and direction?

There are two types of forces:

- Internal forces are those that we generate ourselves, through contraction of our muscles.
- External forces come from outside our body, such as **air resistance**, **gravity** and contact with the ground or some other body.

Forces are vectors and as such have the characteristics of vectors; they have both magnitude and direction and are usually drawn as arrows.

Gravity

Despite what you may think, weight is a force. It is the effect of gravity on a body. Gravity is the force that causes objects that are thrown into the air to be attracted back towards the planet's surface. The gravitational force that is acting on an object is called its weight. This is distinct from its mass. Mass is the quantity of matter in a body, usually measured in kilograms. Weight is the effect of gravity on a body and is equal to the mass of the body multiplied by the acceleration given to that body by the force of gravity.

Friction

Whenever one object moves or tries to move over another, friction occurs as a force, acting parallel to the surfaces in contact and opposing the movement or tendency to move. In a 100 m sprint, there is friction between the performer's running shoe and the track. The runner pushes against the track and a friction force is generated. This force prevents the athlete from slipping. Friction acts to oppose the motion between the contacting surfaces, and its magnitude is proportional to the weight force

> ### Key terms
>
> **Air resistance:** friction between a body and air particles.
>
> **Gravity:** the force of attraction between two bodies; force pulls objects towards the centre of the earth.

that pushes the two surfaces together. The important thing about friction in terms of sport is that movement requires frictional forces. For this reason, the degree of motion you can achieve is, to a large extent, decided by the shoes you wear for your sport. Shoe designers try to achieve as great a value as possible for the degree of friction between the sole of the shoe and the surface on which you are playing for most sports.

Basketball, volleyball, badminton and tennis players all wear different types of shoes with different soles designed to provide maximum grip, which actually means maximum friction. The studs in the boots of outdoor games players serve the same purpose. Players play with different boots for different surfaces to provide differing degrees of friction. In some sports, such as ice-skating and skiing, friction between the performer and the ground surface is reduced to as small a value as possible to enable the performer to slide deliberately over the surface.

Air resistance

Air resistance is essentially friction due to air passing over surfaces. Again in many sports, air resistance is changed by wearing appropriate clothing. In speed-based events, such as sprinting, speed skating and cycling, it helps to wear materials that cling to the body and move through the air in a way that minimises the effects of air resistance. In many airborne activities, such as power kiting, hang gliding and parachuting, the idea is to increase air resistance to provide greater lift.

Inertia

When a body is at rest, it is reluctant to do anything other than remain at rest. A heavy set of weights lying on the floor of a gym shows this resistance when attempts are made to move them. Similarly, when a body is moving, it is reluctant to change what it is doing, and is relatively difficult to stop. Think of something heavy – a ten-pin bowling ball for example – and imagine pushing it in order to get it to move. The ball is initially reluctant to start moving, and it's hard to get it going; but once the ball is moving, it's fairly easy to push. Ever tried stopping a moving ten-pin bowling ball? Once the ball is moving, it is reluctant to change what it is doing. Imagine standing in front of a moving ten-pin bowling ball and trying to stop it with your hands – it takes a great deal of effort and usually results in bruised fingers! This reluctance of a body to change from its existing type of motion is called **inertia**.

Newton's first law

Inertia is not something that can be gained or lost: it is a reluctance to change. It is mass that determines inertia. Extra mass means greater inertia, which in turn means that changes in speed and/or direction will be more difficult. This is the basic idea behind **Newton's first law**, the law of inertia. This law states that:

> A body will remain in a state of uniform motion in a straight line (or remain at rest) unless compelled to change its state of motion by a net external force acting upon it.

This law clearly explains that it is normal for objects to continue travelling in a straight line with constant velocity. When we observe movements in real life, there are always forces such as friction and gravity acting on an object. It can be difficult to appreciate that Newton's first law applies, however small the object. The law also explains that, if an object is changing velocity, either increasing or decreasing, and/or it is changing direction, there must be a net external force acting on it.

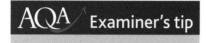

Examiner's tip

Air resistance is totally different from, and should not be confused with, wind resistance.

■ Key terms

Inertia: the reluctance to change the state of motion.

Newton's first law: (the law of inertia) a force is needed to change a body's state of motion.

Conversely, if an object is not changing its velocity, and/or direction, then the net forces acting on it must be zero.

Imagine a snooker ball at rest on the surface of a snooker table. As the ball's motion is not changing, the net effect of all the forces acting on it must be zero. A player now plays a shot and the snooker cue hits the ball. During the short period of time that the cue is in contact with the ball, a force is applied to the ball; and the ball changes its state of motion from being at rest to one of forward motion. The ball is obeying Newton's first law; the ball would remain stationary on the snooker table forever unless a force causes it to change its motion. As soon as the contact between the cue and ball is over, the force causing the change of motion is no longer present, and the ball will travel across the table in a straight line and with constant motion. You have to use your imagination and ignore the effect of friction between the cloth and the ball and the effect of air resistance between the ball and the air! In theory at least, this ball would continue travelling forever with constant velocity and in a straight line, until it is affected by another force.

This will happen when the ball hits the cushion at the side of the table. Whilst it is in contact with the cushion, the ball experiences a force that changes its direction and causes it to rebound from the cushion with a new velocity. Once it leaves the cushion, in theory at least, no forces are acting on the ball and it continues to travel in a straight line with constant velocity. In a similar way, Newton's first law can be applied to the observed changes in the state of motion of a soccer ball when it is kicked.

The law can also be applied to a 100 m sprinter in the set position on the blocks. The sprinter will remain in the set position, not changing their motion, until a force is applied. In order to leave the blocks, the sprinter must generate some force to change their state from rest to forward motion. Although the mechanism by which the sprinter generates forces may not as yet be clear, it should now be obvious that, as there is a rapid change in the sprinter's state of motion, some type of force has been applied to the sprinter in order to cause movement. After the race, the sprinter slows rapidly and then stops. Again, it should now be obvious that, in order to achieve this change in motion, the sprinter must again apply some force.

Note that the inertia of the sprinter remains the same throughout the race, because the sprinter's mass has not altered, and hence their reluctance to change their state of motion remains constant.

Newton's second law

Every object that is in motion, such as a sprinter, a football, or a bowling ball travelling down a lane, has a certain mass and a certain velocity. The product of these two values is known as its **momentum**. Momentum is the quantity of motion that a body possesses; momentum is equal to the body's mass multiplied by its velocity.

$$\text{Momentum} = \text{Mass} \times \text{Velocity}$$

If two objects, for example rugby players, are travelling with the same velocity, the one with the greater mass has the greater quantity of motion, or momentum. Similarly if two objects have the same mass, the one that is travelling with the greater velocity has the greater quantity of motion, or momentum. Objects with high velocity such as a downhill skier, or a large mass such as a rugby scrum, will have a large momentum.

AQA Examiner's tip

Examination questions invariably involve applying Newton's laws to a sporting situation, and this requires you to state the laws. Your definitions of Newton's laws need to be reasonably accurate rather than word perfect.

Activity

Describe in your own words how Newton's first law applies to the different phases involved when kicking a soccer ball.

Key terms

Momentum: the quantity of motion of a body; mass × velocity.

Key terms

Newton's second law: the magnitude and direction of applied force determines the magnitude and direction of acceleration given to a body.

Newton's second law incorporates this concept. It states that:

> The rate of change of momentum of an object (or acceleration of an object of fixed mass) is directly proportional to the force causing the change, and the resulting change in momentum takes place in the direction in which the force was applied.

Linking this complex definition to Newton's first law, it can be seen that a force is needed to change the momentum of an object. In most sports situations, the mass of the objects involved can be assumed to be constant and mass can therefore be removed from the momentum equation; thus, change in momentum becomes the same as change in velocity.

Hence, Newton's second law can be interpreted as saying that the rate of change of velocity is directly proportional to the force causing the change and this change occurs in the same direction as the force. We have previously called the rate of change of velocity 'acceleration'. Hence Newton's second law becomes:

> The rate of acceleration is directly proportional to the force causing the change.

Force = Mass × Acceleration

The important thing to notice from this equation is that, provided that the masses involved remain constant, which they do in all sporting contexts, the observed acceleration of an object is proportional to the net force acting on the object at any particular time. Also, remember that forces are vectors and therefore have direction. Forces produce acceleration and also produce a change in direction. The acceleration given to an object is in the same direction as the force applied. Note that an object is only accelerated whilst a force is being applied to it. When you kick a football, acceleration is only given to the ball while the foot is in contact with the ball.

AQA Examiner's tip

* When describing movement involving Newton's laws, always include the idea that the forces produced by the body to cause movement are muscular forces.

* Newton's second law is complicated but can be simplified, and defining it provides more marks than defining Newton's other laws; don't forget about direction when talking about it.

The sprinter on the starting blocks applies a force that provides them with acceleration. The magnitude of the acceleration given to the sprinter is directly proportional to the magnitude of the force exerted. The direction of the acceleration of the sprinter is also dependent on the direction of the force involved. The force that the sprinter applies is an internal force. Contractions of the various muscles involved (e.g. the gastrocnemius, quadriceps and gluteals) generate a force that is applied to the starting blocks through the foot, and this force causes the performer to accelerate off the blocks.

Newton's third law

There is a certain degree of misplaced logic in the previous sentence. The sprinter applies a force in order to accelerate and this force determines the direction of the acceleration. But, the force and the acceleration appear to be in opposite directions. This apparent anomaly is because of **Newton's third law**, which states that:

> When an object exerts a force on a second object, there is a force equal in magnitude but opposite in direction, exerted by the second object on the first.

Activity

Use Newton's second law to explain how a footballer moves a ball by kicking it.

Key terms

Newton's third law: (the law of action/reaction) to every action there is an equal and opposite reaction.

This law is usually called the law of action/reaction. In the sporting situation, the two objects concerned are often the performer and the ground. Thus, the sprinter on the blocks exerts a force on the blocks, and there is an equal, but opposite, force driving the sprinter forwards; but, as the blocks are attached to the earth and the earth has such a large mass compared with that of the sprinter, the acceleration given to the earth by the sprinter is insignificant. However, the force given to the sprinter by the earth causes them to accelerate. This force is called the **ground reaction force**. In much the same way, the soccer player who kicks the ball applies an **action force** to the ball, and simultaneously receives an equal and opposite **reaction force**, which can usually be felt on the foot.

Applying forces in sport

Sprinting

When a performer runs down a track, several forces are involved in various parts of the movement. Figure 7.3 shows that the performer generates an action or muscular force that is applied to the ground. According to Newton's third law, this force will generate an equal and opposite ground reaction force that causes the performer to accelerate with a magnitude and direction dependent on the action force. While running the performer will also be subject to the force of gravity, which will act on every particle in their body but for clarity is usually shown acting at a single point called the centre of mass. The performer will also be affected by friction and air resistance. There is friction between the track surface and the performer's foot in contact with the ground and there is air resistance between the performer's body and the air. The friction force opposes motion, and the air resistance is usually drawn as only acting from one point on the performer, whereas in real life air resistance affects the whole of the body.

High jumping

During high jumping, Newton's three laws are applied in the instant when the performer applies a muscular force to the ground at the point of take-off. This action force results in a ground reaction force (Newton's third law) that alters the state of motion of the performer (Newton's first law). This ground reaction force has a very large vertical component, unlike the forces involved in sprinting which are trying to move the sprinter quickly down the track and therefore have large horizontal components. The ground reaction force also changes the direction of the performer's motion from essentially horizontal to predominantly vertical. The magnitude of this vertical component of the ground reaction force governs the magnitude of the vertical component of the performer's vertical acceleration (Newton's second law). The interesting thing here is that both the sprinter and the high jumper use essentially the same leg muscles to cause changes in motion. It is simply the direction in which these forces are applied that governs the direction of the ground reaction forces and therefore the direction given to the performer.

Kicking a ball

The forces involved in kicking a ball are more complicated because the ball doesn't move in a nice convenient direction. Forces and their effects are much easier to explain and understand if we only deal with vertical and horizontal directions. When we kick a ball along the ground, we are simply dealing with horizontal motion. The force of gravity acts downwards and therefore remains constant through the motion of a ball being kicked horizontally, and we can therefore ignore its effects. In terms of horizontal motion, the ball is initially stationary as there are no net forces acting on it. The performer then kicks the ball and in doing so applies a force to the ball through contraction of their muscles, which causes the ball to accelerate (Newton's first law). The magnitude and

Key terms

Ground reaction force: the equal and opposite force given to a performer who exerts a muscular force into the ground.

Activity

Use Newton's three laws of motion to explain how a tennis player moves towards the ball.

AQA Examiner's tip

You may be required to apply Newton's laws to different sporting situations. The question will tell you which laws are needed. Defining the appropriate law gains marks, as does explaining its involvement in the sporting situation.

Fig. 7.3 *The forces involved in running*

Fig. 7.4 *A high jumper at take-off developing a large vertical component to their ground reaction force*

direction of the acceleration depend on the magnitude and direction of the applied force. The force applied to the ball causes it to accelerate and the acceleration takes place in the same direction as the applied force (Newton's second law). At the same time as the muscle force is applied to the ball, there is an equal and opposite reaction force applied by the ball to the performer's foot (Newton's third law). Once the ball has left the performer's foot, it is subjected to frictional forces because of the contact between the ball and the ground. These forces will tend to slow the ball down until eventually it stops.

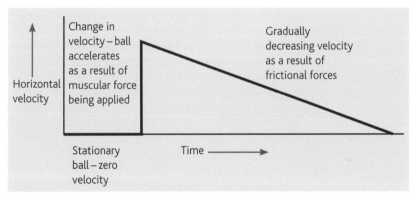

Fig. 7.5 *Changes in horizontal velocity of a ball when being kicked*

Delivering an object into flight

The forces acting on an object in flight are slightly more complicated because there are two dimensions to consider: the horizontal and vertical components. The forces involved in delivering an object into flight are once again the muscles' contraction to produce an applied action force. When an object is in the air, gravity affects the vertical component of the object's flight and, as gravity acts downwards, will act to reduce the vertical component until it becomes zero and eventually negative and causes the object to return to the ground. In flight, air resistance affects the horizontal component, reducing it and thereby slowing the object down. If the time (and/or distance) involved in the flight is short, the effects of air resistance may be negligible (such as during the flight of a shot or a long jumper), but for longer flights (e.g. javelin, rugby penalty kick) air resistance will have an effect.

Impulse is the term for the force applied and the time that the force is applied for, i.e. it is the effect of a force acting over a period of time.

$$\text{Impulse} = \text{Force} \times \text{Time}$$

In simple terms, the greater the force applied, the greater is its effect on an object; also, the longer the duration of the force the greater the impulse. That's why it is often important in sport to maintain contact with an object being thrown for as long as possible, so as to increase the impulse and therefore increase the effects of the forces involved.

☑ *You should now be able to:*

- define and distinguish between velocity, displacement, acceleration, momentum and impulse
- state the differences between scalars and vectors
- define each of Newton's three laws of motion and apply them in different sporting situations such as sprinting, jumping, kicking and flight.

Link

For more information on impulse, see Chapter 8 – Application of forces (pages 108–11)

1   (a)   Figure 7.6 shows a velocity/time graph for an elite 100 m runner. Use Figure 7.6 to determine the velocity of the sprinter after 3 s, and identify the period of time when the sprinter's acceleration was the greatest.   *(2 marks)*

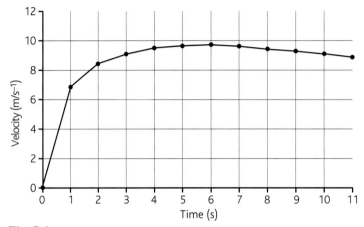

Fig. 7.6

   (b)   The major leg muscles used in the drive phase of sprinting are the gastrocnemius, quadriceps, gluteals and hamstrings. Exactly the same muscle groups are also used in high jumping.

Using the idea of vectors, explain how these same muscle groups can produce both maximal horizontal motion and maximal vertical motion.   *(5 marks)*

2   Use Newton's laws of motion to explain how a sprinter leaves the starting blocks.   *(7 marks)*

3   (a)   As a sprinter accelerates along the track at the beginning of a race, they generate a large impulse. What do you understand by the term 'impulse'?   *(2 marks)*

   (b)   Identify the forces A–E in Figure 7.7 that act on the sprinter during a race.   *(5 marks)*

Fig. 7.7

4   Figure 7.8 shows a high jumper at take-off. Use Newton's three laws of
    motion to explain how the high jumper takes off from the ground.   *(7 marks)*

Fig. 7.8

8 Application of forces

In Chapter 7 – Mechanical concepts, you started your journey towards understanding how forces are used and act on sport performers. You were introduced to the concepts of velocity, acceleration, momentum and impulse. You also looked at Newton's laws of motion and saw how they can explain how forces act on the body and how we use the force generated by muscular contraction. You were asked to apply this theoretical knowledge to human performance; the same will be the case in this chapter.

However, whereas Chapter 7 focused on linear motion, i.e. forces acting in a straight line, in Chapter 8 we shall look mainly at forces that act on a rotating or spinning body. We shall also be seeing what happens when we apply a force to a mass that is able to rotate around an axis, i.e. applying Newton's laws to bodies that can spin and rotate. Finally, we shall be examining how gravity and forces generated by our muscles act on objects that we throw, in particular when putting a shot. At the beginning of the chapter, there is a quick résumé of some of the terms introduced in Chapter 7 and a more detailed look at the concept of impulse and how this relates to our ability to run and jump.

Although some A Level Physical Education students get very concerned about biomechanics and the application of forces, you need not fear this aspect of the specification: in essence, it is quite straightforward. Nothing changes unless a force acts on it – if you bear that in mind all the way through this chapter, things will fall into place. At all times, you will be asked to think about the application of force within physical activity situations – something that you have been doing all of your sporting life.

Running – just an impulse?

When we run, our foot lands on the ground (this is known as **footfall**); our muscles contract; force is applied to the ground; the ground reaction force acts upon the foot, and that force is transmitted to the rest of the body and we move forward to the next footfall. Easy!

Before we bring the concept of impulse into play, let's recap some of the terms that were introduced in Chapter 7 – Mechanical concepts.

Basic concepts

Velocity

Velocity is a vector – it has both magnitude (size) and direction. To find velocity divide displacement (shortest distance between two points) by time.

Acceleration and momentum

So if you want to accelerate yourself or an object you have to change its velocity – you have to apply force to it. The amount of force you applied can be calculated by multiplying the mass of the object by how much it accelerates. Once you have got yourself or the object moving it has momentum, and this can be calculated by multiplying the mass by its velocity.

Key terms

Footfall: the action of the foot making contact with the ground when walking, running or jumping.

Link

For more information on how to calculate velocity, force and momentum, see Chapter 7 – Mechanical concepts (pages 95–103).

AQA Examiner's tip

It will help your understanding to keep on referring back to definitions – in essence, they are quite simple but can seem complex when they are combined.

Once you have reviewed these key concepts, we can re-introduce the concept of impulse.

Impulse

It is important to understand the concept of impulse so that you are able to understand how we apply forces to an object or to the ground. Force is not applied instantaneously; no matter how fast you hit something, the force is applied to the object for a period of time. For example, a tennis ball stays on the face of a racket for 5–8 ms; a middle-distance runner's foot is in contact with the ground for 160–210 ms (or 130 ms for elite sprinters).

> Activity
>
> A 5 km runner, who completes the distance in 16 min and takes 190 steps a minute, totals 3,040 steps from start to finish. Calculate how much time the runner would save if they could reduce each footfall's contact time with the ground by 0.015 s.

Fig. 8.1 *Sprinting – keep your foot on the ground!*

As you can see from Figure 8.1, each sprinter's foot is in contact with the ground and she is able to apply force to the ground. As a result of the ground reaction force and in accordance with Newton's second law, force is applied to the foot and then to the rest of the body. The foot is in contact with the ground for a period of time, therefore force is applied to the body over a period of time, which results in impulse.

$$\text{Impulse} = \text{Force} \times \text{Time}$$

Impulse is measured in Newton seconds, reduced to kg/s.

Impulse is also a change in momentum.

$$\text{Momentum} = \text{Mass} \times \text{Velocity}$$

Therefore,

$$\text{Force} \times \text{Time} = \text{Mass} \times \text{Velocity}$$

So does this lead you to think that the sprinter would do better by extending the time that their foot is on the ground? Well, the answer is no. Analysis shows, as does common sense, that you are better off trying to apply more force for a shorter period of time.

Imagine a sprinter who has just left the blocks and is getting into their running stride. We know that at this point they are accelerating – but

> Link
>
> For more information on reaction force and Newton's second law, see Chapter 7 – Mechanical concepts (pages 101–3).

> Activity
>
> How could a sprinter increase the amount of force that they apply to the ground on each footfall?

Examiner's tip

The AQA specification requires you to understand the concepts of impulse, momentum and acceleration in the context of sprinting.

how is this being achieved? It can be best described using force–time graphs. A force–time graph shows force over time – therefore it shows impulse, see Figure 8.2.

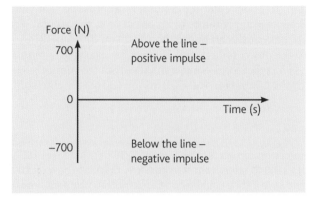

Fig. 8.2 *A force–time graph*

Figure 8.3 shows the force–time graph of the sprinter at the beginning of the race, away out of their blocks. Your own experience will tell you that this is a period of acceleration. Why should this be?

Key terms

Negative impulse: a force generated when absorbing body motion – landing.

Positive impulse: an impulse that moves the body.

Key point

To increase your understanding, think of other sport situations, particularly in your own assessed sport, where you would experience positive and negative impulses.

Activity

Redraw the graph to show the sprinter accelerating at a greater rate.

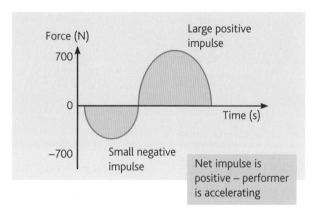

Fig. 8.3 *Force–time graph – sprinter at the start of the race*

From the force–time graph in Figure 8.3 we can see that the **negative impulse** generated on footfall on landing (below the line) is less than the **positive impulse** generated on the push phase of the stride (above the line). With a positive impulse greater than the negative impulse, the result is a positive net impulse – the sprinter has positive momentum and is therefore accelerating.

Figure 8.4 shows the situation during the middle section of the race. What can you tell about the positive and negative impulses? They are in fact the same – the positive impulse from the push phase is the same as the negative impulse from footfall. The result is a zero net impulse. Therefore, there is no change in momentum and the sprinter is running at constant velocity.

Figure 8.5 shows the position towards the end of the race. The negative impulse of the footfall is greater than the positive impulse of the push phase. The result is a negative net impulse. The sprinter has negative momentum and is therefore decelerating. The sprinter who decelerates the least will win the race.

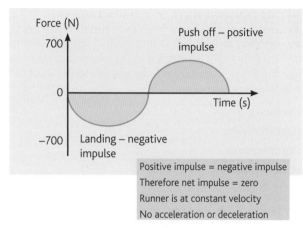

Fig. 8.4 *Force–time graph – sprinter at constant velocity midway through the race*

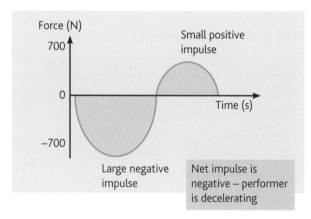

Fig. 8.5 *Force–time graph – sprinter towards the end of the race*

Activity

Using the graph in Figure 8.6, plot force - time graphs for points A, B and C.

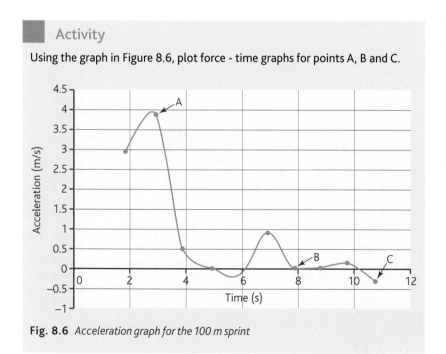

Fig. 8.6 *Acceleration graph for the 100 m sprint*

AQA Examiner's tip

Exam questions may present you with a force–time graph and ask you to describe the athlete's motion. Remember to compare the negative and positive impulses, the areas above and below the line.

■ The body in rotation

Having completed our look at linear motion (i.e. motion in a straight line), we need now to apply the principles to rotating or spinning motion. But first, here are a few more terms to help us describe what is happening to a body that is rotating:

- **angular velocity**
- **angular acceleration**
- **angular momentum**
- **moment of inertia**
- conservation of angular momentum.

You will see that we are using familiar terms – 'velocity', 'acceleration' and 'momentum' – except that we have placed the word '**angular**' in front of them; in this context, 'angular' simply means that the mass is rotating or spinning around an axis. Before we look at these terms we need to understand the concept of inertia in terms of lever systems.

Levers and the principle of moments

In a lever system you have an axis, an effort and a resistance; see Figure 8.7. Levers also involve turning forces – in a lever system, the resistance (the mass) and the effort required to hold it still or to rotate it around an axis or a fulcrum.

■ Key terms

Angular velocity: the rate of movement in rotation.

Angular acceleration: the rate of change of velocity during angular movement.

Angular momentum: the amount of motion that the body has during rotation – angular velocity × moment of inertia.

Moment of inertia: the resistance of a body to a change of state when rotating.

Angular: a word used to describe the motion of a mass when it is rotating or spinning.

Moment: the turning effect produced by a force, measured in newtonmetres (Nm); also known as torque.

Moment arm: the perpendicular distance from the point of application of a force to the axis of rotation.

Resistance arm: the mass and the lever system from the mass to the fulcrum.

Effort arm: the part of the lever system from where the effort is applied to the fulcrum.

Perpendicular: at right angles to.

■ Links

- Angular movement is discussed in more detail later in this chapter (pages 114–15).
- 'Inertia', meaning 'a resistance to motion' was covered in Chapter 7 – Mechanical concepts (page 100).

■ Activity

Put a ball, a shot and a discus on the floor.

1. Apply roughly the same force to each and rank them in order of inertia.
2. Explain why each of the objects exhibits different inertia.

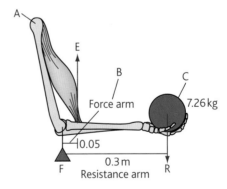

Fig. 8.7 *Levers and the principle of moments*

The amount of turning force that is generated by the resistance is known as the torque or the **moment** of force. The moment of force is calculated by multiplying the resistance by the distance of the load from the axis. This is known as the **moment arm** (MA) and is either a **resistance arm** or an **effort arm**. So in Figure 8.7 the tendency is for the shot to move downwards.

Moment of force (torque) = Resistance × **Perpendicular** distance
from the point of application of a force to the axis of rotation

In Figure 8.7, you can see a hand holding a shot (7.26 kg). In this system, there is a tendency for the moment to turn the object clockwise. Because the weight of the shot is causing a resistance to motion, it is the resistance arm.

The amount of the turning force of the resistance arm can be calculated by:

Moment of resistance (or resistance arm) = Load force × Distance of load from fulcrum

Moment of resistance = 7.26 kg × 9.81 ms^{-2} × 0.3 m

Moment of resistance = 21.4 Nm

AQA **Examiner's tip**

This is a part of the specification where the use of the correct technical terms is going to be very important. It is almost impossible to discuss biomechanical concepts, or the application of force to sport situations, without using the right terminology. To help yourself get to grips with it, prepare your own glossary with, for each term, a definition and a range of sporting examples.

Activity

1. Hold a 5 kg shot with a bent arm. Measure the distance from the shot to the pivot point on the elbow and calculate the moment of resistance.

2. Now hold the shot at arm's length and recalculate the moment of resistance.

3. Repeat the same exercise until you have measurements for the whole group.

4. If you had to hold the shot for a period of time, would you prefer to hold it at arm's length or with a flexed elbow? Why?

5. Would the smaller people in the group find holding the shot at arm's length easier or harder? Why?

Therefore, to hold the lever still, the moment (turning force) of the effort arm's anticlockwise movement must equal the moment (turning force) of the resistance arm's clockwise movement. (The effort arm is the part of the lever system from the insertion of the muscle to the fulcrum at the elbow – see Figure 8.7.)

Moment (Effort arm) = Effort force × Distance from the fulcrum

Moment (Effort arm) = Effort × 0.05 m

To hold the lever system still:

Anticlockwise moment (Effort) = Clockwise moment (Resistance)

0.05 m × Effort = 2.18 Nm

$$\text{Effort} = \frac{21.37}{0.05}$$

Force required from the effort arm (to hold the lever still) = 427 N.

This is known as the **principle of moments**.

To make the lever rotate upwards, the force generated by the muscle must overcome the moment of inertia. The moment of inertia of a body is its resistance to rotational or angular motion.

Moment of inertia = Mass × Distance from the axis of rotation (fulcrum)

This is the same as the resistance arm shown in Figure 8.7. The weight of the shot acts as an inertial force – it resists being moved.

Therefore, the moment of inertia is the resistance of a mass to a change of state (speeding or slowing down) when in rotation. From what we have just looked at in terms of levers, it can be seen that the moment of

Key terms

Principle of moments: for a body to be in equilibrium (balance), the sum of the clockwise moments is equal to the sum of the anticlockwise moments about the fulcrum (pivot).

AQA **Examiner's tip**

You will not be expected to undertake complex calculations in the examination. The reason for asking you to do some calculations within this chapter is to help your understanding – to add some practical applications to the theory.

inertia is dependent on two factors: the mass of an object and how the mass is distributed from the point of rotation. The further the mass from the point of rotation, the greater is the moment of inertia and the greater the force required to make the object spin or to stop it spinning. The gymnast in Figure 8.8 is performing a flip and has their mass away from the centre of rotation. A diver, in the tuck position, would have his mass concentrated nearer to the point of rotation. The gymnast would have a larger amount of inertia.

Angular movement

You have no doubt seen the phenomenon where the performer in the tuck position (diving, tumbling, trampolining) spins faster than the performer in the extended position. This is due to some of the other variables that were mentioned earlier:

- angular velocity
- angular acceleration
- angular momentum.

Angular movement is the movement of a body around an axis – spinning or rotating. Angular velocity is the rate of movement of a body in rotation; it is the same concept as linear velocity except applied to a spinning or rotating body.

Angular acceleration is also similar to linear acceleration in that it describes the rate of change of velocity: in this case, angular velocity of a body over time.

Angular momentum is the amount of motion a body has when rotating. It is a product of angular velocity and the moment of inertia.

Angular momentum = Angular velocity × Moment of inertia

Angular momentum is used in Newton's first law of angular motion which states that:

> A rotating body will continue to turn about its axis with constant angular momentum unless an external force acts upon it.

This law is also known as the law of **conservation of angular momentum**; the law states that a body will keep on spinning or rotating unless some force acts on it. On its own, the body cannot lose momentum, which is conserved unless a force acts on it. The forces that might act on a rotating body are air resistance or friction when in contact with the ground (or ice in the case of an ice skater).

In the light of the law of conservation of angular momentum, let us look again at the calculation for angular momentum.

Angular momentum = Angular velocity × Moment of inertia

Moment of inertia is the product of mass × distance from the axis of rotation. Now a body is unlikely to lose mass during a movement but it can change its distance or distribution from the axis of rotation; (see Figure 8.8). If the mass moves closer to the axis of rotation (tuck position) then the moment of inertia is small (3.5 kg m^2). If the moment of inertia is small the angular velocity is high because angular momentum remains constant – angular velocity and the moment of inertia have an inverse relationship.

If the gymnast changes their shape to a piked or stretched position, the moment of inertia increases (the distribution of mass is larger) and

Key terms

Angular movement: the movement of a body or mass around an axis – spinning, rotating, turning.

Conservation of angular momentum: the principle that the angular momentum of an object remains constant as long as no external force (moment or torque) acts on that object.

Activity

Consider your own sport and see if you can find examples of angular velocity, angular acceleration and angular momentum.

Activity

Explain why a skater spins more quickly with their arms at their side than with their arms outstretched.

therefore the angular velocity decreases. This is why gymnasts (and trampolinists) find it easier to perform tucked somersaults than open somersaults. The gymnast is only in the air for a limited amount of time, and they rotate much quicker in the tucked position.

Key terms

Radian: one radian equals 57.3 degrees.

Angle of release: the angle at which an object is released, measured from the horizontal.

Parabolic curve: the flight path of a projectile in the absence of air resistance.

Tucked shape
– moment of inertia =
3.5 kg m² – rotate quickly

Piked shape
– medium moment of inertia =
6.5 kg m² – rotate at medium speed

Stretched shape
– high moment of inertia =
15 kg m² – rotate slowly

Fig. 8.9 *Moment of inertia changes by moving from the layout to the tuck position*

Fig. 8.8 *These images show how moment of inertia varies in a gymnast depending on the body shape and how that moment of inertia then affects the speed of rotation or angular velocity*

The flight paths of objects in sport

Finally, we have to consider the flight path of an object (e.g. a shot) once it leaves the performer's hand. We are interested in the flight path because it helps determine the optimal **angle of release** of the shot from the performer's hand. By finding the optimal angle of release, the performer will help maximise the distance thrown.

The physics of a shot's flight

Given that the shot travels relatively slowly, we do not have to consider the effects of air resistance on the object. In fact, the shot's flight path is a **parabolic curve** as can be seen from Figure 8.10.

■ **Key terms**

Horizontal component: the horizontal motion of an object in a parabolic flight curve.

Vertical component: the upward motion of an object in a parabolic flight curve.

Height of release: the highest point above the ground that an object is released.

During the flight of a shot, it exhibits both a **horizontal component** and a **vertical component**. In Figure 8.10, you can see that the shot has just left the thrower's hand and is travelling up and away from the thrower – its flight must therefore have vertical and horizontal components.

Fig. 8.10 *The flight of the shot*

During the throw, the force of gravity will continuously be acting upon the mass of the shot, transforming a positive vertical component to a negative vertical component (see Figure 8.11). In terms of gaining the maximum distance (the whole point of the exercise!) the **height of release** is important. Given that gravity is constantly pulling the shot back to earth it is in the shot-putter's interest to release the shot at the highest point above the ground.

■ Remember

Remember that the flight path of the shot starts off at the point of release, some way off the ground, but lands on the ground at a point much lower than the point of release.

■ Activity

Research the heights of male and female elite shot-putters.

1 In terms of biomechanics, do you think that elite talent identification programmes should simply seek out the tallest mesomorphs they can?

2 Would this guarantee Olympic success?

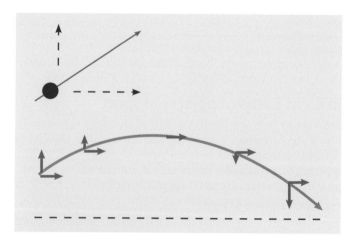

Fig. 8.11 *Parabolic flight path of a shot*

As you can see from the horizontal and vertical component arrows, the horizontal component remains the same, ensuring the motion away from the shot-putter, but gravity is the force that eventually determines the distance.

In terms of the optimal angle of release, it was thought that theoretically a release angle of 45° was optimal, but this does not take into consideration how to achieve maximum release velocity. More important than the angle of release is the **velocity of release**. The steeper the angle of release, the slower the release velocity; release velocity is the most important variable. It has now been calculated that the average optimal angle of release for elite shot-putters, bearing in mind flight path and release velocity, is 34°. It varies between 26° and 38° and is affected by height of the performer, the kinetic chain, the anatomical structure of the shoulder, etc.

Biomechanics and elite sport

We have now completed our look at biomechanics and its relationship to sport. As a support to elite performers, biomechanics has become increasingly important. The use of video to analyse performers' movements – to see whether force is being applied to the ground, an object or another performer as effectively as possible – has become a vital part of an elite coach's strategy. An understanding of how forces act on the body and how the body can apply force is vital for any elite performer or coach.

☑ *You should now be able to:*

- describe what causes a performer to be able to spin and rotate

- describe how a gymnast, diver or trampolinist can alter the rate at which they spin and how this is affected by their body shape

- analyse and explain how a shot-putter can achieve maximum distance by a consideration of the following factors: height of release, angle of release and the efficient use of muscle force.

Key terms

Velocity of release: the velocity of the object when it is released from the hand.

Link

For more information on the kinetic chain, see Chapter 6 – Sports injuries (page 90).

AQA Examination-style questions

1   (a)   In relation to a sprinter describe what is meant by the term
            'impulse' and how it can be shown on a force–time graph.   *(4 marks)*

    (b)   Draw and label a force–time graph to show the impulse of an
            accelerating sprinter.   *(3 marks)*

2   The performer in Figure 8.11 is completing a somersault. Describe what
    is happening to the performer in terms of their rate of rotation and why. *(7 marks)*

Fig. 8.11

3   When learning the shot put, young performers are often given a light
    implement such as tennis ball to practise the action. They often end up
    throwing the shot, rather than putting it with a straight-arm push.

    (a)   Why would this be a bad idea when using the correct weight
            implement? Ignore the laws of the event; your answer should
            refer to the principle of moments and inertia.   *(4 marks)*

    (b)   Why do shot-putters use either a glide or spin technique prior to
            releasing the shot?   *(3 marks)*

4   A number of factors affect the distance travelled by a shot when thrown.

(a)   What are the three most important factors that affect the
distance travelled by the shot?   *(3 marks)*

(b)   With reference to Figure 8.12 explain the variations in the
horizontal and vertical components.   *(4 marks)*

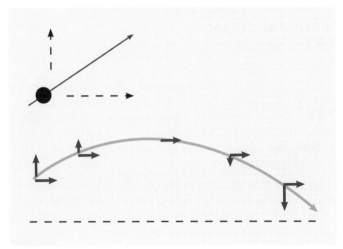

Fig. 8.12

Introduction

In Unit 3 Section 2, the specification requires an understanding of the psychological factors that influence elite-level performance. It is insufficient merely to possess superior anatomical and psychological attributes; if a performer is not able to control and use the internal and external psychological pressures that are always present in elite sport situations, they will fail.

The first psychological factor to be considered is personality. In Chapter 9 we look at whether it is possible to determine an individual's personality and if personality has an impact on performance. Given that success in elite sport requires individuals to take risks, is it possible to identify an 'elite sport personality' or are elite performers just very good at calculating the odds? Chapter 10 continues our look at how individuals manage in elite-performance situations with a consideration of the importance of arousal: the different forms of arousal, how levels of arousal differ from situation to situation and how arousal can be managed. It is vital for the performer to achieve optimal levels of arousal – the peak flow experience, or being 'in the zone'. If the performer is unable to control their arousal, they are likely to suffer from anxiety. Chapter 11 has anxiety as its theme: the forms it may take, its effects and how it may be controlled. The chapter finishes with a look at the role of goal setting.

Our look at the pressures on the individual continues in Chapter 12 with an examination of three other important psychological forces that affect the individual – personal attitudes, aggressive behaviour and how we attribute our successes or failures. Chapter 13 begins our look at the elite performer and their interactions with others as we consider self-confidence, the impact that the presence of others may have and why performers seem to play differently when not in front of their home crowd.

Much elite sport is conducted with others – we play in groups and teams – and Chapter 14 looks at how teams are formed and whether putting all the best individuals together is enough to bring success at the highest level. The final chapter in the section considers the impact that leaders have on teams, how they are selected and the different forms of behaviour that go towards making a success of the role.

The psychological forces that are at play on individuals and groups are less well understood than the physiological ones but are equally, if not more, important.

9 Personality

Key terms

Personality: an individual's predisposition to behave in a certain way.

People are different; in fact, every individual is unique. Because of this uniqueness, it is difficult to generalise about human behaviour. But one thing is clear: many of us share common traits or characteristics and tend to behave in similar ways. **Personality** is the sum of those characteristics that make a person unique. Personality is the distinctive pattern of long-lasting psychological and behavioural characteristics by which each person can be compared and contrasted with others. These characteristics in turn then determine how we behave. No two people are exactly the same: not even identical twins. Some people are anxious, some take risks; some are unflappable, some highly strung; some are confident, some shy; and some are quiet and some are talkative. This issue of differences is fundamental to the study of personality.

Psychologists have been studying personality and its relationship with sport for a long time. These are some of the questions that they have been trying to answer:

- Is there a relationship between personality type and the sport people choose?

- How do people decide which sports to participate in? Is it simply that differing personality types have different sporting preferences or are certain personality types more attracted to certain sports?

- Why do some people prefer individual sports over team sports?

- What do basketball players have in common with other basketball players in terms of their personality?

Research into personality attempts to answer some if not all of these questions.

We use the term 'personality' frequently but what does it actually mean?

- 'She has a wonderful personality.'

- 'He has no personality.'

- 'We seem to have a personality conflict.'

- 'She has her mother's personality.'

- 'He's a real personality.'

Activity

Try the 'I am' exercise. Write 10 honest endings to 'I am …' then, when you have finished, share what you have written with someone.

1. Do your answers sum up your personality? You'll probably have to ask somebody else to answer this for you!

2. Why do your responses sum up your personality, or, if they don't, why not?

What is personality?

Some definitions

Your personality is unique to you. It is what makes you act as you do. Personality is what tends to make you behave in a certain way.

There are many definitions of personality; in fact so many that it soon becomes clear that psychologists are not really sure what personality is! Hollander (1971) says that 'personality is the sum total of an individual's characteristics which make him unique'. Gross (1992) suggests that it is 'those relatively stable and enduring aspects of individuals which distinguish them from others, making them unique, but which at the same time allow people to be compared with each other'. A more contemporary definition is suggested by Carver and Scheier (2000): 'Personality is a dynamic organisation, inside the person, of psychophysical systems that create a person's characteristic patterns of behaviour, thoughts, and feelings'.

Hollander's model

Hollander suggested that our personality is a layered structure, with an inner core of beliefs, values and attitudes (see Figure 9.1). This inner core, which is fairly permanent and unlikely to change, affects the next layer.

The middle layer shows our typical responses to a situation and generally gives a good indication of the inner core; different people, with different inner cores, may have different typical responses to the same situation. It is the outer layer, the role-related behaviours, that shows our actual responses to different circumstances. This outer layer is the most changeable aspect of our personality; Hollander suggests that our behaviour will vary, depending on how we feel and the situation that we are in, and could be different from our psychological core.

As Hollander's work suggests that how we behave depends on our environment and our inner core of traits, it is an example of an **interactionist theory**. There are psychologists, however, who give greater emphasis to our inner core, saying that we inherit certain **traits** that define our personality. Yet others say that how we act is simply down to our environment; we learn to act in different ways in different situations.

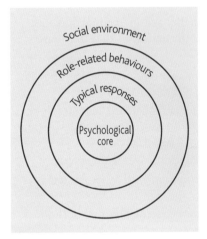

Fig. 9.1 *Hollander's model*

> ■ **Key terms**
>
> **Interactionist theory:** an explanation of behaviour that assumes that our personality depends on our traits and on the environment.
>
> **Traits:** innate, enduring personality characteristics that allow behaviour to be predicted.

Interactionist theories

Interactionist theories suggest that our behaviour depends on the interaction between our inherited, enduring personality traits and the environment or situation in which we find ourselves. In recognising the part played by traits, interactionist theories build on the trait approach, which views personality as a unique combination of tendencies or dispositions to think and behave in certain ways. The three basic assumptions of this approach are that these tendencies to behave in a certain way are stable and unchanging over time, that the tendency to think and behave in certain ways is consistent in many different situations and that each person has a unique combination of these dispositions. However, trait theory cannot explain why we may change our behaviours in different situations. One explanation is offered by social learning theory, which suggests that we learn our behaviours through mimicking or copying others. We especially tend to copy significant others such as our family, peers and role models.

Interactionist theories suggest that our behaviour depends on what traits we have inherited and how these are influenced by our environment. According to Kurt Lewin's (1935) formula, our behaviour (B) is a function (f) of our personality traits (P) and the environment (E) in which we find ourselves:

$$B = f(P.E)$$

From this formula, we can see that the causes of our behaviour can be separated into two classes of variables: personality and environment. The difference is that the personality variables (our traits) are internal causes of behaviour and environmental variables are external causes of behaviour. When we ask ourselves why we do what we do, in other words why we behave in the way that we do, the answers are either personality variables or environmental variables or some combination of both. What interactionist theories tell us is that our behaviour will tend to be predictable in a particular environment; we are likely to behave in similar ways whenever we enter the same environment. But it tells us, too, that an individual's behaviour may well be different in different environments. Someone who is assertive and loud on the rugby pitch may behave completely differently in an office environment. Interactionist theory also tells us that different people will behave differently in the same environment if their personality traits differ; for example, not all people in a netball competition will behave in the same way (they may well have different personality traits).

Can we measure personality?

Measuring personality is difficult, not least because there is no clear definition as to what personality is! Nevertheless, several ways of measuring personality have been devised, and personality tests are frequently used in the sports setting. Personality may be measured by questionnaire, interview or observation; questionnaires are especially popular. But it must be remembered that all psychological tests contain a degree of measurement error.

The ability to predict who will continue to participate in sporting activities and who will drop out would be a useful gift for those responsible for mass participation in sport; it would be possible to reduce drop-out rates and increase initiation into the sports concerned. However, personality tests have so far been unable to identify those who are likely to drop out or those who will regularly participate. The idea of using psychological characteristics such as personality in **talent-identification programmes** is also very attractive. Selection of those who would best fit into a certain situation, such as the best team players, would allow optimal allocation of resources. Some organisations have used personality tests as part of a sport-identification programme where psychological factors have been included. How and if to use the psychological information is hotly disputed, and most coaches and performers would tend to agree with the idea that there is more to a player's suitability for a role than simply their personality!

Validity, reliability and ethics

Much research has been conducted in this area and, overall, it has been concluded that there is no such thing as a clearly distinguishable sporting personality, nor have studies found noticeable personality differences between people who take part in different sporting activities. It is always important to consider the validity of the personality test used in research. Remember from AS Level that validity refers to whether a test measures what it is supposed to measure. The problem is that there is no clear definition of personality. So how can we measure something that we cannot define or explain?

The reliability of personality tests is also open to question. Remember from AS Level that if a test has good reliability, the test results are repeatable; this is not always the case with many tests because the

AQA Examiner's tip

When answering examination questions, remember that personality theory is concerned with how we behave or act.

■ **Key terms**

Talent-identification programme: a systematic method of identifying and selecting those who have the ability or qualities to progress further to a higher competitive level.

respondents are required to interpret their own personality which can be very difficult to do.

Another consideration is ethics. Personality testing is designed to probe into a sensitive area of a person's inner being, and all results must be treated with sensitivity and confidentiality.

Questionnaires

Questionnaires are the most common way of attempting to measure a person's personality; most require some form of self-report. Questionnaires are very popular for research because they are fairly cheap and easy to produce and administer. They are fairly reliable and can be used almost anywhere, including the pitch or court. Questionnaires will produce a considerable amount of data which can then be analysed. However, most people find it difficult to answer questionnaires accurately; it can be difficult to self-assess your own personality. Being asked a question such as 'Are you an irritable person?' leaves the respondent thinking 'Am I? How irritable do I have to be to answer yes?' Often respondents will answer a question in a way that they think will please the person doing the research. But the biggest problem with questionnaires is their validity. How can a personality questionnaire be valid when we don't know what personality is?

Interviews

Interviews try to assess personality through discussions with the respondents. A series of questions are usually asked, or the respondents may be asked to interpret drawings. Interviews tend to have greater validity than questionnaires and can uncover issues within the individual as answers are not limited to yes and no. This tends to give interviews lower reliability than questionnaires. In addition, the method depends on the ability of the interviewer to interpret the answers given. Because in each interview the interviewer works with a single respondent, the method is an expensive and time-consuming way to collect data from a number of people.

Observation

In behavioural observations, the responses and actions of participants are recorded and analysed. Similarities in behaviour between the participant and the behaviour of others, already assessed, are noted; and from this a personality profile can be produced. Observing an individual's behaviour in a real-life setting has the advantage that the person is more likely to operate as they would naturally, whereas questionnaires and interviews are likely to be administered in artificial surroundings. However, observations are also expensive and time consuming and may have low validity. The low validity of observations stems from the difficulty of interpreting the behaviour that is being observed and from the possibility that the participant's behaviour is affected if they know that they are being watched.

Profile of Mood States

Some research has illustrated a difference between successful and less successful sportspeople. This difference is based on mood states and coping abilities as opposed to more enduring personality traits. Studying psychological states or the moods that arise in a particular situation is therefore of interest to sports psychologists. The **Profile of Mood States (POMS)** was designed to measure the following:

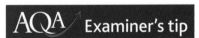
Examiner's tip

Examination questions tend to ask for the advantages or disadvantages of different methods of measuring personality but you could also be asked about other psychological constructs, such as attitudes, aggression, etc.

■ **Key terms**

Profile of Mood States (POMS): a way of measuring the moods of those who participate in sport.

- tension
- depression
- anger
- vigour
- fatigue
- confusion.

Morgan (1979) compared successful elite athletes and unsuccessful athletes on each of these moods. His results showed a difference in their average scores (see Figure 9.2).

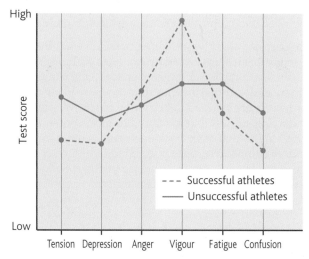

Fig. 9.2 *POMS scores for athletes, illustrating the iceberg profile*

Successful athletes tend to score higher than unsuccessful athletes on measures of anger and vigour; successful athletes tend to score lower than unsuccessful athletes on measures of tension, depression, fatigue and confusion; unsuccessful athletes tend to score approximately equally across all mood states. Morgan called the shape of the results for the elite athletes an **iceberg profile** because of how it looks compared with the almost horizontal line recorded for all moods by unsuccessful athletes. In simple terms, the elite athletes score higher on the positive mood of vigour and lower on the negative moods of tension, depression, fatigue and confusion. Other research has largely confirmed the existence of an iceberg profile for elite performers. There is even the suggestion that lack of an iceberg profile is an indication that something is wrong with the preparation of the performer. For example, overtrained swimmers showed lower than expected scores on vigour and higher scores on fatigue, tension and depression.

There is a problem with utilising the findings of this research: they are not applicable to all performers. It must be remembered that not all elite performers in every sport show an iceberg profile. Looking at the results from a different angle, you could even suggest that, rather than performers having an iceberg profile before becoming elite, it could be that, by becoming successful elite performers, athletes acquire the self-confidence and 'feel-good' factors that lead them to develop positive mood states.

Personality, sport performance and sport choice

Back to some of the questions raised in the introduction to this chapter. Is there a relationship between personality type and sport preference?

Key terms

Iceberg profile: the POMS profile (e.g. higher vigour) that is associated with successful athletes.

How do people choose the sport they participate in? Would it be a matter of personality preference? Are certain personality types more attracted to certain sports, as in careers? Why do some people prefer individual sports over team sports? What do basketball players have in common?

There is disagreement, even among psychologists, as to whether studying personality and sport has any real value. Some researchers, for example Morgan in his research with the POMS, argue that an individual's personality has an influence on their sporting success. This is the 'credulous' view (it holds real meaning for those who agree with it). The other view is the 'sceptical' one held by psychologists who think that personality has no relevance to sporting performance. They argue that we cannot see or measure personality; we can only make inferences about it from people's behaviour and so in some ways it doesn't really exist!

It has been suggested that the traits that make up what the personality theorist Eysenck termed 'extroversion' can be linked to sport. Because extroverts have naturally lower levels of arousal, and can therefore cope with pain more easily, it may be that they are more likely to seek new stimuli. Extroverts are believed to be able to cope with stressful situations and the distracting stimuli that are found in most sports. Research by Cooper (1969) found that athletes do have some common traits – they tend to be more competitive, outgoing and to have high self-confidence – but other research has not confirmed these findings. Following research that found some differences in the characteristics of elite and non-elite performers, it has been suggested that personality testing might be able to identify those who may go on to achieve and those who may drop out early. But summarising the findings of the research into personality traits and sport, Vealy (1992) said that no link had been established between personality and sport choice and that there was no evidence to suggest that a particular personality type was likely to be more successful.

> ### Activity
>
> 1. Using the internet, find a copy of Eysenck's Personality Inventory (EPI) and complete the questionnaire.
>
> 2. Analyse the results for the whole class by comparing the results of those who play team games with the results of those who do not.
>
> 3. Is there a common psychological profile for players of team games? Discuss the results in small groups.

■ Do you take risks in sport?

Competition is an important aspect of sport and a key factor that distinguishes sport from recreation. Some people appear to be more motivated to compete in sport than others. Some people are simply more competitive than others. There is a suggestion that these differences are based on personality types.

Figure 9.3 shows how the major motives for taking part in competitive sport and recreational (non-competitive) sport vary across the general population. It would appear that the major motives for sport participation are recreation, health and fitness, and companionship. There is a significant difference between the competitive and recreational participants in the achievement motive; in some of the other motives there appears to be little distinction between the two categories of participant. Perhaps some people are

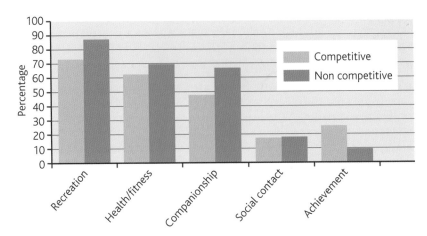

Fig. 9.3 *The major motives for taking part in competitive sport and recreational sport*

more motivated to compete than others; some are simply more competitive than others.

Achievement motivation

Analysis of motives has led some sport psychologists to suggest that people approach sport with either a motive to achieve or a motive to avoid failure. **Achievement motivation theory** states that we have within our personality a need to achieve and a need to avoid failure.

The achievement motive is the need (all motives are based on needs) to overcome obstacles, to strive to do something difficult as well, and as quickly, as possible. The achievement motive is what urges a player to be the best player in a team. The goal of becoming the best player in the team can be achieved by undertaking more training than the rest of the team. Some people have a greater **need to achieve (nAch)** than others and are said to have nAch-type personalities: they appear to seek out competitive situations – they show 'approach behaviours'.

At the other end of the scale, there are those who seem intent on avoiding competitive situations because they have a **need to avoid failure (Naf)**. These people are described as having Naf-type personalities: they show 'avoidance behaviours'.

Key terms

Achievement motivation theory: the theory that an individual's behaviour is determined by their interaction with the environment and their desire to succeed.

Need to achieve (nAch): the motivation to succeed or attain particular goals; people with nAch-type personalities show approach behaviours.

Need to avoid failure (Naf): the motivation to avoid failure; people with Naf-type personalities show avoidance behaviours.

Activity

The following test helps to illustrate the distinction between nAch and Naf.

Imagine that you are taking an exam. This exam has negative marking (if you get a question wrong, you lose marks). After 20 minutes you find that you have done all the questions you knew the answers to or could make an intelligent guess at. There are 10 questions left, what would you do?

- Answer the 10 questions and risk losing marks?
- Sit safely and have a rest?

If you would choose to answer the questions, you probably have high achievement motivation; but, if you would avoid the questions, you probably have low achievement motivation and a stronger need to avoid failure.

How motivated a person is to achieve depends on the relative strengths of the desire to succeed and the fear of failure. Note too that the importance to the individual of the situation – in terms of success or failure – is also a factor. People with high nAch prefer tasks with at least a 50 per cent chance of success, whereas those with low nAch prefer tasks where the outcome is relatively certain, whether it be failure or success.

In a similar vein, people with high nAch would rather play than not, whereas those with Naf-type personalities would prefer to avoid any competitive situation. Whichever of these behaviours predominates in an individual, it is going to be much more likely to occur when a person is in an evaluative situation, i.e. one where others are going to be making judgements about their performance. Sport invariably involves evaluation of performance, which is why it is thought that sport is more attractive to nAch-type personalities.

Table 9.1 *Characteristics of nAch and Naf personalities*

nAch characteristics	Naf characteristics
Shows approach behaviours	Shows avoidance behaviours
Seeks out challenges	Avoids challenging tasks – prefers easier tasks (guaranteed success) or very difficult opposition (guaranteed failure)
Is concerned with standards of performance and excellence – will do extra training	Avoids situations where success is 50:50 and evaluation is possible
Enjoys performing in situations where they are being evaluated	Performs worse when being evaluated
Is not afraid to fail	Tends to be preoccupied with failure
Attributes performance to internal factors	Attributes performance to external factors
Keeps going at task for longer (task persistence)	Lacks task persistence
Values feedback from others	Does not value feedback

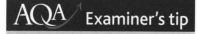

Examiner's tip

It is common for questions to ask for the characteristics of a high nAch performer, although occasionally these characteristics might be linked into a sport-based scenario.

Key terms

Ego oriented: interpreting success as a sign of superiority over others.

Task oriented: interpreting success as playing well.

Interpreting success

However, it has recently been suggested that it is the way in which people interpret success that determines their motivation. For some people, success only occurs if they have beaten somebody else; victory is everything, and a demonstration of their superiority is all-important. Such individuals are said to be **ego oriented**. Others see their success as being predominantly internal, due to their own efforts and abilities, so that they don't mind losing as long as they have gained a personal best; such people are said to be **task oriented**.

Implications for coaching

Achievement motivation theory is another example of interactionist theory. It sees achievement as influenced by the environment as well as by traits. Our behaviour depends on an evaluation of the situation, especially in terms of the likelihood of success (the task difficulty) and the incentive value (the shame or pride felt following the result). The relevance of achievement motivation to the sports setting is, however, somewhat debatable as it is difficult to measure and/or calculate a value for motivation because of its imprecise nature. There is a current tendency to suggest that achievement motivation is not a global concept but rather a sport-specific construct, in other words 'competitiveness'.

Nevertheless, knowledge of the type of motive a person has (gained through administering a questionnaire) can be beneficial in determining what type of motivational strategy should be adopted by a coach. For example, if a performer's motives are essentially ego oriented, they should be set goals or targets that allow comparisons with others to be made. On the other hand, if the performer's motives are task oriented, goals need to be related to personal performance criteria.

☑ *You should now be able to:*

- define personality and describe how trait and interactionist theories may be used to explain behaviour

- discuss whether personality can predict performance

- provide advantages and disadvantages of different ways of measuring personality

- describe the Profile of Mood States and the iceberg profile found in elite performers

- explain achievement motivation and the characteristics of the motives to achieve (nAch) and to avoid failure (Naf), including the development of approach and avoidance behaviours

- explain how the motive to achieve depends on incentive value and probability of success.

Link

For more information on goal setting, see Chapter 11 – The effect of anxiety on performance (pages 153–4).

1   It was previously thought that certain personality types tended to become involved in particular sports, thus those participating in a triathlon may have shared common personality characteristics.

   (a)   In terms of personality, explain what is meant by 'interactionist theories'. *(3 marks)*

   (b)   One aspect of personality is achievement motivation. What are the characteristics of an individual with a motive to achieve success?

(4 marks)
AQA, June 2006

2   Personality profiling can be used to prepare performers who compete at the highest level.

Morgan's profile of mood state (POMS) is a questionnaire given to performers to establish their relative measures on the six mental health states of fatigue, vigour, tension, depression, anger and confusion.

   (a)   Research has shown that the profile for POMS differs between elite and non-elite performers. Describe these differences. *(3 marks)*

   (b)   What are the advantages and disadvantages of using questionnaires to provide psychological information? *(4 marks)*
AQA, June 2005

3   Two footballers are asked to take part in a penalty shoot-out. One accepts the invitation; the other refuses.

   (a)   Explain, in terms of achievement motivation, the decision of each player. *(4 marks)*

   (b)   Discuss how the two footballers would view the next penalty shoot-out against a goalkeeper of a higher standard. *(3 marks)*
AQA, June 2003

4   Hollander (1971) showed personality as a core, a middle and an outer layer (see Figure 9.4).

Fig. 9.4

   (a)   What does the core represent? Give an example to show your understanding. *(3 marks)*

   (b)   What do you understand by a 'typical response'? Give an example for a gymnast successfully completing a vault. *(2 marks)*

   (c)   What do you understand by 'role-related behaviours'? Give an example related to gymnastics. *(2 marks)*
AQA, June 2002

10   Arousal

Key terms

Arousal: the state of general preparedness of the body for action, involving physiological and psychological factors.

Peak flow: a state in which the performance is at its best, achieved without thought, effortlessly and with total confidence.

AQA Examiner's tip

You will not be required to state any particular definition of arousal, but you must be able to show a general understanding of the meaning of the term.

Elite performers are frequently seen 'psyching themselves up', or attempting to get themselves 'in the zone'. Psychological preparation that increases the individual's level of **arousal** is as important – for elite performers – as physiological preparation. In this chapter, we shall start by examining what we mean by arousal and the various psychological theories that have been used to explain the mental and physical processes that are involved. We shall look closely at how arousal can affect performance and learn how important it is to pay attention to the characteristics and demands of the performance and the performer before determining the right levels of arousal and how to achieve them. We shall also see how performance can improve but may also deteriorate if the levels of arousal are not appropriate. Finally, we shall examine what is known as the '**peak flow** experience' or 'being in the zone' – those times when the athlete is so focused, so confident, that optimal performance seems to flow without effort and flawlessly.

Fig. 10.1 *Final thoughts before performance – getting arousal right*

What is meant by 'arousal'?

'Arousal' has many definitions. For some it is simply a state of heightened physiological activity. Singer (1993) considered arousal to comprise a number of factors that energise the mind and body, involving physiological responses (e.g. increased heart rate) and cognitive processes (e.g. excitement). He proposed a continuum for arousal, ranging from deep sleep to extreme excitement. Sage (1984) linked arousal to motivation which directs one to a specific goal, and Cox (1990) linked high levels of arousal to alertness.

As a performer you will no doubt have experienced various levels of arousal and will recognise both the physical (somatic) and mental (cognitive) signs. You may have experienced these prior to an important competition or during a specific moment during a performance. You may have experienced under-arousal, when you felt 'flat' and a coach or a team mate tried to shake you out of your lethargy, or you may have felt over-aroused and someone has tried to calm you down. You may have received training in how to manage levels of arousal for yourself. Most research indicates that we need a certain level of arousal to enable us to perform at our best.

Activity

The next time you are about to be involved in a sport performance:

1. Make a record of your feelings in the 48 hours prior to the performance and in the 24 hours following it.

2. Identify times and occasions when you experienced periods of high arousal (feeling 'up for it') or periods of low arousal (feelings of deflation, not being 'up for it').

3. Plot those times on an hourly timeline and describe the activity or situation that you were in at the time.

4. If possible, compare your timeline with the timelines of others.

■ How do we know when we are experiencing high levels of arousal?

There are physiological and psychological signs of high levels of arousal.

Physiological (somatic) signs

Among the wide range of physiological signs indicating high levels of arousal are some that are fairly easy to spot:

- increased heart rate
- increased breathing rate
- sweating
- headache
- cold, clammy hands
- constant need to urinate
- dry mouth
- dazed look in the eyes
- feelings of nausea
- increased muscle tension
- butterflies in the stomach.

Signs less easy to spot include:

- increased blood pressure
- galvanic skin response – a change in the electrical resistance of the skin
- increased levels of hormones (e.g. adrenaline) in the blood.

Whilst these physiological responses are useful for letting us know that we are experiencing raised levels of arousal, we are more concerned, here, with the psychological responses and signs.

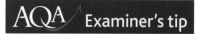

Examiner's tip

It is important to be able to distinguish between cognitive and somatic examples of high levels of arousal (there may not be over-arousal). You should be able to give three or four examples of each.

Psychological (cognitive) signs

Increased levels of arousal can lead to:

- increased focus and concentration
- heightened awareness of important cues in the environment
- narrowing of attention, excluding irrelevant stimuli
- decreased reaction time (as shown in Figure 10.2).

It is possible that a performer can become too highly aroused and can exhibit signs of:

- anxiety and apprehension
- tension
- negative self-talk
- difficulties sleeping
- inability to concentrate
- fear and anger.

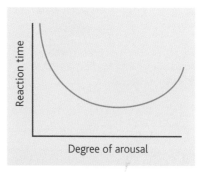

Fig. 10.2 *The relationship between level of arousal and reaction time*

> **Activity**
>
> Look back at the timeline you completed for the activity on page 132. Consider the times when you noted high levels of arousal.
>
> 1 Were the times of high arousal accompanied by any of the cognitive or somatic signs listed above?
>
> 2 Were other people present?
>
> 3 Were those present competitors, spectators, friends or coaches?

Also, with too much arousal, there is likely to be an increase in reaction time (as shown in Figure 10.2).

Over-arousal can lead to anxiety. Performers showing physical signs of anxiety are suffering from somatic anxiety. Those who show mental signs of anxiety are suffering from cognitive anxiety.

In the last learning activity, you were also asked to note if your levels of arousal changed whether or not there were other people present. It is the case that the presence of others, be they rivals, supporters, audience, coaches, friends or family, will have an effect on a performer's level of arousal.

Like over-arousal, under-arousal can have an adverse effect on performance – the trick is to ensure that the performer is at the optimal level of arousal.

■ Theories of arousal

Psychologists have been trying to explain arousal and its relationship to human behaviour for many years. Typically, when psychologists are trying to explain some aspect of human behaviour, a theory is proposed after research; it becomes accepted for a while, but further research calls the theory into question if it is found that not all behaviour fits the model proposed within the theory. The theory is then revised or new theories are generated.

Drive theory

Drive theory was an early theory of arousal. Devised by Hull (1943), it proposed a linear relationship between arousal and performance – as

> **Links**
>
> - For a much deeper discussion of anxiety, see Chapter 11 – The effect of anxiety on performance (pages 142–55).
> - For more information on how the presence of others can affect level of arousal, see Chapter 13 – Confidence (pages 181–3).

> **AQA** Examiner's tip
>
> You will be expected to be able to discuss each of the theories of arousal in depth and to be able to quote examples, from sporting situations, of the relationship between arousal and performance.

> **Key terms**
>
> **Drive theory:** a theory of arousal that proposes a linear relationship between arousal and performance; as arousal increases so does the quality of performance.

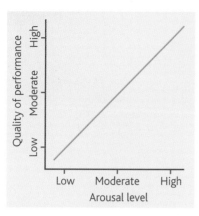

Fig. 10.3 *The relationship between arousal and performance – drive theory*

arousal increases so does the quality of performance (see Figure 10.3). Hull's view was that higher levels of arousal, such as are found in competition, would intensify the dominant response. For an expert, the dominant response is likely to be habitual and the correct one and performance would be improved. For a beginner, the dominant response may be incorrect or inaccurate and a higher level of arousal may cause deterioration in performance. Spence and Spence (1968) adapted the theory and tried to quantify its principles by proposing an equation describing the relationship between habit strength and drive.

$$Performance = Habit\ strength\ x\ Drive$$

$$P = HD$$

Drive theory is now considered to give an inadequate explanation of the relationship between arousal and performance. Observation of even the most talented and successful performers would seem to show that there is a point when arousal reaches a very high level and performance fails to improve – or even deteriorates.

Inverted U theory

Initially developed by Yerkes and Dodson in 1908, **inverted U theory** seems to fit more accurately with observations of performance. According to inverted U theory, performance will improve as arousal increases and a point will be reached where optimal performance is achieved; should arousal increase beyond that point, performance will start to deteriorate (see Figure 10.4).

AQA Examiner's tip

Examination questions will often include an arousal–performance graph for you to interpret.

■ **Key terms**

Inverted U theory: a theory of arousal that considers that optimal performance occurs when the performer reaches an optimal level of arousal.

AQA Examiner's tip

Examination questions involving inverted U theory will only give a few marks for the basic understanding. The higher marks will only be available if you can apply the theory to beginner/expert situations or to different kinds of skill performance.

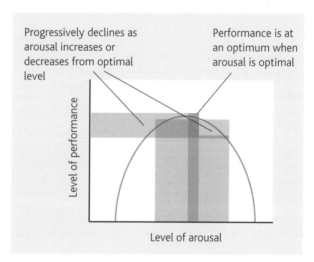

Fig. 10.4 *Inverted U theory – finding the optimal level of arousal*

In many ways this theory would seem to fit our everyday observations of sport performers, but in reality it is too simplistic and we have to adapt the theory to answer two questions:

■ Does inverted U theory apply equally to expert performers and beginners?

■ Does it apply to all sports performances in the same way?

In respect of experts and beginners, research indicates a number of reasons why beginners are not able to perform as well as experts as levels of arousal increase:

■ A beginner does not have the same level of grooving of a skill; it is less habitual (this is similar to Hull's view of dominant responses).

■ A beginner needs to give a greater proportion of their attention to the performance of the skill. Increased levels of arousal may well take a beginner's attention away from the skill performance and the performance deteriorates.

■ Beginners rely heavily on expected cues and signals from within the environment to help them perform a movement at the right moment or in the right situation. As arousal increases, their focus on these expected and essential cues also increases so they miss the unexpected, are unable to react to it and performance deteriorates.

It is therefore likely that beginners normally perform better with a lower level of arousal than an expert would need, but they still need to reach what is for them an optimal level of arousal to ensure that optimal performance is likely to occur (see Figure 10.5).

Activity

If possible, observe a team game (football, hockey, etc.) played by younger players (8 to 12 years old). In such a team it is likely that the players will have a range of experience.

1 Note periods of the game (if possible also listen to the team talks) when the players may be more highly aroused.

2 During those periods do some players increase their level of performance and others decrease?

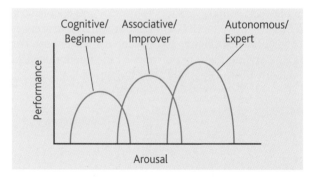

Fig. 10.5 *Optimal levels of arousal – relative to performer (experts and beginners)*

Figure 10.5 shows that beginners and experts exhibit the same pattern of performance linked to arousal but that the optimal levels of arousal are lower for the beginner.

The optimal level of arousal can also vary in relation to the skill being performed. Performers engaged in events that require the use of major muscle groups, or in a gross skill such as the shot put or weightlifting, may benefit from higher levels of arousal than performers using finer skills, such as those involved in target sports like archery or shooting (see Figure 10.6). As you can see from the diagram, even though some skills benefit from higher levels of arousal there is still an optimal level and performers can still be under- or over-aroused, with a subsequent deterioration in performance.

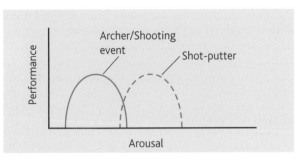

Fig. 10.6 *Optimal levels of arousal – relative to skill type*

> **Activity**
>
> 1 List a range of skills and skill situations (both individual and group/team) that are common in your chosen physical activity.
>
> 2 Place them on an arousal–performance graph with those that may benefit from higher levels of arousal towards the right end of the graph and vice versa.

Catastrophe theory

> **Key terms**
>
> **Catastrophe theory:** a theory that predicts a rapid decline in performance resulting from the combination of high cognitive anxiety and increasing somatic anxiety.

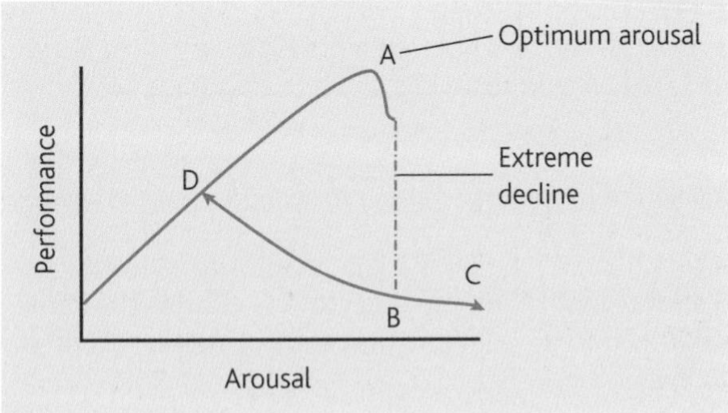

Catastrophe theory is a development of inverted U theory. In inverted U theory, there is a steady fall-off in performance following over-arousal (see Figure 10.4, page 134). Catastrophe theory involves a much faster and more dramatic reduction in performance – hence the name 'catastrophe'. In reality, it is more a model than a theory in that it attempts to predict human behaviour and performance rather than explain it. The model proposes that performance is affected by the relationship between somatic anxiety (physical) and cognitive anxiety (mental). When cognitive anxiety is high but somatic anxiety is low, performance is enhanced (Figure 10.7, Point A). When both cognitive and somatic anxiety are high, performance can suddenly deteriorate (Figure 10.7, Point B).

AQA Examiner's tip

Candidates frequently fail to understand that there are two alternative outcomes after the sudden drop in performance and that the outcome is dependent on how much and how quickly a performer can lower their arousal levels.

Fig. 10.7 *Catastrophe theory of arousal*

> **Activity**
>
> Try and describe, for your chosen physical activity, a portion of a performance that would reflect the changes in arousal and performance given in the description of catastrophe theory.

Following this sudden decrease in performance, the performer tries to regain control by decreasing arousal. When they attempt to do this, their performance does not immediately return to its original level but remains low and only gradually starts to rise as arousal and anxiety return to much lower levels (Figure 10.7, Point D). It is also possible that performance will continue to deteriorate (Figure 10.7, Point C).

According to this multi-dimensional view of arousal, a high level of cognitive anxiety produced by arousal can be beneficial, as long as it is accompanied by low somatic anxiety – this is most likely to occur some days before an event. As the event gets nearer, somatic anxiety increases to a peak just prior to performance and then normally declines once the performance begins (see Figure 10.9). If the somatic anxiety does not decrease or it increases again during the event, the performer may suffer a catastrophic decline in performance – they 'fall apart'.

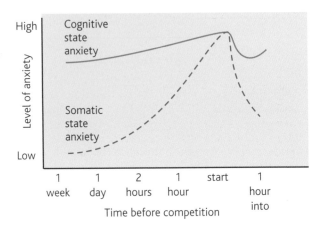

Fig. 10.9 *The relationship between cognitive and somatic anxiety – changes in cognitive and somatic anxiety pre- and post start of competition*

Fig. 10.8 *A sudden collapse of performance – catastrophe theory*

What effect does arousal have on performance?

Optimal level of arousal

Based on the various theories of arousal and your own observations, it should be clear that there is an optimal level of arousal, a point when a performer is in an optimal state of readiness for the sport performance. Their reaction times are at their fastest, and they are able to screen out irrelevant information but do not suffer from **attentional narrowing**. Attentional narrowing occurs when the performer is so tightly focused on performing the skill, or on a small part of the display (e.g. the defender in front of them), that they do not attend to other important aspects or they miss important cues (e.g. team mates they could pass to).

Key terms

Attentional narrowing: focusing on too narrow a range of information or on the performance of a skill; this causes the performer to ignore important cues or information.

Activity

1. Describe a situation, from your own sport/physical activity, and identify information that a performer should attend to and information that they should ignore or filter out.

2. Imagine the performer's attention narrowing – list the information they may begin to ignore and describe how that might have an impact on performance.

When in a state of optimal arousal a performer's heart and breathing rates are sufficiently elevated to prepare the body for action, and levels of emotion are at a peak in relation to the performer, their skill level and the type of activity they are engaged in. We have already seen that performers engaged in activities requiring finely controlled movements work best at a lower level of arousal than those performing activities requiring gross

AQA Examiner's tip

Arousal is closely linked to a number of other areas within the psychology elements of the specification – information processing, anxiety, social facilitation, evaluation apprehension, stress and stress management. When answering questions on arousal, bring these other areas into discussion – as long as they are relevant to the question.

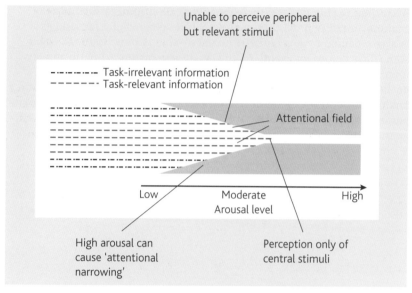

Fig. 10.10 *Missing important information – attentional narrowing*

muscle movements. Beginners, or those with a lower skill level, operate better at a lower level of arousal than highly skilled performers. Beginners are consciously processing more information and over-arousal will involve loss of concentration.

Interpreting arousal

A performer's personality and attitudes may affect how they react to arousal. If a performer interprets the arousal as pleasant and exciting, it is likely to help performance and vice versa. This is known as **reversal theory**. It is also believed that performance is likely to be enhanced if a performer views arousal or anxiety as being helpful ('it is getting me ready to perform') and if they interpret their arousal or anxiety as not being high.

Much has been written about whether or not there is a relationship between an individual's personality and how they react to increasing levels of arousal. There is some support for the view that elite athletes tend to fit Morgan's iceberg profile (Morgan, 1980); Morgan believed that elite athletes suffer from low levels of anxiety and are therefore able to utilise higher levels of arousal. Performers who have high levels of trait anxiety are more prone to state anxiety and will perform better with lower levels of arousal.

Zone of optimal functioning

Whatever the skill or activity type, whether the performer is an expert or a beginner, whether they view arousal and anxiety as being beneficial, or whether their personality makes them prone to anxiety, they all seek to be in the **zone of optimal functioning**. This represents the area between the upper and lower limits of arousal, within which the performer is sufficiently aroused to perform at their best. Given the many variables involved, sports psychologists refer to 'individual zones of optimal functioning' rather than trying to group performers together.

Is arousal the same for all performance situations?

We have already seen that in performance situations the level of arousal that is most effective may depend on the type of skill involved.

■ Key terms

Reversal theory: the proposal that whether a performer views arousal as pleasant (or unpleasant) is likely to have a positive (or negative) impact on performance.

Zone of optimal functioning: the area between the upper and lower levels of arousal within which optimal performance takes place.

■ Links

■ For information about the iceberg profile and the personality traits of elite performers, see Chapter 9 – Aspects of personality (pages 125–9).

■ For more information about state anxiety and trait anxiety, see Chapter 11 – The effect of anxiety on performance (pages 142–4).

The nature of the performance situation itself also has a bearing. For example, if the performer feels that they are being evaluated during the performance they may be suffering from **evaluation apprehension**, which will be raising their levels of arousal; they may therefore wish to take steps to return to a lower level of arousal. The importance of the sport situation or performance will also have an impact on arousal; other factors influencing arousal include opponents, actions by team mates and referees, and the nature of the crowd or audience. Zajonc (1965) proposed that the presence of others either as audience or as coactors raises the level of arousal, and this increase in arousal makes the performer's dominant response more likely. If the skill is easy or the performer is an expert, performance will improve; there has been **social facilitation**. However, if the required skill is complex or if the performer is a beginner, the dominant response is likely to be incorrect and performance will deteriorate; the audience or coactors cause **social inhibition**.

The peak flow experience – what is it?

Fig. 10.11 *In the zone*

The peak flow experience is sometimes called 'being in the zone' – the two terms are interchangeable. It refers to a period during participation in sport when the performer experiences a heightened state of consciousness; the performance might be the pinnacle of their achievement, a state in which they perform to the best of their ability. It is a 'special place where performance is exceptional and consistent, automatic and flowing. An athlete is able to ignore all the pressures and let their body deliver the performance that has been learned so well' (Murphy, 1996). When experiencing a peak flow experience, or when in the zone, performers report that they are so focused that they are oblivious to anything else; all that matters is the performance. The performance seems effortless; the performer is totally confident; movement seems to be automatic; they are on autopilot yet totally in control, in charge of their own destiny. Performers who have experienced a peak flow state report that they really enjoyed the performance, during which they felt immense satisfaction and accomplishment. Research indicates that this experience is connected to alpha brain wave activity. A self-report test, the Flow State Scale version II, is designed for performers

■ Key terms

Evaluation apprehension: a sense of anxiety caused by a performer's thinking that their performance is being watched and judged by somebody.

Social facilitation: the beneficial influence of the presence of others on performance (the others can be in the audience or coactors who are doing the same activity).

Social inhibition: decrease in performance due to the presence of others.

■ Link

For fuller explanations of evaluation apprehension and social facilitation, see Chapter 13 – Confidence (pages 181 and 183).

to rate nine specific factors associated with flow state or being in the zone:

- challenge – skill balance
- merging of action and awareness
- clear goals
- unambiguous feedback
- concentration on the task at hand
- sense of control
- loss of self-consciousness
- transformation of time
- intrinsic rewards.

Performers who achieve this state are able to undertake a range of mental strategies and exercises which help them achieve the state. They are high in confidence and show a positive mental attitude, have high levels of achievement motivation and a high motivation to perform, successfully use goal setting, are able to achieve optimal arousal level before competition and can peak under pressure. It was also found that being able to get into the zone is highly dependent on the performer's awareness of the challenges and on their having the skills to meet them.

Achieving the correct level of arousal, or maintaining an optimum level of arousal, is critical for all performers, in all performance situations. It is a popular misconception that all performers 'psyche' themselves to frenzy prior to a match, or stay icily calm throughout a performance. You should now understand that there is a complex and dynamic interaction between the performance situation, the skills being utilised, the personality of the performer and their level of experience.

✅ *You should now be able to:*

- describe what is meant by the term 'arousal'
- explain arousal in terms of psychological theory and be able to apply theories of drive, inverted U and catastrophe to performance
- recognise the mental and physical effects that arousal can have on the individual
- from a coaching perspective, know the correct levels of arousal for different individuals and for different sporting situations
- recognise and explain what is meant by the peak flow experience and being 'in the zone'.

1   Explain the inverted U theory of arousal and how it relates to different physical tasks, skills or performance situations. *(7 marks)*

2   After a highly successful performance, a performer stated that they had been 'in the zone'.

    (a)   Explain what is meant by the term 'in the zone'. *(3 marks)*

    (b)   What factors are necessary for a performer to achieve this state? *(4 marks)*

3   Performers can become over-aroused prior to or during a performance.

    (a)   What cognitive and somatic signs might a coach see to indicate that their performer is over-aroused? *(4 marks)*

    (b)   How might over-arousal cause performance to decline? *(3 marks)*

4   Answer the following questions in relation to Figure 10.12.

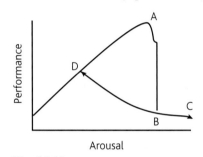

Fig. 10.12

    (a)   What theory of arousal is being shown in this diagram and what is occurring in the area marked B? *(2 marks)*

    (b)   What is being shown by the line D–C and what factors will determine whether D or C is the outcome? *(3 marks)*

    (c)   What combination of factors may have caused the situation shown in Figure 10.12 to occur? *(2 marks)*

The effect of anxiety on performance

In this chapter you will:

- understand what anxiety is and what forms it can take

- explain how anxiety may affect performance

- describe how levels of anxiety can be measured

- explain the different ways in which performers may try to control high levels of anxiety

- evaluate the benefits of goal setting and the methods used to set goals.

Link

For more information on evaluation apprehension, see Chapter 10 – Arousal (page 139).

Key terms

Cognitive anxiety: thoughts, nervousness, apprehension or worry that a performer has about their lack of ability to complete a task successfully.

Somatic anxiety: physiological responses to a situation where a performer feels that they may be unable to cope; symptoms include increased heart rate, sweaty palms, muscle tension and feelings of nausea.

State anxiety: (A-state) anxiety felt in a particular situation.

In this chapter we are going to look at anxiety and at some ways of combating anxiety. Most performers who are involved in a competition will have some concern about their chances of performing well or winning.

> When an athlete's performance suffers in an important event, it is often because of too much worry about the outcome … being solely concerned with winning causes an increase in anxiety.
>
> T. Orlick, Psyching for Sport, Mental Training for Athletes, *1986*

Anxiety has been defined as the negative aspect of experiencing stress. Anxiety is the worry – that unpleasant feeling – experienced because of fear of the possibility of failure.

The causes of anxiety vary greatly from individual to individual. The merest hint of an audience at a low-key event might cause an inexperienced performer to become anxious. Performing in front of your friends (peers) can turn out to be the most stressful situation you can experience. Even if you know that you are better than they are, you still feel that your team mates are evaluating or checking you out. Your perceptions of their higher expectations can make you unduly anxious. This has been referred to as evaluation apprehension.

Different types of anxiety

Cognitive and somatic

Anxiety is seen as having two components: **cognitive anxiety** and **somatic anxiety**. 'Cognitive' refers to thoughts and 'somatic' to the body's physical responses. More accurately, we should say that cognitive anxiety is psychological and somatic is physiological.

Activity

Read the following passage carefully and identify the symptoms of cognitive and somatic anxiety that Paul is experiencing:

Paul Smith is a cricketer who confides in his coach that he has a general feeling of anxiety. Paul may be referring to a temporary state in which he feels worried or apprehensive in response to a specific situation, such as a difficult training session, or he may be referring to a more permanent feeling of agitation and uncertainty which he experiences much of the time. It is likely that the coach will perceive Paul's anxiety as a negative influence affecting Paul's ability to concentrate, increasing his heart rate and possibly affecting his energy levels.

State and trait

Researchers have distinguished between two further types of anxiety. Anxiety can be an emotional state. It is the emotional reaction of someone to a situation that they experience as threatening. This is known as **state anxiety**. This state is:

characterised by subjective, consciously perceived feelings of apprehension and tension, accompanied [by] or associated with activation or arousal of the autonomic nervous system.

C. D. Spielberger, *Theory and research in anxiety. In C.D. Spielberger (ed.)* Anxiety and Behaviour. *1966*

For example, a player's level of state anxiety would change from moment to moment during a basketball match. They might have a slightly elevated level of state anxiety (feeling somewhat nervous and noticing their heart pounding) prior to tip off; a lower level once they settle down into the match; and an extremely high level in the final seconds of a very close game when faced with free throws to win the game.

Anxiety as a personality trait is a tendency to react to situations in an anxious way. This is known as **trait anxiety**. Trait anxiety is

a motive or acquired behavioural disposition that predisposes an individual to perceive a wide range of objectively non-dangerous circumstances as threatening and to respond to these with state anxiety reactions disproportionate in intensity and magnitude of the objective danger.

C. D. Spielberger, *Theory and research in anxiety. In C.D. Spielberger (ed.)* Anxiety and Behaviour. *1966*

For example, two rugby players, who normally kick penalties with equal technical skill, may be put under the identical pressure of having to kick the last-minute goal to win a match and yet have entirely different state anxiety reactions to the situation because of their personalities – that is, their levels of trait anxiety. One is more laid back (low trait anxiety) and does not perceive kicking the match-winning penalty as overly threatening. Thus, he does not experience more state anxiety than would be expected in such a situation. The other has high trait anxiety and therefore finds all situations threatening.

Very anxious people achieve optimal performance at low levels of arousal, whereas people who can tolerate high levels of anxiety require high arousal in order to perform at their best. Better performers are able to control arousal in anxiety-producing situations, and it is likely that this control is predominantly cognitive; they are able to control their negative thoughts. These performers can easily control their anxiety with simple techniques and have few problems during competitions. Other sports performers, however, including some professional athletes, have considerable difficulty in controlling their anxiety. Many performers help themselves to reduce their own pre-competition anxiety through a carefully developed warm-up. Exercise itself can produce relaxation and reduce symptoms of anxiety.

Key terms

Trait anxiety: (A-trait) an enduring personality trait, giving a tendency to view all situations as threatening.

Activity

Using the inverted U theory, described in Chapter 10 – Arousal (pages 134–6):

1. Sketch the optimal performance levels for two types of performer: one who has high trait anxiety and one who has low trait anxiety.

2. Repeat for a performer who can control their anxiety and another who cannot.

A direct relationship exists between a person's levels of trait anxiety and state anxiety. Research has consistently shown that those who score high on measures of trait anxiety experience more state anxiety in highly competitive, evaluative situations. This relationship is not, however, perfect. Through experience, an athlete with high trait anxiety can learn to cope with a particular situation and reduce their state anxiety. Generally speaking, knowledge of a person's level of trait anxiety will enable a prediction to be made about how they will react to competition, to being assessed and in threatening conditions.

■ Measuring anxiety

Both state and trait anxiety affect performance; psychologists have therefore tried to devise ways of measuring a person's state and trait anxiety. Examples of such measures include:

- physiological measures of somatic anxiety (e.g. measurement of heart rate, muscle tension and sweating)
- observation
- questionnaires.

However, problems are associated with these types of measurement:

- Physiological methods put the performer in the artificial situation of being 'wired up' to devices that measure physiological changes caused by anxiety, such as increased heart rate, increased sweating and increased muscle tension. But simply putting the performer in such a situation tends to create anxiety in itself.
- Observation involves looking for the symptoms of changes in anxiety in a performer, such as increased bodily movements and increased agitation. But the observation also tends to take place in artificial environments, which leads to extra anxiety.
- When answering a questionnaire, the respondent's responses may not be a true reflection of their feelings. Nevertheless, self-report questionnaires are popular for research because they are quick to administer, cheap to produce and evaluate and can be relatively accurate.

Questionnaires

Three questionnaires used to measure anxiety are:

- the State–Trait Anxiety Inventory (STAI; Spielberger, 1970)
- the Sport Competition Anxiety Test (SCAT; Martens, 1977)
- the Competitive State Anxiety Inventory-2 (CSAI-2; Martens, 1990).

The STAI

The STAI is a self-report questionnaire in which people rate how nervous they feel both in general and in specific situations. The scoring system for the questions gives an indication of both the state anxiety and the trait anxiety of the performer.

The SCAT

Simple observation of a competition will show you that some performers are able to cope with anxiety and remain calm, while others can become highly stressed, even ill. Martens developed the SCAT to find out which competitors are likely to become too anxious in competitive situations. The SCAT also uses self-report but applied specifically to sports competitions. Scoring then gives an indication of that person's level of state anxiety in competition-specific situations. According to Martens, four factors are related to competitive anxiety:

- individual differences in how performers interact with different situations – some events are more important than others and therefore cause more anxiety
- the different types of anxiety (state and trait) that a performer experiences
- a specific anxiety trait that only occurs in competitive situations (Martens called this 'competitive trait anxiety')
- the competition itself, which involves interaction between the performer's personality traits, their own competitive trait anxiety and the specific situation involved.

The SCAT questionnaire has been shown to be a reliable means of measuring a performer's tendency to become anxious about competition and is thought to be a valid means of predicting competitive state anxiety. The performer's competitive trait anxiety and the competitive situation together generate a threatening situation, which in turn increases the performer's competitive state anxiety.

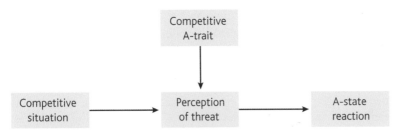

Fig. 11.1 *The relationship between the situation and personality factors*

Activity

1. Complete a SCAT questionnaire.

2. Comment on your results compared with those of the rest of your class. What similarities and differences have you found?

The CSAI-2

The CSAI-2 uses self-report to measure each of the three components of anxiety proposed by Marten: cognitive state, somatic state and self-confidence in a competitive situation. The CSAI-2 questionnaire is usually given out before a major competition, but more than once, such as a week before, a day before, and half an hour before the competition. This enables the researcher to discover the baseline level of anxiety and compare it with the pre-competition levels to see if they differ. It also allows the researcher to see whether any aspect of anxiety becomes more evident in the pre-competition period.

Typical results of CSAI-2 questionnaires are shown in Figure 11.2. These results are fairly consistent and suggest that cognitive state anxiety increases in the days prior to competition and fluctuates during competition, as the likelihood of success or failure changes. Somatic state anxiety tends to be lower than cognitive state anxiety in the days leading up to the competition, but it increases in the hours before the event as the event approaches; generally, it decreases during competition. Both types of anxiety can affect performance, as both increase arousal.

Link

For more information on the effects of arousal, see Chapter 10 – Arousal (pages 137–40).

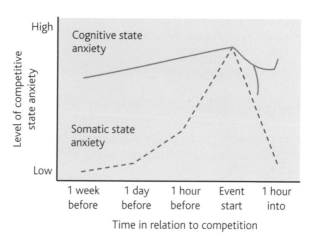

Fig. 11.2 *Typical results of CSAI-2 questionnaires*

■ Stress

It should now be apparent that it is beneficial for performers if they can try to eliminate anxiety and control their levels of stress. Often what separates the very good performer from the good performer is the ability to control their anxiety when there is a need to do so.

Today the term 'stress' is in common usage in the world of sport and in society in general. However, what is usually being referred to is distress (negative responses to a situation that places demands on us). When people say that they are 'suffering from stress', what they mean needs to be clarified. Selye (1976) defined stress as 'the non specific response of the body to any demand made upon it'.

Stress depends on a number of components. These components cannot be seen as separate forces; Figure 11.3 illustrates how they interact.

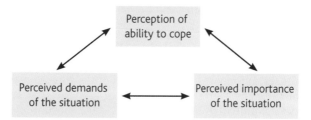

Fig. 11.3 *The components of stress*

The perceived demands, called stressors, are what set off the stress. A stressor could be anything that:

■ threatens our self-esteem

■ causes us personal harm

■ develops fear of the unknown or uncertainty

■ causes frustration

■ increases pressure.

How an individual perceives a potentially stressful situation depends on:

■ trait anxiety

■ self-confidence

■ interpretation of arousal

■ the importance of the event.

Pressures from the environment may result in the individual's becoming optimally aroused as opposed to being stressed.

Having the ability to cope with a particular environmental stressor will stop an individual becoming stressed from that source. In some activities, stress appears to be integral to the activity as it is associated with the thrill and excitement of participation. This is called eustress and is associated with activities such as bungee jumping. In general, however, stress is something to be avoided as it inhibits performance.

Responding to stress

The way we respond to stress is partly instinctive and partly to do with the way we think. Some of the early research on stress showed the existence of the now well-known 'fight-or-flight' response. Humans release hormones such as adrenaline to help us to run faster and fight harder. These hormones increase heart rate and blood pressure, delivering more oxygen and blood sugar to power important muscles. They increase sweating in an effort to cool these muscles and help them stay efficient. They divert blood away from the skin to the core of our bodies, reducing blood loss if we are damaged. As well as this, our attention is focused on the threat, to the exclusion of everything else. All of this significantly improves our ability to survive life-threatening events.

It is not only life-threatening events that trigger this reaction: we experience it almost any time we come across something unexpected or something that frustrates our efforts to attain our goals. When the threat is small, our response is small and we often do not notice it among the many other distractions of a stressful situation. Unfortunately, this mobilisation of the body for survival also has negative consequences. In this state, we are excitable, anxious, jumpy and irritable. This actually reduces our ability to work effectively as part of a team. With trembling limbs and a pounding heart, we can find it difficult to execute precise, controlled movements. The intensity of our focus on survival interferes with our ability to make fine judgements that involve drawing information from many sources. We find ourselves more accident prone and less able to make good decisions.

Controlling stress

Stress-management techniques can assist in improving personal sporting performance through controlling the pressures that the competitive environment brings. The optimal psychological state for most sports tasks is a state of relaxed concentration. Performers must be alert and attentive to the task, but they should also be free of excessive muscle tension: in other words, relaxed but in control. Simply telling athletes about the importance of relaxation and control is usually sufficient to eliminate some ineffective psychological approaches.

The coach and performer can control stress through approaching the problem in two ways:

■ controlling or redirecting the performer's thoughts and attention – reducing cognitive anxiety

■ reducing or controlling the physiological components of anxiety – reducing somatic anxiety.

AQA Examiner's tip

As each of the following stress-reduction techniques is included in the specification, you will need to understand all of them. Note that they have aspects in common: they are trying to reduce either somatic or cognitive anxiety; they all require learning; they all use some method of distracting the performer from the stress-causing situation to allow their anxiety to reduce.

■ **Key terms**

Imagery: creating mental images to escape the immediate effects of stress.

Visualisation: the process of creating a mental image of what you want to happen or feel.

The following strategies can help the performer to achieve the optimal performance 'zone'. All the strategies need to be learned and developed through practice. They all involve some means of redirecting thoughts away from the cause of the stress and by so doing reducing the cause of any anxiety. Many performers combine two or more of the techniques to produce their own, personalised anxiety-reducing method.

■ Cognitive techniques for controlling anxiety and stress

Imagery

One way of reducing stress is by changing the environment that is causing the stress, but often in sport you cannot change the environment. **Imagery** can be a useful method of relaxing in such situations. As you will be aware, particular environments can be very relaxing, while others can be intensely stressful. The principle behind the use of imagery in stress reduction is that you can use your imagination to recreate and enjoy a situation that is very relaxing.

When using imagery in relaxation, a common method is to imagine a scene, place or event that you remember as safe, peaceful, restful, beautiful and happy. You can bring all your senses into the image, including, for example, sounds of running water and birds, the smell of cut grass, the warmth of the sun, etc. The imagined place is then used as a retreat from stress and pressure. It is important to the effectiveness of the technique that you come up with the image rather than have someone else choose it.

You can also use imagery in rehearsal before a big event, allowing you to run through the event in your mind. Aside from enabling you to rehearse mentally, imagery also allows you to practise in advance for anything unusual that might occur, so that you are prepared and already practised in handling it. This is a technique used very commonly by top sportspeople, who learn good performance habits by repeatedly rehearsing performances in their imagination. If unusual eventualities that they have rehearsed using imagery occur, they have good, pre-prepared, habitual responses to them.

Imagery also allows you to pre-experience achievement of your goals, helping to give you the self-confidence you need to do something well. This is another technique used by successful athletes.

Steve Backley, a GB international javelin thrower, suffered from a series of debilitating injuries that severely restricted his training. Although he was able to remain fit, he was unable to actually throw a javelin for the six months leading up to a world championship. But through the use of imagery he could mentally practise, to the extent that despite being unable to throw prior to the competition he still finished with a silver medal!

Visualisation

Another form of mental rehearsal uses **visualisation** to lock in on 'perfect performance' as a way of focusing on controlling the performance. This reduces anxiety by diverting attention away from the cause of the anxiety, and blocking out anxious thoughts. It depends on previous learning of visualised sequences of perfect movements.

Many athletes routinely use visualisation techniques as part of training. Generally speaking, visualisation is the process of creating a mental

AQA Examiner's tip

Terms such as 'imagery', 'visualisation' and 'mental rehearsal' tend to be used interchangeably for the processes of using the mind to create an image. There are two types of image: the calming image, to reduce anxiety; and the image of success, to increase confidence.

image of what you want to happen or feel. An athlete can use this technique to imagine the intended outcome of a race or training session, or simply to rest while enjoying a relaxed feeling of calm and wellbeing. When imagining a scene, complete with detailed images of a previous best performance, the athlete is instructed to 'step into' that feeling. These scenarios can include the visual, kinaesthetic and auditory senses. Using the mind, the performer can call up these images again and again, improving the skill through repetition, similar to physical practice. With mental rehearsal, minds and bodies become trained ready for the actual performance of the imagined skill.

Research is finding that physical and psychological reactions in certain situations can be improved with visualisation. Repeated imagery can build experience and increase the athlete's confidence in their ability to perform certain skills under pressure, or in a variety of possible situations. The most effective visualisation techniques result in a very vivid sport experience in which the athlete has complete control over a successful performance and a belief in this new 'self'.

Attentional control and cue utilisation (focusing)

If you're a performer, you will have often been told by your coach to concentrate. So you do your best. But what are you then concentrating on? The most common answer is that you're concentrating on concentrating, which defeats the object somewhat. The concepts of concentration and attention are closely connected.

Attentional control aims to improve the performer's ability to focus on the appropriate cues (cue utilisation). In doing so, the number of errors caused by other distractions is reduced. Concentration is the ability to sustain attention on selected stimuli for an extended period of time. Although this might appear to involve great strain and exertion, the reverse is actually true. Effective concentration has been described as 'being in the zone', or a flow state, of being totally absorbed in the present. Concentration is difficult to master because the mind tends to shift its focus when presented with novel stimuli. This bias toward new sights and sounds is known as the orienting response. Although this response was valuable in pre-history as it alerted our ancestors to dangers in the wild, in terms of sport it is not such a great asset as it often makes us susceptible to meaningless distractions on the playing field. A split-second loss of concentration at a critical point can often spell the difference between winning and losing.

Careful planning and practice are required to gain control over our attentional faculties. Fortunately, selective attention and concentration can be learned, refined, and perfected just as easily as the skills required when playing sport. This is the important point: attentional control, like all other stress-management techniques, needs to be learned and refined through practice.

To improve attentional control, the performer has to avoid negative thoughts and feelings, as these are needless distractions which rob us of limited attentional resources. The performer must remain focused on the present, attending to what is immediately important and blocking out past and future concerns. It is often useful to use key words or phrases such as 'focus' or 'control' to remind yourself to concentrate. The performer should be oriented on the task rather than the outcome. Thinking about the score or how you look are common distractions. The performer needs to relax whenever they have the chance. If a skill is repeatable, such as a tennis serve, add a ritual or consistent routine

▪ **Key terms**

Attentional control: maintaining concentration on appropriate cues.

▪ **Link**

For information on 'being in the zone', see Chapter 10 – Arousal (pages 139–40).

Activity

Watch a performer who has to keep repeating specific skills (e.g. a field-event athlete, a tennis player preparing to serve, a golfer). Each will have a 'routine' that they go through before attempting the skill. Explain in your own words what they are trying to achieve in terms of attentional control.

Key terms

Positive self-talk: developing positive thoughts about one's actions.

Thought-stopping: conditioning the mind to think of alternatives to the anxiety-causing negative thought.

to your game (e.g. bounce the ball the same way) to help avoid needless distractions and keep your mind from wandering. Pay special attention when fatigued because players often lose their focus when tired. Attention and arousal are closely related, so try to avoid becoming overly aroused while remaining focused. Brief breathing and/or relaxation exercises can help lower arousal.

Thought-stopping

This relaxation technique uses a simple physical or mental 'action' (e.g. clenching a fist, or imagining a picture or sign) as a means of switching your attention into a controlled mental state and hence reducing cognitive anxiety. For example, when you experience a negative or unwanted thought (cognitive anxiety) such as 'I just don't want to be here today' or 'She beat me by five seconds last time we raced', think of something distinctive and memorable. Something like a large red stop sign should be pictured in your mind's eye. This is where the practice comes in. Every time a negative thought comes into your head, you must try to picture the same image. Try to hold this image for a few seconds then allow it to fade away along with the negative thought. If you wish, you can follow this with a **positive self-talk** statement such as 'I am going to get off the line quickly and run by her shoulder!' **Thought-stopping** involves conditioning in that you condition your mind to think of a large red stop sign instead of a negative thought; as the conditioned image fades so does the attention on anxiety-causing stimuli. Thought-stopping can be used to block an unwanted thought before it escalates or disrupts performance. The technique can help to create a sharp refocus of attention, keeping you engrossed in the task at hand. It depends on prior learning or conditioning to associate the response of the calm mental state with the stimulus of the physical/mental 'action'.

Self-talk

This is another method of taking your mind off the cause of anxiety and is often used if your concentration strays or you start to feel fatigued. It is vital that self-talk remains positive and focuses on self-instructing, motivational content. Because of this, performers can actually plan and even rehearse what they are going to say to themselves beforehand, just like you might rehearse an important telephone call in order to remember it. The key is to stay positive even when the situation is less than ideal; this is not easy to achieve and will take considerable time to learn.

The first step in learning to use positive self-talk is to become more aware of your thoughts during training and competition. If you want to gain more control over your own thoughts, try to work out a simple plan for how to record them. This should then be tried over a number of weeks during training. If you notice any undesirable patterns in your thinking, such as negative self-talk or loss of focus, you can try to combat these by planning more positive alternative thoughts. You can, for example, design positive statements that you repeat to yourself regularly. These can be written down and left around to remind you to use them. Work on recalling these statements when you become aware of negative thoughts or feelings. This might seem a little strange at first, but you are actually programming your brain to notice more 'positives' and, over time, this will become a habit. So instead of thinking 'Am I ready for this?' try saying 'I've trained hard and am really fit and raring to go for the win!' Elite performers often recall that their very best performances were accompanied by very few thoughts, a feeling of complete control, effortless movements and a sense of being 'on automatic pilot'.

Somatic techniques for controlling anxiety and stress

Biofeedback

Biofeedback uses the monitoring of a physiological variable that is affected by somatic anxiety; examples are:

■ heart rate, using a pulsometer or heart rate monitor

■ muscle tension, using electromyography (EMG)

■ sweating, using a galvanic skin response (GSR) meter

■ blood pressure, using a sphygmomanometer

■ breathing rate, using a spirometer.

The performer is attached to the monitoring device and has to learn to reduce the physiological variable by trying to think pleasant thoughts, thereby reducing the anxiety state associated with the high level of the variable. The method most commonly used in sport is the heart rate monitor. As the heart rate increases because of anxiety caused by the situation, the performer concentrates on the monitor and tries to calm themselves to such an extent that their heart rate falls. The reduction in heart rate shows that somatic anxiety is reducing. It only works if the performer has already learnt to use the monitoring process as a means of diverting attention away from the anxiety-producing mental stimulus.

■ Key terms

Biofeedback: information about changes in physiological variables; the patient watches a monitor displaying changes in readings of a variable associated with somatic anxiety and tries to lower the reading by distracting their attention away from the cause of the anxiety.

Breathing control: using diaphragmatic breathing as a means of focusing on relaxation.

■ Activity

1. Wear a heart rate monitor. Usually, just putting on a heart rate monitor causes anxiety and a corresponding increase in heart rate. Look at the read-out from the monitor. Think calm thoughts. Try to relax. Watch your heart rate read-out decrease. This needs to be attempted several times before the hard part!

2. Repeat as above, but this time make sure the situation is stressful. Try using this biofeedback technique while standing in front of your classmates. Can you ignore them and reduce your heart rate?

Breathing control

Breathing control also focuses on an aspect of physiology to distract the mind from the anxiety-inducing situation. Breathing control is a common feature of several techniques, as it causes a relaxation response. The first step involves learning to breathe deeply. Deep breathing is also called 'diaphragmatic breathing'. When you breathe deeply, the air coming in through your nose fully fills your lungs, and the lower belly rises. When first practised, deep breathing seems unnatural. One reason for this is that body image has a negative impact on respiration in our culture. A flat stomach is considered attractive, so people tend to hold in their stomach muscles. This interferes with deep breathing and gradually makes shallow 'chest breathing' seem normal, which increases tension and anxiety. Shallow breathing limits the diaphragm's range of motion. The lowest part of the lungs doesn't get a full share of oxygenated air. That can make you feel short of breath and anxious. Deep abdominal breathing encourages full oxygen exchange: that is, the beneficial trade of incoming oxygen for outgoing carbon dioxide. Not surprisingly, it can slow the heart rate and lower or stabilise blood pressure.

Breathing control helps you concentrate on slow, deep breathing and helps you to disengage from distracting thoughts and sensations. It is especially helpful if you tend to hold in your stomach. Find a quiet, comfortable place to sit or lie down. First, take a normal breath. Then try a deep breath; breathe in slowly through your nose, allowing your chest and lower belly to rise as you fill your lungs. Let your abdomen expand fully. Now breathe out slowly through your mouth (or your nose, if that feels more natural).

Once you've taken the steps above, you can move on to regular practice of breath focus. As you sit comfortably with your eyes closed, blend deep breathing with helpful imagery and perhaps a focus word or phrase that helps you relax. Deep breathing is a simple, but very effective, method of relaxation. It is a core component of everything from the 'take 10 deep breaths' approach to calming someone down through to yoga relaxation and Zen meditation. It works well in conjunction with other relaxation techniques, such as **progressive muscular relaxation (PMR)**, relaxation imagery and meditation, to reduce stress.

Centering

Centering is used to interrupt a stressful situation and regain your concentration. It requires the performer to focus particularly on the rate of breathing and maintaining a slow, steady pace. It involves a deep abdominal breath with the performer concentrating on the breath and then switching concentration back to the important external cue. Centering during sports is critical in helping you to stay focused and avoid distractions. It helps the performer stay in the moment and release past and future thoughts, worries and plans. Centering techniques help reduce anxiety and stress and allow athletes to pay attention to their body and breathing, redirecting their focus from the negative or anxiety-causing event to the present task.

Often centering involves repeating a key word (mantra) that helps you refocus on what you want to do. For example, 'relax' or 'steady'. To do this automatically when you need it (during the stress of competition or training), you must practise it often. Training sessions can be used to try various centering techniques and find the best one for you. Refocus and get 'centered' at every break, rest period or when there is a pause in the action. Like all the other techniques described, centering aims to keep you in the present, help you drop any 'baggage' you carry about performance anxiety, expectations or 'what-ifs'. If you develop an automatic relaxation response, it will change how you feel about what you are doing. Then, you will have less stress and more enjoyment when performing and, as a result, have more success.

Progressive muscular relaxation

Progressive muscular relaxation is useful for relaxing your body when your muscles are tense (muscular tension is associated with somatic anxiety). PMR alternates tension and relaxation in muscles of body parts; this is coupled with a breathing rhythm as a means of progressively reducing tension in the whole body. In PMR, you tense up a group of muscles so that they are as tightly contracted as possible and hold them in a state of extreme tension for a few seconds. Then, you relax the muscles normally, before consciously relaxing the muscles even further so that you are as relaxed as possible. As the name suggests, relaxation should be progressive: you should start at the extremities of the body and, as muscles relax, move the alternating tension and relaxation more

Key terms

Progressive muscular relaxation (PMR): learning to be aware of the tension present in muscles and removing it by relaxing.

Centering: using deep breathing as a way of refocusing your concentration.

towards the centre of the body. By tensing your muscles first, you will find that you are able to relax your muscles more than would be the case if you tried to relax them directly. Success depends on learning to concentrate systematically on tension reduction in muscles, starting at the periphery and working towards the centre/head.

Goal setting

The sprinter Michael Johnson rewrote the record books when, at the 1996 Olympics, he became the only man ever to win Olympic gold medals for both the 200 m and the 400 m. At times he was, quite literally, 'in a class of his own' and until the Beijing Olympics he still held the world records for both events. However, in his book *Slaying the Dragon*, Johnson says that his achievements were based not so much on talent but on hard physical conditioning, mental strength, a clear vision of where he wanted to go, and a plan of how to get there. Johnson's book is an insight into how one man mobilised his talent through effective **goal setting**. Not everyone has the talent to be a Michael Johnson, but anyone can achieve significant improvements in performance by means of effective goal setting.

Goal setting works by providing a direction for our efforts, improving selective attention, increasing our motivation, promoting task persistence, increasing our self-confidence and reducing anxiety. When coaches and performers set goals, those goals must be realistic and achievable. There are different types of goal depending on the nature of the task, the abilities of the performer and their levels of anxiety.

Outcome goals

Fulfilment of an outcome goal depends on the performer's achieving a particular result, such as qualifying for the next round by winning an event. The method of achieving that result is not important: it is the outcome that counts. Achieving such a goal will increase the performer's motivation; a performer who is motivated by this type of goal is said to be outcome-goal oriented. The trouble with outcome goals is that quite often the result is outside the performer's control. The performer is unable to do anything about the opposition, the officials or the weather, and so they may not always win, however hard they try. If, after repeated attempts, the performer is still unable to achieve the desired result, there will be an increase in anxiety. This is especially true of performers with avoidance behaviours. Therefore, outcome goals are not always the best way forward.

Performance goals

With performance goals, the performer's attempts are judged against others or even against themselves. A performance goal may be as simple as achieving a certain time in a competition, regardless of whether the performer wins (or not). A performance goal could be to run the first 400 m of a 1500 m race in under 60 s. By setting realistic performance goals the performer can concentrate on that aspect of their performance and in doing so distract themselves from any stress-inducing happenings such as only finishing third in the race. By achieving the set performance goal, the performer's motivation will be maintained, if not increased.

Process goals

Process goals concentrate on the performer's techniques and tactics. Process goals will often influence performance goals. For example,

Activity

Experiment with PMR by forming a fist and clenching your hand as tightly as you can for a few seconds. Relax your hand to its previous tension, and then consciously relax it again so that it is as loose as possible. You should feel deep relaxation in your hand muscles.

Key terms

Goal setting: a technique used to control anxiety by directing attention away from stress and towards an achievable target.

Link

For information on avoidance behaviour, see Chapter 9 – Personality (pages 127–9).

giving the performer the process goal of a slower backswing during a bunker shot in golf may well improve the overall efficiency of the stroke, resulting in achievement of the performance goal of getting the ball within 2 metres of the hole.

✅ *You should now be able to:*

- define and explain the different types of anxiety – somatic, cognitive, trait and state – and their effects on a performer
- explain the different ways of measuring anxiety – observations, questionnaires and physiological measures
- outline different cognitive and somatic anxiety-reducing techniques
- explain the different types of goals that may be used to reduce anxiety.

1 The nature of the event and its positioning within a stadium often mean that the shot-put competition for elite athletes may take place in front of many spectators.

Competing in the shot put may cause anxiety in the performer. Figure 11.4 shows the relationship of competitive anxiety to the competition process.

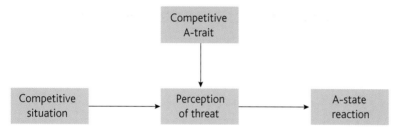

Fig. 11.4

    (a)   Using the diagram, explain why the competitive situation invariably leads to anxiety, and how and why these anxiety levels may vary between competitors. *(4 marks)*

    (b)   Martens (1977) developed a Sport Competition Anxiety Test (SCAT). Outline the use of this test and its effectiveness. *(3 marks)*

AQA, January 2002

2 Research on athletes has found differing effects of somatic state anxiety and cognitive state anxiety on performance.

    (a)   Comment on the levels of somatic state anxiety and cognitive state anxiety that an athlete might experience leading up to and during a major competition. *(3 marks)*

    (b)   Explain, with appropriate examples, how an athlete could control cognitive anxiety. *(4 marks)*

AQA, June 2003

3 Prior to important competitions, cyclists tend to become anxious.

    (a)   Name and explain the different forms of anxiety that a performer may experience. *(4 marks)*

    (b)   Various tests have been designed for measuring anxiety in sport. Name one of these tests and explain how it is administered and what aspects of anxiety it measures. *(3 marks)*

AQA, January 2006

4   (a)   Explain the difference between outcome, performance and process goals. *(3 marks)*

    (b)   Which of these tends to be best at reducing anxiety? Explain your answer. *(4 marks)*

12 Changing behaviour

In this chapter you will:

- understand what attitudes are and how they are made up

- understand how attitudes are formed and influence our behaviour, the importance of developing positive attitudes and how attitudes can be changed

- understand what is meant by aggression in sport and the different psychological theories that are used to explain aggressive behaviour

- be able to describe how players, coaches and officials might try to control aggressive behaviour

- understand what attributions are and Weiner's theoretical model

- understand how attributions are used to explain success and failure, how this impacts on a performer's future success or development, and how attributions may be altered.

Key terms

Aggression: in sport, behaviour intended to harm another person, physically or psychologically, outside the laws of the game.

Attribution: the perceived cause of an event, e.g. a win or a loss, as given by a participant.

Attitude: a complex mix of feelings, beliefs and values that predisposes somebody to behave towards something or someone in a consistent way.

Sport performance is often about how a performer behaves within a competitive situation, or the approach that a performer has to a competitive situation. A performer's attitude to an opponent, a venue, a competitor or to training and preparation will have a significant effect on the outcome. An attitude is a complex mix of feelings, beliefs and values that predisposes the individual to behave towards something or some person in a consistent way.

During match situations players can exhibit both **aggression** and assertion and it is very important to know the difference between the two. It is equally important, when coaching or officiating, to know how to control aggressive behaviour, whether yours or another's. After an event, we all have a tendency to seek reasons for the outcome – be it a win or a loss. The factors to which you attribute your win or loss can have a significant impact on the next performance. In this chapter, you will learn how these aspects of a performer's behaviour can be changed or modified to help them play better; effecting such a change involves a sound knowledge of the various psychological theories that underpin our understanding of attitudes, aggression and **attribution**.

Our first topic is attitudes: what they are, how they can affect behaviour and how they can be changed.

Fig. 12.1 *A positive attitude towards training – a necessity*

Attitudes

What is an attitude?

People talk frequently about attitudes, usually commenting on an individual's positive or negative **attitude**. An attitude is a view held by an individual towards an **attitude object**; this view might be positive, negative or neutral. The existence of an attitude predisposes the person holding the attitude to behave in a certain way towards the attitude object.

For example, an athlete may have a poor attitude towards weight training, resulting in a half-hearted approach. A team game player may have an attitude towards a certain official which causes them to act in a particular way towards that official, such as disagreeing with their decisions. This attitude may stem from an earlier encounter with that official. Does this mean that the player would have the same attitude to all officials? This is unlikely – Gill (1986) considers that attitudes tend to be specific rather than global.

An attitude can become a **prejudice**. A prejudice is a value judgement about someone or something made before you have the full picture and is most likely based on incomplete, inaccurate or stereotypical views. Prejudices are attitudes as they predispose the holder of the prejudice to behave in a certain way.

Attitudes are multi-dimensional, which means that they are made up of a combination of some knowledge, some emotional feelings and some behavioural intentions.

Attitudes and social norms

People are often told to change their attitude if they hold one that is not approved of or is thought to be unhelpful. The National Curriculum for PE encourages schools to instil positive attitudes towards sport and physical activity. Unfortunately, those that recommend such changes of attitude rarely suggest ways in which that might be achieved. Often, when someone is accused of having a poor attitude it is because their attitude leads to behaviour that goes against **social norms**. Social norms are rules, normally unwritten, about a person's behaviour, values, beliefs or attitudes. They help control social behaviour and are often based on consensus – they become rules because enough people consider them to be useful. These rules, which are enforced through social disapproval or approval, can lead to social acceptance or rejection.

Key terms

Attitude object: a person, event or behaviour towards which a person has an attitude.

Prejudice: a preformed opinion or judgement of someone, based on irrational, incomplete or inaccurate stereotypical views.

Social norm: a rule that is socially enforced, or a standard of behaviour; can apply to appropriate or inappropriate values, beliefs or attitudes.

Fig. 12.2 *Prejudice – a judgement made without thought or reason?*

Activity

1. Undertake a survey about physical education and sport with two groups of children (one group who are 11 to 12 years old and the other 14 to 15 years old), either at a club or in school. Share the data gathering as a group. The questions are given below; ask the pupils to respond on the scale shown. You will have to prepare the actual questionnaire yourself. You may add to the questions and should include age group and whether the respondent is male or female.

Scale
1 Strongly agree
2 Agree
3 Do not agree or disagree
4 Disagree
5 Strongly disagree

Questions
1 I think exercise is good for you
2 I enjoy taking exercise
3 I enjoy PE
4 I enjoy physical activity outside of lessons/outside of school

> 5 I think I am good at sport
> 6 I think I am good at PE
> 7 I think everybody should participate in physical activity
> 8 I enjoy the challenge in adventure activities
> 9 I feel relaxed after participating in sport
> 10 I enjoy sport
>
> **2** Answer the following questions after analysing the data:
>
> a What do the data tell you about attitudes towards PE, sport, and physical activity?
>
> b Do the two age groups differ in attitude?
>
> c Are attitudes the same for boys and girls?
>
> d Were there any surprises?

Attitude components

According to the **triadic model**, attitudes have three elements (these are also referred to as the attitude components).

The three components of an attitude are:

■ the cognitive component – what we know and believe about the attitude object

■ the affective component – how we feel about the attitude object

■ the behavioural component – how we actually behave towards, respond to, or intend to respond to the attitude object.

For example, a hockey player may know that training will improve their performance: they understand that doing interval training will improve their recovery processes during a match – this is the cognitive component. They enjoy the improved feelings of fitness in the game and their improved performance – this is the affective component. Finally, they plan their interval training sessions, monitor and record their heart rate and alter their training load to reflect increased levels of fitness – this is the behavioural component. In this instance, all three components are positive and consistent with each other.

■ **Key terms**

Triadic model: a hypothetical, testable proposition that holds that attitudes are made up of three components – cognitive (what we think), affective (what we feel), behavioural (how we behave).

AQA Examiner's tip

■ Marks are often lost because candidates are not able to discuss an attitude in terms of its components. Ensure that you understand the description of each of the components. Use the learning activities to become familiar with breaking down an attitude into its component parts.

■ When answering examination questions, you do not need to remember the names of the various psychologists. They may be referred to in a question but all you need to understand is the thrust of their arguments or hypotheses.

■ **Activity**

Take some of the attitudes you analysed in the previous activity. Try and break them down into the three components. Alternatively, take some of your own attitudes to PE, sport and physical activity and try and break them down into the three components.

You may think that if our cognitive and affective components are in agreement about the attitude object then we will behave in accordance with those components. But our behaviour is not always consistent with our attitude – young people may have learnt that physical activity is good for them and they may have experienced some enjoyable physical activity sessions but they still do not participate or exercise voluntarily.

Fishbein and Ajzedn (1975) found that, to predict behaviour, a high degree of specificity of both attitude and behaviour is required. For example, an intention to train for a specific match or purpose gives rise to more predictability than just a general intention to train. A stated intention to behave in a certain way was found to be a strong predictor of actual behaviour, and it was found that attitudes towards behaviour, specifically

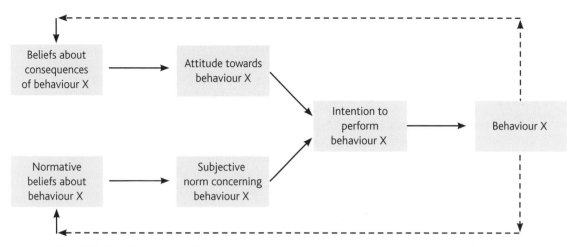

Fig. 12.3 *The Fishbein and Ajzedn model for predicting specific intentions and behaviours*

focused on sport, and generally accepted beliefs or values (normative beliefs, see Figure 12.3) both contribute towards predictability. If they are in agreement, predictability is greater. If they are not in agreement, the intention to train may not be strong enough: for example, the case of a teenage girl who understands the need to train and enjoys it but knows that the normative values of her peers are in conflict with this. The behaviour itself provides feedback to both personal attitude and generally accepted beliefs (norms). To get performers to behave in accordance with a set of general values and their own attitudes, we must ensure that:

- they understand the specific goals of a training session
- they have a positive experience and reinforce their attitudinal intentions
- any negative attitudes or negative experiences from the behaviour are recognised and dealt with.

How attitudes are formed

Attitudes are formed by experience and learning. This is influenced by a number of factors:

- **Peer groups** – friendship groups and wider peer groups strongly influence an individual's attitudes. An acceptance of the group's attitudes towards an attitude object is a way of gaining membership of a group and gaining a sense of identity. A team that has a shared set of attitudes will show a high degree of cohesion.
- **Conditioning** – rewards will strengthen existing attitudes. A performer who is praised for training will have their attitude towards training strengthened, which in turn will strengthen the intention to train and therefore the likelihood of training.
- **Socialisation and social learning** – we learn a lot from significant others – parents, teachers, coaches, wider role models and the **media** – and they are powerful formers of attitudes, including negative ones that may lead to prejudice and stereotyping.
- **Familiarity** – the more a person experiences an attitude object, the more likely the person is to develop a positive attitude towards it. For example, the more often a child is taken to a sports club or to matches by their parents, the more likely the child is to develop a positive attitude towards that sport and to take it up themselves.

Key terms

Media: the collective name for the means of mass communication of information, usually taken to mean television, newspapers and radio.

Links

For more on the influence of the media, see Chapter 19 – Commercialisation of elite sport (pages 276–7).

We begin forming attitudes very early in life and they continue to change and develop, form and reform, all through life. Players are strongly encouraged to develop good attitudes towards opponents and officials and to adopt the ethic of the sport in which they are involved, or to change their attitude if it is negative. We try to encourage children and young people to develop good attitudes towards participating in physical activity.

■ Activity

Review the attitudes you analysed in the first two learning activities. How do you think those attitudes were formed? It will be easier to start with your own, then speculate about some of the attitudes that you encountered in others.

AQA Examiner's tip

In an examination answer, you do not need to put forward what you think are acceptable attitudes (what is acceptable is a moral or ethical debate that goes beyond the scope of a psychology question) but you do need to understand why coaches, teachers and captains may try to instil what they believe to be good attitudes (i.e. for what purpose?).

■ Why is it necessary to form good attitudes?

We try to develop good attitudes because attitudes are a good predictor of behaviour. We try to develop good or preferred attitudes because there is a high probability that this will lead to good or preferred behaviours, such as participating in physical activity, showing a high level of sportsmanship or being a dedicated trainer. As well as being beneficial to the individual these attitudes are also socially valued; they abide by preferred norms and allow individuals to become part of a group, to feel valued, to be accepted. This is also known as socialisation – the process by which we learn the values, norms and culture of our particular society. We learn to conform to the way of life in our society.

Fig. 12.4 *Good attitudes help us be accepted*

We know that to become an elite performer, individuals need to develop the correct attitudes. For example, in a team situation a coach might find it useful to know what an individual's attitude is towards new members joining the squad, or their attitude towards referees and officials or towards unknown situations. A coach would find it useful to be able to measure the strengths of an individual's attitudes. This would allow the coach to modify those attitudes that were hindering the performer from giving of their best.

1 What attitudes would you expect somebody joining your team or club to have?

2 What attitudes would be essential for them to become a fully accepted member of the group?

3 How similar are the attitudes you have identified to those that might have occurred during the group formation processes covered in Chapter 14 – Group success?

Measuring attitudes

Psychologists have developed various methods of determining the strength of an individual's attitudes. A person's attitude towards an attitude object may be measured in two ways:

- Observation of behavioural signals – a highly negative or positive attitude may manifest itself in an individual's becoming overly aroused, including changes to heart rate, or in changes to their body language, such as failing to make eye contact. These behavioural signs are very hard to measure and rarely give anything other than a general indication.

- Questionnaires – this is a far more common method. Often the questionnaire takes the form of an **attitude scale** that attempts to probe an individual's attitudes towards a range of objects by asking them to respond to a set of statements (you used an activity scale in the activity on pages 157–8). Other questionnaires ask respondents to describe how they feel about something. An analysis of their responses is used to determine their attitude.

Issues with attitude questionnaires and scales

Any questionnaire that asks individuals to discuss how they feel about something or to express their strength of preference will have its limitations:

- Some respondents give the answer they think is wanted or which will paint them in the best light, depending on what they think the questionnaire is for.

- Not all respondents may understand the question/statement in the same way, or understand the scale.

- The gap between the statements in a **Likert scale** are not necessarily the same – the difference between 'agree' and 'strongly agree' may not be the same as the difference between 'agree' and 'neither agree nor disagree'.

- The way the statement is phrased may affect how the respondent thinks about the issue – it may change their attitude.

- Most attitude questionnaires and scales are not specific to sport, making the results harder to interpret.

- The knowledge and skill of the person analysing the responses can affect their interpretation.

Changing attitudes

If we accept that the assimilation of certain attitudes may be beneficial to an elite performer, we need a means of changing unhelpful attitudes. Sports psychologists use two main methods of changing attitudes:

Key terms

Attitude scale: a form of question design used in questionnaires to gauge an individual's attitudes; using a pre-set scale of measurement, the respondent is asked to agree or disagree with a set of statements.

Likert scale: a method of attitude measurement involving a number of statements with which respondents are asked to agree or disagree by choosing one of five positions: 'strongly disagree', 'agree', 'neither agree nor disagree', disagree' and 'strongly disagree'.

AQA Examiner's tip

With attitude measurement as with much psychological theory or research, there are limitations, and to gain the higher marks you should be able to comment on those limitations. This does not mean that a theory or a research procedure is wrong or of no use, but that the conclusions that are drawn should always be treated with caution.

■ persuasive communication

■ **cognitive dissonance**.

■ **Key terms**

Cognitive dissonance: tension resulting from having contradictory thoughts or beliefs about something or someone.

Persuasive communication: an active, non-coercive attempt to reinforce, modify or change the attitude of others.

Persuasive communication

Persuasive communication is very much what it sounds like: for example, the coach is able to persuade the performer to alter their attitude by discussion, argument or debate. For persuasive communication to be successful, a number of preconditions apply to:

■ the persuader – the person attempting the change (coach, team manager, teacher, captain)

■ the receiver – the person whose attitude the persuader is trying to change

■ the quality of the **message** the persuader is giving.

These three factors inter-relate, as shown in Figure 12.5.

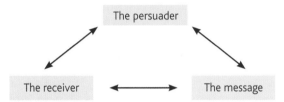

Fig. 12.5 *Persuasive communication*

The persuader

For the persuader (i.e. the message giver; most often coach, captain, teacher, etc.), these are the most important factors:

■ Their status in the eyes of the person to whom they are communicating – a person with higher status is more likely to persuade.

■ Their popularity – role models such as high-profile performers can be effective message givers and persuaders. Sport England's 'Sporting Champions' programme uses high-profile sports personalities to change people's attitudes to sport and to encourage participation.

■ Their credibility – this is linked to their status but also to feelings of trustworthiness and whether they have given helpful or accurate advice in the past. It is also linked to the perceived or actual intentions of the persuader – does the listener believe that the persuader is acting in their best interests?

■ Social or cultural background – if there is a wide difference between the background of the persuader and the background of the receiver, the persuader may lack credibility or status in the eyes of the receiver.

The message

These are very important factors relating to the message:

■ The accuracy of the message – is it obviously correct?

■ Is the message stated with confidence and enthusiasm (but being careful not to overstate or oversell)?

■ The clarity of the message – is the argument well constructed and logical?

■ Is the message logical and factual, appealing to the receiver's intellect; or is it emotional, appealing to feelings of loyalty, duty and responsibility?

Fig. 12.6 *Persuasive communication – the message, the message giver*

The receiver

Finally, factors relating to the receiver of the message must be considered:

- Are they ready for the message – are they able to understand the arguments in terms of their own emotional, intellectual or educational development?
- How strongly held is the current attitude; how persuadable is the receiver? Why do they hold their current feelings and beliefs?
- Are they motivated to change or at the very least are they open to the possibility? Pushing someone too hard to change their attitude could make them feel defensive about their current position, making them more resistant to change.

> **Activity**
>
> You play in a team that is in a lower division than your opponents in the next round of the cup. One of your team mates is doubtful that your team will win. Using the information about persuasive communication, write notes on how you would persuade your team mate that it is possible to beat that team.

Although persuasive communication seems to be a common-sense way of getting individuals such as elite performers to adopt more positive attitudes, it can fail in the light of strongly held beliefs; this is where a more focused approach, such as one based on the ideas of cognitive dissonance theory, can be more successful.

Cognitive dissonance

This theory was first developed in 1957 by psychologist Leon Festinger. According to cognitive dissonance theory, individuals like to be consistent in what they do, feel and believe. If they do something that goes against their beliefs, or if they encounter new knowledge or feelings that are counter to their current state of mind, they feel

> **AQA Examiner's tip**
>
> Weaker responses to questions about persuasive communication fail to understand the inter-relatedness of the three components: the persuader (message giver), the message and the receiver. To gain high marks, you must mention all three unless the question requires a more limited response.

Fig. 12.7 *Sporting Champions – an example of persuasive communication*

uncomfortable: they feel dissonance (a lack of consistency). This lack of consistency is uncomfortable and individuals are then motivated to reduce the discomfort by change their existing attitude or belief or by acquiring new ones. Earlier in the chapter we encountered the idea that an attitude has three components – the cognitive (what we know), the affective (what we feel) and the behavioural (what we do). For a person to feel 'comfortable', each of these three components must be consistent with each other. If an attitude is one that is not helpful to the individual, it may be changed by causing one of the components to be inconsistent with the others, thereby creating cognitive dissonance.

For example, imagine that a group of boys is being introduced to dance in a PE class but the group has a poor attitude towards dance and is not being cooperative. Using the triadic model (see page 158), the boys' attitude may be explained as follows:

- Cognitive – they may know that dance is not highly thought of by their peers; they may believe it to be for girls; they may have heard their father make disparaging remarks about dancers on television.
- Affective – they may have tried dance before and been unsuccessful – they did not enjoy it.
- Behavioural – they may not have tried dance before and they refuse to try now.

The boys' refusal to do dance is consistent with the other two elements and therefore they do not feel any tension.

To make progress with these lessons, the teacher must set up a state of dissonance, an inconsistency, so that the boys can begin to change their attitude towards dance. To do this, there must be a change to one of the components:

- Cognitive – change their knowledge of dance, for example by bringing in a dancer to demonstrate; show different dance forms including modern and popular dance; show all-male dance groups; emphasise the physical demands of dance, etc.
- Affective – engineer a situation where the boys enjoy dance or a dance-type experience; use music that is popular; keep the required responses at a level where success can be almost guaranteed; and then use positive reinforcement.
- Behavioural – use rewards and incentives to get them to have a go.

By changing one of the three elements, so that there is no longer consistency within the triad, dissonance is created. To reduce the feelings of inconsistency and imbalance that accompany dissonance and to return to a state of balance or harmony, the individual is motivated to alter what they believe, feel or do.

Evaluation

Cognitive dissonance theory has been criticised for being too simplistic and not taking into account each individual's personality, motivation and whether they have a need for consistency. Both persuasive communication and cognitive dissonance are useful when understanding what may cause a negative attitude. In addition, they give insights into the factors that should be considered when trying to alter that attitude and offer a range of strategies that might help cause change. Attitude change is a long process and there is never any guarantee of success.

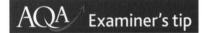
AQA Examiner's tip

Ensure that you can give practical examples of how you would use cognitive dissonance to change an attitude.

Activity

Taking the situation outlined in the previous learning activity (page 163), how would you change that person's attitude using a cognitive dissonance approach?

Aggression in sport

A player's apparent aggressiveness when competing is often ascribed to their attitude. Aggressive behaviour in sport is talked about in many ways, both positively and negatively. Players who are aggressive in defence are often praised, but if their aggression leads to an injury, even if unintended, they are criticised. Players are referred to as being overaggressive or insufficiently aggressive, and what is acceptable can vary between sports or at the different levels at which the sport is played. There is clearly a tendency to understate what constitutes aggression, or aggressive behaviour, in sport.

Activity

1 Read the following list of sporting situations and decide which ones you think involve the use of aggressive behaviour.
   a A boxer delivers a right uppercut which knocks out his opponent.
   b A hockey player strikes the ball at an opponent, breaking the opponent's finger.
   c A footballer disagrees with a decision made by the referee and swears at the referee.
   d A rugby player tackles a player and in the process the opponent becomes injured.
   e A basketball player pulls the opponent's shooting arm so that they miss.
   f A tennis player hits the ground with their racket, smashing it in the process.
   g A shot-putter shouts and thumps their chest before they step into the shot circle.
   h A footballer deliberately goes over the top of the ball but the opponent gets their leg out of the way.
   i In a football match, a foul occurs and both players involved end up punching each other.
   j The situation described in (i) happens in a rugby match.
2 When you have made your decisions, discuss them with a partner or with the rest of your group. How consistent were the group in deciding what was aggressive behaviour and what was not?

It is likely that the last learning activity caused a fair amount of discussion and disagreement. This is not surprising as there are many different definitions of aggressive behaviour in sport and the word 'aggression' is used by spectators, players, coaches and the media very loosely. We should therefore define what we mean by aggression in sport.

For 'aggression', the *Collins Dictionary* gives us the following definition:

> Aggression – an unprovoked attack (1), any offensive activity, practice (2), a hostile or destructive mental attitude or behaviour (3).

Collins Dictionary, 2007

For the purposes of the AQA specification and examination, aggression in sport is defined as:

- behaviour that harms another human being
- behaviour that is intentional
- behaviour that is outside the laws or rules of the game or activity.

Fig. 12.8 *Is this aggression?*

■ **Activity**

Now that you have a definition for aggressive behaviour, revisit the activity on page 165 and reconsider your decisions.

Fig. 12.9 *Aggressive behaviour in sport – compare with the dictionary definition*

■ **Key terms**

Assertive behaviour: the use of physical force that is within the rules or ethics of a sport and is therefore legitimate.

Channelled aggression: feelings of aggression that are diverted into useful, positive actions.

AQA **Examiner's tip**

■ The concept of aggression may seem a confusing one. In your examination answers, you must stick with the definition given in this chapter. This is not an area where you have latitude or will gain marks by applying your own subjective judgement.

■ To gain the higher marks in the examination, you must be able to refer to the subtypes of aggression: hostile, instrumental and channelled.

You may still find it difficult to determine what constitutes aggressive behaviour. A further differentiation may help; we can differentiate between hostile aggression and instrumental aggression.

■ Hostile aggression is the intention to harm outside the rules, often as an emotional response to another performer or situation, the sole purpose being to cause hurt or injury.

■ On the other hand, instrumental aggression is aggression that intends to harm as a means (instrument) to another goal. For example, if you rugby tackle an opponent with great force with the intention of making them fear you or be winded and out of the game, the primary motivation is to put them out of the game.

In the definitions we have used so far, aggressive behaviour has negative connotations – it is harmful, against the rules and liable to lead to negative consequences for the individual or team. Yet you no doubt still feel that aggression (in its everyday use of the word) is a valuable and useful attribute if used in the right way. Within sport this more constructive use of what is seemingly aggressive behaviour is often labelled **assertive behaviour.** Assertive behaviour is behaviour that may involve the use of physical force but is within the rules or ethics of a sport and is therefore acceptable, and indeed may be welcomed or even demanded.

Fig. 12.10 *Aggressive behaviour or assertive?*

Channelled aggression is another more positive form of aggression. When a performer is able to divert aggressive feelings into positive actions – working harder, concentrating better or striving for more accuracy –this is helpful to the team or individual.

■ **Activity**

View a video of an invasion game. Using the definitions and descriptions of the various types of aggression, identify examples of each of the following:

■ aggression

■ hostile aggression

■ instrumental aggression

■ channelled aggression

■ assertive behaviour.

What causes aggression? A theoretical approach

Now that we have defined aggression and differentiated between different types of aggressive behaviour, we should consider the possible causes of such behaviour. It is hard to be absolutely sure what causes aggressive behaviour as we are dealing with the behaviour of human beings with different personalities, backgrounds, and motivations in what are often rapidly changing situations. There are a number of theoretical explanations for why aggression occurs:

- instinct theory
- the frustration–aggression hypothesis
- cue arousal (a development of the frustration–aggression hypothesis)
- social learning theory
- deindividuation theory.

Instinct theory

According to instinct theory, aggressive behaviour is inherited not learnt. Writing in the 1920s, Sigmund Freud expressed the view that we all possess the potential for aggressive behaviour which cannot be eliminated. Freud believed that aggressive impulses build up within the individual and, if not released, can be directed inwards, which would be psychologically damaging. It is therefore necessary to release that destructive energy away from the individual and this can occur through aggressive acts either in legal and acceptable ways (sport, adventure, etc.) or in illegal and/or unacceptable ways (criminal activity, violence). Freud believed that individuals displace their aggression from non-acceptable to more acceptable situations: for example, away from the home and on to the sports pitch. This displacement of aggression with the accompanying release of the driving force is known as **catharsis**. A cathartic experience is supposed to allow a release of emotion and tension so that the individual feels less aggressive. Whilst this cathartic effect is often quoted, there is little evidence to support it.

In the past, instinct theory was criticised for several reasons:

- No biological basis for aggressive behaviour had been found (but see below).
- Research has shown that societies do not show similar levels of aggression.
- Instinct theory implies that aggressive behaviour is emotional or spontaneous (hostile or reactive) whereas there are times when it is clearly preplanned (instrumental).
- Social learning clearly has an inhibiting or controlling effect on people – even if it is highly variable.
- Social studies show that aggression can also be learnt.

However, recent gene research has reawakened interest in the instinct theory. Geneticists have isolated a gene (PET-1) that seems to have a controlling effect on levels of neurotransmitters such as serotonin. When that gene is absent or defective, individuals may be more prone to anxiety or aggression. The debate now revolves around the interaction between genetic inheritance and environmental factors such as social learning.

The frustration–aggression hypothesis

This hypothesis is based on the work of Dollard *et al.* (1939) who stated that 'aggressive behaviour always presupposes the existence of frustration'

Key terms

Catharsis: the release of pent-up emotions or feelings of aggression through harmless channels, such as the physical and emotional activity of sport.

and that the 'existence of frustration always leads to some form of aggression'. In a sporting context, being prevented from achieving our goal leads us to feel frustration. Frustration then leads to aggression. The levels of frustration are increased if it is unexpected or if it occurs when we are nearer to our goal. The foul that stops the goal is more likely to lead to aggressive behaviour than the foul that occurs 60 m from the goal line. The hypothesis then goes on to state that if aggressive behaviour occurs it will have a cathartic effect, reducing the level of frustration and therefore aggression. This is shown diagrammatically in Figure 12.11.

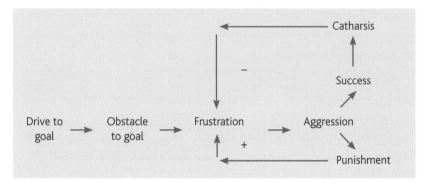

Fig. 12.11 *The frustration–aggression hypothesis*

There are a number of reasons why the frustration–aggression hypothesis cannot be the sole explanation for why an individual displays aggressive behaviour:

■ Not all individuals who experience frustration or blockage exhibit aggressive responses or behaviour.

■ Individuals who become aggressive when frustrated do not do so on every occasion; they can find alternative ways to deal with their frustration.

■ Individuals display aggression even when there is no obvious obstacle to cause frustration.

In addition, it is not clear that the use of aggressive or even assertive behaviour has a cathartic effect. Research has shown that aggressive acts can actually increase levels of aggression in those who commit them. Many performers report feeling more anxious, stressed, frustrated or aggressive after a sports contest than they did before it. Spectators who witness aggressive acts in sport or view aggressive sports exhibit higher levels of aggression or become more prepared to commit aggressive acts.

Aggressive cue (cue-arousal) theory

Aggressive cue, or cue-arousal, theory was developed in response to the criticisms of the frustration–aggression hypothesis. Berkowitz (1994) stated that, although obstacles can lead to frustration, arousal and anger, this does not always lead to aggressive behaviour but only predisposes the individual to aggressive behaviour. For aggressive behaviour actually to occur, socially learned cues or certain stimuli must be present within the environment (see Figure 12.12).

In a sport situation, socially learned cues might include encouragement from the coach to act aggressively, previous praise from team mates for aggressive responses to a similar situation or seeing role models act

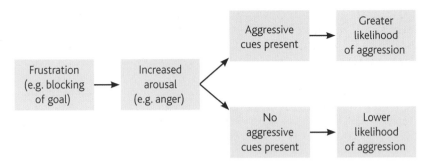

Fig. 12.12 *Aggressive cue theory*

in such a way. Stimuli that can act as a trigger for aggression might include:

- aggression-related objects (e.g. guns, bats, boxing gloves)
- aggression-related sports (e.g. rugby, boxing)
- aggression-related people (e.g. specific player, coach or fan)
- aggression-related places (e.g. a pitch where an aggressive incident had previously occurred).

It has also been found that certain environmental conditions such as high temperature and humidity (relative to the performer's normal conditions) can act as stressors and become cues for aggression.

It is clear from Berkowitz's work that individuals can learn to be aggressive, or to be aggressive in particular situations. This leads us on to the social learning theory of aggression.

Social learning theory of aggression

This theory contends that learning in social situations influences individuals towards or away from aggressive responses. According to social learning theory, we learn by observing others when those others are receiving reinforcement for their behaviour; for the observer, the reinforcement is vicarious (experienced at second hand). So if we observe a significant other (a role model), such as a high-profile sport performer, behave in a certain way, we may learn to copy them. If we then imitate that behaviour and receive praise or reward we are likely to repeat the behaviour. If we see role models punished for aggressive behaviour, we may conclude that this is behaviour that we should not follow.

If an England player injures an opponent, and is praised by the crowd or team mates, it is possible that younger players will copy this action and be aggressive on the pitch. The likelihood that they will continue to do so is dependent on whether they receive praise or a punishment as a result of that behaviour.

Deindividuation theory

According to this theory, individuals will, in certain situations, act differently when in a crowd than they might as an individual. The larger the group or crowd, the more likely it is that individuals will act as the crowd does rather than in accordance with their own beliefs and values. This is relevant to football crowds and football hooliganism where individuals may not take responsibility for their own actions.

Link

For more information on hooligan behaviour, see Chapter 18 – Deviance in sport (pages 259–64).

Fig. 12.13 *Deindividuation, a loss of personal responsibility*

Which theory?

As is often the case, psychologists and sports psychologists put forward a range of theories, each one building on the criticisms or weaknesses of existing theories. So how should we view aggression?

■ There is some evidence to suggest that genetic inheritance can predispose some people towards aggressive behaviour.

■ Obstacles to success can make us become frustrated, which can also predispose us to aggressive behaviour, especially if within the environment there are cues for aggression.

■ When in a crowd, our loss of self-identity and the ability to become anonymous can lead us to follow the actions of the crowd rather than our own inclinations.

■ Finally, socialisation probably has the greatest influence on whether we will act aggressively or not in sporting situations. It will significantly affect our ability to channel arousal into acceptable and legitimate actions, to be assertive. It can give us the strength to act as an individual either when in a crowd, or when asked to act against our own beliefs by a coach or captain. It allows us to view the actions of a high-profile player and measure them against our own moral and ethical sporting code before deciding whether or not to imitate them.

■ Controlling aggression

Aggressive behaviour can often be non-productive for the individual or their team. To be sent off for a bad foul or to be 'sin-binned' will affect the team's success. To cause injury to another player through a deliberate action will bring the individual, the team and the sport into disrepute. This may have long-term financial implications in terms of fines, loss of sponsorship or endorsements for the individual, team or the sport. It is clearly therefore in everybody's interests to be able control their own, or others', aggressive behaviour.

Do the learning activity before going on.

Activities

1 Consider how aggression is controlled within your own sport activity. Think of the actions of captains, managers, local and national governing bodies, officials, etc. Research examples at a national level.

2 In discussion with others, or by preparing a presentation, compare the methods used in your sport activity with those used in other sports.

Controlling aggression is vitally important, given that aggression can lead to serious consequences and outcomes for the individual performer, opponents, the team or club and indeed the sport. Whose responsibility is it? As your study of the various theories shows, attempts to control aggression must involve two components:

- The individual – each individual is responsible for their own actions. In a sporting context, individuals will form their own personal code of conduct, based on the ethics of the sport, their own personal morality and what they have learnt from others. Individuals have a responsibility to recognise their own levels of arousal, however caused, and to act accordingly.

- Significant others – parents, coaches, team managers and teachers have the opportunity to set the standard, to indicate what is acceptable or not acceptable and to provide the environment within which the desired behaviour can develop. It is the responsibility of national governing bodies, clubs, and Sport England to see that high-profile performers become role models and exhibit the desired behaviour.

What practical steps may be taken to control aggressive behaviour or to change a performer's responses in specific situations? Table 12.1 shows the range of options available; these are based on four principal strategies: punish aggressive play; reinforce assertive play; reduce or control arousal levels; avoid aggressive situations.

Fig. 12.14 *Controlling aggressive behaviour – direct action and/or a calming word*

Table 12.1 *Managing aggressive performers*

Strategy	Individual's actions	Coach/manager actions	Governing body actions
Punish aggressive play	■ Peers discourage aggressive behaviour	■ Substitute, fine, transfer aggressive players ■ Draw up player-conduct contract	■ Code of conduct ■ Support referees ■ Punish aggressive players, especially role models
Reinforce assertive play	■ Praise others	■ Talk about, praise, reward assertive play in team talks, practices, etc. ■ Show assertive role models	■ Fair play awards
Reduce/control level of arousal	■ Use mental rehearsal and stress-management techniques ■ Channel aggression ■ Be aware of aggression cues	■ Do not over-arouse pre-match ■ Focus on process as well as outcome ■ Not 'win at all costs' ■ Understand each individual player's aggression level and cues	■ Educate referees to lower match temperature ■ Discuss with coaches ■ Coach-education programmes
Avoid aggressive situations	■ Learn to walk away ■ Mark another player	■ Move player to another role ■ Ask player to take on position of responsibility ■ Substitute the player ■ Change tactics	■ Stagger derby matches ■ Play at neutral grounds

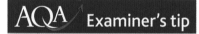

AQA Examiner's tip

How to control the behaviour of aggressive players is a popular examination question. Make sure that you have a range of strategies, with examples, to use in an answer. You will be most familiar with the ones from your own activity.

Getting the balance between assertion and aggression right, i.e. getting players to play and strive to win without crossing the aggression–assertion boundary, is a complex process requiring an understanding of the causes of aggression, a range of methods of dealing with aggressive behaviour and an in-depth knowledge of yourself as an individual or of the players as a coach, manager or teacher.

■ Attributions and sport

After any high-profile sporting encounter, eager television commentators interview players, managers or coaches about the event and why they or their team won or lost, played better or played worse. Responses will mention many factors – team spirit, referee, luck, the hard work done on the training pitch, the quality of the opposition, or moments of individual brilliance.

When we identify the factors that we believe have contributed to the outcome of a sporting contest, we are making attributions. These attributions are important in that they hint at the underlying beliefs of the players and coaches about the reasons for success or failure and knowing these can help when preparing for the next contest.

■ Activity

Think back to recent sporting events that you have been involved in as a performer; choose one when you won and one when you lost.

1 Write down the reasons that you think were important in determining the outcome.

2 Compare the reasons you have written down for when you won or when you lost – are they same?

3 Compare the reasons for winning or losing with those given by other members of the group.

4 If there are some events in which you have performed together either as team mates or as opponents, to what extent are your reasons common or shared?

Weiner's attribution theory

The most important and widely used theory of attribution was formulated by a social psychologist Bernard Weiner in the 1970s.

Weiner's attribution theory (Weiner, 1974, 1985) was not specifically developed for sport, but sports psychologists quickly saw its value in terms of understanding the reasons that performers give for their performances, what caused them to win or lose. The process of attributing one's performance (behaviour) to specific causes has three stages:

■ As the performer, you must be aware of your performance or behaviour.

■ You must accept that the behaviour was intentional.

■ You must accept that behaviour is caused either by internal factors (within you) or external factors (outside you, such as other people).

You can probably see that attribution is closely related to motivation (the reasons why we do something).

Although people give many reasons for success or failure, Weiner argued that there are four categories of attribution:

■ ability (your own or the team's)

■ effort (your own or the team's)

■ luck

■ task difficulty.

Initially, Weiner devised a model (a hypothetical, testable proposition) in which the four categories are placed on two dimensions:

■ the causality dimension (internal or external causes), known as the **locus of causality**

■ the **stability dimension** (relatively unchanging or changing causes).

Figure 12.15 shows Weiner's model with the two dimensions: locus of causality and locus of stability.

Weiner later added a third dimension:

■ controllability (the extent that the behaviour or consequences were within the control of the performer), known as the **locus of control**.

Most of the time when we succeed, we tend to attribute our success to internal factors (e.g. our own skill or effort). This is known as the **self-serving bias.** When we lose or an opponent wins, we tend to credit

■ Link

For more information on motivation, see Chapter 9 – Personality (pages 127–8).

■ Activity

Look back at either your own or the group's analysis of their recent sporting contests and the reasons given for success or failure. Can you group them into the four categories?

■ Key terms

Locus of causality: the internal/external factors that a performer believes caused an event or an outcome.

Stability dimension: the stable/unstable factors that a performer believes caused an event or an outcome.

Locus of control: the extent to which a performer believes that the outcome was within their control (or not).

Self-serving bias: the tendency to attribute success to internal factors and losses or failures to external factors; protects our self-esteem.

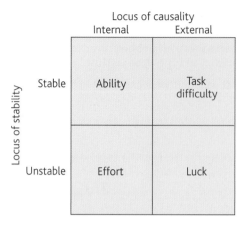

Fig. 12.15 *Weiner's two-dimensional model of attribution*

external factors (e.g. luck). When we fail or make mistakes, we are more likely to make an external attribution and blame factors outside ourselves rather than blaming ourselves. But this may not always be the case.

The factors to which we attribute our loss or failure, whether those are internal or external (locus of causality), or whether they can be changed or not (locus of stability), and to what extent those factors are within our control (locus of control), can have a significant effect on our future motivation to train and compete and even influence whether we continue to participate or give up.

Attributing our successes to internal factors (skill and effort) will develop our self-esteem, and we are likely to become increasingly motivated. If, on the other hand, we attribute loss or failure to internal and stable factors, we come to believe that we do not have the ability and that we cannot change this, so we might as well give up. Performers are therefore encouraged to view failure as a result of factors that are unstable and can be changed, such as effort and luck. This prevents damage to self-esteem. Coaches will also refer to external factors beyond the control of the performer, such as the difficulty of the task. If you played against a team from a much higher division and lost, you can point to the difficulty of the task and prevent damage to self-esteem. It is, however, better to attribute success to factors within the performer's control.

Weiner believed that unsuccessful individuals would try and protect their self-esteem by attributing failure to external factors beyond their control. Later research showed that, within sport, unsuccessful performers do not always do this: they often see success or failure in terms of mastery goals or task goals. If they lose but actually performed better and could attribute that improvement in performance to internal, controllable factors, self-esteem and motivation would be improved.

Learned helplessness

Performers who attribute loss or failure to internal factors and view the task as impossible to achieve suffer from **learned helplessness**. Learned helplessness, first identified by Dweck (1975), is an acquired condition where the performer believes that change is impossible, that events, or the performer's ability to affect the future, are beyond their control and they are doomed to lose. Learned helplessness is often acquired after an initial lack of success in a hard task.

The characteristics of learned helplessness are as follows:

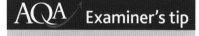

Examiner's tip

Attribution theory is a popular topic for question setters. Practise applying the three dimensions – locus of causality, stability and controllability – to as many sport situations as possible to become familiar with the terms.

■ **Key terms**

Learned helplessness: the state that occurs when a performer believes that failure is inevitable and that they have no way of changing that outcome.

- The performer believes that they have limited ability.
- They are focused on outcome goals (win or lose) rather than process goals (how many tackles, accuracy of passing, etc.).
- The performer is unwilling to try new skills or situations, believing that the skills will not work or that they cannot do it.
- They attribute performance to stable, uncontrollable factors.
- They do not believe that the things they have control over (e.g. effort) will make any difference.

Learned helplessness can be limited to a specific situation (specific learned helplessness), or occur in a wider range of sport situations or in all sports (global learned helplessness). If players are suffering from learned helplessness, or lack motivation because of the reasons that they give for their success or failure, changing those attributions could lead to improvement and to greater sporting success.

How to avoid being a failure – changing attributions

In **attribution retraining**, the performer is helped to look at how they explain success and failure; they are encouraged to focus on explanations which allow for future success. In particular, they learn to attribute failure to factors over which they have control: for example, after a game that went badly the performer may be told, 'You didn't lack ability but were possibly playing in the wrong position. Let's change that.'

The following are specific strategies that a coach could use:

- Observe and listen to what players are saying; monitor their attributions.
- Draw attention to progression or change.
- Focus on process, task and mastery goals rather than on outcome goals.
- Collect and use statistics about a player's contribution (passes made, tackles put in, etc.); this will allow changes to be noted and future attainable targets set.
- Try and ensure initial success to avoid learned helplessness.

Research into children's involvement in sport has shown that they enjoy

■ **Key terms**

Attribution retraining: methods of helping the performer to change the way that they explain the causes of success and failure; in the case of failure, they are encouraged to focus on factors that can be controlled.

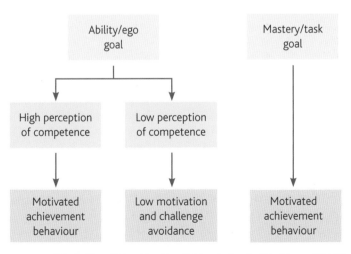

Adapted from M. Lee, Coaching Children in Sport – Principles and Practice, *1993*

Fig. 12.16 *Possible consequences of different goal orientations in sport*

GOWER COLLEGE SWANSE
LEARNING RESOURCE CENTRE
GORSEINON
SWANSEA SA4 6RD

their sport experiences more if they are set mastery or task goals rather than what are known as ego goals, such as beating another person (Duda *et al.*, 1992). This is demonstrated in Figure 12.16. Ego goals may work with those who perceive that they are highly competent but can lead to learned helplessness for others.

Summary

During this chapter, we have looked at the wide range of factors that can affect how performers make use of their skills and abilities in performance situations and how these are influenced. We have seen that attitudes can have an impact even before the performer steps on the pitch, that our reactions to events on the pitch or court have significant effects on our own performance and the performance of others, and that how we view our own performance has an impact on the future. Finally, we have seen that all those factors can be changed or improved with skilled coaching and if performers are willing to listen.

You should now be able to:

- understand what attitudes are, how they are formed (including the triadic model), and how you can change them by practical applications of persuasive communication and cognitive dissonance theory

- explain why developing positive attitudes contributes to sporting success

- recognise aggression in sport and explain why it occurs, using a range of psychological theories such as instinct theory, frustration–aggression, aggressive cue and social learning

- describe practical ways in which coaches, performers and officials can control aggression in sporting situations

- explain why we attribute our wins and losses to different factors and how an understanding of attribution theory can help prevent a performer from labelling themselves as a failure

- give practical methods for changing somebody's attributions.

1   Most elite performers have positive attitudes to their preparation and performance.

   (a)   What is meant by the term 'attitude' and how might an elite performer have developed such a positive attitude? *(4 marks)*

   (b)   Using an example from sport and with reference to the triadic model, discuss how a negative attitude could be altered. *(3 marks)*

2   Players are sometimes thought to be not aggressive enough whilst others can be punished for being overaggressive.

   (a)   In the context of sport, what do we mean by 'aggressive behaviour'? Use an example to illustrate your answer. *(2 marks)*

   (b)   Sport is often claimed to be a useful way for young men to 'let off steam' and to help prevent incidents of social misbehaviour. Using your knowledge of the psychological basis for aggression, discuss whether or not this is a reasonable assumption. *(3 marks)*

   (c)   How may a coach help a player desist from engaging in aggressive behaviour? *(2 marks)*

3   Players, coaches and managers will always give reasons for successful or unsuccessful performances.

   (a)   Using examples from sport, give an explanation of the different attributions labelled B, C and D in Table 12.2. *(3 marks)*

Table 12.2

	Internal attribution	External attribution
Stable attribution	A	B
Unstable attribution	C	D

   (b)   Using your knowledge of attribution theory, explain why a performer may begin to suffer from the condition known as learned helplessness and how they could be helped to overcome it. *(4 marks)*

4   A player is often punished by referees for aggressive acts on the field of play. With reference to the various theories of aggression, discuss why this might be the case. You should also discuss the validity of such theories. *(7 marks)*

13 Confidence

In this chapter you will:

- understand the need for high self-confidence and self-efficacy

- describe how various factors can affect self-efficacy

- explain how the presence of an audience may affect performance

- explain how to reduce the effects of an audience on performance.

Key terms

Self-confidence: a person's belief in their ability to achieve sucess.

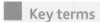

Examiner's tip

When explaining self-confidence, just remember the three words – 'belief', 'ability', 'succeed' – and then complete the definition.

Link

For more information on cognitive anxiety, see Chapter 11 – The effect of anxiety on performance (page 142).

Picture the moment: November 2003 in Australia and the Rugby World Cup final. Just a few seconds of extra time remaining and Jonny Wilkinson kicks the match-winning drop goal, a performance that demonstrated not just immense skill on his part but also the confidence of a winner.

It is easy to forget that Wilkinson had failed with three previous attempted drop goals prior to this point in the match. These failures might have dented the confidence of a player with a more brittle temperament, resulting in more tentative and indecisive future actions. But, in an interview following the final whistle, Wilkinson revealed that, having missed his previous three attempts at drop goals during the match, he still felt he was going to make the fourth one count. The rest, as they say, is history. This one example shows the importance to the sports performer of confidence and self-belief.

Of course, having high levels of **self-confidence** (i.e. a strong belief in one's ability to achieve success) is no guarantee of success and will not compensate for lack of skill, but in situations where competitors are evenly matched it can be the crucial determinant. In research, confidence has consistently been shown to be the main feature distinguishing highly successful athletes from less successful performers (Gould, Weiss and Weinberg, 1981; Mahoney and Avener, 1977). Although many people mistakenly assume that confidence reflects performance, i.e. we become confident once we have performed consistently well, it is becoming increasingly evident that confidence can be established beforehand. Self-confidence may be the most important cognitive factor in sport. Most participants recognise the importance of a positive attitude. Coaches and teachers tell performers to 'think like a winner', or 'believe you can do it'.

Self-confidence and self-efficacy

Sports psychologists define self-confidence as the belief that you have the ability to succeed when performing a desired behaviour. Confident athletes expect to do well and have a high level of self-belief, and this appears to be crucial in determining how far they strive towards their goals. It is largely confidence that determines whether people give up or remain committed to their goals following a series of setbacks.

For the sake of simplicity, self-confidence can be considered as conceptually opposite to cognitive anxiety (negative beliefs and worries about performance).

Both of these psychological constructs are related to our beliefs and both, ultimately, influence our performance. Coaches can often see fluctuations in the balance between the opposing states of cognitive anxiety and self-confidence reflected in the behaviour of their athletes. While confident athletes are not afraid of making mistakes, often taking calculated risks in order to take charge of a situation, self-doubters often avoid responsibility, becoming overly conservative and paralysed by fear of failure. As an example, consider the football striker who has not scored for a number of successive matches and is riddled with self-doubt. When faced with a half-chance, which he would usually take on with a shot towards goal, he may be lacking so much in confidence that instead he chooses to avoid responsibility and passes to a team mate.

Factors affecting self-efficacy

According to Bandura (1977), a performer's situational-specific confidence, or **self-efficacy**, is based on four primary sources of information (see Figure 13.1).

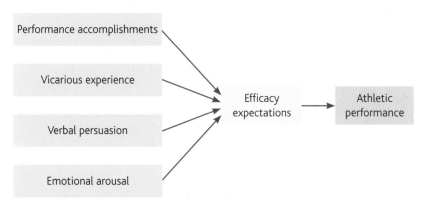

Fig. 13.1 *Factors affecting self-efficacy*

Performance accomplishments

The first and most important factor is previous **performance accomplishments**. What you have achieved in training and competition forms the basis of future expectations as to your success or failure. Repeated success naturally leads to positive expectations of further success, higher motivation and enhanced self-belief.

Unfortunately, the flip side of this principle is that repeated failures can give rise to a downward performance spiral and a 'snowball effect' whereby a performer starts to believe that success is not possible. Of course, the athlete does not mysteriously lose their physical skills and talents but, without confidence in these abilities, high-level performance is rarely achieved.

The implication of Bandura's work is that it is vital for coaches to make sure that their athletes achieve success, even if this means changing previously agreed goals that may now be thought to be too ambitious.

The most important thing here is how you perceive the task. Are you confident that you can achieve success?

Vicarious experiences

Research has also suggested that performers can gain confidence from viewing other people achieving their own successful performances. However, it is important that the success is achieved by a performer of similar ability to the person observing the achievement. This second source of information is known as **vicarious experience**. For example, a tennis player lacking confidence in her serve will gain confidence if she sees another player of similar standard demonstrate the skill. The tennis player begins to think, 'Well, if she can do it, then so can I!' Viewing others succeed lets us see that, with effort, success is attainable. The very common use of celebrities in fitness videos is an example of vicarious experience.

Key terms

Self-efficacy: situation-specific self-confidence.

Performance accomplishments: previous successes at the task.

Vicarious experience: watching others of similar standard successfully perform a skill.

AQA Examiner's tip

Definitions of self-efficacy should include the concept of situation-specific self-confidence and a definition of self-confidence (the belief in your ability to achieve success).

Links

For more information on goal setting, see Chapter 11 – The effect of anxiety on performance (pages 153–4).

For information on vicarious learning, see Chapter 12 – Changing behaviour (page 172).

■ Key terms

Verbal persuasion: encouragement from significant others.

Emotional arousal: perceiving physiological arousal as indicating emotion.

■ Links

- For more information on positive self-talk, see Chapter 11 – The effect of anxiety on performance (page 150).

- For more information on how arousal can affect performance, see Chapter 10 – Arousal (pages 131–40).

- For more information on anxiety-reducing techniques, see Chapter 11 – The effect of anxiety on performance (pages 148–53).

AQA Examiner's tip

Bandura's four primary sources of information are easily remembered as quotes: 'I've done this before'; 'If they can do it so can I'; 'Go on, you can do it'; 'I'm feeling good at this moment'.

Verbal persuasion

Verbal persuasion is a third way for coaches to help build confidence. By means of careful reasoning, performers can be shown that other people (i.e. the coach) have confidence in their abilities and believe that they can achieve the goals that have been set for them. Verbal persuasion can also take the form of positive self-talk: athletes convince themselves that success will follow.

Emotional arousal

Bandura also suggested that how you interpret your own **emotional arousal** can influence confidence. Although this is the least influential factor, it is important that physiological symptoms are perceived positively rather than negatively. Confidence can be enhanced by perceiving increases in heart and respiration rate as the body's natural preparation for top performance rather than as triggers for anxiety. Over-arousal will hinder performance by making the performer less confident in their actions. Anxiety-reducing techniques should therefore increase self-efficacy, but the individual's interpretation of arousal must also be considered.

Strategies to increase self-efficacy

Clearly, confidence is enhanced by good preparation, planning and a sense of optimism. Conversely, negative thinking and pessimism can undermine performance and limit progress. By expecting failure, you set your belief system to a negative channel and start favouring information that is consistent with these beliefs. During a training session you may have done some things well and struggled with others. When you have a negative mindset, you tend to focus only on the things that went badly, leading to what psychologists call negative self-fulfilling prophecies and psychological barriers.

Research into Bandura's self-efficacy model has found that self-efficacy alone cannot predict performance. Other aspects of performance, like skill level and incentives, have to be taken into consideration alongside cognitive processes. To increase a performer's self-efficacy, the following strategies should be included as part of their preparation:

- Ensure that the individual achieves performance accomplishments through manipulation of the environment (ensure that competitions can be won and training drills can be completed). At the elite level, it is more difficult to manipulate the environment to provide success for athletes. Imagine the response of the Australian cricket team if they were asked to take it easy so that the younger players of the English cricket team could gain success!

- Goal setting should be effective. This is achieved through ensuring that the individual's goals are realistic, thereby maximising the likelihood of success. The goals should emphasis individual performance targets, rather than group or team targets. This means that the goal setting must be done in consultation with the performer.

- Encourage the performer to use cognitive techniques to gain control of their mind. One way of achieving this is through self-talk. Performers say positive things to themselves, but not so much that it distracts them.

- Routines can also help to ensure that the individual achieves control over sporting performance. A tennis player may have a pre-competition routine, a routine between games and routines for between points.

■ Imagery and/or visualisation can also help, either as a means of perfecting performance or as a means of perfecting preparation for performance.

Link

For more information on imagery and visualisation, see Chapter 11 – The effect of anxiety on performance (pages 148 and 149).

Activity

Watch a video of an elite performer preparing to perform a closed skill. A tennis player serving, or a golfer addressing the ball would be good. Note how, each time, they go through a practised routine to control their anxiety.

■ Extrinsic motivation is known to produce short-term improvements in self-confidence, but only if the performance targets set by the coach are achievable. Thus, self-confidence can also be decreased by the use of extrinsic rewards, especially if the rewards begin to have a controlling effect.

The following are possible causes of a reduction in self-efficacy:

■ The coach's goal setting becomes too outcome oriented rather than performer oriented (e.g. the coach's desire to win a championship causes them to have unrealistically high expectations of the performer).

■ The feedback from the coach becomes too negative.

■ External rewards are restricted to the 'best' performers rather than being given to all who achieve their targets.

Activity

Consider the following scenarios and suggest whether each is likely to cause an increase or a decrease in self-efficacy. Explain each answer:

1 Your coach enters your team into a higher league in order to improve his prestige.

2 You are watching your friend successfully complete a gymnastics move.

3 You are told by your neighbours that you have the ability to beat an opponent whom you have never beaten before.

4 You feel nervous but relaxed prior to a big match.

■ The effect of an audience on performance

Social facilitation

Sport by its very nature is a social activity. Whether we are talking about a child's first tennis lesson, a kick-about game of soccer or the World Athletics Championships, the athlete's performance is on display for others to see. It is rare for an athletic event to be performed in social isolation. Even when other performers and spectators are not present, quite often some aspect of an individual's performance (time, distance) will be subjected to the scrutiny of others.

Zajonc (1965) called the behavioural effects due to the presence of others, social facilitation. Social facilitation entails two forces, audience and coaction. In this context, audience refers to the presence of passive observers. Coaction refers to the presence of others independently undertaking the same task (team mates or opponents).

Zajonc noticed that, in general, the presence of observers or coactors facilitated (helped) the performance of simple or well-learned tasks but inhibited (hampered) the acquisition of new skills. He explained that the presence of others could produce two types of effects:

■ improved performance on simple or well-learnt tasks

■ decreased performance on complex tasks or ones that had not been well learnt.

In summary, he found that the presence of others, as spectators or coactors, enhances the emission of dominant responses. Zajonc linked social facilitation to Hull's drive theory. The presence of others results in an increase in drive or arousal level. This increases the chance of the habit being strengthened and affecting performance. In other words, when the correct response is dominant (e.g. when a skill is mastered or is very simple), increased drive benefits performance. On the other hand, when the incorrect response tendencies are dominant (e.g. when a skill is complex or is not well learnt), increased drive hinders performance.

The reason that this might happen is distraction. When others are present, we are torn between concentrating on the task in hand and concentrating on other people. This leads to conflict, which increases arousal, which in turn can lead to a decrease in performance; Zajonc called this social inhibition.

> **■ Link**
>
> For definitions of social facilitation and social inhibition, see Chapter 10 – Arousal (page 139).

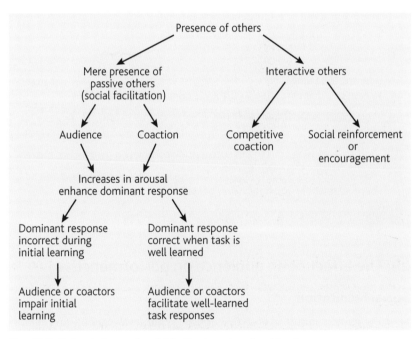

Fig. 13.2 *Zajonc's theory of social facilitation related to drive theory*

> **■ Activities**
>
> **1** Explain how, according to Zajonc, the presence of others may affect performance.
>
> **2** Using inverted U theory, explain why performance is likely to improve on simple or well-learnt tasks and decrease on complex tasks or tasks that have not been well learnt.

It has, however, become apparent that it may not just be the presence of others that is significant; the nature of their presence is more important. Specifically, social facilitation and social inhibition effects increase in proportion to the extent to which we perceive that those who are watching us are evaluating us!

Evaluation apprehension

Evaluation apprehension (Cotterell, 1968) is caused when we think people who are watching us are assessing our performance. An audience of one, who is perceived to be evaluating you, might have the same effect on your arousal level as 50 spectators! Even accomplished performers may crack if performing in front of people with high expectations of their performance or in a situation where evaluation apprehension is high.

Baron's distraction–conflict theory

Baron (1968) linked the presence of an audience to information processing, suggesting that an audience takes up much of what little attentional capacity we have. We may have sufficient attention left to cope with a simple task, but a complex task requires much more attention and, as the presence of an audience creates additional competing demands on our attention, which in turn increase arousal, performance is therefore affected. Baron also suggested that anything that distracts us (audience, lights, sounds, etc.) affects performance.

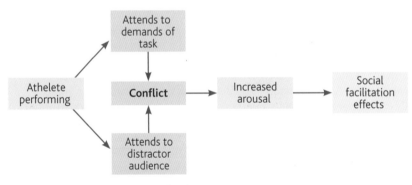

Fig. 13.3 *Baron's distraction–conflict theory*

Strategies to limit the effects of an audience on performance

The following strategies will help the performer cope with audience effects:

■ Because the presence of an audience may affect performance, it is probably best to learn new skills in the absence of an audience.

■ Once a performer has become accomplished at a skill, an audience should gradually be introduced; but this should be during training, rather than during competition.

■ Strategies, such as self-talk and imagery, should be developed to help the performer 'block out' the audience.

■ Prior to the actual performance, the performer should visualise performing the skill in front of an audience.

■ Self-efficacy should be improved through performance accomplishments, vicarious experiences or verbal persuasion.

Link

For a definition of evaluation apprehension, see Chapter 10 – Arousal (page 139).

Activity

Explain to a classmate the effect that knowing you are being watched by national selectors might have on your performance.

Activity

Explain, using Baron's distraction–conflict theory, how playing a racket game with a slightly torn grip might affect performance.

Link

For information on information processing, see *AQA Physical Education AS*, Chapter 8 – Information processing (pages 87–100).

■ Home-field advantage

There is a common feeling in the world of sport that the team playing a game at home has an advantage. While research has shown that the home team does indeed win the majority of contests, studies have not yet been able to pinpoint the potential causes and explanations for the phenomenon.

Generally speaking, the more crowd support a team receives, the better they perform. In many sports, fans take the bandwagon approach to choosing which team to support. Whichever team is winning at the time seems to be the team that everyone is following and rooting for. Conversely, if a team is having a losing season, they are abandoned. In some sports, fans tend to be more loyal to their home team, regardless of past and present performances. Audience support definitely increases players' confidence and motivation. Playing at home has also been shown to increase players' confidence: not only was individual players' self-efficacy found to be higher at home but there was also a positive effect on the team's collective confidence in its abilities.

Having an audience can create 'functional assertive behaviour' in the home team, causing them to play more aggressively, helping them towards their goal of winning. Remember that the presence of others creates arousal or drive which increases the likelihood of a performer exhibiting their dominant response. Because, in many sports that have audiences, the skills are well learnt, the dominant response should be the correct one, enhancing the quality of performance.

An audience can also have a negative influence on the visiting team, causing them to perform poorly, therefore increasing the home-field advantage. The support that is given to the home team is withheld from the visitors. Negative feedback from the crowd, such as taunts or booing, can invoke anxiety in the visiting team, causing them to perform beneath their capabilities. Another psychological aspect of home advantage is anxiety. Research has shown that somatic anxiety can be triggered by something in the environment, such as a particular stadium, and is usually highest around the start of the game. However, the most significant variable in this research was how the team rated the ability of its opposition. Cognitive anxiety and self-confidence are related to ability and expectations. Therefore, cognitive and somatic anxiety levels should be higher and self-confidence levels should be lower for away games when compared with home games.

Another effect that an audience has on performance is the 'choke' effect. When it comes to home field advantage, this only seems to happen in very important games, i.e. the more importance the game holds, the less likely the home team will be to win it. The bottom line is that fans don't necessarily want wins: they want championships. Audiences can be exceptionally supportive in important games but unintentionally increase the pressure felt by the athletes.

So why do some home teams still lose if home-field advantage is supposed to give a boost to their performances? Some stadiums are large and hard to fill. This can make the crowd look and sound very spread out and small, even with several thousand people in attendance, leading the players to feel a lack of support. Secondly, because the stadiums are so large, the crowd is relatively far away from the action of the game and therefore has less influence on the players.

It also seems that audience characteristics may play a role and influence the extent of home-team advantage:

- The more supportive the crowd is of the home-team and the more it is involved and attentive to the game, the better the home team's performance, and the more the performance of the visiting team is hindered.
- Crowd size can play a role in player performance: the bigger the crowd, the more likely the home-field advantage.
- The proximity of the crowd also affects home-field advantage: home teams have a greater advantage in grounds where the crowd is very close to the action than in grounds where the crowd is some distance from the pitch.
- The more hostile the crowd is to the visiting team, the greater is the audience's effect on home-field advantage.

Yet other research has shown that the distance travelled to an away fixture has an effect on the outcome of the match. The further the distance travelled by the visiting team, the more likely a home win is. There is also the influence that crowds may have on officials, with the home team being favoured.

However, performing in their home ground may have a negative effect on the home team, as performing in front of a large, evaluative and expectant crowd may increase the anxiety of the home performers and cause pressure that adversely affects their performance.

In summary, however, home-field advantage generally exists and is probably due to psychological aspects, such as increased confidence and reduced anxiety for the home team and reduced confidence and increased anxiety for the away team. The most advantageous scenario for home-field advantage would appear to be a stadium where the players are close to a large crowd that is supportive of the home team and very hostile to the visiting players.

☑ *You should now be able to:*

- define and explain self-confidence and self-efficacy
- explain the different ways of improving self-efficacy
- explain how the presence of an audience may affect performance
- explain the different strategies that may be used to reduce audience effects
- explain the phenomenon of home-field advantage and suggest circumstances in which it is more likely to occur.

1 Elite performers will train hard and develop high self-efficacy.

    (a)   What do you understand by the term 'self-efficacy'?   *(2 marks)*

    (b)   What strategies may be used to improve the self-efficacy of a performer?   *(5 marks)*

                                                      AQA, January 2007

2 Some weightlifters appear to perform well in front of an audience, while others seem to perform badly, 'choking' under the pressure. Use social facilitation theory to explain this observation.   *(7 marks)*

                                                      AQA, June 2004

3 Elite performers are invariably required to perform in front of an audience, even when undertaking physiological tests. The following diagram shows the possible effects, according to Zajonc (1965), of the presence of others on sports performance.

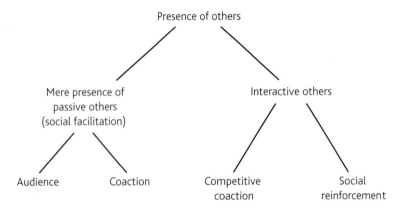

Fig. 13.4

    (a)   Explain, using appropriate examples, what is shown in the diagram and how the presence of others affects performance.   *(4 marks)*

    (b)   Recent research has pointed to distraction as being the main effect of the presence of others. How could performers reduce the effects of distraction?   *(3 marks)*

                                                      AQA, June 2004

4 Research has consistently suggested that in most sports there is a home-field advantage.

    (a)   What aspects of the audience contribute towards the likelihood that a home team will win?   *(3 marks)*

    (b)   In terms of psychology, what would appear to be the most likely cause of this home-field advantage?   *(4 marks)*

14 Group success

Key terms

Group: two or more individuals interacting with each other – or connected to each other via social relationships – often with a common objective.

Many elite performers participate as a member of a team, with their success being dependent upon the performances of others, and how well the members of the **group** perform together. The old saying that the 'sum is greater than the parts' was never more true than in the case of elite sport. Sporting history and literature is full of extraordinary successes gained by teams playing above themselves: FA Cup Finals being contested by teams from lower divisions, teams of semi-professional and amateur players performing in Cricket World Cups, and so on. Golfers who normally play solely for themselves find that when they come together as a Ryder Cup team they are subject to the most powerful of emotions and a determination to perform for the team. Performers in sports such as athletics and swimming, seemingly performing alone and for themselves, frequently rely on a support team to get them to the elite competition.

This chapter will begin by considering what we mean by a team or a group and how a team or group differs from a collection of individuals who happen to be in the same place at the same time. We shall then consider how groups and teams come about, what processes are at work that cause individuals to bond together and perform as a unit. We shall consider what makes for a successful team and the benefits that teamwork can bring to the group, i.e. how the sum becomes greater than the parts. Finally, we shall look at the factors that can interfere with the smooth running of the team, factors that cause a downturn in the team's performance, and how those problems can be overcome.

Group (or team) formation

First, we must be clear about our definition of a group. To be classified as a group, two or more individuals need to interact with each other, to be interdependent, to have a social relationship and to share a common objective. They will almost certainly have a sense of group identity and share norms and values. A collection of people at a bus stop does not

Fig. 14.1 *Bus queue – a group?*

■ AQA Examiner's tip

This whole chapter is concerned with the functioning of groups or teams. Spend time observing and analysing, either live or on TV or video, how teams work together and the efforts of individuals within the team. This will give you a range of examples to use in examination answers.

■ **Key terms**

Sociogram: a chart showing the inter-relationships within a group.

Fig. 14.2 *A group – interacting and sharing goals*

■ AQA Examiner's tip

Rather than asking you just to identify the various profiles within a sociogram, an examination question is more likely to ask you to discuss the effect that each of the profile types might have on team performance.

constitute a group. Although they are there for a common objective (one criterion for a group), they are almost certainly not interacting with each other (another criterion).

What about a crowd of supporters at a match? There is undoubtedly some interaction, and they are all there to see the match. But they do not all share the same objective; they do not have an interpersonal relationship with each other, nor will they all have the same norms or values – all necessary criteria for a group. On that basis, a crowd of supporters cannot be classified as a group.

Groups are often identified by means of a **sociogram**. A sociogram is a chart that shows the inter-relationships, connections and shared objectives that exist within a group.

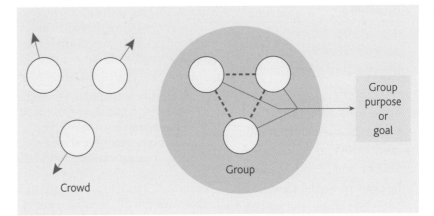

Fig. **14.3** *A sociogram*

In Figure 14.3, the broken lines represent the inter-relationships or interactions between individuals within the group; the large circle represents the group's sense of self-identity, whilst the unbroken lines represent the contributions to a common goal. A sociogram can also show the relationships within a group and whether all members of the group are closely bonded to each other.

■ **Activity**

Construct a sociogram of your learning group or a team that you are involved with.

1 Start by devising a questionnaire using the following questions:
   ■ Who do you most like in the team?
   ■ Who do you most often pass to in the team?
   ■ Which player would you most like to have in your team?

2 Identify team members by letter, and use those letters on the sociogram. It is vital that the responses are treated with great confidence, that no individual is aware of the responses of the others, and that no individual is identified by name, or could be identified.

3 Identify:
   ■ stars – highly popular members
   ■ isolates – infrequently chosen individuals
   ■ pairs – reciprocal partners
   ■ clusters – subgroups or cliques.

Your sociogram from the learning activity may look like the one in Figure 14.4.

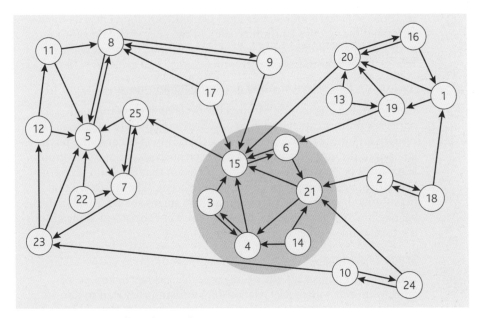

Fig. 14.4 *Sociogram of a rugby squad*

In Figure 14.4, the following conclusions can be drawn:

- The stars (highly popular members) would be numbers 5 and 15, especially 15 as he is selected by people outside his subgroup.
- Numbers 9, 18 and 23 would be identified as the isolates as they are infrequently chosen. Pairs (those that choose each other) are represented, for example, by numbers 15 and 6, 20 and 16, and 25 and 7.
- Finally the blue circle indicates a cluster, a subgroup within the squad. The point of doing a sociogram is that it allows the coach to examine the **group dynamics** that exist within the team.

Group dynamics is the study of groups and is also a general term for interactive processes that occur within a group. Because individuals interact and influence each other, groups develop a number of dynamic processes; these include:

- norms (the expected behaviour)
- roles that individuals play within the group
- relationships between individuals
- how the group develops
- the need to belong to the group
- the social influences on each other
- the effects on the behaviour of people within the group.

Each of the profile types in the sociogram (stars, isolates, pairs, clusters) can have an impact on the team's performance. Do people always try and pass to the stars, whether that is the most appropriate tactic or not? Does the contribution of an isolate get overlooked? How might a clique within the team have a detrimental effect? Do pairs exclude others and try and get things to work their way by mutually supporting each other?

> ### Key terms
>
> **Group dynamics:** the study of, and a general term for, the interactive processes that occur between people in a group.

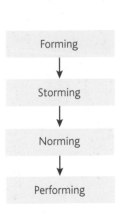

Fig. 14.5 *Tuckman's four stages of development*

Tuckman's model of group development

One of the leading theorists of group dynamics was Bruce Tuckman, who in 1965 proposed a four-stage model of group development. His model suggested that groups go through each of the stages while in a process of development, and as a consequence the norms, roles, individual relationships and effects on each other change and evolve.

Tuckman's four stages of group development are shown in Figure 14.5.

Groups and teams may go through the cycle or, if something adverse happens, revert to an earlier stage. A change of coach or captain or the retirement of experienced members of the group may cause the team to go back to the storming phase. It has been suggested that the storming stage must be actively re-engaged in to ensure that the team keeps on being creative and does not become complacent. The stages are not necessarily distinct: they may overlap. The stages are described in detail below; for consistency, 'team' has been used but the stages apply also to the formation of other types of group.

Stage 1 Forming

During the forming stage, the members of the team get to know each other, with some early social relationships evolving; they start to gain an understanding of the task or objective and begin to tackle the problem. At this stage, everyone is on their best behaviour and, although working independently of the others, is beginning to be aware of how the others in the team work. During this stage, a coach may act in quite a directive manner.

Summary of actions during the forming stage

- Get to know each other.
- Find out about the task or objective.
- Show respect for each other (but not working together).
- The coach tells the team what to do.

Stage 2 Storming

Next is the storming stage. As this point, ideas for solutions, put forward by individuals, begin to compete for adoption. The ideas of others are criticised or discarded; small alliances may form; rivalries and power struggles occur. Different types of leadership behaviour may become apparent. Less experienced members of the team may stick fiercely to their ideas and fail to see the value of others' input. More experienced team members will know the need for tolerance and patience if the team is to move forward. This stage can be difficult and unpleasant, and some teams founder here. Once again, the coach has a pivotal role in helping the team go forward.

Summary of actions during the storming stage

- Team members compete with each other, forming alliances; there may be power struggles.
- Different types of leader emerge.
- Less experienced members will not compromise.
- It is a difficult stage; the team may fail.
- The coach must help the team through this stage.

Stage 3 Norming

If the team survives the traumas of the storming stage, it will at some point go into the norming stage. During this stage, the members agree the rules, behaviours, methods of working together and things that are

■ Link

For information on types of leadership, see Chapter 15 – Leadership (pages 203–4).

'off limits' or taboo. Trust begins to develop and motivation levels are high as the team becomes more successful. Although the norms are important, they must not be so strong as to limit creativity or the need to be critical of team performance. Leaders will have emerged, and the team can begin to take more responsibility for decision making. The coach's role becomes less directive and more consultative.

Summary of actions during the norming stage

▨ Team members agree how to work together, rules develop; acceptable and non-acceptable behaviour are defined.

▨ There is development of trust, ability to accept criticism and new ideas.

▨ Leaders emerge and start to take responsibility for decision making.

▨ The coach becomes more of a consultant.

Fig. 14.6 *Even elite teams can go back to the storming phase*

Fig. 14.7 *A group at the performing stage*

Stage 4 Performing

In Tuckman's early model, the performing stage was the final one. This stage, which is not reached by all, is exhibited by high-performing teams, working as a unit and showing high levels of interdependence and motivation. The team and its members are knowledgeable, experienced and highly competent and very independent in terms of decision making. Leadership is devolved, consultation is the norm, but the team will accept direction in crisis situations. Dissent is encouraged as long as it is evaluative and the aim is better solutions or performance.

Summary of actions during the performing stage

▨ The team works as a unit, with high levels of interdependence and motivation.

▨ Experienced, skilled and knowledgeable team members are able to make decisions independently.

▨ Consultation is expected and leadership is devolved, but authority and direction are accepted in times of stress.

▨ Dissent is used in an evaluative manner to improve performance.

Stage 5 Mourning

Later, Tuckman introduced a fifth stage, sometimes known as the mourning stage. This occurs when the team breaks up because the task has been completed. After the 2003 Rugby World Cup, it is likely that the England team went through the mourning stage.

■ Activity

Try and observe a group of young players in a team – ideally a school team that has recently begun to play together.

1 What stage is the group of players at?

2 What behaviours have you observed that have led you to that conclusion?

3 Did the stage of formation of the group have a negative or positive effect on the team's performance?

4 If you were the coach of the team, how would you help the group move to the next stage or become more cohesive?

■ Cohesion

As the team or group moves through Tuckman's stages, it begins to develop what is known as **cohesion**. Teams that are successful are often described as being very cohesive. Carron *et al.* defined cohesiveness as:

> a dynamic process which is reflected in the tendency for a group to stick together and remain united in the pursuit of its goals and objectives, and/or for the satisfaction of its members' needs.

A. V. Carron et al., The measurement of cohesiveness in sport groups. In J. L. Duda (ed.) Advances in Sport and Exercise Psychology Measurement, 1998

Carron felt that individuals choose to stay together because either:

■ they find the group attractive and value being a member of the group or

■ the group helps them achieve an objective.

This was further developed into two clear categories of cohesion – **task cohesion** and **social cohesion**. When there is task cohesion, the team or group works well together to achieve a task, an objective or a goal, for example winning a cup, gaining promotion, etc. Social cohesion occurs when members of the team like each other and are drawn together socially, with a high level of social and interpersonal interactions. Most researchers have concluded that task cohesiveness is far more important than social cohesiveness. Widemeyer *et al.* (1993) and Carron (2002) found that there was a strong correlation between task cohesiveness and team success. Initially it was thought that this relationship only applied when looking at cooperative sports, such as basketball, football and hockey, and was much less evident in coacting sports such as bowling. Later research using the Group Environment Questionnaire (GEQ) has found that this is not the case, with similar levels of task cohesiveness found in cooperative activities (basketball, hockey, rugby) and coacting activities (athletics, swimming, gymnastics).

Carron proposed that cohesiveness is founded on four elements:

■ individual attractions to the group – task (how much a team member is involved with the group's task)

■ individual attractions to the group – social (how a team member feels about their personal social interactions with the group)

■ group integration – task (how much a team member feels that the group is focused and unified in its pursuit of an objective)

■ group integration – social (how much a team member thinks that the group is unified socially).

■ **Key terms**

Cohesion: the dynamic forces that cause a team to stick together.

Task cohesion: found in a group that is bound together in a drive to achieve a common objective, a focus on the task.

Social cohesion: found in a group that is bound together by social bonds, social attractiveness and relationships.

Examiner's tip

Whilst task cohesion is the most important, ensure that you mention both types of cohesion in a general answer about cohesiveness. The response to the question 'Does cohesion produce success or does success bring cohesion?' is: both!

Activity

1 Use a copy of the Group Environment Questionnaire as developed by Carron, Brawley and Widemeyer (1985). Ask members of one of your school or college teams to complete the questionnaire.

2 Analyse the results.

3 Discuss with the team members and the coach:

a the levels of cohesion

b if there are variations between task and social cohesion

c the four elements as defined by Carron.

Fig. 14.8 *A cohesive group – highly focused on the task*

In his 2002 research, Carron concluded that the first and third elements (listed above) are the most important, i.e. are those that contribute to team cohesiveness. This would also seem to be borne out by observations of highly successful teams. In the main, they demonstrate high levels of focus on the objective, and they seem able to bury personal differences or dislikes when engaged in the pursuit of the objective: they do not need to like each other to be able to work together. The former England football manager Sven-Göran Eriksson lists eight key attributes of an effective team and none has anything to do with social relationships:

1 A common vision

2 Clear and definite goals clearly linked to the vision

3 A shared understanding of strategy and tactics

4 Inner discipline – acting professionally together

5 Players with characteristics which complement each other

6 A division of roles among the players such that all team members are treated equally

7 Players who put the team's objectives and welfare before their own interests

8 A no blame culture – everyone taking responsibility for the whole team and accepting others' mistakes as long as people are doing their best.

Sven-Göran Eriksson, Sven-Göran Eriksson on Football, 2001

Carron proposed that there are four key antecedents to the development of cohesiveness. (An antecedent is something which comes before, or is pre-existing.) The antecedents to the development of cohesion are:

■ environmental factors
■ personal factors
■ leadership-based factors
■ team-based factors.

Their relationship to cohesion and group formation is shown in Figure 14.9.

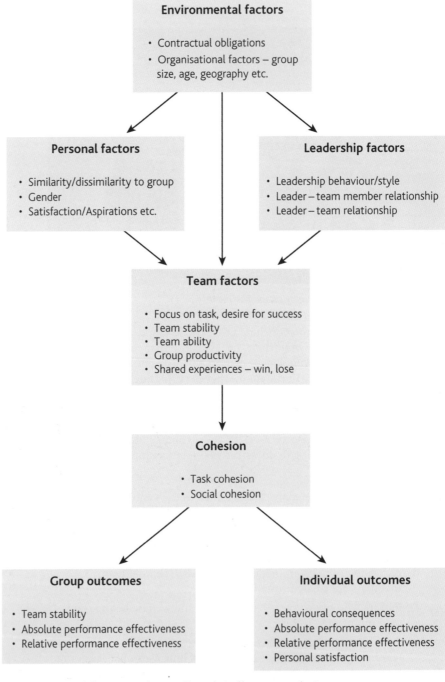

Fig. 14.9 *Carron's four antecedents and how they affect group cohesion*

The following strategies, which build on the work of Carron and Spinks (1991) and of Yukelson (1984), could be applied in a practical context by leaders and team members to achieve cohesion and contribute a great deal to team success:

- Maintain open communication channels, with open and honest discussion in an atmosphere of trust and respect.
- Set challenging but realistic individual, team and unit goals.
- Set and strive for agreed norms of behaviour.
- Ensure role clarity and acceptance of role by team members.
- Provide evidence of, and value, personal contributions by each team member.
- Reward exceptional individual contributions (e.g. player of the match).
- Strive for consensus and commitment by involving all in goal setting.
- Use team meetings to resolve conflicts and forge togetherness; travel together.
- Stay in touch with formal and informal leaders within the group; use them to implement necessary changes and avoid the development of cliques.
- Create a sense of distinctiveness (e.g. team uniforms, routines, etc.).
- Encourage self-sacrifice – performers who are more skilled help the less skilled; sacrifice personal success for team success.

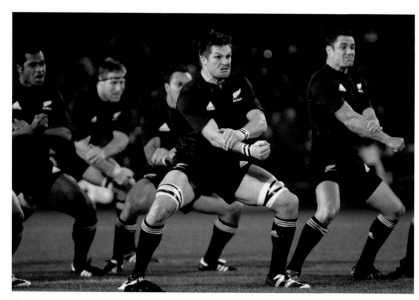

Fig. 14.10 *Team rituals develop cohesion*

AQA Examiner's tip

Questions frequently ask you to describe or explain a theoretical concept and then apply it to a performance situation. Practise this in relation to a team you know and include plenty of examples.

Group performance

Even in the most cohesive and well-led teams, there will be times when there is a drop in performance and the team becomes less than 'the sum of its parts'. In this section, we look at some reasons why that may happen.

Faulty group processes

Steiner (1972) proposed a theoretical model to relate the potential productivity or effectiveness of a team (based on the collective nature of its talents) and the actual productivity (how well they do). This model is expressed as a formula.

Actual productivity = Potential productivity – Losses due to faulty group processes

The term 'faulty group processes' refers to such things as lack of coordination, due to poor communication or strategies, and loss of motivation due to lack of recognition or benefit. Coordination losses come about when the group's timing or strategies do not function well; this may occur during set moves, say a hockey penalty corner or a rugby line-out.

Steiner also noted that the level of cooperation between players varies with the type of activity. For example, basketball and volleyball teams require a high level of interaction or cooperation, whilst athletics relay teams and cricket teams require less. Those sports where a higher level of cooperation is required are more likely to suffer from losses due to poor coordination than are activities where less cooperation occurs. In those highly interactive sports, a coach would therefore need to spend more time practising team drills and set plays to get the timing and player movement patterns right.

The Ringelmann effect

Motivational losses tend to occur more as group size increases. As a group grows larger, the contribution of individuals diminishes; this has an adverse effect on output or productivity and is known as the **Ringelmann effect**. Ringelmann observed the efforts of groups of men pulling on a rope. He found that in larger groups each individual pulled less hard than when in smaller groups. It was once thought that the Ringelmann effect occurs because coordinating the group's activities becomes more difficult as group size increases. Now, however, it is thought to be primarily the result of motivational losses. The Ringelmann effect is linked to **social loafing**.

> ### Key terms
>
> **Ringelmann effect:** the diminishing contribution of each individual as group size increases.
>
> **Social loafing:** loss of individual effort in a group due to a reduction in motivation.

Fig. 14.11 *Could the Ringelmann effect be happening here?*

Social loafing

After researching the effect of group processes on group performance, Latané *et al.* (1973) coined the phrase 'social loafing'. They concluded that the performance drop was due to motivational losses. Some people in a group may feel that their own personal contributions have little effect so try less hard; others may perceive that others are not trying hard so they feel justified in working less hard themselves. For either reason, individuals feel less motivated to work hard and are more likely to engage in social loafing. Latané noted that social loafing was eliminated or dramatically reduced when individuals believed that their efforts and contributions were monitored or noticed.

This identifiability factor also goes some way to explaining why social loafing is less prevalent in coaction situations; indeed as the number of coactors increases there is less evidence of social loafing affecting group performance. This is because there are more people to observe an individual's performance, whereas in a cooperative, interactive situation the increase in numbers and therefore interactions can mask an individual's efforts.

Activity

Observe a team playing an invasion game such as football, hockey, basketball, etc.

1. Can you indentify any opportunities or situations when social loafing, or other faulty group processes, could occur?

2. Can you identify any players engaging in social loafing?

3. What is it about their behaviour that leads you to this conclusion?

4. Is this due to motivational or coordination faults?

5. If you were the captain or the coach of the team, how would you overcome this problem?

AQA Examiner's tip

Remember that Steiner's faulty group processes, the Ringelmann effect and Latané's social loafing are inter-related. A full answer would expect you to be able link them together.

■ Achieving a team's potential

An essential part of a coach's role is helping a team to reach its potential, play to the best of its collective ability and be more than the sum of its parts. A coach could employ a range of strategies to overcome coordination losses and the motivational losses that occur as a result of social loafing.

Link

The role of the coach is covered in more detail in Chapter 15 – Leadership (pages 201–6).

Reducing coordination losses

■ As part of team selection, take note of individual interactive skills – timing, vision, ability to learn set plays etc. Clive Woodward, coach of the England team that won the 2003 Rugby World Cup, brought in a vision coach.

■ Engage in drills that develop interactive play – set plays, passing drills, etc.

■ Ensure that all members of the team understand their role and how it relates to, or interacts with, other roles.

Reducing motivational losses

■ Ensure that each individual's contribution is noted and identified – use team and match statistics, videos of games, etc.

■ Develop both intrinsic and extrinsic motivation via praise, acknowledgement of the importance of a player's role and contribution, and rewards (such as player of the match, tackle of the day, etc.).

■ Be aware of situations or occasions where social loafing may occur or is a danger.

■ Ask all team members to acknowledge and value the contribution of other members – especially those doing the less glamorous roles.

■ Develop team cohesion, especially task cohesion, by ensuring that the team objective is clearly understood as is who must do what to achieve that goal.

■ No matter how hard a coach works to enable a team to work effectively together, in most sports they can have little effect once the game has started, and here the role of captain becomes vital. An effective captain can do much to ensure that the team's effectiveness is not diminished by social loafing or by other faulty processes.

■ Link

For information on intrinsic and extrinsic motivation, see *AQA Physical Education AS*, Chapter 9 – Learning and performance (page 103).

Fig. 14.12 *A successful team is more than the sum of its parts*

Setting the scene for success

To succeed as a team requires more than just bringing together the most talented individuals. Sport is littered with examples of managers, directors or rich philanthropic owners who have failed to achieve success despite bringing together the most expensive talent they can find; having done so, they expected the league and cup trophies to follow but took no steps to ensure success. The best coaches and managers understand that it is their role to create the environment in which each individual can fulfil their promise but in concert with others and in coordination with each other. In an environment where each member of the team trusts their team mates to carry out their role and understands the value of their own role, the likelihood of individual and group success is increased.

☑ *You should now be able to:*

- differentiate between a group and a crowd or loose collection of individuals

- describe the developmental stages that a collection of individuals goes through to become a high-performing group or team

- understand how you can help the group-formation process

- understand what is meant by cohesion and the difference between task and social cohesion

- describe a range of strategies to develop cohesion

- understand the reasons why a team may not be fulfilling its potential and may be less than the sum of its parts

- apply a range of strategies to overcome faulty group processes such as social loafing.

1   Sport performers often work as groups or teams.

       (a)   What criteria would you use to determine if a collection of individuals is a group?   *(3 marks)*

       (b)   A coach decides to use a sociogram to help get players to work together more effectively. How might use of a sociogram achieve this?   *(4 marks)*

2   A keen hockey coach decides to set up a new team and advertises for players; approximately 15 people join.

       (a)   What stages would these players go through when going from being individuals to becoming a cohesive team?   *(2 marks)*

       (b)   What strategies could the coach use to help in this group-formation process?   *(5 marks)*

3   Successful teams are said to show good cohesion.

       (a)   What is meant by the terms 'social cohesion' and 'task cohesion'?   *(2 marks)*

       (b)   The manager of a team was concerned that members of the team did not get on well together. Was he right to be concerned? Give reasons for your answer.   *(3 marks)*

       (c)   How might the manager develop task cohesion?   *(2 marks)*

4   It is often said that highly successful teams are greater than the sum of their parts.

       (a)   A team of highly talented individuals may not be performing as well as they might. Explain the group processes that may be causing this to happen.   *(3 marks)*

       (b)   With reference to group processes, what actions might the coach take to improve the performance of the team in this situation?   *(4 marks)*

15 Leadership

We have seen in the previous chapter that, when a group is involved in sport, the way they behave and interact will be in some way affected by others in the group. Probably the most important 'other' will be the leader. In sport, we tend to emphasise the importance of the coach, the trainer and the captain, praising them for their contribution to the team or for their individual performance.

Barrow (1977) defined leadership as 'the behavioural process influencing individuals and groups towards set goals'. The leader is expected to give clear guidance to the rest of the group, influencing their decisions and directing their performance towards their goal. Leadership has many dimensions including decision-making processes, motivational techniques, giving feedback, establishing interpersonal relationships and directing a group or team effectively. In summary, the leader knows where the group is going (its goals and objectives) and provides the direction and resources to help it get there.

What makes leaders effective?

It is not always the best player who makes the best leader, in much the same way as the best footballer does not necessarily become the best manager. Certain qualities are expected from an effective leader; these include:

- good communication skills
- effective decision making
- enthusiasm
- knowledge of the activity
- empathy/understanding of others
- clear goals or vision of what is needed
- charisma
- ability to motivate/inspire
- good organisational skills
- confidence.

Martens (1987) suggested that effective leadership depends on four factors:

- the leader's qualities
- the style of leadership that the leader adopts
- the type of situation involved
- the follower's qualities.

There is no one effective form of leadership. Good leadership depends on the interaction between personal factors (the leader's style and qualities) and situational factors (the follower's qualities and the situation). A coach need not necessarily adopt one leadership style; different styles can be blended. The challenge for the leader is to adopt a style that best suits the circumstances. The style that is appropriate depends on situational factors and the follower's qualities.

Many leadership qualities are learned over a period of time; some may appear to be natural. The question of whether leaders are 'made' or 'born'

Fig. 15.1 *The four components of effective leadership*

has interested psychologists. If leaders are born, this would suggest that leaders have certain personality traits. Early ideas on this theme (the 'Great Man' theory) suggested that good leaders in one field, such as sport, should, because of their leadership traits, become good leaders in other fields, such as politics.

Although there may be some similarities in leadership traits – leaders tend to be intelligent, articulate, ambitious, assertive, etc. – there has never been sufficient evidence that certain traits are common to all leaders to justify the idea that leaders are born. As an alternative, research has tended to study the behaviours of leaders rather than the traits of leaders.

Leaders need to be aware of the different situations in which they are involved. For example, are they dealing with a team or an individual? What is the size of the team? How much time is available? Is the activity interactive or coactive?

The characteristics of the follower or followers are also important in determining how effective the leadership is. There is an important interaction between the characteristics and style of leaders and those of followers.

Leaders tend to be chosen, either by being voted for by their peers or by being selected by others. It is usual for leaders to be appointed by someone in authority; these are called **prescribed leaders**. For example, in health clubs, the owners choose the manager; in schools, the headteacher chooses the teacher; in football, the manager chooses the captain; in athletics, the national governing body chooses the team captain. Prescribed leaders are thought to be good for bringing in new ideas, but they may tend to be somewhat disruptive to group harmony.

Sometimes, however, leaders simply emerge from the group and take charge (**emergent leaders**), as in the case of the captain of a local club team. Many emergent leaders are more effective than prescribed leaders, because they have the respect and support of the team members. They probably have recognisable leadership skills or high levels of ability in their particular sport. Emergent leaders are thought to be good for a group as they maintain group harmony, but they tend not to bring any fresh ideas.

■ Leadership as an interactive process

Researchers have tried to identify the special skills that make an effective leader. Some researchers have adopted a behavioural approach

Activity

What qualities would you expect leaders to have?

Link

For more information, on coaction, see Chapter 13 – Confidence (page 181).

Activity

A leader needs to be sensitive to the specific situation and environment. What types of different situational factors might affect the way a leader acts?

Key terms

Prescribed leader: a leader who is appointed by an external source.

Emergent leader: a leader who comes from within the group through possession of some skills.

to leadership, suggesting that the behaviours that make a leader effective can be learned. However, most psychologists now propose an interactional model of leadership, where successful leadership is thought to be determined by the interacting characteristics of the leader (leadership style), the task (situational characteristics) and the team members (member characteristics).

These theories of leadership suggest that, because of the interaction of the three characteristics, there is no one leadership style that makes a leader effective and leaders cannot be predicted by their personalities. Effective leadership fits the specific situation involved. Some leaders function better in certain situations than in others. For example, football managers can be sacked from one job because of poor results and then immediately find success at another club; or one manager is sacked, then another takes his place and finds success with exactly the same group of players.

Lastly, leadership styles can change and good leaders will change their style of leadership to suit a particular situation. Fiedler (1967) identified situations when a certain style of leadership would be most effective.

Fiedler's contingency model

Fiedler's contingency model suggests that leaders should decide whether to be task or person oriented in their leadership style, and that the decision should depend on the 'favourableness' of the situation. A **task-oriented leader** focuses on the performance of the team. For example, in a sports club facing relegation, the leader would focus on what needs to be done for the team to win its forthcoming games. A **person-oriented leader** develops interpersonal relationships, keeps open lines of communication and maintains positive social interactions (this is sometimes referred to as relationship-oriented leadership).

Leaders can change from a person-oriented to a task-oriented style (or vice versa) depending on the situation. Task-oriented leadership is best when the situation requires discipline, members have a high level of ability, their motivation is high and there are good resources to work with. Person-oriented leadership is best when physical resources and external support are limited. Task-oriented leadership is required when there is poor discipline in a group of low ability, resources are limited and the task is unstructured. Thus leaders need to adapt their style to meet the demands of the situation.

◼ Three leadership styles

However, although successful leadership usually requires some flexibility of style, some leaders tend to favour one of three styles:

- The **autocratic style of leadership** is leader centred, employing the 'command' approach and stressing the personal authority of the leader. Autocratic leaders are characteristically task oriented, rarely getting involved with group members on a personal level. Autocratic approaches are most likely to be effective in team sports, when greater numbers of performers are involved.

- A leader with a **democratic style of leadership** employs a more cooperative approach and is more person oriented. The leader only makes a decision after consulting the group. Democratic leaders strive to keep open lines of communication, maintain positive social interactions and ensure that everyone is involved. Democratic styles of leadership are more likely to suit individual sports and coaching situations.

◼ Key terms

Task-oriented leader: a leader who concentrates on setting goals and completing the task as quickly as possible.

Person-oriented leader: a leader who concentrates on developing interpersonal relations within the group.

Autocratic style of leadership: in sport, a style that is usually win oriented, very structured and task oriented.

Democratic style of leadership: in sport, a style that is athlete centred, cooperative and person oriented.

AQA Examiner's tip

In simple terms, leaders need to adapt their style of leadership to suit the situation and group members.

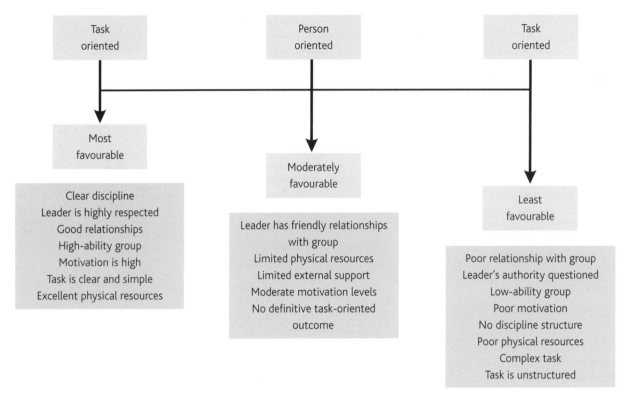

Fig. 15.2 *Fiedler's contingency model of leadership*

■ Key terms

Laissez-faire style of leadership:
the leader makes few decisions,
provides little feedback and lets
the group do as it wishes.

AQA Examiner's tip

To a large extent, the concepts
of 'task-oriented leadership'
and 'autocratic style' are
interchangeable. (Similarly, a
person-oriented leader adopts
a democratic style.) Exam mark
schemes tend to accept these terms
as synonyms.

■ The **laissez-faire style of leadership** is one in which the group members
get on with the task by themselves and the leader generally plays a
passive role. This style of leadership is not recommended in sport.

The amount of time available for decision making is a factor in
determining which style would be most appropriate. A democratic style is
only workable when there is ample time to make decisions; an autocratic
style may be more appropriate on the field of play when there is limited
time. A democratic style better suits off-field coaching or social situations
when time is not so much of a problem.

■ Leadership in sport

Chelladurai (1980) argues that effective leadership can and will vary,
depending on the characteristics of the athletes and the constraints of
the situation. Sports leaders have therefore to be more dynamic and
changeable in relation to the characteristics of the situation. He suggested
that there are various types of leadership behaviour and developed the
Leadership Scale for Sports to measure leadership behaviours. The
Leadership Scale for Sports has five dimensions:

■ Training and instruction behaviour – a structured approach to training
  improves performance through emphasising hard training, providing
  technical instruction on skill development and coordinating the
  strategies of team members.

■ Democratic behaviour – the involvement of the group in decision
  making about the group's goals, practice methods and tactics is
  emphasised.

■ Autocratic behaviour – the leader emphasises their own authority by
  making the decisions and stressing their personal authority.

- Social support behaviour – the leader has concerns over the wellbeing of the group and emphasises the warm, welcoming atmosphere within the group. The leader's behaviour tends not to be dependent on the individuals' performances.
- Rewarding behaviour – the leader emphasises and reinforces good performances through positive feedback and thus depends on individual performances.

The results of Chelladurai's research are shown in Figure 15.3.

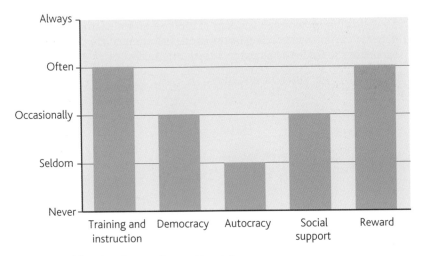

Fig. 15.3 *Athletes' preferences for teaching styles*

Who coached you, how they coached you and the specific situation involved will probably have influenced how you felt in your last involvement in an activity. In general, the following apply:

- Novices prefer more extrinsic feedback in the form of rewards, whereas experts tend to prefer a more democratic approach with social support behaviour.
- Performers involved in individual sports tend to prefer democratic coaching and social support, whereas members of teams prefer training and instruction through autocratic coaching.
- Females prefer a democratic style, whereas males prefer a more autocratic style.
- Older performers prefer a democratic style with social support and training and instruction, whereas all performers seem to value rewarding behaviours.

Group members also have preferences for specific leader behaviours. This is known as the **preferred behaviour** of the leader. Some group members might want to stress achievement, others affiliation. Factors such as the age, gender, skill level and experience of the group influence its preferences, dictating the type of guidance, social support and feedback preferred. Sometimes, group members come to prefer a certain type of leader, usually the one they have become used to.

Chelladurai's research shows that members of a group prefer coaching that emphasises skill development through hard training, where positive feedback reinforces good performances. Certain situations demand a certain type of behaviour from a leader. Chelladurai called this the leader's **required behaviour**. Coaches are expected to behave in certain ways with, for example, their players, the media, the spectators and other coaches.

Key terms

Preferred behaviour: behaviour of the leader that is demanded by the group members.

Required behaviour: behaviour of the leader that is demanded by the situation.

Key terms

Actual behaviour: the behaviour shown by the leader.

The **actual behaviour** is the behaviours that the leader exhibits, such as being responsive or considerate. According to Chelladurai, the leader's characteristics, such as personality, ability, and experience, affect these behaviours directly. Actual behaviour is thought to be indirectly affected by group preferences and what the situation dictates. For example, a Premiership team usually has winning as a goal, and its manager would probably adopt task-oriented behaviours, because the team and the situation dictate this.

How well required behaviour, preferred behaviour and the leader's actual behaviour match affects both performance and satisfaction. Performance and satisfaction are not independent of each other: for example, if athletes are task oriented, satisfaction and performance are both enhanced if the leader's behaviour is task oriented too.

Chelladurai's multidimensional model of leadership is shown in Figure 15.4.

AQA Examiner's tip

You may need to interpret Chelladurai's model of leadership. In simple terms, this involves the actual behaviour of the leader, the behaviour required by the situation and the preferred behaviour of the members. If they match, good performances follow.

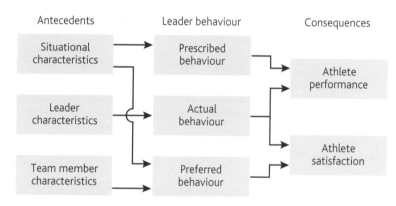

Fig. 15.4 *Chelladurai's model of leadership*

As we saw, Chelladurai suggests that athlete satisfaction and performance depend on three types of leader behaviour:

- required
- preferred
- actual.

The situational characteristics, leader characteristics and members' characteristics lead to these three kinds of behaviour and are therefore called antecedents. Chelladurai theorises that a positive outcome – optimal performance and group satisfaction – will occur if the three aspects of leader behaviour agree. In other words, if the leader shows the appropriate behaviour for that particular situation, and these behaviours match the preferences of the group members, members will achieve their best performance and will feel most satisfied.

Activity

Use Chelladurai's model to explain what type of leadership would be most beneficial to an AS Level student who has just enrolled at a college and is playing in a trial game of basketball for the college.

☑ *You should now be able to:*

- explain the qualities that are required to become a good leader
- explain the different types of leader
- explain the effectiveness of the different styles of leadership
- describe how leaders are appointed
- explain the need for leaders to be adaptable according to Fiedler's and Chelladurai's models.

1   Team-game players often look to their leader to assist their performance.

    (a)   Distinguish between 'emergent' and 'prescribed' leaders.   *(2 marks)*

    (b)   Figure 15.5 shows three main factors affecting leadership.

Fig. 15.5

Using Figure 15.5, discuss the idea that leaders need to be adaptable in their approach.   *(5 marks)*

AQA, June 2005

2   The members of a sports team are usually led by a captain, manager and/ or coach. Fiedler (1967) suggested that such leaders had one of two types of leadership style.

    (a)   Identify Fiedler's two leadership styles and describe the situations in which each type of leader would be most effective.   *(4 marks)*

    (b)   'In order to be effective, leaders need to be sensitive to the characteristics of the group members.' (B. Woods, *Applying Psychology to Sport*. Hodder and Stoughton, 1998).

    (c)   Explain how leadership styles should be adapted depending on the different characteristics, such as size, age, gender and skill level, of a team.   *(3 marks)*

AQA, June 2006

3   Success in sport is often linked to effective leadership. Fiedler (1967) suggested that the effectiveness of a leader depended on the extent to which the leader's style fitted the situation that the team were in.

    (a)   Name the two styles of leader that Fiedler identified and describe the different situations where each style is most effective.   *(5 marks)*

    (b)   Chelladurai suggested additional factors, other than the leader's characteristics and different situations, which must be taken into account when assessing the effectiveness of leadership. Identify and explain one of these factors.   *(2 marks)*

AQA, January 2004

4   A hockey coach has worked with the same squad for a number of years, taking them from the youth section through to adult.

(a)   Discuss, in terms of leadership, how this relationship between the coach and squad would have developed over this period of time.

(3 marks)

(b)   Figure 15.6 shows Chelladurai's multidimensional model of leadership. Explain, with reference to Chelladurai's multi-dimensional model of leadership, how the captain can affect the quality of the performance of the team.

(4 marks)

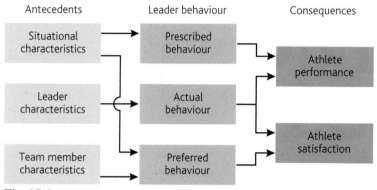

Fig. 15.6

AQA, June 2003

Evaluating contemporary influences

Introduction

Elite performers, despite their physical and psychological gifts and attributes, cannot succeed in isolation from society, whether local, national or global, and this section considers the importance of the social context in which elite performers operate.

We begin by taking a look at what we mean by elite sport and how we as a nation find, support and develop our elite performers. Chapter 16 opens by examining what is meant by the term 'World Games' and the pathway that the individual treads to reach that level. The chapter examines in detail the various agencies, governmental and non-governmental, that contribute to the support and development of elite performers. Chapter 17 gives us a historical perspective on the development of sport, tracing its development from the spread of rational recreation in the public schools of the 19th century to the global phenomenon that it has become. We also engage in an in-depth analysis of the ethics and philosophy of elite sport – the Olympic ideal, the amateur–professional divide and the bonds that exist and are sometimes broken when we play at the highest levels.

Although we have expectations of those who play sports and elite sport performers in particular, our heroes sometimes let us down. Chapter 18 takes a look at the darker side of sport – the use of drugs, the impact of hooliganism and violence, and the increasing use of civil and criminal law to resolve issues in sport. The section concludes with the impact of the commercial and technological world – sponsorship, the media, clubs as global businesses – and the impact of technology on spectators, players and officials.

Sport at the highest level is a high-stakes element of the entertainment and business world but nevertheless is able to stir us with fantastic feats of strength, endurance and determination. Despite knowing that there are some who cheat their way to the top, we can still be excited by the Olympic message and the numerous examples of sportsmanship and fair play. Sport, like all human endeavours, reflects the world in which it exists, for better or for worse.

16 Elite performers and World Games

In this chapter you will:

- understand the nature and characteristics of World Games

- explain the role of World Games in society and the impact they have on individuals and the country

- understand the social, cultural and personal characteristics that are required to become an elite performer

- describe the principles behind elite-performer development

- understand the role of UK national agencies in developing elite performers.

Key terms

National Lottery: a national form of gambling, regulated by the government, where the proceeds are divided between prize money and good causes such as sport.

World Games: sport competitions involving individuals, clubs or national teams in world, continental or regional championships.

Link

For a definition of elite sport, see Chapter 4 – The elite performer: food, supplements and performance-enhancing drugs (page 53).

AQA Examiner's tip

World Games are events above national level (i.e. international); elite level would include competing at national level.

To be able to perform at an Olympic Games or in a World Cup match is the dream and aspiration of many sportspeople. Not only do countries and their citizens desire sporting success but also many jobs may depend on such success. Thousands of young and not so young people in the United Kingdom strive to fulfil their potential and play or perform at the highest level. As a nation, we agonise any time we fail to win a cricket test series, fail to qualify for European tournament finals or see our favourite marathon runner unable to run. We spend a great deal of money from taxation or the **National Lottery** on supporting the development of elite performers, and much time and energy has been devoted to putting in place better structures for talent identification and development. We have examined all those countries that seem to be more successful than we are and over the last 20 years have engaged in a radical shake-up of our sport infrastructure so that we may be a more successful nation on the stage of world sport.

In this chapter, we shall begin by studying the nature of **World Games**: what we mean by the term 'World Games', their characteristics and the impact that they have on individual people and national economies, and the social effects of developing national self-confidence or feelings of self-worth. We shall then go on to look at the general principles underpinning the identification and development of sporting talent, and the individual, social and cultural prerequisites for developing elite performers. Finally, we shall untangle the web of national policies, strategies and programmes that are designed to help those with talent, and look at the organisations that are responsible for implementing those plans.

World Games

In the AQA specification, the term 'World Games' is used to describe the level of competition engaged in by elite performers beyond their own national boundaries. It implies a coming together of elite teams or individuals in a range of elite sport competitions. To allow students to focus more on what might be needed when answering examination questions, the following paragraphs identify the nature and characteristics of World Games as they apply to the AQA specification.

What are World Games?

For the AQA specification, the term 'World Games' refers to any sporting competition that takes place at world, continental or regional level, either on a single-sport or a multi-sport basis. Such games may involve individuals, clubs or national teams, and performers with a disability.

Single-sport

Examples of single-sport World Games include:

- football – the FIFA World Cup
- hockey – the World Hockey Champions Trophy (men and women)
- swimming – the Oceania Swimming Championships (Oceania – Pacific Ocean countries)
- rugby – the Heineken European Rugby Cup

- gymnastics – the African Gymnastics Championships
- volleyball – the European Champions League
- badminton – the International Badminton Association for the Disabled (IBAD) European Championships.

Fig. 16.1 *Beijing Olympics 2008 World Games*

Multi-sport

Examples of multi-sport World Games include:

- the Olympic Games
- the Paralympic Games
- the Commonwealth Games
- the Pan American Games
- the Special Olympics Latin America Games
- the All-Africa Games.

> **Link**
>
> The Olympic Games are discussed more fully in Chapter 17 – The Olympic ideal and modern sport (pages 247–8).

> **Activity**
>
> Take an example of a multi-sport and a single-sport international championship and give a breakdown of its characteristics. You should include such details as:
>
> - number of teams or competitors involved
> - number of sports involved (if multi-sport)
> - structure of competition (pools, knock-out, etc.)
> - television audience
> - cost of staging the championship
> - length of the event.

Characteristics of World Games events

The characteristics of World Games events will vary with the popularity and commerciality of the sport and the economic and physical resources available. For example, the Olympic Games involves 11,000 athletes,

Fig. 16.2 *Success at the highest level – a national effect*

■ **Key terms**

Sponsorship: provision of funds or other forms of support to an individual or event in return for some commercial return.

3.5 million spectators, with costs ranging between £2.3bn (Sydney) and £20bn (Beijing) and 50,000 volunteers to help run the events; it has a world-wide television audience. For international competitions, on the other hand, performers pay their own transport and accommodation costs and only friends, family and others involved in the sport know that it is taking place.

However, we can identify a range of characteristics that would be typical of World Games. World Games:

- involve elite performers
- often require pre-event qualification or meeting a pre-set standard
- become a shop window for the city or country holding the event
- are often highly commercialised, involving high levels of **sponsorship** and the selling of franchises
- if large, will involve significant infrastructure development (transport, permanent living accommodation, hotels, health care, etc.)
- are likely to involve the development of sport facilities for the competition events and training
- often involve large numbers of spectators.

■ What impact do World Games have?

Owing to the size and scope of World Games competitions and the commercial, social and political interests that surround them, they now have a significant effect on participants, spectators and on the countries that host and participate in the various competitions. Few elite competitions are free from the tug-of-war between commercial interests and the interests of the performers; few governments ignore the opportunity to use the success of their international performers to advance their own political interests; and millions and sometimes billions of people become part of the theatre via their television screens. We shall now examine the impact that World Games have on individuals (participants and spectators), the impact on nations and the way that national governments make use of these international competitions.

Activity

1 Imagine that you are participating at the London 2012 Olympics. Prepare a newspaper article, describing (using words and pictures) what it might feel like to compete in the final event of your sport and win a medal; you should consider the following:
   - final preparations
   - the actual event
   - what would happen afterwards
   - the experiences you would share with others
   - how it might affect your life in the future.

2 Print your article and those of the rest of your group and pin the articles up on a board, or compile an online newspaper.

Impact on individuals

World Games impact upon individuals as either performers or spectators:

- Performers wish to become the best; they are highly motivated to succeed.

- They wish to compete against other elite performers and to test themselves against the best.
- They wish to fulfil their potential, to make the most of their abilities.
- They may be driven by personal gain, a desire to make their living as a professional performer.
- They gain pride and satisfaction from representing their country or nation.
- They strive to meet the expectations of family, peers, teachers or coaches.
- As players or spectators, individuals may have been inspired by role models.
- Spectators feel a pride in their country after successful international sporting performances.

Fig. 16.3 *An elite performer – a combination of many factors*

Achieving the ambition of performing at a World Games will require great sacrifices and may mean giving up many aspects of a normal life. Those attempting to reach elite level often have to give up or restrict their social life and even put other career development plans on hold, sometimes cutting short their time in school or higher education and giving up or postponing the opportunity to gain qualifications. Some individuals delay starting a family or move away from friends or family to live near training facilities or their coach. All these sacrifices may be in vain as only a small percentage of those who aspire to reaching elite level are able to do so. There are many reasons why an individual may not reach an elite level, despite having the necessary ability:

- Individuals may lack the self-discipline to make the sacrifices needed.
- They may not have sufficient motivation to keep pushing performance boundaries.
- They may not receive the necessary financial, coaching or technical support.
- They may suffer a career-ending injury.

- They may decide to fulfil themselves as individuals via another career or life path and participate in sport at a lower level, perhaps part time.
- The combination of the highly competitive demands of elite sport and the high levels of motivation of those who compete, or aspire to compete at that level, has led some performers to use illegal methods, such as performance-enhancing drugs. Should a performer use such methods, they run the risk of being caught and the consequent ban from competition, loss of sponsorship or other forms of financial support and loss of status and reputation; and of course there may be side effects that are detrimental to their health.

Impact on the country

International sport has a significant impact on the cultural, social and economic life of a country.

Cultural effects

Many countries place significant emphasis on being successful and on the desire to be successful; competitive sport seems to be a part of their national character. This is demonstrated by the resources that are devoted to achieving that success, the impact that international success or failure has on the nation's mood, often reflected through the media, and the levels of primary and secondary spectator support when national teams or elite clubs are playing. International teams or performers who do well become national heroes; those deemed to have failed can be vilified and scorned.

Social effects

Socially, international sport can help unify a country. The West Indian cricket team, particularly when it was being very successful during the 1970s to 1990s, had the effect of bringing together into a more socially cohesive unit people from the very many different islands, which often thought of themselves as mini-states. In the run-up to the Beijing Olympics, the international criticism of the Chinese government's record on human rights had the effect of unifying the Chinese people behind their government. Individuals who had previously been publicly acclaimed for speaking out in favour of more democracy and individual freedoms found themselves isolated and rejected. The sense of national pride about staging the Olympic Games provided a strong, if somewhat temporary, unifying force. Conversely, the need to look unified in the eyes of the world can cause a government to clamp down on human rights and dissent (see page 215).

Economic effects

International sport can have a significant economic effect on a country. Many nations now seek to stage large international sports tournaments, such as the Olympic Games, World Cups and international club tournaments or finals. They do this because staging the event:

- has a 'shop window' effect, placing the country in the international limelight
- encourages inward financial investment
- has a beneficial effect on tourism
- provides a stimulus for the development of sports facilities
- can be used to increase levels of participation in sport and physical activity

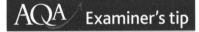

Link

The use of performance-enhancing drugs is discussed more fully in Chapter 18 – Deviance in sport (pages 264–70).

AQA Examiner's tip

Questions relating to World Games and the Olympics will generally require a discussion about the benefits **and** the disadvantages of staging them.

Fig. 16.4 *Politics and sport – never far apart*

- provides a stimulus for infrastructure development, for example roads, public transport and social housing
- can provide a focus for regional regeneration.

Whilst there can be many benefits to hosting an international sports event, many countries and cities have encountered significant difficulties:

- The cost of the event can far exceed revenue, leaving either the government or the local community with debts to pay off in the future.
- The legacy facilities that are left are not always in the right location, or of the right design, to be used successfully in the future.
- If there were construction delays in the run-up to the event, there may be adverse comment in the international press, damaging the reputation of the host nation.
- If the event has not been well run and does not go smoothly, there can be damaging press coverage.

Impact on the government

No international event can be bid for or brought to a successful conclusion without the active support of the government of the host nation or city. Governments will generally support the bidding, planning and bringing to fruition of the staging of an international event because they believe that the event will bring long-term benefits to the country. A government may be keen to stage the event to demonstrate the effectiveness of its political philosophy. During the Cold War of the 1960s and 1970s, both the USA and the USSR staged the Olympics and used them to promote their different political philosophies and systems. More recently, Beijing in China won the right to stage the 2008 Olympics. At the time, the Chinese government stated that this would help with the development of human rights and yet Amnesty International constantly reported that as the Games approached more and more dissidents and protestors were arrested.

A government's own political future can be influenced: when a country wins the right to stage an international event, there is almost always a feeling of joy and success within the country. The ceremony at which the winner of the bid to stage the 2012 Olympics was announced was televised worldwide. In the UK, huge television screens showed the broadcast and large crowds awaited the result. When it was announced that London had won the bid there was much celebration. In the aftermath of the announcement, political pollsters reported that there had been an increase in the popularity of the government. The political protests against the Chinese government's treatment of dissidents in Tibet that followed the Olympic torch on its journey to Beijing had the effect of bringing many Chinese people behind what had been an unpopular government.

Fig. 16.5 *Elite sport and politics – a mutual need?*

Conversely, if the planning of an international event causes disruption to the lives of local residents, or costs overrun significantly and have to be paid for through local or national taxes for many years after the event, the government in power at the time may find its support dropping.

Activity

1. Since London won the right to stage the 2012 Olympics, fierce debate has raged over whether or not it will be beneficial to London and the UK. Prepare notes to speak either for or against the following motion: 'This House believes that the London 2012 Olympics will have a beneficial effect'. Your research could include facts on the following and you may also think of other areas:

    ■ costs

    ■ income

    ■ improvements to infrastructure and sporting facilities

    ■ media impact

    ■ an increase in participation in sport and improved levels of performance

    ■ improvements to sporting infrastructure – coaching, technical, scientific and medical support.

2. Stage your debate and vote – who won?

Becoming an elite performer – influential factors

Many young people dream of becoming an elite performer and strive to achieve that dream. Many factors can determine whether or not an individual achieves their goal (apart from the necessary physical and psychological attributes).

Fig. 16.6 *Kelly Holmes – no easy path to glory*

Social and cultural factors

A range of social and cultural factors may influence a talented individual's progression to elite-level status.

- Whether they have the support of their family – this goes beyond financial support. An individual who does not have the emotional support and encouragement of their family will find it much harder to progress.

- The status of elite or professional sport within their family or community – if elite sport is not viewed as a high-status or worthwhile vocation by a performer's family, local community or culture, the performer's progression will be hampered.

- Their experience of sport at school –if their school has the policies and strategies in place to encourage talented individuals to aspire to and progress towards elite status then progress is more likely.

- Whether or not the individual has the financial resources to enable them to pay for the necessary equipment, training facilities, travelling expenses, coaching, medical support, etc. – their personal **socio-economic status** is important as not all sports activities receive lottery or government support.

- Whether or not a country has the willingness or the resources to provide the necessary support – the elite performer needs high-class specialist facilities, world-class coaching, medical and technological help, and funding to allow them to train full time.

- Whether or not there is the infrastructure for elite-performer development – talent-identification programmes (TIPS) and the opportunity to progress from one level of performance to another

> ### Key terms
>
> **Socio-economic status:** an individual's position in the social structure; it depends on a combination of occupation, education, income and where they live.

through clubs or representative teams are essential, as are structured levels of competition.

■ The amount of media exposure that sport generally and specific sports receive – high-profile sports with plenty of role models will motivate aspirant individuals to strive to improve.

■ Various barriers to progression – social class, gender, ethnicity, and the effect of disability – have significant effects and will be covered in more detail later in the next section (see below).

■ Antidiscrimination policies – whether or not these are in place and their effectiveness in counteracting the barriers to progression can significantly affect an individual's progression through the sport.

The report *The Performance Environment – A Study of the Personal, Lifestyle and Environmental Factors that Affect Sporting Performance* (UK Sport, 2006) indicated that family involvement with sport and having and gaining friends through sport were the two most important factors in the early stages of becoming an elite performer.

In terms of maintaining a performer's development and then sustaining their performance, a number of other factors were identified:

■ an attitude of resilience and determination

■ strong friendships within their sport or training group and the support of those friends

■ maintaining a balance between training and performing and the other elements of life (education, family, etc.)

■ continuing education – for personal fulfilment and to achieve qualifications for non-sport career options later in life

■ having ownership, by having a degree of control over training regimes and decisions over competition route

■ a balance between creativity and individuality and the use of science and technology to rationalise training and performance strategies

■ not being required to specialise in their sport at too young an age.

Barriers to progression

Obviously, should any of the social and cultural factors identified in the previous section work against an individual, there may be a barrier to progression to elite-level success. However, a number of factors have been formally identified as being barriers to success, and national polices have been established to overcome them. These barriers are based on discrimination involving:

■ sex or gender

■ ethnic differences

■ some form of disability

■ social class.

These barriers are the same as the ones identified as impeding participation, which you looked at during your AS Level studies. This chapter will include a brief recap for each of the barriers and then examine the steps that are being taken to overcome them in terms of elite performer development.

Sex or gender discrimination

'Sex' refers to whether an individual is biologically male or female. 'Gender' refers to the culturally determined roles that men and women

> **Activity**
>
> Prepare a short presentation to your group, reflecting on the factors (positive and negative) that have contributed to your own sport progression.

play in a particular society. Women's progression to elite-level status is affected by issues of **sexism**. In sport, sexism occurs when women are discriminated against as a result of stereotypical views of the strengths and qualities of women in a sport and the gender role that women are expected to fulfil within society.

What evidence do we have that women suffer discrimination in elite sport?

▧ Although more and more women's events have been added to the Olympic programme, in Beijing 2008 45 per cent of the events were for women compared with 55 per cent for men.

▧ In the British Olympic team for Athens 2004, there was evidence of a bias in favour of men in terms of the proportion of athletes participating and, interestingly, the percentage in debt (see Table 16.1).

▧ Overall in Athens, 31 per cent of the competitors were women.

Table 16.1 *2004 Athens Olympics – GB team male/female data*

	British team	Average age of athletes	Income (£)	Percentage of athletes in debt
Men	60	27.5	19,194	35
Women	40	26.5	16,161	46

The Athens Athlete Report. Produced by the Olympic Committee of the British Athletes

▧ In national and International Olympic Committees and Commissions, only about 14 per cent of members are women.

▧ Women's elite football in England is still semi-professional even at the highest level.

▧ It was only in 2007, when Wimbledon became the last tournament to offer equal pay, that all the tennis Grand Slams paid equal prize money to men and women.

▧ In golf, the European tours show a stark difference in total prize money with the men earning £82m and women £10m. Individual prize money was also very different. In the Women's Open the winner received £106,000 whilst the winning man earned £740,000.

Clearly there are fewer women at the elite level, and those who reach that level earn less. Why should this be the case?

▧ Women's elite sport has less social status than men's. This acts as a disincentive for women to pursue elite sport. Sport is still seen as a male-dominated activity.

▧ Women have had to battle to be allowed to legally participate in certain sports. It was not until 1973 that women were officially allowed to participate in the marathon (it took until 1984 for the women's marathon to appear in the Olympics); first participation in some other sports was:

– wrestling, 1987

– pole vault, 1992

– triple jumping, 1994

– boxing, 1996

– weightlifting, 2000.

▧ **Key terms**

Sexism: discrimination on the basis of sex, especially the oppression of women by men.

■ Developing one's ability to elite level requires a huge investment in time and the sacrifice of the usual social life. If doing so is less socially acceptable for girls and young women, this will act as a disincentive.

■ The media portrayal of elite female performers often focuses on factors other than their performance, such as their appearance and whether or not they have children.

■ Female athletes who have developed their physique and strength to enable them to perform better have had their sexuality called into question by the media; this creates a fear among younger performers that they may experience homophobic reactions whatever their sexual orientation (what the Women's Sport Foundation refers to as 'homo-negativism').

■ Some women may suffer from a double barrier – in combination with facing sexual discrimination, they may be subject to racial discrimination, or be from a lower socio-economic background, or have a disability. In 2004, Islamic groups in Bangladesh forced the cancellation of the Women's National Wrestling Championships.

■ Women's sport is less well reported by all forms of the media than men's. This has a knock-on effect in gaining sponsorship and in the development of role models.

■ Tournament organisers may say that it is harder to find sponsors, or that they can only obtain lower levels of sponsorship for women's events, thereby depressing the amount of money available for the performers.

■ Female performers seem to find it harder to get state sponsorship. In 2006, the four home sports councils supported 571 women in comparison with 832 men.

The United Kingdom has enacted legislation that outlaws sex discrimination and is designed to allow women equal opportunity. The four home sports councils and UK Sport have set equity targets for all sport national governing bodies. The Women's Sport and Fitness Foundation is a pressure group whose role is to improve the participation of women and girls in sport and enable more women to have the opportunity to proceed to elite level. It tries to do this by influencing sports policy and pressuring strategy makers at national and regional levels.

Racial discrimination

The United Nations Convention on the Elimination of All Forms of Racial Discrimination defined racial discrimination as:

> any distinction, exclusion, restriction or preference based on race, colour, descent, or national or ethnic origin which has the purpose or effect of nullifying or impairing the recognition, enjoyment or exercise, on an equal footing, of human rights and fundamental freedoms in the political, economic, social, cultural or any other field of public life.

United Nations High Commissioner for Human Rights, UN-OCHR, 1966

The cultural field would obviously include sport. You will have studied the effects of racial discrimination in sport participation as part of AS. At A2 we are specifically concerned about progression to elite level and here the picture is more mixed.

A look at a range of elite sports within our own country would seem to show marked differences in the numbers representing ethnic minority groups at elite level. Twenty-five per cent of English footballers from the Premiership, along with 30 per cent of the England team, are from UK Caribbean or African origins; almost none are from UK Asian. In the UK athletics team, the same can be said of the sprinters and jumpers; yet ethnic minority representation in other events is markedly less. In tennis there is only one representative from an ethnic minority background in the UK top 10 for either men or women and there are similarly few in badminton. In general, members of the UK Asian community are under represented.

Fig. 16.7 *Do some sports present more racial barriers than others?*

Why should there be this variation in representation? In relation to athletics and football, the response often given to this question is that people from UK Caribbean and African groups have the right physiological or anatomical attributes, owing to their genetic make-up – i.e. they have a genetic advantage. Athletics and football often require speed, power and strength, and claims are made that those ethnic groups have a higher proportion of fast-twitch muscle fibre, have a longer Achilles tendon allowing for greater power transfer, or have a higher ratio of muscle to other body tissues.

At the time of publication there is no research evidence to substantiate these claims. No valid or peer-reviewed piece of research has been able to show that people from the UK Caribbean or UK African ethnic groups have genetically derived physiological and anatomical characteristics that predispose them towards sports that require power, speed and strength. There are of course many other sports that require these physiological characteristics, for example tennis and rugby union, yet we do not see the same 'over' representation there.

It is true that to be an elite athlete (in the explosive or speed events) or an elite footballer you are very likely to have a higher proportion of fast-twitch muscle fibres. Indeed, for sprinters it is the most important single factor, so all elite sprinters have a high percentage of fast-twitch fibres – a genetically endowed factor that is then honed by training. It has not been shown that one ethnic or racial group has a higher incidence of those than any other.

So what factors may account for this higher than average representation?

AQA Examiner's tip

In response to an examination question that asks why elite finals seem to favour certain ethnic groups it is common to see students give the stereotypical explanation. Ensure that you have a clear understanding of the arguments and counterarguments and do not rely on stereotyping.

■ The role model effect – the existence of high-profile elite performers who are members of these communities encourages others to take up those activities with more coming through to the elite level. This is further enhanced by a lack of role models in other sports or walks of life. Certain sports may seem to offer opportunities for social and economic advancement and will encourage those with the ability to choose that path.

■ Young people from these ethnic groups may be encouraged, or even pressured, to undertake certain activities based on the mistaken belief that they have the 'genetic advantage' that we discounted earlier.

■ Athletic achievement is based on objective, factually based outcomes – times, distance, height and a clear rank order based solely on performance. There is less likelihood that talented performers can be overlooked or ignored – there is much less room for selection to be based on prejudiced or discriminatory views.

■ The socio-economic groups from which the largest proportion of elite footballers and athletes come have a higher than average percentage of members of the UK's Caribbean and African communities within them. Conversely, we have no member of our elite tennis squads from those socio-economic or ethnic minority groups.

In 2008, Sporting Equals, the UK body charged with eradicating racial discrimination in sport, began a research project into the representation of black and minority ethnic (BME) groups in sport, including their progression to elite level.

Disability and elite sport

In the 2008 Beijing Olympics, British Paralympians were second in the medal table with 102 medals (42 gold, 29 silver, 31 bronze); in the main event, Britain was fourth in the table with 47 medals. Would this comparison suggest that, in the UK, athletes with a disability are relatively well advantaged and do not suffer from any barriers to progression?

Fig. 16.8 *Paralympians win more medals than Olympians*

It is true that those with a disability do not participate in the same numbers as those without. Evidence from Sport England's *Active People Survey 2006* shows that only approximately 9 per cent of people with a

---

AQA **Examiner's tip**

Remember that questions about disability require responses that go beyond issues of mobility involving wheelchair athletes. Look back to the classification information in the AS book.

■ Links

Detailed information on the nature of disability, disabled sports, the profiling system and general levels of participation can be found in *AQA Physical Education AS*, Chapter 13 – Equal opportunities (page 187 and from page 196).

longstanding illness or disability participate regularly in sport, compared with 23 per cent who do not have such a condition. A Sport England survey in 2001 concluded that people with a disability are 39 per cent less likely to participate in sport and active leisure. But how well do we support those who do participate and wish to progress to elite level?

A number of organisations support disabled performers. The British Paralympic Association (BPA) is responsible for selecting, preparing, entering, funding and managing Britain's teams at the Paralympic Games and Paralympic Winter Games. The athletes are funded by the usual route: exchequer funding, lottery funding via the World Class Performance Plan, sponsorship and fundraising. Disability Sport Events is responsible for putting on international, national and regional events as well as helping local volunteers run local events. Sport England's 'Awards for All' programme looks favourably on applications from disabled sports groups. For elite performers or potential elite performers, the World Class Programme provides a level of funding as it does for non-disabled performers. The age limit for the Talented Athlete Scholarship Scheme (TASS), which helps potential elite athletes when in education (see page 239), is extended for those with a disability to 35. **SportsAid** helps support performers in 25 disabled sports (50 non-disabled sports).

One common complaint from disabled performers is the lack of television exposure even of the top events such as the Paralympics and the World Paralympic Championships. Lack of media exposure leads to lower levels of sponsorship of both competitors and competitions. Some media coverage focuses on the adversity that disabled athletes have to overcome rather than on the quality of their sport performance and achievement.

Social class

The effect of social class on a talented individual's progression to elite status is a complex one. Clearly, lack of financial support and resources is an obvious barrier that might affect those from lower socio-economic groups.

Table 16.2 shows that, in general, those from a lower socio-economic group tend to participate less. The table uses the National Statistics Socio-economic Classification (NS-SEC).

Table 16.2 *Participation by social class*

Adults' percentage participation rates in previous 4 weeks (excluding walking)			
Socio-economic group	At least once (%)	4 times or more (%)	12 times or more (%)
NS-SEC (1 & 2)	54	39	18
NS-SEC (3 & 4, 5)	40	29	12
NS-SEC (6, 7, 8)	30	21	10

Participation in Sport in England – Sport Equity Index 2002, Sport England

However, whether or not it is more difficult for an already participating performer from a lower socio-economic group to progress to elite level is a more complex issue. Clearly, lack of financial resources will be an impediment to progression and those from lower socio-economic groups have less disposable income. Certain sports, such as professional football, are so focused on unearthing talent that they will provide the

Key terms

SportsAid: a charitable organisation that raises money to support talented young performers, or those with a disability not supported by national programmes such as the World Class Performance Programme.

Links

- For more information on lottery and exchequer funding, see this chapter (pages 238–9).
- For more information on the World Class Performance Programme, see this chapter (pages 232–4).

necessary resources. In general, it is in the amateur or semi-professional sports that lack of financial resources will have the most impact on an individual, and this is where state and lottery funding attempts to bridge the gap.

Financial support is provided by national funding and community funding. National funding comes from two distinct sources: from the government via national taxation, known as 'exchequer funding'; and from the National Lottery, known as 'lottery funding'. The money for elite-performer development, made up of both exchequer and lottery funding, is routed through the World Class Programme and the World Class Pathway. In England UK Sport has the responsibility for all Olympic and Paralympic performance support, and resources are spread between 10 UK-wide priority sports and 10 English priority sports as shown in Table 16.3.

Table 16.3 *UK and English priority sports*

UK-wide priority sports	English priority sports
Athletics	Golf
Gymnastics	Badminton
Canoeing	Hockey
Cycling	Netball
Equestrian	Rugby league
Judo	Rugby union
Rowing	Squash
Sailing	Tennis
Swimming	Cricket
Triathlon	Football

The range of financial support available will be discussed later in the chapter (page 239) but there may be other factors that present a barrier to development for those with ability. As you saw at AS Level, various factors have an effect on levels of participation:

■ Some physical recreation activities are associated with specific social classes. For example, golf and yachting are perceived as middle-class activities and individuals from other socio-economic groups may believe that they will be rejected or discriminated against if they attempt to engage in the activity.

■ Individuals from a socio-economic group that differs from the one that is predominant within the activity may suffer actual discrimination and be prevented from participating. For example, a club may have membership application processes that are open to discriminatory practices.

■ Individuals from socio-economic groups 3 to 7 may have less leisure time available to spend on physical recreation and therefore their participation levels are lower.

There is little or no research to give us a definitive answer as to whether or not these factors have an impact on the progression to elite level of those already engaged in a sport.

Fig. 16.9 *Lawn tennis – socially restrictive?*

Activity

1 Research the sporting life story of an individual performer from one of the groups who typically suffer discrimination or face barriers to progression – women, people from ethnic minority backgrounds, those with a disability, those from lower socio-economic backgrounds or those who experience a combination of those factors.

2 Present your research in one of the following ways:

- a magazine article
- a photo news story
- a podcast
- a video interview/presentation.

AQA Examiner's tip

Remember that many individuals may suffer from multiple barriers: for example, they may suffer from sexual discrimination as well as the effects of social class.

■ Becoming an elite performer – a route map

Having examined the barriers that inhibit the development of elite performers, we shall now consider the various ways in which elite performers are developed and supported.

The Sport Development Continuum

The stages on the route to becoming an elite performer are reflected in the Sport Development Continuum, which was first developed in 1997 by the English Sports Council and describes the progression from the early acquisition of skills to the highest levels of performance.

Within the continuum there are four stages: Foundation, Participation, Performance and Excellence:

- **Foundation** is the early development of sporting competence and physical skills on which all later forms of sports development are based. Without a sound foundation, young people are unlikely to become long-term sports participants.

- **Participation** refers to sport undertaken primarily for fun and enjoyment, at basic levels of competence. However, many very competent sports people take part in sport purely for reasons of fun, health and fitness.

- **Performance** signifies a move from basic competence into a more structured form of competitive sport at club or county level and implies regular training and coaching, and a desire to win competitions and progress.

■ **Excellence** is concerned with reaching the top and applies to performers at the highest national and international levels.

It is thought that, if the right conditions exist, the larger the participation base (the more people who are engaged at Foundation or Participation level), the greater the number of people who will come through to the Performance and Excellence stages.

AQA Examiner's tip

When answering questions about the 'route to elite level', you will be expected to have a general understanding of the stages and routes that a performer may take, and to be able to support that understanding with concrete examples. These examples are best found from within your own sport activity.

Activity

Reflect on your own sport progression; then describe to a partner your own experiences of each of the stages of the continuum.

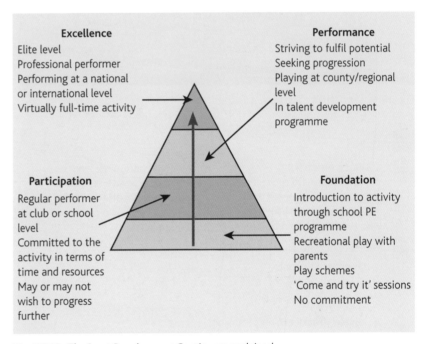

Fig. 16.10 *The Sport Development Continuum explained*

Strategies for advancing along the sport development continuum

If you are a performer within the World Class Programme or if you have taken a look at the websites for Sport England or UK Sport you will be aware of the large number of resourcing strategies, campaigns and linked organisations that are involved in trying to support the development of elite performers. Advancement along the continuum is based on a set of fairly simple processes, which are shown below.

Creating the foundation base

It is Sport England's primary function to get more people to participate in sport, and all sport national governing bodies (NGBs) are charged with encouraging more people to participate in their sport. If an NGB wishes to be in receipt of Sport England lottery funding, it will have to have a development plan for increasing participation – this is now part of what is called a '**Whole Sport Plan**' (see page 237). Apart from the benefits to personal and community wellbeing and health if more people take up a sport, the more that do, the greater is the chance of finding and developing high-level performers.

Finding the talent

Having a large participation and foundation base will not help if there is no way of identifying which of those performers may have the necessary

Key terms

Whole Sport Plan: a four-year plan produced by an NGB for the development of its sport; it determines the level of funding from Sport England.

qualities to go to the top. TIPs are fundamental to this process and formally became part of the overall sport strategy in 2002 when the **Department for Culture, Media and Sport (DCMS)** published its document, *Game Plan: a Strategy for Delivering the Government's Sport and Physical Activity Objectives*, which said:

> Talented young athletes need to be helped to reach the elite level. We propose a more systematic approach to talent identification and development, led by governing bodies on a sport by sport basis.

DCMS, Game Plan: a Strategy for Delivering the Government's Sport and Physical Activity Objectives, 2002

NGBs have the primary function of putting TIPs in place. They work with clubs and schools to set up local and regional TIPs. School and club players are sent to trials for district or regional teams, and these will often be linked to development squads. Occasionally, attempts are made to unearth latent talent by means of programmes such as London County Cricket's 'Search 4 a Star', which describes itself as the *'Pop Idol* for cricket', with bowling hopefuls turning up to be assessed for their potential.

The difficulty that the UK has had in producing elite performers has suggested to some that our talent identification may be at fault. In 2004, Sport Scotland published a research document *Talent Identification and Development*, which critically reviewed the various methods used to identify talent. Sport Scotland's findings included the following:

- Some TIPs used physiological or anthropometric data (measurements of skeletal size, musculature, etc.) to select young performers for development programmes. This was criticised for favouring children or young people who had physically matured earlier and also because it is not a measure of future potential.

- Some TIPs used current performance measures: they attempted to assess and select those who are already performing better than others. This method was criticised for favouring those who have had early opportunities, supportive parents, specialist coaching at school, etc. and because it is not a guarantee of future progression – it is not an indication of potential. Also, this approach can result in overspecialisation at an early age, which has been linked to high rates of drop-out.

- Although psychological factors are thought to be highly important in the development of skills and the ability to sustain training and practice over long periods of time, there were as yet few TIPs in the UK that used any form of psychological testing or profiling.

- TIP models were mostly focused on whether the performer currently has the right skills or physiological requirements for performance rather than whether or not an individual has the ability to learn and consolidate skills.

- The emphasis on achievement of success at an early age (and the pressure on NGBs) confuses performance with talent. If future funding is partly dependent on success at junior levels, resources will go to the current performers (with possible high levels of drop-out) rather than allowing talent to flourish, albeit at a later stage.

In conclusion, the report stated that there seemed to be no true talent identification programmes functioning within the UK and that the focus must shift from current performance to future performance.

Key terms

Department for Culture, Media and Sport (DCMS): the government department that oversees government policy for sport.

Game Plan: a strategy for delivering Government's sport and physical activity objectives

A JOINT DCMS/STRATEGY UNIT REPORT – DECEMBER 2002

Fig. 16.11 *Game Plan – a strategy for sport*

AQA Examiner's tip

For higher-level marks, students will often be required to look critically at a national policy or strategy. You will need to know what the weaknesses may be and be able to suggest improvements.

However, even with the best methods of identifying talent there remains the issue that if you cannot develop talent after you have found it, your sport will not be successful at the highest levels.

Activity

1 For your own sport activity, devise a method of talent identification for youngsters between the ages of 12 and 15 years. Consider the following questions:

   a What characteristics are important for future success?

   b Rank these characteristics in order of importance.

   c How would you test for these characteristics or identify them?

2 Compare the system that you have devised with your own experiences or with the systems currently used within your sport. What differences can you see?

Providing the development structure

To enable a performer to move on from the Foundation or Participation stage there must be routes for them to follow, competitive structures to allow them to play at higher levels and places where they can receive coaching and support. In other words, there must be:

- opportunities for playing at a higher level – the sport must have structured layers of competition (leagues, cup competitions, etc.)
- a representative structure where, through the selection process, individuals can play for their district, their region or their country
- development squads linked to TIPs to bring together the best, or the performers with the most potential, to give them high-quality coaching and training.

Setting up such a structure is not particularly difficult and most sports in the UK now have a well-defined and logical progression from the grass roots (e.g. playing on a Sunday morning) to representing the country. So how can we ensure that individuals are able to take advantage of this structure?

Supporting performer development

Providing the necessary levels of financial, technical and expert support is fundamental to developing elite performers. Since publication of the report *Raising the Game* (Department of Heritage, 1985), the UK has spent a great deal of time and money putting in place the necessary support structures for developing elite performers. For a while, this led to so many programmes from such a very wide range of providers that there seemed to be no coherence in what was being offered. Gradually, the system has been clarified and key organisations now have direct responsibility for elite-performer development.

The main players are:

- the NGBs of individual sports
- UK Sport
- the English National Institute of Sport
- the Sports Councils of Wales, Northern Ireland and Scotland plus their own Institutes of Sport
- the British Olympic Association (National Olympic Committee for Great Britain), the British Paralympic Association

Activity

Draw a diagram to show the competitive structure of your own sport activity, from grass roots to national champions.

Fig. 16.12 *Badminton – whole sport plan*

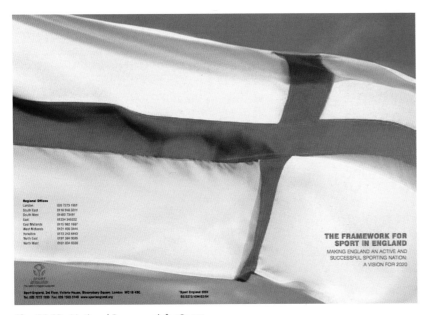

Fig. 16.13 *National Framework for Sport*

Great Coaches...Great Sport

Fig. 16.14 *Elite performers – the main players*

■ sport coach UK

■ SportsAid.

The role of each of these bodies is covered in more detail later in the chapter (pages 232–8). Each has a quite specific role but all work in harmony with what is known as the Long Term Athlete Development (LTAD) model.

The Long Term Athlete Development (LTAD) model

The LTAD model was developed by worldwide expert on LTAD Dr Istvan Balyi in 1990 and focuses on maximising player development to encourage a lifelong commitment to sport and exercise.

> LTAD outlines a staged approach to appropriate training, competition and recovery programming in relation to the developmental age of the individual. LTAD is not just another plan, it is a philosophy, a real tool for change.

Istvan Balyi, www.cwsportspartnership.org

AQA Examiner's tip

Many national documents are very long! Most have a much shorter executive summary which will tell you all you need to know.

In simple terms, LTAD is intended to produce a long term approach to maximising individual potential and involvement in sport.

I. Stafford, Coaching for Long-term Athlete Development: To Improve
Participation and Performance in Sport, *2005*

Link

For more information on periodisation, see Chapter 5 – Specialised training (pages 69–71).

The LTAD underpins the government's publication *Game Plan: a Strategy for Delivering the Government's Sport and Physical Activity Objectives* (DCMS, 2002) and the *National Framework for Sport* (Sport England, 2004). It derived from Balyi's work on periodisation. The LTAD model divides sports into two categories and therefore proposes two models: the early specialisation model and the late specialisation model.

The early specialisation model

Early specialisation sports include diving, figure skating, gymnastics, rhythmic gymnastics; sports which (in Balyi's view) require early sport-specific specialisation in training.

There are four phases in early specialisation:

1 Training to Train

2 Training to Compete

3 Training to Win

4 Retirement/Retainment.

The late specialisation model

Late specialisation sports include athletics, cycling, racquet sports, combat sports, rowing, and all team sports; these require a more generalised approach to early training, with the emphasis on the development of general motor, technical and tactical skills.

There are six phases in late specialisation:

1 FUNdamental stage (boys aged 6 to 9 years; girls aged 6 to 8)

Development of fundamental movement skills such as running, jumping, throwing, agility, balance, and hand–eye coordination: the focus is on the acquisition of basic motor skills, fitness and fun rather than on competition and winning, providing a sound base for continued involvement in sport or other forms of recreation. Participation in as many activities/sports as possible is encouraged to ensure experience of a wide range of sports and to reduce the likelihood of specialising too early.

2 Learning to Train (boys aged 9 to 12 years; girls aged 8 to 11)

The major emphasis is on the acquisition of basic skills and fitness. The stage coincides with peak motor learning; therefore skill development is a priority. Ideally, there is a balance of 75 per cent training to 25 per cent competition. Emphasis is on learning how to train and not on results or performances. Participation is in complementary sports that use similar energy systems and movement patterns. This is a vital stage of development.

3 Training to Train (males aged 12 to 16 years; females aged 11 to 15)

The focus is on aerobic conditioning and individualisation of specific sport fitness and technical training. The emphasis is on training rather than competition; however, the quality and focus of the competition is important. Strength development may be undertaken towards the end of this stage, depending on the player's maturation as well as the development of suppleness. There is real danger of overcompeting and undertraining.

4   Training to Compete (males aged 16 to 18 years; females aged 15 to 17)

The focus is on sport-specific skills and techniques, developed alongside tactics and game strategies and individualised conditioning programmes. About 80 per cent of activities should be sport and individual specific. Young players are likely to be involved in selected competitions in this phase and overtraining or too much competition has to be avoided.

5   Training to Win (males aged 18+ years; females aged 17+)

At this stage of player development, all of the young player's physical, technical, tactical and mental capacities are now fully established and the focus is on specific training to achieve optimal performance at key competitions and maintenance of the capacities needed to compete successfully. About 80 to 85 per cent of training at this phase is likely to be sport specific.

6   Retirement/Retainment

This phase involves keeping the performer involved via coaching, administration, officiating, veterans' competitions, teams, etc.

The LTAD also provides the basis for Whole Sport Plans and One Stop Plans constructed by sport governing bodies (see page 237).

Activity

1   How does the LTAD model match your own sport development? Were you doing what was recommended or did you have quite a different experience? Discuss your findings and thoughts within your group.

2   Now research the LTAD model for your own sport activity – you will probably find it on the NGB website.

3   Compare the LTADs for the different sports played by members of your group. Are there similarities and differences?

Is the LTAD working?

The theoretical basis for the LTAD has been criticised and there are some who think that changes to NGBs' young performer development strategies have been detrimental. The rationale behind Balyi's conversion of a periodisation regime designed for the Canadian alpine ski team into a generalised model for all sports has been questioned. There seems to have been no longitudinal research into the effectiveness of the LTAD model, little academic peer review of the original model, and no research with established elite performers to consider their experiences in relation to the LTAD. Chris Earle, Director of Sports Development at Loughborough University, considers that the model should be thought of as an athlete-retention model rather than one for the development of elite performers (Earle, 2001). Believing that passage through the FUNdamental stage is vital, Earle argued that it is wrong to drop the FUNdamental stage in the early specialisation model.

This is not to say that the LTAD is not a sound basis on which to plan the development of young performers; nevertheless, at the very least, the progress of those who have been trained and developed within the LTAD

■ Link

For information on use of the LTAD model for injury prevention for young athletes, see Chapter 6 – Sports injuries (page 84).

AQA Examiner's tip

You must know something about the work of each of the bodies named within the specification – their general role and some examples of actual policies and strategies. Questions about the role of these organisations are very common.

overall strategy should be monitored long term, and the biomechanical, physiological, psychological, skill learning and nutritional rationale for its use should continue to be researched.

■ Becoming an elite performer – who does what?

In the final sections of this chapter we shall consider the roles of various UK organisations concerned with elite-performer development and how the funding is provided.

UK Sport

UK Sport was established in 1996 and works in partnership with the home-country sports councils and other bodies to lead UK sport to world-class success. It is responsible for distributing both exchequer funding (money from the government raised by taxation) and money from the National Lottery. It currently distributes over £100m a year. UK Sport is answerable to parliament via the Department for Culture, Media and Sport.

UK Sport has three major goals:

- **World Class Performance** – development of world-class performers and the UK expertise to support them. This means primarily winning more Olympic and Paralympic medals.
- **Worldwide Impact** – bringing the best practice from other sporting nations to the UK and providing support to enable sports to bid for and stage major events in this country.
- **World Class Standards** – promoting the highest standards of sporting conduct including a world-class anti-doping programme for the UK and ethically fair and drug-free sport via education and information.

To fulfil the primary goal of delivering UK success at the Olympics and Paralympic Games, a 'no compromise' approach is taken, which targets resources at those sports and athletes capable of delivering medal-winning performances. Individual sports are allocated funding through the World Class Performance Programme, with the amount determined by their immediate past and current levels of success (or failure).

In April 2006, UK Sport became responsible for the high-performance pathway at a UK and England level, including the World Class Development Programmes for Olympic and Paralympic Sport, the TASS schemes, Athlete Personal Awards and the **English Institute of Sport**. The Sports Councils of Northern Ireland, Wales and Scotland retained responsibility for the development of their own performers up to **World Class Performance Pathway** standard.

Key terms

English Institute of Sport: a distributed network of support centres providing facilities and services to develop elite performers in England.

World Class Performance Pathway: the template by which support is provided to elite performers, depending on how close they are to winning medals at international level.

The World Class Performance Pathway

The World Class Performance Pathway is directed by UK Sport and the National Institutes of Sport and is focused on Olympic and Paralympic sports and on non-Olympic sports in England. Within the World Class Performance Pathway, there are three distinct levels of support, determined by how close the sport is to winning medals:

- World Class Podium – capable of winning medals at the next Olympics, therefore within the next four years
- World Class Development – typically six years away from winning medals, the next wave after Podium
- World Class Talent – performers who have the potential to progress to the next two levels.

In the period 2001 to 2009 (which includes the run-up to the 2008 Beijing Olympics as well as the first year of the 2012 cycle), UK Sport had nearly £200m at its disposal. In the same period, over £36m was dedicated to Paralympians.

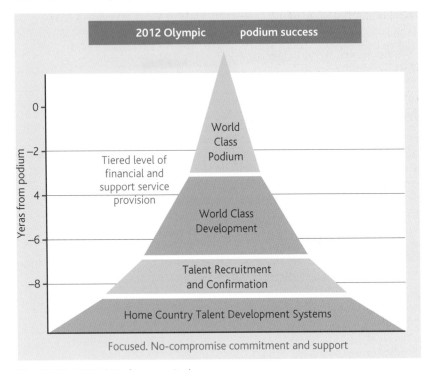

Fig. 16.15 *UK High Performance Pathway*

Funding is applied for and delivered by the sport's NGB in conjunction with the National Institutes of Sport, the British Olympic Association and the Paralympic Association. Since the Athens Olympics in 2004, UK Sports has operated what has been called the 'no compromise' strategy, which in simple terms rewards sports on the basis of how well they meet their medal targets. If a sport fails to meet its target then its funding will be reduced. UK Sport's rationale for this is that there are limited resources available and these must be spent as effectively as possible – it is not prepared to reward failure. An example of this policy is shown in Table 16.4, which gives the level of funding pre- and post-Athens Olympics.

Table 16.4 *UK athletics funding 2001–09*

Athens Performance	3 gold, 1 bronze
Athens Target	5–7 medals
2001–05 WC Programme funding	£8.3m
2005–09 WC Programme funding	£7.2m
2001–05 Athlete places (average)	82
2005–09 Athlete places ('up to' figure …)	40
2001–05 Exchequer funding	£1.8m
2005–09	£1.6m

Performers will need to go through an assessment procedure set down by the sport's NGB to receive their World Class Performance Pathway funding, or to have it extended for future years. Each NGB will set its own criteria, overseen by UK Sport.

As well as centralised support, including training centres (for example the National Badminton Centre in Milton Keynes), medical support, training camps, coaching and technological support, developing elite performers can receive subsistence allowances for personal living and training costs. These are known as Athlete Personal Awards and are given and assessed annually; the amounts given can rise or fall, depending on performance.

National Institutes of Sport

National Institutes of Sport are the organisations responsible for delivering the high-class support services – training facilities, medical and nutritional advice, and biomechanical, scientific and technological support – that are needed by elite performers. In Northern Ireland, Scotland and Wales, the institutes are managed via the region's Sports Council and have one centralised base, but in England the English Institute of Sport (EIS) is structured somewhat differently.

English Institute of Sport

The EIS is a nationwide network of support services, delivered from nine regional multi-sport hub sites and a range of satellite centres, and is currently supporting over 2,000 performers. The EIS provides a whole range of sports science support, including applied physiology, biomechanics performance analysis, and strength and conditioning coaching. Sports medicine services include screening and consultations, nutritional advice, sports massage and podiatry. The Performance Lifestyle programme offers performers career and education advice.

In concert with UK Sport, the EIS manages a talent-identification and development programme with four phases:

■ talent identification
■ talent selection
■ talent confirmation
■ Olympic/Paralympic development.

Prior to the 2012 Olympics, the EIS is also managing three specific programmes:

■ talent transfer – examining whether recently retired or about-to-retire performers can succeed in another sport
■ flat-water canoeing or kayak transfer – looking for performers who can transfer from a related discipline, such as international swimmers, rowers or surf life-savers
■ sporting giants – looking for performers with good all-round ability who are already 5 feet 11 inches (180 cm) or above (females) or 6 feet 3 inches (190 cm) or above (males) for rowing, handball and volleyball.

Performers are nominated for support from the EIS via their NGB and will normally be within the World Class Programme. The EIS is funded by Sport England with lottery funding and is grant aided by UK Sport.

Sport England

Sport England is the Sports Council for England; its major responsibility is to develop participation in sport at grass roots level and to produce a community sports development programme. Its motto is 'producing an active nation through sport'. It is a nongovernmental organisation and is responsible for distribution of lottery funds. In 2008, it published its four-year strategy for the run-up to the 2012 London Olympics. The major objectives of its revised strategy are:

■ To focus exclusively on sport and sport participation for sport's sake. Although sport contributes to wider social benefits, Sport England's role is to concentrate solely on sport, leaving the physical activity agenda to the Department of Health.

■ To provide a seamless pathway from school to community to elite levels of performance. The Youth Sports Trust retains responsibility for sport in schools, with Sport England developing opportunities beyond the school so that children and young people can move from school sport to community sport. Sport England will work with NGBs to improve participation in NGB-accredited clubs to 33 per cent of 5- to 16-year-olds by 2010.

■ UK Sport is responsible for elite sport but Sport England will work with NGBs to ensure that talent-identification systems are closely linked with elite-development programmes and increase the pool of talent coming into those programmes.

■ NGBs will become more accountable and responsible for delivering greater participation and diversity via their Whole Sport Plans, which must include sport equity targets for under-represented groups. NGBs will have greater control over the money allocated to them, to be given in single four-year grants, but future funding will be determined by how well they meet their objectives.

■ Sport England is to work with sport coach UK and NGBs to ensure that sufficient coaching resources are developed and employed, and with the Youth Sports Trust to provide high-quality coaching to children at a young age, as part of the Five Hour Sport Offer. It will also work to develop 4,000 more volunteer coaches under the Recruit to Coach Scheme.

■ Nearly 2 million people already volunteer to help with sport. Sport England is to work with sport NGBs to attract and retain more volunteers.

■ Sport England is to work with NGBs to develop a modern, accessible sports club structure in each sport, and also to develop multi-sports clubs where appropriate.

Sport England has committed itself to a set of targets to be achieved by 2012:

■ 1 million people doing more sport by 2012–13

■ A reduction in post-16 drop-off in at least five sports by 25 per cent by 2012–13

■ a quantifiable increase in satisfaction (actual measure to be determined)

■ improved talent-development systems in at least 25 sports

■ a major contribution to the delivery of the Five Hour Sport Offer.

By increasing participation in sport, reducing the post-16 drop-out rate and improving talent-identification and development systems, Sport England will support the development of elite performers within England. Sport England, the non-governmental body responsible for developing participation and the standards of sport in England, has invested over £2.2bn in community sport since the start of the National Lottery in

1994 and is set to invest another £1bn before the start of the 2012 Olympic and Paralympic Games in London. Sport England's annual budget (from lottery and exchequer) is approximately £250m. Sport England currently funds 31 priority and development sports for the four-year period (2005 to 2009) through Whole Sport or One Stop plans.

> ### Activity
>
> How much money does your sport receive from Sport England or UK Sport?
>
> 2 Compare the findings for your sport with the findings of those in the group who do different sports.

British Olympic Association/Committee (BOA)

The BOA selects (in conjunction with the NGBs) and manages Britain's Olympic teams prior to and during the Summer and Winter Games. The BOA is independent of government, has no political interests and receives no government funding, being funded via commercial sponsorship and fundraising. The BOA has responsibility for developing the Olympic movement and spreading the Olympic message throughout the UK.

In the run-up to an Olympic Games, the BOA provides an extensive and wide-ranging number of support services to the selected athletes:

■ The Olympic Training Centre provides world-class training and preparation facilities in Austria and Cyprus for the use of British high-performance athletes and coaches from across a wide range of sports.

■ The Olympic Passport Scheme allows Olympic and Paralympic athletes access to national and local sports centres at reduced costs or free of charge.

■ The Olympic Medical Institute based in London and in partnership with the EIS provides medical and rehabilitive services to those on the World Class Programme or who are on the BOA Passport scheme.

■ Planning for Success Workshops provide athletes with advice from experienced Olympians to help with goal setting and time management throughout the Olympic cycle.

■ The Olympic and Paralympic Employment Network (OPEN) helps elite athletes establish a career path or employment opportunities outside of sport whilst they are still training and performing.

■ Performance Lifestyle is a programme designed to help athletes balance all other aspects of their life with their sport.

■ The Athlete Medical Scheme provides comprehensive medical cover to over 1,500 nominated and potential Olympians, ensuring that the athletes have access to the best sports-specific medical advice when it is needed.

Sport national governing bodies

Sport national governing bodies are at the heart of identifying, developing and supporting elite-level performers. They have a wide range of roles:

■ meet sport participation and sport equity targets as contained within their Whole Sport Plan

■ develop an accessible club structure

- provide a competition structure for all levels of performance
- develop TIPs
- develop a coaching structure and qualifications to provide coaches for all levels of performance
- manage representative teams and entries to international competitions
- develop and manage performer-development strategies, including nominating performers for the World Class Performance Pathway, Athlete Personal Awards and the TASS scheme
- set a code of ethics for all those involved in the sport and manage child protection measures
- enforce the rules and regulations of the sport
- promote the sport.

To receive funding from Sport England, an NGB has to agree a Whole Sport Plan.

Whole Sport Plans/One Stop Plans

To qualify for Sport England funding, an NGB must produce a Whole Sport Plan or One Stop Plan for its sport. Whole Sport Plans and One Stop Plans are four-year plans showing how a sport intends to achieve key objectives in terms of increasing participation and success. A Whole Sport Plan is for NGBs that are just responsible for England, and a One Stop Plan is for an NGB responsible for the sport across Great Britain. The success of the plan is measured against key performance indicators to ensure delivery; Sport England will use these indicators – how successfully they have been met – to determine future funding.

In 2006 to 2007, Sport England invested £64,045,589 in 30 NGB Whole Sport Plans.

A Plan for the Development of Gymnastics in England 2005-2009

Unlocking the Potential to Start, Stay & Succeed

Fig. 16.16 *Gymnastics Whole Sport Plan*

Activity

1 Research the Whole Sport Plan for your own activity and present it to the rest of the group.

2 How do the plans of the various NGBs vary?

---

sports coach UK

sports coach UK is leading on the development and implementation of a coaching system for the United Kingdom through the UK Coaching Framework. The vision of The Framework is to create a cohesive, ethical, inclusive and valued coaching system where skilled coaches support children, adults, players and athletes at all stages of their development in sport. The Framework will be world-leading by 2016 and aims to:

- Enhance the quality of coaching at all stages.
- Provide active, skilled and qualified coaches to meet demand. This will lead to:
  - Sustained and increased participation
  - Improved performances in sport underpinned by clear career structures from coaches within a professionally regulated vocation.

Gower College Swansea
Library
Coleg Gŵyr Abertawe
Llyrfgell

sports coach UK and Leeds Metropolitan University are working in partnership to establish The UK Centre for Coaching Excellence in sport and disability sport. As well as benefiting elite-sport coaches, The Centre will also offer training to high-performing children, community and talent development coaches to improve the quality of the sport experience for all, and help identify potential British sport stars of the future.

The coach education system develops a hierarchical model of coaches: Assistant Coach, Coach, Senior Coach and Master Coach. It would be possible for a coach working solely with young children to achieve Master Coach status.

Activity

1 You wish to become a coach in your own sport activity. Prepare a route map showing your progression, including qualifications.

2 What role would have been played by the NGB and sport coach UK?

SportsAid

SportsAid, previously known as the SportsAid Foundation (SAF), was founded in 1976. Its principal role is to raise funds from the private sector to provide financial assistance to Britain's amateur sportsmen and women. The aim was to help them prepare for competitions against better-funded, overseas athletes. In 1997, lottery funding changed SportsAid's role and it has focused on giving grants to youngsters aged 12 to 18, from 50 able-bodied and 25 disability sports. The athletes compete in national squads, and these grants, generally worth £500, help with costs such as travel, training, accommodation, competition fees and equipment.

Since 1976, SportsAid has distributed around £20m and now gives 1,500 grants a year.

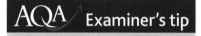

Examiner's tip

The role of all the organisations mentioned in the specification will change, sometimes quite radically. It is good practice to look at the websites on a regular basis, say once a term.

Activity

Imagine that you are an elite performer who has won medals at World or European Championships. Prepare bullet-point notes for a speech that you are going to give at a £500-a-head dinner for 150 leaders of industry, education and commerce. Your motivational speech is designed to show them the value of sport and why they should donate more money to the charity SportsAid.

■ Where does the money come from?

Money for elite-performer development comes from two sources: exchequer funding and lottery funding.

Exchequer funding

The government sets the overall policy and objectives for sport in the UK and this is overseen by the DCMS; within the Department, sport is represented by a Minister for Sport. The government provides money to UK Sport and the four home-country Sports Councils to develop sport participation and levels of sport performance. This money is raised from general taxation and is known as exchequer funding. In 2006, the total government expenditure on sport (including Olympic preparations) was £165m.

Talented Athlete Scholarship Scheme (TASS)

The Talented Athlete Scholarship Scheme (TASS) is a government-funded programme; it is a partnership between sport and higher and further education. TASS provides 16- to 24-year-old athletes with services such as coaching, strength and conditioning training, Talented Athlete Lifestyle Support, physiotherapy and sports medicine whilst they are in higher or further education. It also provides support for competition and training expenses. The level of support can be up to £3,000 a year. It is the responsibility of the NGBs to identify and nominate performers in higher and further education.

Fig. 16.17 *TASS – elite sport and higher education*

National Lottery funding

The National Lottery distributes funds to sport as one of the four 'good causes' – the others being the Arts, Heritage, and Charities and Community groups. Since 1995, sport has received £3.5bn in lottery funding. All the major UK sport bodies receive lottery funding – UK Sport and all the Sport Councils.

Over the last 20 years, much more attention and greater resources have been given to developing our high-level international performers. One reason is that Britain wishes to be a successful sporting nation; it is considered that this would bring social and economic benefits. Another is that developing our elite performers contributes to a broad government objective of producing opportunities for individuals to fulfil their talents and maximise their opportunities. There have been, and still are, a huge range of initiatives and at present it is too soon to determine whether we are being successful. There is no doubt that we do have a much more coordinated system that greatly increases the possibility that talented individuals will find their route to the top.

AQA Examiner's tip

Many students lose marks because they do not have a clear enough picture of the respective roles of government funding and lottery funding.

✓ *You should now be able to:*

- identify and describe a World Game or World Games event

- describe the benefits that World Games can bring to individuals and to societies and explain why governments feel that they have a vested interest in successful international events

- evaluate the impact of events such the Olympic Games

- describe the characteristics that are required for an individual to progress to elite-performer level, especially those other than physiological and anatomical advantages

- understand the broad principles of how elite performers are identified, developed and sustained, and give examples of strategies used within the UK and critically evaluate their effectiveness

- describe the role of the various UK and national agencies in the development of elite performers.

1   Describe the strategies or processes that must occur to allow a talented performer to progress through the sport continuum. Comment on their effectiveness within the UK.   *(7 marks)*

2   Not all those with the necessary physical attributes to succeed make the elite level.

    (a)   Ignoring matters of financial support, what cultural, social or personal characteristics may an individual require if they are to become an elite-level performer?   *(4 marks)*

    (b)   What external financial support is available to support elite-performer development outside of exchequer or lottery funding?   *(3 marks)*

3   What factors, both positive and negative, would the United Kingdom government and the city of London have considered before making the bid for the 2012 Olympics?   *(7 marks)*

4   A wide range of UK government and non-governmental agencies support the development of elite performers.

    (a)   Name and briefly describe the role of four of those agencies   *(4 marks)*

    (b)   Talent identification is an important first step in elite-performer development. What criteria should be used or included in a talent-identification programme (TIP)?   *(3 marks)*

17 The Olympic ideal and modern sport

In this chapter you will:

- describe the early development of sport in the UK
- explain the ways that sport spread throughout the world
- understand how the status of amateur and professional sportspeople has changed
- understand the importance of the need to play fair
- evaluate the differences between sportsmanship and gamesmanship.

Key terms

Popular recreation: recreation for the masses, involving violent, unruly 'mob games'.

Industrialisation: (of the workplace) mechanisation of the manufacturing industry.

Rational recreation: the development of rules and organisation of sport.

AQA Examiner's tip

You may be required to identify the characteristics of mob games. Be able to list four or five of these characteristics.

Activity

Do some research into existing mob activities such as the Haxey Hood game, Shrove Football at Alnwick, the Eton Wall game or Shrovetide football at Ashbourne. Which characteristics of mob games do they demonstrate?

In this chapter we shall be looking at how sports developed from their early beginnings in the 18th and 19th centuries, becoming the modern sports that were being played in recognisable forms before 1900. We shall then look at how that peculiarly British way of playing fair and to the letter of the law – the ethic of sports – came about.

Before beginning to try and understand how sports have developed, you must realise that sport is an important aspect of life within society and, as such, tends to reflect society. Thus, when society was cruel and riotous, so was sport. When society was becoming civilised, sport became civilised, and when society began to recognise and appreciate the place of women within that society, so did sport. It may be easier to understand if you suppose that sport, like society, has been through several clear stages of development:

- **popular recreation**
- **industrialisation**
- **rational recreation**
- post-industrialisation.

Pre-industrialisation

Popular recreation was a feature of life before the industrialisation of the workplace. The term 'popular recreation' means 'recreations for the populace'; however, the different classes within society were involved in very different forms of recreation.

The upper classes – the aristocracy – played refined games with complex rules, such as real tennis and fencing, while the working classes – the peasants – were limited to so-called 'mob games'. Most of the peasants lived a rural life, based on the farming year and dictated to by the seasons. What little time they had for recreation was provided by the Church's holy days and festivals. Thus popular recreations were occasional happenings where people met as a community to let off steam and challenge others to sporting activity. These early games had no clear rules and were often more like a free-for-all kick-about. Popular recreations, such as mob football, had the following characteristics:

- local, often rural
- disorganised and/or unstructured
- few and/or simple unwritten rules
- working-/lower-class involvement
- violent, many injuries
- for the participant rather than the spectator
- used limited equipment or facilities
- played only occasionally on festivals or holidays
- based on force not skill.

Industrialisation

From about 1860 onwards, society began to change and, as it did, so did sport. The Industrial Revolution was in full swing, with machines

Fig. 17.1 *Mob football*

carrying out many tasks that had previously been done by people. Factories were employing thousands of people, who needed to live close to their work, and so rows of terraced housing were built in cities for the factory workers. In these terraces, there was little or no space for recreation. Factory employees worked long 12-hour shifts for six days a week. Leisure time was scarce, with Sunday the only day off, but this was a day of rest.

The upper and middle classes continued to play their sport. They were unaffected by the **urbanisation** that was occurring

Urbanisation affected sport. Typically, rural life was based on the seasons. The villages were the centres of the local communities, and these were the structures on which sporting rivalry was based. The rural location of the communities also provided the space to play. The move to towns meant that the traditional sports had to change to suit a new environment. There was insufficient space for most traditional sports.

With the industrialisation of the workplace, machines dictated the working hours in factories. In the early days, the factory working week could easily reach 72 hours; it was eventually reduced to 56 hours and the standard six-day week was reduced to five and a half. The Church had a great influence over the population and there was no Sunday sport; Sunday was a day of rest and reflection.

Participation in sport was expensive. The working classes were very poorly paid and overtime was usually taken whenever offered. There was a general lack of facilities for sport, but the middle-class factory owners began to establish sports clubs as a means of developing morale and loyalty within the workforce. The same owners would often provide the land on which sports could be played. The Church too was an important provider of land and organiser of teams.

Sport was seen as way of improving health and loyalty within the workforce and also as a means of social control. This led to the sponsorship or patronage of factory teams by the owners, which was also a means of satisfying the workforce. During this period, working conditions in the factories gradually improved and, with the five-and-

Key terms

Urbanisation: development of cities caused by the movement of the working population from rural areas (where jobs were disappearing because of mechanisation) to towns (where new jobs were being created in factories).

a-half-day week, sport could be played on Saturday afternoon. But as space was at a premium, only a few could play and the main form of involvement was as spectators.

As wages increased, workers could afford to watch and play sport. At the same time, the railways developed and communications improved. This assisted the development of fixtures, competitions, leagues and cups, and, with the ease of travel and the establishment of more and more clubs, often based on factory teams, spectator sport blossomed. Competitions grew in size and, as they did, so too did spectator interest, leading to professionalism and increased media interest.

The middle classes controlled sport. They dictated the hours worked, which were long and tiring, allowing little leisure time. Women and children were used as cheap labour, and malnutrition and disease were common. The working classes had very, very little disposable income and few leisure facilities. Initially there were no parks, and street games were declared illegal because of the damage they would cause to shops and onlookers. Pubs were the cultural centres of the working population. Sports were developed to suit this new environment.

The emergence of rational recreation

In the Victorian era, the traditional aspects of popular sport (revelry, debauchery, gambling and drunkenness) became less of a force because of the moralising influence exerted by the middle classes via the developing traditions of public school education. The middle classes redefined their sport to include **fair play**, through the strict regulation of the rules and the enforcement of a strict amateur ethos. The middle classes played sport for pleasure and as a form of character-building.

There were three major contributions to the emergence of rational recreation:

- **codification**
- competitions
- organisations.

Activity

Invent a game! Arrange to meet a group of other students. Bring a tennis ball and two waste-paper bins. Choose an area to play on. Discuss with other players the limits of the playing area, the method of scoring, the limitations to movement with and without the ball, and what constitutes a foul. Play the game. Does it need adapting? You are going through the processes that occurred as codification.

Without rules, sports could not exist. Rules permit participants to compete on equal terms and can be applied to all levels of involvement. The major influence on the codification of rules came from the public schools, where sports were promoted as a means of providing boys with discipline; the schools encouraged the formation of a code of practice for the conduct of activities.

Boys who played sports took their games and their rules to the universities and armed forces, where they established sports clubs. Influential members of the leading clubs became involved in the

AQA Examiner's tip

A typical question may ask why the working classes were generally excluded from early forms of rational sport. Be prepared to suggest three or four reasons.

Activity

Research the living conditions of the poor by reading the books of Charles Dickens and Elizabeth Gaskell.

Key terms

Fair play: allowing all the performers an equal chance of success and treating other performers with respect.

Codification: the gradual organisation and defining of rules, including rules for the actual playing of the sport and the conduct and behaviour of participants.

Fig. 17.2 *An early association football match – sport has become rationalised*

standardising of an agreed set of rules. This development led to the formation of national governing bodies (NGBs). These NGBs promoted the development of regional and local organisations, with competitions to allow more teams to play matches.

Coinciding with the development of sport and physical activity was the British dominance of the world in terms of industrialisation. Owing to the demand for machinery and organisation, the British way of life was exported to Europe and further afield. With it went British sports and games. European and South American football and athletics clubs soon developed, in many cases to provide recreation for the British who were abroad at that time; however, many were also for local people who soon saw the fun and physicality of the new games. In the far-flung corners of the world, British dominance of local society was evident, whether in the country's armed forces or through the work done by British missionaries, engineers and administrators. As an example, consider cricket: this sport is played at an international level by very few countries, all of which were part of the British Empire.

Fig. 17.3 *England v. Scotland (1872)*

Activity

Research into the history of a famous football club from Europe or South America. How does its founding fit into the development of sport in the UK?

Public school influence on sport and the gentleman amateur

The public school ethos

Victorian society was class oriented, and this both reflected and was promoted by the educational system; the public schools were only available for the fee-paying middle and upper classes. The schools aimed to produce further generations of men who would guide the government and industry of the United Kingdom (UK) and the developing Empire. In these establishments, qualities such as leadership, loyalty, courage, discipline and commitment were encouraged, and the schools saw the potential in developing these characteristics through participation in sport, especially team games.

The cult of **athleticism** developed, with its emphasis on goodness, manliness, restraint and discipline. The public school sportsmen went to universities and following graduation many returned to schools to teach or entered the clergy. Knowing the benefit of organised competitive sport, they encouraged more to join them to form clubs. Clubs played each other and by 1890 most sports were being played in organised way.

Professional or amateur?

The individuals who played were keen to maintain the class divide and used sport as a means of social control, maintaining a clear distinction between **amateurs** and **professionals**. A **gentleman amateur** was a gentleman of the upper and middle classes who played sport with strict adherence not only to the rules of sport but also to a strict ethical code determining the manner in which the sport should be played. 'Not playing the game' is an expression describing the spirit in which someone was playing; it is not a reference to the rules of the game.

■ **Link**

For information on public school sports, see *AQA Physical Education AS*, Chapter 12 – National Curriculum Physical Education and school sport (pages 164–7).

■ **Key terms**

Athleticism: a fanatical devotion to sport that developed the physical, social and moral aspects of young men.

Amateurs: a person who plays sport for fun and for no financial gain.

Professional: a sports performer who is paid to play their sport.

Gentleman amateur: a sportsman who, because of his social position and financial situation, had no need for monetary reward from participating in sport.

Fig. 17.4 *Middle-class sport – Blackburn Olympic F.C. (founded 1877)*

Professionals were paid to play and invariably came from the working classes. Men were employed to play sport, usually because of a talent for that sport. The distinction between amateur and professional was enforced through strict rules about membership. The middle classes excluded the working classes. The sport of rowing remained amateur by refusing to admit to its clubs those involved in any form of manual labour. The governing body of athletics, the Amateur Athletic

Association, excluded 'any tradesman, mechanic, artisan or labourer'. Cricket maintained its amateur and professional divide into the 1960s. The upper classes managed not only to play sports the way they wanted, but they also managed to keep the working classes out of their sport.

Football was slightly different. The early administrators eventually had to admit that the better players were unable to take time off to play for their clubs. Not only that, but the clubs had sufficient spectators to be able to afford to pay them to play. Somewhat reluctantly, the amateur football administrators had to accept professionalism in 1885 when the Football League was established.

Various current Football League clubs originated at this time from a variety of backgrounds (see Tables 17.1, 17.2 and 17.3).

Table 17.1 *Current football teams derived from associations with churches*

Football team	Church
Fulham	Fulham St Andrew's Sunday School
Aston Villa	Villa Cross Methodist Chapel
Bolton Wanderers	Christ Church Sunday School
Birmingham City	Trinity Church, Bordsley

Table 17.2 *Current football teams derived from associations with workplaces*

Football team	Workplace
Manchester United	Yorkshire and Lancashire Railway Company
West Ham United	Thames Ironworks
Arsenal	The Royal Arsenal, Woolwich
West Bromwich Albion	Salters Spring Works

Table 17.3 *Current football teams based on Old Boy associations from various schools*

Football team	School
Blackburn Rovers	Blackburn Grammar School
Tottenham Hotspur	St John's Presbyterian School and Tottenham Grammar School
Sunderland	Sunderland and District Teachers Association
Leicester City	Wyggeston School

The difference between classes was never more apparent than in this period, owing to the increasing affluence of the middle and upper classes while the working classes were becoming more impoverished.

The professional performer in the 19th century had limited earning potential, but his earnings were still better than the normal wage for the working classes. The middle and upper classes remained firmly entrenched in their amateur ways. In fact, until quite late into the 20th century, the broad generalisation was that the professional performer was from the working classes; the agents, managers and promoters (the

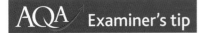

Examiner's tip

A typical question may ask you to explain how the middle and upper classes prevented the working classes from taking part in many sports.

businessmen) were from the middle classes; the sponsors and patrons were from the upper classes.

Owing to the rise in media interest in sport, the income of the various agencies involved in sport has increased to the extent that most sports are now able to support professional performers. In those sports where amateurs and professionals coexist, it is invariably the professional who tends to play at a higher standard. This increased media coverage has also increased the status of professional sportspeople. Professionals have become role models and media personalities; indeed, most people can name sporting personalities more easily than they can name people from other walks of life. In today's society, many young people aspire to emulate their sporting heroes. This may be for the financial rewards that are available but also for the social mobility that is much more possible now than in the 19th century.

Activity

Work in small groups to produce a poster that highlights the ways in which the status of amateur and professional performers changed in the last 100 years.

Olympism

Prior to the 1970s, the intention of the Olympics was to promote friendship, international harmony and understanding. The Olympics existed within a Victorian ethos: fair play and sportsmanship. Performers not only played within the rules and laws but also within the etiquette of the sport. The performers were amateurs; there were no financial rewards for winning – 'It's the taking part that counts'.

The symbols of the Olympics are designed to reinforce this ideal. There are doves of peace, the intertwined Olympic rings to show harmony, and the athlete's Olympic oath: 'We swear that we will take part in these Olympic Games in the true spirit of sportsmanship and that we will abide by the rules that govern them, for the glory of sport and the honour of our country.' These various symbols identify the values of **Olympism**.

Key terms

Olympism: competing in the spirit of sportsmanship with the emphasis on taking part rather than winning.

Fig. 17.5 *Great Britain's team at the London Olympics of 1908*

For the more recent Olympic Games, there has been a vast increase in money from TV rights because the games are highly telegenic and attract large viewing audiences. As this increase in audience numbers must be maintained, the different countries need to achieve sporting success in order to sustain interest and finance the games. The staging of the

Link

For more information on the Olympics as World Games, see Chapter 16 – Elite performers and World Games (pages 210–40).

Olympics provides the host city with the potential for substantial revenue through tourism, employment, prestige and facilities. Media coverage has increased the earning potential of successful athletes, and many sports now involve professional competitors. The Olympics have become hugely nationalistic, with countries spending millions of pounds on bringing their competitors to the highest possible level of physical prowess. The Olympics are now elitist.

The Olympic ideal

When the Olympics were originally established by Baron Pierre de Coubertin in 1896, the underlying philosophy was that the games would bring nations together, allowing the youth of the world to compete across national boundaries and increasing cross-cultural tolerance. In this respect, participation was regarded as being far more important than winning. Gradually over time, there has been an eroding of this amateur ethos and the Olympic ideal of competing fairly, i.e. with respect for others and succeeding as a result of one's own efforts and ability. In today's world, the amount of financial support available for the preparation of performers varies considerably among different countries.

Contract to compete

Key terms

Contract to compete: an unwritten code governing how to strive to play fairly, within the rules.

Sportsmanship: conforming to the rules, spirit and etiquette of a sport.

The **contract to compete** is an unwritten code whereby performers agree to strive against each other to win. Acceptance of this contract involves an expectation of how the opposition will play: it is assumed that they will play within the rules, with appropriate ethics and with sportsmanship. People talk about playing to the spirit of the contest. There is also recognition that the opposition should be allowed to play and, within the laws of the activity, possibly win. This concept is based on the culture that pervades the UK: the Victorian ideas of fair play, amateurism, athleticism, respect for the opponent, sportsmanship and that the taking part is important, not the winning. On the basis of the contract to compete, we expect performers to:

- try their best
- show **sportsmanship**
- respect the rules and officials.

Links

For more information on the contract to compete, see Chapter 18 – Deviance in sport (pages 255–6).

Sportsmanship (conforming to the rules, spirit and etiquette of the sport) is usually regarded as one of three overlapping components of morality in sport; the others are fair play and character:

- Fair play refers to allowing all participants an equal chance to achieve victory and acting towards other performers in an honest, straightforward, and dignified manner even when others do not play fairly. It assumes respect for others, including team members, opponents, and officials.
- Character refers to those values and habits that determine the way that a person normally responds to fears, challenges, failures and successes; character is typically seen in polite behaviours toward others, such as helping an opponent up or shaking hands after a match. An individual performer is believed to have a 'good character' when these tendencies and habits are part of their core values. This is important to a lot of sports.

However, over time a more negative ethic has invaded sports, involving for example:

Fig. 17.6 *Sportsmanship – England v. South Africa (2007 Rugby World Cup Final)*

- prize money
- **gamesmanship** (e.g. over-aggressiveness, foul play)
- the idea that winning is everything
- the use of drugs (breaks the rules and has potential side effects).

> ### Key terms
>
> **Gamesmanship:** 'bending the rules' – often seen as time wasting in some sports.

> ### Activity
>
> Arrange to play a game such as badminton with some friends who are not doing A Level Physical Education. As soon as the game begins, start cheating! Call your opponent's shots out when they are in. Serve incorrectly. Break as many rules as you can! Watch how the opposition reacts. How did you feel about not playing properly?

The modern performer is under pressure to perform to the highest level, and these pressures can lead to deviant behaviour. There are pressures from within the performer themselves, such as an overly strong desire to win because of the need to increase income or maintain their own self-esteem. Sometimes, the performer lacks the moral or ethical restraints that might be expected to govern their personal behaviour. Players can lose control of their own performance in response to the actions of the referee or through frustration with the opposition, possibly leading to retaliation. These pressures will increase as the importance of the occasion increases and will also increase with age as the performer's prowess diminishes.

Some pressures are external and outside the performer's control, such as the demands of the sponsor, the intrusion of the media into areas of the performer's life that are not directly related to performance, the expectations of the organisers of the event and the crowds as to how the player will perform, and the demands of coaches and team mates.

> ### AQA Examiner's tip
>
> A typical question may ask you to explain the difference between sportsmanship and gamesmanship.

Examples of functional actions

Here are some examples of functional actions in sport that are within the contract to compete:

- returning the ball to the opposition after an injury break
- clapping the opposition after losing
- 'walking' in cricket
- clapping the opposition's century
- exhausting yourself in the attempt to win
- lending the opposition a player if they are short
- admitting fouls in snooker.

Dysfunctional actions in sport

The following are some examples of dysfunctional actions in sport:

- arguing with the referee
- appealing for a throw when you know it's not yours
- deliberately fouling to prevent good performance
- diving in a game to gain a foul
- tying laces to get a rest
- using drugs.

There are reasons why some of the dysfunctional actions in modern sports are contrary to the contract to compete:

- An act of violence is outside the rules of the activity and also outside the characteristics, etiquette and ethics of the activity.
- In general, violence will deprive the victim of a free and fair opportunity to win.
- Violence is often against the law.

However, some games will allow a violent act within mutually agreed, accepted limits that are set by the participants, and a 'violent act' is within the rules of some sports (e.g. in boxing).

Link

For more information on the dysfunctional aspects of sport, see Chapter 18 – Deviance in sport (pages 252–70).

✔ *You should now be able to:*

- describe how and why various social and cultural factors led to sports developing in the UK as they did
- explain how the playing of organised sports spread from their early beginnings in the UK to become commonplace throughout the world
- explain how the status of professional sportspeople has changed over the last 150 years
- understand the importance of fair play in the playing of sport
- explain the difference between sportsmanship and gamesmanship.

1   The opportunity for sporting and recreational activities has varied since the 19th century, and many sports have undergone dramatic changes since the middle of the 19th century.

    (a)   Mob football was an example of popular recreation. What were the characteristics of mob games?   *(3 marks)*

    (b)   Figure 17.7 depicts a football match between England and Scotland at the Oval in 1875 (an early example of rational recreation).

Fig. 17.7

            Using the information provided in Figure 17.7 as a guide, describe the characteristics of rational recreation.   *(4 marks)*

            AQA, January 2007

2   At the beginning of the 20th century, the extent and nature of a person's participation in sport were influenced by their social class and gender.

    (a)   Describe the differences in the sports played and the roles undertaken by the upper/middle classes and the working classes. Illustrate your answer with examples.   *(4 marks)*

    (b)   Discuss the reasons why people from the working class had fewer opportunities to participate than those from the upper and middle classes.   *(3 marks)*

            AQA, January 2004

3   Many elite sports have a high public profile and offer the performers extrinsic rewards. Violence may sometimes occur in elite sport, both on and off the pitch.

    (a)   Discuss whether an act of violence would be acceptable within the concept of the 'contract to compete'.   *(4 marks)*

    (b)   Explain what is meant by the term 'gamesmanship' and give examples of its use in different sporting situations.   *(3 marks)*

            AQA, June 2003 and June 2006

4   (a)   The desire to win a gold medal may be taken too far and have detrimental effects for both the performer and society in general. What might these detrimental effects be and how may they go against the Olympic ideal?   *(5 marks)*

    Violence may sometimes occur in elite sport, both on and off the pitch.

    (b)   Why might an elite performer commit an act of violence on the pitch?   *(2 marks)*

            AQA, June 2003

18 Deviance in sport

Link

For more information on the influence of the public schools and on Baron de Coubertin and the rebirth of the Olympic Games, see Chapter 17 – The Olympic ideal and modern sport (pages 245–8).

Often the highest of motives are claimed for sport whether played at grass roots level or at international level. When those who make such claims point to the ethical and social values inherent in sport, they may be looking back to the roots of rational sport in the English public schools of the 19th century and the philosophy of athleticism. In the modern era, the Olympic Games still strives to present itself in the highest moral light – the Olympic oath being an example of this desire:

> In the name of all the competitors I promise that we shall take part in these Olympic Games, respecting and abiding by the rules which govern them, committing ourselves to a sport without doping and without drugs, in the true spirit of sportsmanship, for the glory of sport and the honour of our teams.

www.olympic.org.uk

Officials also swear an oath:

> In the name of all the judges and officials, I promise that we shall officiate in these Olympic Games with complete impartiality, respecting and abiding by the rules which govern them in the true spirit of sportsmanship.

www.la84foundation.org

When studying definitions of sport at AS Level, we noted that sport helps us learn the norms of society, that it gives us something to strive for and an opportunity for better international relationships and improved morale. When studying the history of sport, we looked at the development of athleticism in the 19th-century public schools and how the Victorians valued sport for the opportunities that it gave to develop leadership, courage and sportsmanship. When reviving the Olympic Games in the early 20th century, Baron de Coubertin valued the participation beyond the result when he said: 'The most important thing is not to win but to take part, just as the most important thing in life is not the triumph but the struggle'.

Wimbledon finalists, on their way to Centre Court, still pass Rudyard Kipling's words: 'If you can meet with triumph and disasters and treat those two impostors just the same'.

Our language is littered with sporting metaphors, giving us guidance in how to conduct our lives (e.g. 'batting on a sticky wicket', 'being on the ropes', 'the final hurdle'). Our culture puts sport on a pedestal; our sporting heroes are influential role models; sports stars become our gladiatorial representatives; and billions watch the Olympic closing ceremony, looking forward to the next time the youth of the world are gathered together. Unfortunately, however, human nature being what it is, there are times when the actions of our sporting elite disappoint us.

Nobody who has had the slightest interest in sport can have failed to notice that international sport and elite performers have frequently fallen short of the lofty ideals described above. Examples are plentiful: the use of performance-enhancing drugs, underhand transfer payments, betting scandals, cricketers throwing matches, hooliganism at football matches, corruption during the Olympic bidding process, players arrested after on-field player violence, the bribing of match officials and deliberate cheating within a match or contest. In this chapter, we shall look at the nature of **deviance** in sport, examine the causes of such behaviour and see how the authorities are trying to deal with deviant behaviour. Finally, we shall ask ourselves if sport has lost its value for society, lost its moral justification and its ability to act as a guiding force in the development of young people.

Activity

1. Find examples of the deviant behaviours listed below, by researching online news archives:
   - use of performance-enhancing drugs
   - bribery of officials or players
   - hooliganism
   - illegal betting on sport, or betting on sport that contravenes the laws of a sport
   - corruption in the Olympic bidding process
   - illegal payments to agents, players or managers during player-transfer activity
   - player violence and the law.
2. Present your research as a poster – either as hard copy or electronically.

Deviance

The term 'deviant' or 'deviance' refers to any social behaviour that is different, or departs from, what is regarded as normal or acceptable within society. Behaviour in sport is governed by what are considered to be reasonable actions within society at large and what is acceptable within a sporting context. It is possible to find examples of behaviour in sport that would not be acceptable in wider society. It is clear that punching somebody in a boxing ring, within the laws of the sport, would not be considered deviant behaviour, but to do it in the street, unless in self-defence, would be deviant behaviour. Any behaviour that in our day-to-day life breaks the law of the land is clearly deviant, as is, in a sporting context, any action that breaks the rules or laws of a sport. However, we are not just concerned with the behaviour of players – deviant behaviour can be exhibited by spectators, managers, coaches, and officials.

Types of deviance

Most of the time, deviant behaviour is given a negative connotation: breaking the social norms or rules; doing harm; known to be wrong. Some deviant behaviour can be viewed in a more positive light, however, and we need to differentiate between positive deviance and negative deviance. Sports sociologist Jay Coakley (1992) considered that, in this context, there are three types of behaviour:

- **positive deviance** (overconforming to what is expected)
- normal behaviour
- **negative deviance** (underconforming to what is expected).

Coakley suggests that there is a normal distribution for these behaviours (see Figure 18.1) with most behaviour being within the normal category.

Key terms

Deviance: behaviour that falls outside the norms or outside what is deemed to be acceptable.

Positive deviance: behaviour that is outside the norm but with no intention to harm or break the rules.

Negative deviance: behaviour that goes against the norm and has a detrimental effect on individuals and on society in general.

AQA Examiner's tip

Questions relating to the topic of deviance in sport will often require you to give examples of such behaviour, the methods used to control it and possible reasons for the behaviour. It is vital that you have **debated** the issues as part of the learning process; otherwise you will find it hard to answer the questions.

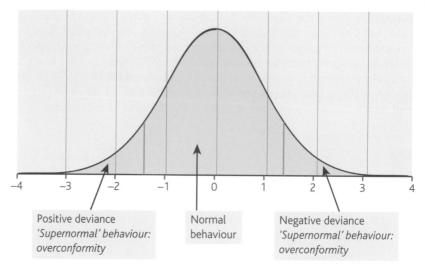

Adapted from R. Hughes in J. Coakley, Sport in Society, 2006

Fig. 18.1 *The distribution of behaviour*

Positive deviance

We have defined deviance as not keeping to the norms of behaviour expected within society or within a subsection of society (sport can be seen as a subsection of social behaviour). It is possible therefore to move away from the expected norms but without the intention to do harm or break the rules. For example, an individual who trains or plays so hard that they injure themselves is certainly not acting within the sporting norm, therefore they are being deviant. Such behaviour can lead to a disruption of normal life, or can drive a performer to play when injured (often to praise from the media). Because their actions are for positive reasons – they are striving to win, or to improve within the ethical guidelines of the activity – these actions, although deviant, can be seen in a positive light. They would be exhibiting positive deviance. One could also argue that the player who is striving to win within the rules and etiquette of a sport and who accidentally and without intent injures another player is also exhibiting positive deviance.

AQA Examiner's tip

Students often forget the issue of positive deviance, focusing solely on negative deviance. Ensure that you have examples of both and can discuss possible causes.

Fig. 18.2 *An accidental foul – then look after the player*

Activity
Look back at the examples of deviant behaviour that you found for the previous learning activity (page 253). Did you find any examples of what you may now consider to be positive deviance? If not, can you now recall any behaviour from your own sporting experience that falls within this category?

Negative deviance

Negative deviance occurs when a player, spectator or anybody else involved in sport behaves in a way that knowingly and intentionally breaks the rules and ethics of sport. We have already identified the types of behaviour that this would include:

- using performance-enhancing drugs
- cheating within a contest, e.g. deliberately fouling another player, 'diving', injuring another player, etc.
- being bribed to influence the outcome of a match (official or player)
- fan violence or **hooliganism**
- illegal betting on the outcome of a contest
- financial irregularities in the transferring of players
- player violence.

Relative deviance

Some actions that in sport are deemed to be within the 'normal and acceptable behaviour' category would be considered both deviant and illegal if they took place in wider society. For example, when rugby players use their fists either in the open or in the dark confines of the scrum, officials, commentators, and players deem this to be quite acceptable as long as the level of violence does not breach an unwritten rule or limit. On the other hand, biting and gouging are definitely off limits. The average person in the street may struggle to understand this concept of **relative deviance** (i.e. that a behaviour is acceptable in a subculture but would not be acceptable outside the confines of that subculture). Sport often prefers to deal itself with those who break its rules and etiquette, but the police are increasingly less willing to look the other way when a breach of the law occurs, even though the behaviour in question has occurred within a sporting context.

Whether or not the behaviour is viewed within a sporting context is determined by whether or not it breaks the contract to compete.

Deviance and the contract to compete

The contract to compete is an understanding shared by players (and by association coaches, managers, etc.) with regard to their obligations (see Figure 18.3).

The contract sets out the following obligations for those engaged in sport:

- In a sporting contest you agree to strive against each other to win. If you fail to do that you are depriving the other person of their sense of achievement and cheating the spectators and all those who have supported you. If you deliberately do not try, or try to lose, you are exhibiting negative deviance.
- If, within the rules or ethics of the activity, you are trying so hard to win that you break the rules (e.g. by deliberate cheating) or

Key terms

Hooliganism: the behaviour of those who engage in unruly, destructive or violent acts, often lnked to supporters of professional football.

Relative deviance: deviant behaviour that is not acceptable in wider society but may be deemed to be acceptable by those involved in a sub-culture.

AQA Examiner's tip

When discussing concepts of deviance (negative, positive and relative), it is essential that you look beyond your own experience. Exam questions expect a balanced response that goes beyond your own experience and, possibly, stereotypical views.

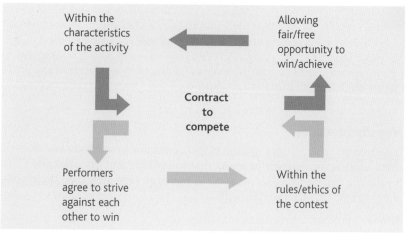

Fig. 18.3 *The contract to compete*

transgress the ethics of the activity through unacceptable physical conduct (e.g. by biting) then you are again exhibiting negative deviance.

■ Within the contract, you are expected to allow your opponents a free and fair opportunity to win. The taking of drugs, for example, or bribing an official, does not allow this and therefore exhibits negative deviance.

■ However, within the characteristics of the activity, you may use all the tactics, strategies and skills that you have to prevent your opponents from defeating you as long as you operate within the expectations of the activity (relative deviance).

The concepts of a contract to compete and relative deviance are strongly connected; both imply that somehow sport exists within in its own moral subculture. However, such a notion is increasingly being challenged as sport becomes ever more high profile within the media and society in general.

Link

The idea of a contract to compete is linked to the concepts of sportsmanship and athleticism that are discussed in Chapter 17 – The Olympic ideal and modern sport (pages 248–9).

AQA Examiner's tip

Students' responses to questions about the contract to compete are often very limited. You will find it easier to express the theoretical elements if you place the contract in a personal context by relating it to your own sport experience.

Activity

1. Watch an elite-level contest, either live or on television. What evidence can you see for the existence of the contract to compete?

2. Note examples of the contract's being adhered to and examples of when it might have been broken.

3. Do you think the contest could have taken place without the contract's being adhered to?

4. Be prepared to discuss your findings with the rest of your group.

Causes of deviant behaviour

The causes of deviant behaviour will vary depending on the context but there are some commonly identified general causes:

■ Individual players lack the moral restraint to keep to a code of conduct.

■ Individuals may value winning above the loss of respect or punishment that may occur as the result of deviant behaviour.

- The rewards of winning may be so great that a larger number of individuals are prepared to cross the line. This may be particularly true for what is considered positive deviance.
- Deviant behaviour may have become less socially unacceptable and cause less negative comment than in the past.
- Sport governing bodies may feel less able to punish deviant behaviour, owing to the power of commercial interests or fear of being taken to the courts by the performers whom they wish to punish.

Link

For a more detailed discussion on the effects of commercial pressure, see Chapter 19 – Commercialisation of elite sport (pages 276–85).

Violence in sport

In this section we shall be considering violence between participants and violence among spectators (hooliganism). We shall see that these two issues are connected.

Violence between players

Violence between players generally occurs in two ways:

- as a spontaneous outburst
- as a premeditated and planned action.

The causes of violence between players

Most violence between players occurs as an aggressive act by one player to another. As Chapter 12 – Changing behaviour discussed aggressive behaviour and its causes at some length (from page 165), there is no need to repeat the material in detail here. However, briefly, aggressive behaviour may be caused by:

- genetic inheritance predisposing some people towards aggressive behaviour
- frustration – for example, frustration in a competitive situation can predispose us to aggressive behaviour, especially if there are cues for aggression within the environment; we may also act aggressively in retaliation or reaction to crowd abuse; it may be thought that the more important the contest, the greater the potential for frustration and therefore aggression, but this does not seem to be the case
- loss of self-identity, leading us to follow the actions of the crowd rather than our own inclinations
- social learning, imitating the actions of a respected role model whose aggressive behaviour has been positively reinforced (rewarded) in some way.

It is also the case that violent acts are perpetrated in a cold and deliberate manner, not as a result of heightened emotions. Within some teams there are well-known characters, sometimes known as 'enforcers', whose role is to physically intimidate the opposition or to act in retaliation on behalf of others.

Dealing with violence between players

Controlling violent behaviour is the responsibility of individual performers, team managers or coaches and the national governing bodies (NGBs) of sport.

NGBs are obviously keen to diminish violent player behaviour that will bring the sport into disrepute, and they have a responsibility to protect individual players from being the victim of a violent action by another player. It is also increasingly evident that the police and the legal system are becoming more involved with acts of violence that may be termed

Fig. 18.4 *Violence – the stress of the situation?*

Fig. 18.5 *Controlling players – are referees always supported?*

assault, and NGBs would much rather be seen to be dealing with such incidents themselves. An NGB may take a range of actions when dealing with player violence:

- ensuring that match officials and their decisions are supported when dealing with violent behaviour by players
- punishing players post match
- being prepared to use post-match video evidence or have a citing system
- upholding players with a good disciplinary record as role models
- using 'fair play' awards to reward clubs with good disciplinary records
- training officials in player management and how to defuse situations between players.

Activity

1. Research the codes of conduct and the national disciplinary procedures of your own sport.

2. Create a short handout to give to other members of the group. (This will give you a range of examples to use in an examination question.)

Team managers, coaches and captains have a great responsibility for player conduct. The instructions that are given during training or in pre-match meetings, what is said about what is expected of players and the singling out of behaviour for praise or criticism will have a significant effect on how players behave, especially the younger players. To ensure good player behaviour, individuals in leadership roles can:

- set a good example themselves before and during contests
- establish a clear code of expectations and conduct
- criticise or punish players who fail to meet the code of expectations; play substitutes in their place
- praise or promote those players who set a good example
- where possible, ensure that players who have a low flash point are kept away from high-stress situations
- stress appropriate behaviour in team talks
- understand each individual player's level of arousal and try to avoid overarousal
- train players to manage their own level of arousal
- avoid an attitude of winning at all costs.

Activity

1. Devise a code of conduct for players or performers in your own sport or for your own club or team.

2. Compare your code to those written for other sports.

   a. What were the major differences in the codes of conduct?

   b. Do different sports seem to have different expectations? (Use the national guidelines researched in the previous activity.)

In reality, it is the individual player who has the greatest responsibility for their behaviour; player behaviour should reflect a clear understanding of their responsibilities and be founded on a moral and ethical code. Through the process of social learning, a player develops their own set of personal guidelines which enable them to make the right decisions. A sufficiently strong personal code of conduct should enable a player to take an independent stand even if they are asked to behave in a way that they know to be wrong. A player develops such a code by:

■ being exposed to good role models from a young age

■ receiving a set of expectations (from parents, coaches and others in leadership roles) that are in accordance with the rules, ethics and code of conduct of the sport

■ understanding how to control their own level of arousal and how to reduce anger and frustration

■ knowing what leads to anger and frustration and finding ways to avoid those situations.

Activity

Review competitive games or situations in which you have been personally involved.

1 Were there any situations that caused you to feel anger and frustration?

2 How did you deal with those situations? Were your actions in accordance with a player code of conduct or your own expectations of yourself?

3 If a similar situation arose in the future, how might you deal with it differently?

 Examiner's tip

Violence in sport is a subject that can spark emotional debate from those who are passionate about sport – and that includes you! Remember that you have to use reasoned debate and good examples when answering a question.

Violence among spectators

Spectator violence has been a problem for football for the last 50 years. It is not confined to the UK but is a worldwide phenomenon and although acts by hooligans can be serious they are often over-reported and sensationalised by the media. A distinction should be drawn between hooligans, fans and supporters. Most people can support their club or country at football matches, or be a football fan, without ever being involved in behaviour that in any way could be described as hooliganism. Hooligans use football as a stage and a justification for the abusive and violent acts in which they are engaged.

Where does hooliganism take place?

First, we should establish what we mean by 'hooliganism' or 'hooligan behaviour':

■ racist and/or obscene chanting

■ fighting with other hooligan groups

■ vandalism and destruction of property

■ interference with the match (pitch invasions etc.)

■ violence against non-hooligans (members of the public, other fans, etc.).

Hooligan confrontations are often:

■ pre-organised

■ looking for conflict with the authorities, especially the police

■ linked to consumption of alcohol

Fig. 18.6 *Hooliganism – what, where and why?*

■ large scale, with many people being involved and evidence of a 'herd' effect.

This behaviour can take place:

■ in football grounds and stadiums

■ in the streets within the vicinity of the ground

■ in city centres

■ in local pubs

■ on public transport such as trains

■ abroad when attending international matches (club or country).

Hooligan behaviour takes place in a variety of locations, often in reaction to the ways in which the police and authorities are dealing with the problem.

Given the long-standing nature of fan violence and hooligan behaviour, the phenomenon has been studied by sociologists and other academics in an attempt to discover its causes.

Activity

Elite rugby and cricket matches attract large numbers of spectators. Alcoholic refreshment is freely available and supporters from different teams sit together. There is little poor behaviour from spectators during these matches and no history of hooliganism.

1 Research details of fan misbehaviour in cricket and rugby – is the above statement true?

2 Assuming it is true, why should this be the case?

The causes of hooliganism

Many explanations have been offered, but none gives a full explanation.

■ It is a form of ritualised behaviour with much posturing and shouting, engaged in as an expression of masculinity, and being part of a group. Committing a hooligan act is seen as a rite of passage.

This may give some explanation but hooligan behaviour goes beyond the ritualistic, is not solely engaged in by males and does not always involve membership of a group.

- It acts as an outlet for young working-class males who are often aggressive and feel themselves restricted by the constraints and limits of an increasingly 'safe' society.

  The counterargument to this is that not all young males feel the need to engage in such behaviour, and hooligans come from a much wider social group than just the working class.

- Hooliganism is a form of tribal behaviour with membership of the group being granted to those who have proved themselves. The group perceive themselves as protecting their local area or patch from fans from the away teams and as establishing national superiority when abroad.

  This may explain some aspects of the behaviour, but hooligans often come from different parts of the country; they are not all 'local'. Not all fans from the local area take part in hooligan acts; fans from other national groups do not engage in such behaviour; and the supporters and fans of other sports do not act in this way – rugby matches have no fan segregation at all.

- Football used to be predominantly a working-class sport, but in recent years it has increasingly become the preserve of a wealthier, more middle-class fan base (a process known as 'bourgeoisification'). It is suggested that hooligan behaviour is a reaction to this on the part of the traditional working-class fan group and also a reaction to the de-skilling and loss of traditional working-class jobs, unemployment and boredom.

  Whilst it is true to say that the spectator balance has changed, particularly for a number of the clubs in the higher divisions, hooligans are not exclusively working class or from lower socio-economic groups.

- Tension on the pitch, violence by one player to another or an officiating decision can act as triggers to fans who are passionately connected to the success of their team.

  There are many fans in football and in other sports equally passionate about their team and engaged in the drama on the pitch, but who never feel the need to resort to an act of hooliganism.

- Some clubs have had their supporter groups infiltrated by extreme political groups which use matches as an opportunity to distribute racist or fascist literature and to incite violence against others who do not share their views.

  Such infiltration is restricted to a few groups and cannot account for hooliganism in general.

- The close rivalry between local teams in derby matches can inflame fans' passions, as can playing against teams from other countries when excessive nationalistic feelings may spill over into violent behaviour. This is often picked up on by the print media in an attempt to increase sales.

  Other sports have derby matches or play against rival nations without there being disturbances between rival fans; in many sports they sit together and enjoy the banter.

In essence, it is not possible to identify a single cause of hooligan behaviour in football. It would seem to be multi-causal with each explanation adding something to our understanding of what may cause such behaviour.

AQA Examiner's tip

An exam question on the causes of hooliganism will expect you know some of the explanations given and the counterarguments. It is always correct to say that it is multi-causal.

Combating hooliganism

Fig. 18.7 *Combating hooliganism – ruining the spectator experience?*

During the 1970s and 1980s, football hooliganism became a significant problem for the football authorities and for wider society and it was clear that action had to be taken. The government, the football governing bodies and the police cooperated to put in place a range of strategies that have resulted in a significant reduction in football-related violence. Those strategies are:

■ prevention of known hooligans from travelling to matches, by requiring them to report to police stations during match times or by applying banning orders.

■ control of alcohol – not serving alcohol within grounds or requiring local pubs to close early

■ segregation of fans travelling to the match and within the grounds

■ the introduction of all-seater stadiums for teams playing in the higher divisions (reduces movement within a stand and gives better control over ticket distribution)

■ improved levels of policing and stewarding, allied to better training of stewards (improves crowd control and can lower tension)

■ introduction of closed-circuit television (CCTV) cameras at grounds and entrances to stadiums (resulting in more information about individuals engaged in hooligan behaviour; when CCTV is coupled with modern-day face-recognition software, known hooligans can be identified and, if appropriate, prevented from entering the ground)

■ sharing of police intelligence across police forces within the UK and abroad (UK police officers travel to other countries to help spot known troublemakers and to advise local police forces; some officers have gone undercover to infiltrate violent fan groups or extreme political groups to gain intelligence)

■ not allowing players to make any kind of action or gesture to the crowd that might cause crowd disturbances

■ responding to the poor behaviour of fans or supporters of a club by banning or removal from competitions, fines, or playing matches away or behind closed doors

- use by the football authorities of high-profile role models to appeal for better supporter behaviour (campaigns such as 'Kick racism out of football' attempted to diminish the influence of racist movements within groups of football supporters).

Activity

All of the above measures have been put in place at elite-level football matches but very few have been introduced for other sports. It is likely that you have attended elite-level matches or contests, or have family or friends who have done so. Research the following questions and then give a presentation to other members of the group.

1. Either from your own experience or that of others, describe the experience of attending an elite sport contest.

2. How does the experience of the football fan differ from the experience of fans and supporters of other sports?

3. If you have attended an elite-level football match, how did the measures for crowd control etc. make you feel?

The effect that violence has on individuals, sport and wider society

Violence of any kind, whether involving players or fans, brings a sport into disrepute and damages its ability to encourage children, young people and families to participate. If parents believe that a sport is likely to bring their children into contact with violence and put their wellbeing at risk, they are highly unlikely to allow their children to take part in that sport. A similar reaction is likely if poor behaviour occurs during local matches, for example if children are encouraged to play inappropriately or parents and other supporters abuse officials, opponents or each other. As was seen during the 1970s and 1980s, violence on the football field can have far-reaching effects:

- Fan violence may lead to poor treatment of legitimate fans and supporters, who are held in the grounds until other fans have left, herded through the streets to get to the stadium or treated with suspicion and distrust, especially when abroad. Significantly, camaraderie between fans and supporters is less evident than in other sports.

- Individual players who are injured as a result of deliberate foul play may have their career and therefore livelihood curtailed.

- Individual players may have their chance of international recognition damaged if their team is not allowed to play in an international competition as a result of the behaviour of their supporters.

- There is a huge cost involved in terms of policing and stewarding football matches. Although clubs and the Football Association (FA) bear some of the cost, some costs are borne by the budget of the area's police force, which reduces resources to be used elsewhere or requires an increase in taxation.

- The reputation of the country as a whole can be affected by the disorderly behaviour of football fans when they travel abroad or their behaviour is seen on television screens worldwide. The banning of teams from competing in European competitions can have social and economic effects that go beyond the club or the individual players.

■ The poor behaviour of those who support our international team can also have an effect on national morale (just as significant as the (opposite) effect of achieving international success).

Effects such as those listed above prompted the range of countermeasures that are now in place (see page 262) and it is clear that the actions of the authorities have achieved much in terms of reducing violence among fans and on the field. However, another aspect of deviant behaviour, the use of performance-enhancing drugs, is proving far more difficult to solve.

■ Sport and the use of drugs

Sports performers have been tempted to use drugs to enhance their performance since the Ancient Olympics, and it is a major problem for elite sport in the 21st century. In Chapter 4 – The elite performer: food, supplements and performance-enhancing drugs (pages 56–8), we had a close look at the types of drugs that are being used and the effects on the performer, both in terms of short-term gains in performance and the more long-term, health-related issues. We are now going to examine the ethics of drug use, the methods of testing and the policies that have been put in place to eradicate their use in sport.

We are concerned with drugs that produce an ergogenic effect or act as an ergogenic aid – they improve performance above what might be achieved normally. This therefore excludes what might be termed 'recreational drugs', unless they have an abnormal effect on performance, and excludes food supplements, although performers are advised to check the World Anti-Doping Agency (WADA) banned substances list.

 Link

For more information on WADA, see Chapter 4 – The elite performer: food, supplements and performance-enhancing drugs (page 58).

Fig. 18.8 *The World Anti-Doping Agency*

■ **Link**

For definitions of these drugs, their effects on performance and their long-term effects on health, look back at Chapter 4 – The elite performer: food, supplements and performance-enhancing drugs (pages 56–8), before you carry on with this chapter.

The following drugs are covered within the AQA specification:

- ■ erythropoietin (EPO)
- ■ anabolic steroids (testosterone)
- ■ human growth hormone (HGH)
- ■ beta blockers
- ■ diuretics
- ■ stimulants.

Why do performers use drugs?

The reasons for performers being tempted to use banned performance-enhancing drugs (PEDs) are broadly similar to the ones given for any deviant behaviour:

■ Some performers may lack the moral and ethical boundaries that prevent others from engaging in an action that most performers would consider to be wrong or to be cheating.

■ They may believe that 'everybody else is doing it' and that they therefore cannot win unless they do so too.

■ They lack the physical and psychological attributes to get to the top without the use of banned drugs.

■ They may not be fully aware that they are using drugs, choosing to give all control over medication, diet and the use of supplements to their coach.

■ The rewards for winning are so great that they are tempted to go beyond what they know to be acceptable, or they attempt to maintain their livelihood as a professional performer by using drugs to stay at the top.

▪ They receive the wrong guidance or educational programmes or have the wrong role models when young.

▪ They are not fully aware of the long-term health risks associated with many PEDs.

▪ They may be pressured by coaches or team managers to use drugs.

▪ They may be tempted to use them to speed recovery from injury.

It should be noted that the use of a PED does not guarantee success. To be an elite performer still requires the performer to have extraordinary physiological and psychological qualities and to train hard to develop them – no drug can replace that. But it is clear that the range of PEDs available does enhance performance and can make the difference between a gold medal and coming fourth (that difference may only be a few hundredths of a second and some performers are tempted to go to any lengths to make it). You should also understand that the use of PEDs seems to be most common in sports that have a high proportion of closed skills – where the relationship between physiological attributes and success is most clearly linked and direct. There is less evidence of their use in highly interactive spots with many open-skill situations – although this may be as a result of weaker testing regimes, as we shall see next.

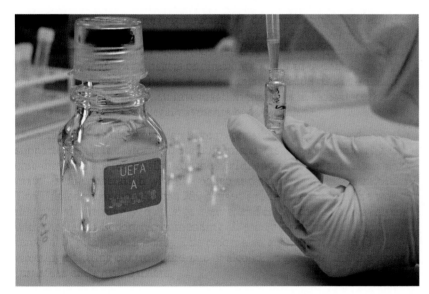

Fig. 18.9 *Drugs and sport – can the battle be won?*

The battle against performers' use of drugs

Every sport, every country and every national and international sport governing body is engaged in trying to find, punish and prevent the use of PEDs by performers and coaches. They do this in a number of ways:

▪ providing testing regimes and laboratory facilities to test performers to see if they are using drugs

▪ taking punitive action against those who have been proved to have used banned substances or have them within their body

▪ trying to educate young performers in the ethical and moral case against the use of drugs and ensuring that they are aware of the consequences for their future as a performer and for their health if they take PEDs

■ ensuring that performers are aware of what is allowed and not allowed and what their responsibilities are.

> ■ Activity
>
> 1 Research the drug control measures for your own sport. What sanctions are you likely to face should you be tested positive?
>
> 2 Prepare your findings as a bullet-point revision sheet for the rest of your teaching group.

Who is involved in the battle against drugs?

WADA

WADA is the foremost international body involved in the battle and is responsible for promoting, coordinating, and monitoring at international level the fight against the use of drugs in sport. In 2003, it introduced a World Anti-Doping Code which provides the framework for anti-doping policies, rules, and regulations. Eighty governments signed up to the code, as did the International Olympic Committee, the International Paralympic Committee, all Olympic sports, national Olympic and Paralympic committees and national and international anti-doping organisations. WADA promotes research into the detection of drugs and produces a list of banned substances; it also helps national bodies to produce coordinated anti-drug policies and regimes in accordance with the code. In addition, WADA helps poorer nations with limited facilities to test their performers and is working to get more compliance for out-of-competition, no-notice testing.

UK Sport and the NADO

In the UK, UK Sport has the primary responsibility for anti-doping policy and strategy. The Drug Control Centre at King's College London was established in 1978 to analyse samples collected from sports competitors. At present (2008), UK Sport continues to support the Centre and the anti-doping programme which covers events and training in the UK. However, in 2009, UK Sport will hand over management of the UK testing programme to a new organisation, the National Anti-Doping Organisation (NADO):

■ The NADO will determine which sports will be required to provide information on players' whereabouts.

■ The athletes on the system will be agreed between the NADO and the sport's NGB.

■ Performers will be required to provide quarterly information on their exact whereabouts for one hour a day, seven days a week, and full details of their training and competition schedule as well as full contact details.

■ Missed tests and filing failures (failure to provide sufficient information) will count as a strike – three strikes over an 18-month period will mean that an anti-doping rule violation has possibly been committed.

■ This will lead to a sanction of one to two years' suspension, depending on degree of fault.

AQA Examiner's tip

As a performer, or an official or coach, you should be aware of the regulations and rules concerning the misuse of drugs. Ensure that you have looked carefully at the websites for UK Sport, WADA and your NGB to have a clear picture of your responsibilities.

What is being done to deter performers from taking drugs?

In an attempt to stamp out the use of banned substances within sport, a whole range of approaches are being taken:

- NGBs are doing more to educate performers, especially younger performers, about the long-term hazards to an individual's health of using PEDs.

- Efforts are being made to ensure that all performers are clear about the testing regime, their responsibilities and the possible outcomes for a positive test. All performers are responsible for what they put in their bodies.

- There has been an increase in the number of out-of-competition, no-warning tests. Many sports now demand that performers are available to take a drug test at any time of the day or night and must inform their NGB or the testing authorities of their whereabouts.

- The severity of the punishment for proven drug use has been increased.

- Efforts are being made to achieve a more consistent approach among countries in relation to the testing regime (how often, with/without notice, etc.) and the sanctions to be taken in the event of a positive test result.

- Use is being made of positive role models to educate and encourage young performers not to use PEDs.

- There is continuing development of more sophisticated tests, or tests for new drugs; this is an ongoing battle as chemists continuously research new ways of manipulating chemicals to aid human performance. Many of the drugs that are used by sport performers were originally devised for use in a medical context, and many are still used for this legitimate purpose.

- More use is being made of the law, so that both those who supply and those who use these drugs are open to prosecution and the possibility of a prison sentence. By 2008, only Italy has made the taking of PEDs illegal. Some countries will prosecute the supply of prescription drugs without a licence.

If a performer has tested positive for a banned substance and this has been confirmed with a test on the 'B sample', the performer will face a range of sanctions. These are agreed between the NGB and the international body and are in accordance with the nature of the offence. For example, missing three random tests is an offence under the code; but the level of sanction will range from several years' suspension to lifetime bans as given by the British Olympic Association.

Testing for PEDs

Although there is a worldwide body, not all countries adopt the same level of rigour towards anti-doping testing programmes or in the way that offenders are punished. Even within countries that are fully committed to the WADA code, different sports may have different approaches. This leads to an unevenness of approach, allowing performers to argue that they are being unfairly treated and possibly forming the basis of legal appeals.

Within the UK, performers have to submit themselves to a drug-testing regime as agreed with their NGB. This will include the following:

- notification by the performer of their whereabouts to UK Sport (from 2009 to the NADO)

Fig. 18.10 *Drug testing – an ongoing battle*

■ **Activity**

For discussion or debate: 'Is using a decompression chamber the same as using erythropoietin or blood doping?' Prepare arguments for and against each side of this question. Be prepared to speak either for or against the motion.

AQA **Examiner's tip**

The socio-cultural element of the specification often deals with issues that require opinion, debate and matters of conviction. Candidates will frequently be asked to discuss the underlying issues and reasons and to show an ability to weigh up the evidence to reach a personal conclusion. On these kinds of issues, there may not be a simple right or wrong response – it is the quality of the argument that is being marked.

- the drug tester turning up unannounced at any time, day or night
- taking the samples as laid down by the NADO, including the choosing of sample pots, observation of the sample being given, the taking of a B sample, and the signing of the sample form by the performer
- asking the performer if they have taken any medication in the last seven days
- bar-coding the sample so that the athlete's identity is not known by the laboratory where the test is done.

The use of drugs – a legal or a moral issue?

Despite the resources that are being used to try and stamp out the use of PEDs in sport, it is clear that many performers still use them. There are mixed feelings over the length of punishment for drug taking, whether bans should be permanent and for all time, and whether or not the taking of a drug is different from using other sophisticated training aids such as decompression chambers.

Is the taking of drugs wrong simply because the governing bodies of sport say that it is or is there a moral issue to be debated? If you accept that laws are enacted to provide control over an individual's actions then those laws have to be based on a clear moral and ethical rationale. So what is the argument for the banning of PEDs?

If you asked a range of elite performers – and those who prepare them – the question 'Should PEDs be banned?', they will instinctively answer yes. But there are some coaches, performers and those who have a deep interest in sport who will argue that there is a case for not banning the use of drugs. They make the following points:

- The battle against drugs, the development of new tests for new drugs, the testing regime and the occasional need to defend a decision in the courts are all expensive and time consuming. The money would be better used in improving support for all performers.
- The detection of drug use is not always effective; tests are not always undertaken properly; and in some countries sports detection is not

as effective as in others. This makes drug detection a lottery, and performers are not therefore treated the same, which is unfair.

- The drug testers are always behind the chemists, playing catch-up to devise new tests for new drugs or masking agents. Therefore those athletes with enough resources and access to the most up-to-date drugs will be able to use them undetected for a while.

- Nutritional supplements are claimed to have a beneficial effect on performance, and the line between what is a drug and what is a nutritional supplement can be difficult to define and may be arbitrary. This does not seem logical to some.

- Performers put themselves through years of hard training and effort. The playing of many sports places a performer at risk of serious and permanent injury, even death. The sacrifices that a performer is prepared to make to achieve success are a personal decision; why should the taking of PEDs with their associated long-term health risks be any different?

- If the use of PEDs leads to improved performances and the setting of new records, this will make sport more exciting and attractive, which will in turn attract more spectators, TV viewers and ultimately sponsors, bringing more money and allowing more people to make a living from sport.

- If the use of PEDs is made a personal decision for the performer, you achieve a level playing field for all.

- The argument that there is not a level playing field, as PEDs are not available to all performers because of the cost, applies not only to drugs. Sport scientists are continually devising more methods of helping performers improve their performance, and those performers with the greatest resources available to them have a greater chance of fulfilling their potential.

Having considered the reasons that some performers might give for not banning the use of PEDs, we should now consider the other side of the debate.

- Whilst most training or playing injuries are temporary, they are not a predetermined side effect of playing high-level sport. The permanently damaging side effects for health of using drugs are known and inevitable, and on that basis should not be allowed.

- If the use of PEDs becomes legalised, it will be assumed that you could not succeed without them. This would pressure all performers into taking them, particularly the young and uninformed who may do so without full knowledge or consideration of the side effects.

- Similarly, performers may come under increased pressure from coaches and team mates, especially within professional/commercial sport.

- There is a cost element in developing and using PEDs; therefore, there cannot be the level playing field that the pro-use argument has claimed; the drugs would not be available to all.

- The final argument, and perhaps the most powerful, is that sport is about the utilisation and development of natural talents and the use of drugs does not sit well with that. Using a PED is not the same as using a training aid. A training aid is used to enhance and develop the existing physiological or psychological abilities already within the performer. PEDs give the performer something that was not already there and therefore boost performance artificially.

> **Link**
>
> For a more information on nutritional supplements, see Chapter 4 –The elite performer: food, supplements and performance-enhancing drugs (pages 50–3).

For these reasons, using PEDs is seen to be unethical; it is perceived as going against the very nature of what sport is about and is clearly cheating.

As part of the fight against drugs a number of countries have now made the use and possession of a wide range of PEDs illegal unless they are being used for certified medical purposes. This brings us to the final part of this chapter, the developing involvement of the law in sport.

Sport and the law

Over the last few decades, elite sport and the law have become more and more entwined. We have seen headlines about illegal betting within sport, prosecutions of players for violent behaviour, bribery allegations, prosecutions for drug offences, and professional players using employment legislation (the **Bosman ruling**). As elite sport becomes more commercialised and more a part of the news and entertainment industry, the stakes become higher for players, officials and spectators, and any transgressions by individuals involved in sport are more likely to attract the attention of the police and the courts.

Not only is a huge amount of national and international case law and legislation solely concerned with sport but it is possible for a lawyer to specialise in **sport law**. Players, team managers, match officials, agents and negotiators now need to be well versed in the law so that they know how they should act to stay within it.

It is also the case that both international and national sport governing bodies are fighting to hold on to their right, as they see it, to determine the rules, and to self-regulate their sport. In many ways, they wish to see sport act as its own law maker, judge and jury, immune from the normal legal processes, but increasingly they are having to operate within the normal legal systems, and we need to understand why this is the case.

Prosecutions in sport – why?

Fig. 18.11 *The law on the pitch – who is responsible, governing bodies or the state?*

Sport is played within a social and cultural environment. It involves interactions between individuals or groups of individuals. International and national laws exist to protect the rights of individual citizens; if all individual interactions are covered by

Key terms

Bosman ruling: the ruling by the European Court of Justice, giving a professional player the right to a free transfer at the end of their contract.

Sport law: the body of legislation, case law, and precedence that applies to sport.

national and international laws, this would of course include sport. As the stakes in sport become higher, with greater exposure to media attention and the increasingly high profile of elite performers, the possibility that players are treated unfairly, incorrectly or illegally will increase. Should this happen, there is now a much greater chance that individuals or groups of individuals will use the law to protect themselves or to gain recompense.

How far that should go and whether all sport interactions can be covered by the same law that operates within the home, the streets or corporate boardrooms are matters of debate. Where should the line be drawn between a few punches traded between opposing forwards in a game of rugby and a physical assault on a pitch that leads to a court case? And does it matter if the action occurs on a Sunday morning in front of two men and a dog or in front of 65,000 spectators and a nationwide TV audience?

The law in relation to performers

Performers may interact with the law in a number of ways:

- They have employment protection. The Bosman ruling gave professional footballers within the European Union (EU) the right to move freely to another employer (football club) at the end of their contract. Their existing club cannot demand a transfer fee or retain the individual's playing licence.

- Players within the EU have the right to work anywhere within the EU without restriction. If, for example, the FA wished to restrict the number of non-England qualified players in the Premier League, it could not do so at present without breaking European employment law. Players from outside the EU still need a work permit and they and the club wishing to sign them must prove that they have skills that are not otherwise available (e.g. not possessed by an existing national within the country). In the UK, this is usually judged by how often the foreign national has represented their country.

- If a performer has been found to have taken a banned substance, they will face a range of sanctions from the NGB or their National Olympic Committee. If the performer believes that they are not guilty of an offence or believes that the test procedures were incorrect or have given an erroneous result, they have a right of appeal. If the appeal has failed, some performers have decided to resort to legal proceedings. The most high-profile performers to have done so in the UK are Diane Modahl and Dwaine Chambers. In 1994, Diane Modahl received a four-year ban after having been sent home from the Commonwealth Games for testing positive for testosterone. In 1995, the British Athletics Federation (BAF) lifted the ban after the test results, supposedly showing that she had 42 times more testosterone than normal, were dismissed owing to the mishandling of her urine sample in a Portuguese laboratory. In March 1996, the International Association of Athletic Federations (IAAF) also accepted the report and cleared her to compete internationally. In 2000, she sued the BAF for compensation totalling £1m but lost the case. Defending the case almost bankrupted the BAF.

- Most NGBs have rules that prevent players from betting on matches in which they are involved and many prohibit them from betting at all on matches in their sport. The reason is that players may affect the outcome of a match (match fixing) if they have bet on it, which

Activity

If you don't know of the Dwaine Chambers case, use the internet to find out about it.

would be illegal. Players have been prosecuted for match fixing; this was often related to illegal gambling syndicates. Hansje Cronje and Salim Malik, who were convicted of match fixing in cricket in the late 1990s, are high-profile examples; as are a wide range of players and clubs in the Italian football league Serie A that were prosecuted, fined and had points deducted.

■ Sport governing bodies and the legal authorities are divided, even between themselves, as to how player violence should be dealt with. Most issues of player violence are handled by the relevant sport national governing body. But in 2005 the UK Crown Prosecution Service stated its intention to prosecute more players involved in on-pitch violence. In 1995, Duncan Ferguson served 44 days of a three-month sentence after being convicted of head butting another player. In 2003, El Hadj Diouf of Liverpool was fined £5,000 after being found guilty of assault after spitting on a Celtic fan during a Uefa Cup match.

More and more players are bringing civil claims against clubs and players for injuries sustained from acts that go beyond the rules of the game. In 2008, the courts were involved after a rugby player was left with a broken eye socket after being punched by an opponent in a skirmish after a scrum; the High Court ruling made the opposition club legally responsible for compensation.

Activity

 Research your own sport for recent examples of player violence and how they were dealt with.

2 Prepare a short presentation of your findings (e.g. a PowerPoint slide).

The law in relation to officials

Referees and other sports officials need to be aware of their responsibilities under the law and know what is legal or illegal:

■ Officials in sport, particularly match officials, are open to investigation if it is thought that they may have been bribed; if so they can be prosecuted for corruption. In 2005, German referee Robert Hoyzer confessed to trying to fix matches in the national second and third divisions and the German Cup.

■ Referees have a duty of care. If a player is injured in a match, and it can be shown that through faulty refereeing the referee has allowed a dangerous situation to occur, the referee may be liable for prosecution. In 1998, the Law Lords upheld a negligence case against a referee and the Welsh RFU for not applying the laws about non-contested scrums correctly.

■ Organisers of sports events have a duty of care towards competitors and spectators to ensure that they are not put at risk though avoidable or predictable events.

Activity

 For your own sport, research the safety issues that referees or other officials should be aware of.

2 What advice and support do they receive from the sport NGB?

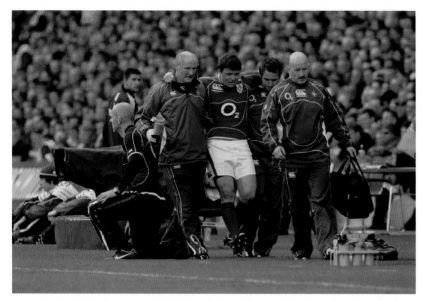

Fig. 18.12 *Player injury – who is responsible, officials or players?*

The law in relation to managers, agents, directors and club owners

As sport has become more commercialised, dealings between players, their agents and the directors and owners of clubs have become more complex. Any breaking of the commercial rules relating to players' transfers, agents' fees and payments to managers or directors could lead to charges of corruption and possible fines or imprisonment. In 2008, the culmination of 'Operation Apprentice', an investigation into alleged football corruption, found that a number of illegal payments had been made.

Owners and club directors also have responsibilities to fans and supporters – their customers. Stadium managers, event organisers and club directors are responsible for the health and safety of spectators at matches, in cooperation with the police and other emergency services. The Hillsborough disaster of 1989 caused a radical rethink in the way that crowds are managed at large events, and in the design of stadiums, with the Taylor Report recommending all-seater stadiums and the removal of pitch-side fencing. The report also resulted in changes affecting ticketing controls, the sale of alcohol in grounds and the use of turnstiles and crush barriers.

The law in relation to spectators

Spectators at sports events must act within the law and with due regard for their own safety and the safety of others. Invasion of playing surfaces, use of foul language and racist chants could be dealt with under various Public Order Acts. Hooligan behaviour, as defined earlier, clearly breaks the law and would be dealt with by the courts.

Maintaining standards of behaviour – whose responsibility?

Elite sport has a huge potential to benefit society and culture. Played in accordance with its highest ethical and moral traditions, sport provides role models for good behaviour. As talented individuals who have striven

AQA Examiner's tip

The topic area of 'Sport and the law' is new; it has not appeared in specifications and exam papers in the past. It is an area that is becoming ever more relevant to a study of elite sport – make sure that you understand the issues and can quote examples.

Fig. 18.13 *Hillsborough – a disaster that changed the way we spectate*

to develop their abilities and produce sporting performances of the highest standards, elite performers can provide all of us with examples of how to deal with both success and disappointment at the highest level. But, as we have seen, that same driving ambition can lead performers, and all those associated with elite sport, to use methods to succeed that are not in accordance with the ethical and legal standards that have been set. The sport authorities, both national, and international, will need to continue to take the lead to maintain those standards. Ultimately, however, the decision as to how to act rests with the individual, and that decision can only be made when the issues have been explored and debated; that has been the point of this chapter and it is why the issues are included in the specification.

☑ *You should now be able to:*

- identify what is meant by deviant behaviour and how it has an impact on sport and on society

- critically evaluate the reasons why individuals engage in deviant behaviour in the context of sport, including hooliganism and the taking of performance-enhancing drugs

- describe the methods used to combat deviance in sport including the methods of drug testing, management of football hooligans and the use of the law in relation to individuals in sport

- comment on those control measures, including the effectiveness of drug testing and the punishment of offenders, and the methods used to deter hooliganism

- discuss the use of the law of the land in the context of the behaviour of those involved in sport, and be able to debate the issue of who should exercise control in sport – the sport's authorities or the police and the courts

- express clearly a view on how the value of sport and its beneficial effect on society can be damaged by the deviant behaviour of a few

- debate issues surrounding performer behaviour and come to a judgement based on an examination of facts and the ethical values of sport.

AQA Examination-style questions

1 The taking of performance-enhancing drugs is a serious issue in elite sport.

(a) Outline the major steps in the drug-testing procedure that may be faced by an elite-level performer. *(3 marks)*

(b) In 1998, the then Head of the IOC, Juan Antonio Samaranch, told a newspaper 'that substances that do not harm an athlete's health should not be banned and should not be considered as a case of doping'. Discuss this statement. *(4 marks)*

2 In 2005, the Crown Prosecution Service (CPS) stated that it intended to prosecute more players who were involved in on-pitch violence. Gordon Taylor, head of the Professional Footballers' Association, considered that such incidents should be left to sport governing bodies.

(a) On what basis does the CPS think it should prosecute players involved in on-pitch violence? *(3 marks)*

(b) How do you respond to the comment made by Gordon Taylor – give reasons for your answer. *(4 marks)*

3 Hooliganism has affected football for over 40 years.

(a) Define the term 'hooliganism' and discuss the reasons why it may occur. *(4 marks)*

(b) What steps have been taken to reduce the incidence of hooliganism? *(3 marks)*

4 Elite sport, both amateur and professional/commercial, has suffered from deviant behaviour by a wide range of people – performers, coaches, agents and officials.

What is meant by 'deviant behaviour' and why should elite sport suffer from such behaviour? To what extent is the contract to compete relevant? *(7 marks)*

Commercialisation of elite sport

Key terms

Pay-per-view: a system by which the television viewer can pay for a private telecast to their home of an event.

Media

Spend a few minutes thinking about your favourite sport. More than likely you can name the best British performers in that sport, possibly even describe what they look like, have an idea about their personality and even have some notion about how much they earn. For the majority of you, this information is known not because you know the performer personally but from what you have gleaned from the media: you have gained your knowledge from television, the newspapers, magazines, the internet and possibly the radio. We live in a media-driven society. Most people are informed by the media, and the media have become the most important influence on society and therefore sport of the 21st century. The presence of the media as an influence on sport has turned sport into a marketable commodity that is worth millions of pounds.

Television

Television tends to be viewed as the 'best' medium as it provides images that can be transmitted live, i.e. as the event happens, but it should be remembered that television is not as 'handy' a means of providing information as radio or newspaper.

The development of satellite television as competition to the traditional terrestrial channels has been based on sport, with Sky Sports invariably topping the viewing figures for satellite programmes. Such is the extent to which Sky Sports has begun to dominate the range of sports that are televised, that the government has deemed it necessary to ring-fence certain traditional sporting events to make sure that Sky Sports does not develop a monopoly and deprive the majority of living-room fans of a chance to see the most popular sporting occasions free on terrestrial television.

Pay-per-view represents a progression from the monthly subscription that the customer pays to view sports on Sky TV. The rationale for pay-per-view is that sports fans are willing to pay special prices to see the most important sporting events live in their homes. Currently, it is boxing that dominates the pay-per-view market in the UK, with additional subscriptions being required to see the latest Championship matches. How soon pay-per-view comes into use for other important sporting events is a matter for Sky TV, the organisers of the event and, unless ring-fencing remains, government policies.

Newspapers

British newspapers tend to appear in one of two forms, broadsheet and tabloid (although some broadsheets are now being published in condensed versions). Both types of newspaper have to sell issues to make a profit, and to do so they adopt different strategies to attract readers. Broadsheet newspapers, which tend to focus on providing an information service, generally have a middle-class readership. In broadsheet newspapers generally, less of the total paper is devoted to sport but the coverage is more varied as the range of sports is wider. The broadsheets also tend to provide critical analysis of events and issues affecting

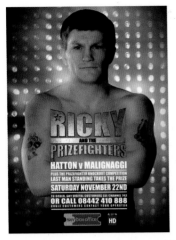

Fig. 19.1 *Sky TV offers both monthly subscription and pay-per-view services*

sport. The tabloid newspapers (sometimes called the redtops) tend to sensationalise events and personalities and traditionally have a more working-class readership. The tabloids tend to focus on a narrow range of popular sports (e.g. football, horse racing), with little coverage of minority sports. Most tabloids have a sizeable proportion of the total newspaper (up to a quarter) devoted to sport.

Fig. 19.2 *There is a range of newspapers available, all offering different perspectives on the same events*

The commercialisation of sport

Television companies have found sport to be a fairly cheap form of entertainment, especially in comparison with the costs of producing a drama or wildlife programme. Sport tends to have all the requirements of a 'good' programme, with lots of excitement and only a few periods when the action slows. It is also the sort of programme that can easily be left for a few minutes without losing the plot. Sports coverage has benefited from developments in technology, with action replays leading the way. Television's love affair with sport seems insatiable, with ever-more hours devoted to matches and competitions. The **commercialisation** of sport has grown; and with the mass use of sport as an entertainment package came the realisation that sport could also

Activity

Compare the amount of coverage given to different sports by a tabloid newspaper and a broadsheet newspaper for the same day. This can easily be done by using a ruler to measure the number of inches devoted to the different sports.

Key terms

Commercialisation: the treating of sport as a commodity, involving the buying and selling of assets, with the market as the driving force behind sport.

make money from television, with the sale of television rights to the highest bidder. The televising of sport has become one of the major contributors to sports funding: for example, at the time of writing (2008), the broadcasting rights to Premier League football were worth £1.1bn a year.

Televised sport offers businesses an investment opportunity. Businesses can invest via sponsorship (see pages 282–4), where financial input into sport is made in return for advertising. Using sport to advertise goods or services for sale can make a product known to the public or promote it. Endorsement involves giving approval to a product or service and receiving payment in return. Those involved in sport, or the sport itself, can also receive income from spectators' fees and from **merchandising**.

Key terms

Merchandising: the practice in which the brand or image from one product is used to sell another. The most common adult-oriented merchandising is that related to professional sports teams and their players.

Golden triangle: the link between sports events, sponsorship by businesses and the media.

Fig. 19.3 *The merchandising of sports clothing generates a lot of cash within sport*

Today, sport is inextricably linked to the media and to sponsorship in what is known as the **golden triangle**.

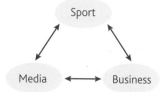

Fig. 19.4 *The golden triangle*

Activity

1 Make a list of ways in which commercialisation benefits the performer, the coach and the spectators.

2 Are there any potential disadvantages?

How commercialisation has affected sport

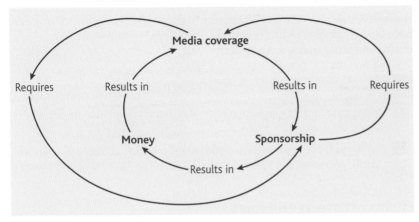

Fig. 19.5 *The influence of media coverage on sport*

Commercialised sport is driven by the requirement to make a profit for the **stakeholders** and the need for instant success. In turn, this may lead to a change in attitude because winning becomes an obligation. Performers are much more likely to be treated simply as commodities to be bought and sold for purely economic reasons. These same performers then have to provide a level of service (performance standard) that satisfies their employers. The employers are themselves under pressure from the stakeholders (sponsors, banks, shareholders) whose needs may often come before those of the fans and most certainly before those of the players.

Commercialisation has changed sport. In order to be commercial and generate more income and make more profit, sports have to appeal to a wider audience. At one level, sport has become much more professionally managed. Gone are the days when clubs or national governing bodies (NGBs) were run by amateur ex-players. Nowadays, because of the commercial nature of sport, it is much more likely that the people in charge will have a business background. As businessmen, these administrators can see that in order for a sport to make money it must attract sponsors. But a sponsor is only really interested if the sport gets good media coverage that will advertise the sponsor's product; therefore, it is necessary to make the sport attractive to the media.

Key terms

Stakeholder: a person, group, or organisation that affects or can be affected by an organisation's actions.

How media coverage has affected sport

Making sport attractive to the media

The media require sport to fit with their needs. Sport that is attractive to the media has the following characteristics:

- demonstration of skill strength and physical fitness
- well-matched competition
- demonstration of aggression and/or physical challenge
- visual spectacle with detail available
- uncomplicated rule structures
- fits into a reasonable time scale
- identification of personalities and/or nationalistic relevance
- traditional

■ ease of televising (e.g. cameras are able to keep up with the speed of play; there is a reasonably sized playing area to make televising easier).

For sports that were already of interest to the media, fairly minor changes have been sufficient to increase their attractiveness; but some have undergone fairly major reconstructive surgery.

Activity

1 Make a list of the changes that have occurred in cricket over the last 20 years.

2 Which of these changes have made cricket more attractive to the media? Justify your choice(s) by referring to the characteristics listed in the text.

Effects of coverage on sport

People played sport long before newspapers and television decided to follow and report the action. Many people participate in sporting activities where there is no media coverage; however, media coverage is necessary at elite level, in order to provide the funding needed to pay the players. Several activities have lost popularity owing to lack of media attention (e.g. table tennis). Other activities are promoted by the media to the extent that it almost guarantees their success (e.g. snooker).

Some NGBs encourage the media to concentrate on the more exciting events within their particular sport, because the money generated can be used as capital to allow further investment at grass roots level.

In 'good-to-watch' sports, excitement is maximised (e.g. sprinting). There have even been new forms of activity created, simply because they were more attractive to a television audience. In skiing, it was decided that the technical brilliance required for the slalom event was slightly lost on a television audience and the sheer speed of the downhill event meant that many viewers thought that it required little skill. Therefore, the skiing administrators invented the giant slalom as a compromise event, primarily to appeal to a television audience.

Many sports have now been adapted for appearance on television (e.g. with coloured shirts in cricket, a white ball in football, the summer rugby league, and kick-off times altered to suit peak viewing times in Premier League football and rugby union).

The largest televised sporting events are the Football World Cup and the Olympics. The organisation of the Football World Cup has been changed to generate more television income. The number of teams involved has been increased from 16 to 24, giving not only more matches but also more teams and therefore providing interest for the supporters from those extra countries. Kick-off times are scheduled to guarantee maximum viewing figures; for example, football has its biggest television audience in Europe, so, wherever the finals are held, the European teams involved will kick off at a time that presents them playing at about 8pm in Europe.

The Olympics are becoming controlled by the American television networks. They pay over £1m for the rights to show each Olympics and then influence the scheduling of the 'big' events for themselves. This usually involves the men's and women's 100m final being held at such a time that it can be shown live in the USA during the early evening. Unfortunately, because of time differences, the men's 100m final at the 2008 Beijing Olympics was run at 10.30 local time. This corresponds to viewing in Europe at 3.30pm and at breakfast time in the USA. If the final had been held at a 'normal' time of between 5 and 8pm, the viewers in the USA would not have been able to see it live unless they were willing to get up in the middle of the night! That was not going to happen with the US television companies paying.

Men tend to control the media and therefore the selection of media coverage in sport is largely made by men. Men still suppress a large amount of women's sports coverage. There is a tendency for the media, and therefore society as a whole, to regard women's sport as being less exciting and less skilful and it is therefore assumed to be less popular with the public. This seriously affects financial investment in women's sport. Women's sport gets less money than men's sport.

How media coverage has affected performers

The media want to focus on individual personalities at the expense of the event. Because of this, performers have to be aware of the need to entertain in order to increase their marketability. The high income of many elite performers and the lifestyle that offers are offset by the amount of media intrusion into their personal background that occurs. Quite often, the focus is on the performer's private life in preference to sporting ability, especially among female sports stars.

Activity

Think of a famous sports personality (footballers are usually the best choice for this activity). Write down as much as you know about them. You should easily be able to identify their sporting exploits, but what about them as a person? Most of the information you have comes from the media.

Does media coverage give a true picture of sport?

The simplistic idea that full, live coverage of sport gives the viewer a true record of events is untrue. Most television commentators may give an unbiased analysis of events, but they will normally exaggerate the action and the incidents in order to attract viewers. One of the problems with sport is that it tends to last a long time; think of the length of football, rugby and cricket matches. In addition, the match cannot end at a guaranteed time: there could be injuries or extra time; the cricket match will finish at the end of the innings. The problem for the television companies is sustaining interest for the duration of the occasion and making sure that the sport does not interfere with their programme schedules. Therefore, television prefers to present 'highlights' rather than the whole event. This allows the television company to maintain control of the programme. What is shown can also be used to influence the viewer. For example, the boring draw can be condensed into a 90 s clip of the near misses and the major incidents. Television can be used to deliberately sensationalise an incident to increase viewing figures.

In much the same way, newspaper journalists can influence a reader's interpretation of events. This is done by the use of dramatic headlines, style of writing and photographs.

Activity

1 Make a list of ways in which commercialisation benefits the officials and the sport.

2 Are there any potential disadvantages?

Table 19.1 *Arguments for and against televised coverage of sports*

For	Against
▓ Provides an information service, e.g. results, tables, and fixtures	▓ Limits participation to a few male sports
▓ Provides an entertainment service, e.g. excitement, drama, and spectacle	▓ Sensationalises: controversies may be created
▓ Provides an educational service, e.g. teaching, coaching, debates, issues, highlights, minority sports	▓ Highlights personalities rather than the team effort
▓ Provides an advertising service, e.g. for sport, goods, business	▓ Possibility of boredom owing to saturation coverage of sport
▓ Aids sponsorship	▓ Minority sports suffer because of lack of interest
▓ Creates role models, personalities, heroes	▓ Possible loss of gate money
▓ Draws attention to top-level sport	▓ Needs of television may dictate the selection of sport action

We mentioned before that several sports struggle to find the media coverage that they need in order to generate income; swimming is one. As swimming is primarily a participant sport, it attracts relatively few spectators and therefore does not generate much gate money.

Activity

1 Work with a partner and, referring back to Table 19.1, suggest reasons why swimming does not attract a large spectator following.

2 Working with your partner, think of ideas to make swimming more telegenic and produce a presentation of your ideas to the rest of the group.

There are several ways of helping underexposed sports:

▓ marketing of minority sports
▓ rule adaptation to create more exciting games for spectators
▓ sponsorship deals.

▓ Sponsorship

Companies invest in sport for several reasons:

▓ The sponsor's name and product is given publicity.

▓ An association is developed between product and performer in which the performer's popularity and prowess reflects favourably on the product's quality.

▓ The sponsor is associated with supporting the community or country.

▓ Sponsorship reduces the amount of tax paid by the company.

The result of sponsorship should be that sales of the company's products are increased and new products can be introduced.

Fig. 19.6 *Companies invest in sportspeople through sponsorship*

Sponsorship and sports organisations

Table 19.2 *The advantages and disadvantages of sponsorship*

Advantages	Disadvantages
■ Sports are expensive to run; extra money allows a more professional approach	■ Sport becomes associated with the product; this may not be desirable
■ Sport is promoted through extra publicity	■ Sponsors gain control over organisation of sport
■ Sponsorship helps create atmosphere at events	■ Sponsors gain control over timing, seasons and location of events
■ Sports are organised better; more efficient management techniques are used	■ There is financial interdependence between media and large sporting events
■ Improved facilities benefit performer and spectator	■ Sports rely too heavily on sponsors; withdrawal of funds can be disastrous
	■ Team selection may be affected – Team Nike *v.* Team Reebok

Several important factors have to be considered by a company when it is considering whether or not to become a sponsor. These include:

■ the success of the team or individual

■ the popularity of the sport, team or individual

■ media coverage

■ participation levels in the sport

■ the suitability of the sport for the product.

Most aspects of sport within the UK receive sponsorship:

■ events – competitions, finals, internationals

■ governing bodies and coaching schemes

■ stadiums, stands, etc.

■ amateur teams and/or individuals (training and equipment costs)

■ professional teams and/or individuals.

Table 19.3 *Ethical aspects of sponsorship: positive and negative*

Positive aspects	Negative aspects
■ Sponsorship promotes individuals and teams	■ Attention is on high-profile individuals or teams
■ Individual sponsorship allows the performer to train longer, facilitates improvement	■ Product association is an intrusion into sport
■ Sponsorship allows the development of new competitions and tournaments	■ Sponsors can gain too much control over a sport
■ Sponsorship allows the development of better facilities and equipment	■ The sponsor may influence choice of performers
■ It helps create atmosphere at events	■ Sponsors can give sport a bad image
■ It attracts high-class performers	■ Sponsors control the timing of events to obtain peak viewing time
■ It generates additional media interest	
■ Sport can be expensive to run and income from traditional sources is not enough	

In 1985, the Institute of Sports Sponsorship (ISS) was established. This is a non-profit-making group of companies, run by a committee, with links to Sport England and the Central Council for Physical Recreation (CCPR). The aims of the ISS are to:

■ bring sports and sponsors together

■ ensure that companies receive a fair return on their investment

■ try to preserve the traditional nature of sport

■ run the Sportsmatch scheme with government.

■ Activity

1 Make a list of ways in which commercialisation benefits the organisation of World Games.

2 Are there any potential disadvantages?

■ Technological developments in sport

Over the years, sport has seen many changes; one is the advent of technology, which has made an impact on many sports. More and more professional sports, especially in the United States, have used instant replay and other high-tech aids to help referees make the right decision. Rugby league and rugby union have, for many years, used video replay systems to check whether a try has been scored. In international cricket, the **television match official** (third umpire) has been used. This umpire sits off the ground with access to television replays of certain situations (such as disputed catches and boundaries) and advises the two central umpires out on the field who are in communication via wireless technology with the third umpire. The third umpire is also asked to adjudicate on run-out decisions, which he makes without consultation with the central umpires. The use of very accurate timing devices is now common in sports such as athletics and swimming. Most sports use video cameras to record performances for later viewing and possible fault correction.

One criticism of technology is that it can slow down the speed of the game, and the one sport that has resisted the use of high-tech assistance is football. Replays could be used to decide off-side decisions, whether a ball passes over the goal line and to clarify penalty decisions. The problem that football has is that reference to technology is time consuming, and waiting for the video official would add a completely different dimension to the flow of the game, possibly changing its very nature. Some might feel that a major appeal of football is that lack of a definite result, so that the fans can argue for days (years!) whether 'it was a goal' or not.

Hawk-Eye technology can trace the flight of a ball. Hawk-Eye comprises a computer and camera system; several cameras take 600 frames a second to give a computer-generated image of the predicted flight of the ball. Hawk-Eye is being used in international cricket and tennis, and many other sports are also looking at utilising this technology. The system is able to give a definite decision as to whether the ball had hit the stumps or crossed a line. In tournament tennis, when players wish to appeal against a line judge's decision, use of Hawk-Eye is permitted to see whether the ball was actually in or out. In cricket, however, Hawk-Eye is only available to the commentators, so that they can comment on the umpires' decisions.

Technological influences have also crept into the lives of athletes. Some elite performers are willing to do whatever it takes to accomplish success, whether that is risking their health by taking the latest drug on the market or experimenting with the most up-to-date equipment. Innovations include the use of the carbon fibre racing bike in place of the

---

■ **Key terms**

Television match official: (TMO/ video referee) a sports official called upon to help adjudicate a sports match by using television footage.

traditional aluminium bicycle, and changing the texture of a golf ball to take full advantage of its travelling distance. There have been changes in hockey, in the size and shape of pads and in goalie equipment; even the sticks have been changed from wood to graphite. All of these efforts are in an attempt to 'improve' the performance of athletes. Even figure skating is using technology to advance its skaters: there isn't just one brand of skate; there are numerous different boots. Which skaters choose depends on what category of skating they do: for instance, a dancer and a singles skater would not have the same skate. Each boot and blade is fitted in order to maximise the skater's performance. A singles skater's boot would be incredibly padded, sturdy and strong in order for them to land those powerful jumps. Yes, there is a safety issue as well, but it is technology that has led skating to the level it is at today.

Another relatively recent innovation is the use of artificial surfaces. These are now used extensively in hockey, have been tried in football, and, as they become increasingly 'grass-like', are being used for rugby training. Synthetic grass can be played on more frequently and for longer than natural grass. Just like the players, a natural pitch needs rest after the competition. However, on a synthetic pitch, another set of players can start training immediately after the match.

With synthetic grass you can always expect the same good conditions. Natural grass becomes too worn out after around 250 hours' play per season, whereas artificial grass can be played on 24 hours a day, seven days a week, although this is, of course, dependent on good, regular maintenance. Synthetic turf is unaffected by the weather; it is an **all-weather surface**. Heavy showers, long drought or snow and frost: the condition of a natural pitch is very sensitive to the weather. An artificial pitch drains well in wet weather; players will not kick up divots, as the tufts of grass are securely anchored in the turf. Competitions can go ahead on artificial grass despite the weather; the schedule does not become disrupted and there is no need to cancel training sessions. Artificial grass is maintenance friendly. Grass needs a lot of effort, time and money. Artificial grass does not.

Artificial surfaces are a benefit to all those involved in sport. Their only problem is that they do not all reflect the bounce of grass, especially its cushioning effect. But the more recent sand-based surfaces are going some way to rectify that and even rugby is now being played indoors on artificial surfaces.

The aims of using of technology in sport are to increase speed, competitive edge and spectator interest. None of these takes into consideration the traditional role that sport once had within society: amusement, diversion, fun or a simple pastime. All in all, it is quite hard to say whether we should be accepting these new technological advances or whether we should be sticking to the traditional model of sport. We are currently in the middle of an era marked by both drug use and the use of new and innovative equipment.

✅ *You should now be able to:*

- explain the role that the media now has in sport and how elite sport is becoming increasingly commercialised

- define sponsorship and explain how sport is now virtually dependent on sponsorship

- describe how technology is changing sport and be able to discuss the benefits of technology to sport.

Key terms

All-weather surface: a synthetic (artificial) playing surface, used instead of traditional grass.

Link

For information on the use of drugs in sport, see Chapter 18 – Deviance in sport (pages 264–70).

1   In the UK, a number of international sporting events are being 'ring-fenced', meaning that they must be available for viewing on terrestrial television rather than on satellite or cable subscription channels.

    (a)   Why should this restriction exist?   *(3 marks)*

    (b)   'Modern television and broadcasting technologies can give the same spectating experience as actually attending the sport event.'

            Discuss this statement using appropriate examples.   *(4 marks)*

            AQA, June 2004

2   Elite sport is always highly competitive and increasingly commercial. Elite performers often attempt to make a living from sport and may be driven to use both legal and illegal methods to become successful.

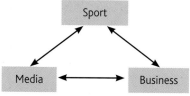

Fig. 19.7

Discuss the relationships shown in Figure 19.7. Comment on the benefits and disadvantages of these relationships to elite sport.   *(7 marks)*

            AQA, June 2004

3   (a)   Elite sports performers rely on sponsorship as part of their income. Discuss whether an individual should consider the nature of a sponsor's product before accepting sponsorship.   *(4 marks)*

    (b)   Discuss the suggestion that modern-day sponsorship deals have positively and negatively influenced the behaviour of elite sports performers.   *(3 marks)*

            AQA, June 2005
            and June 2006

4   What are the potential benefits to performers, organisers and spectators of using artificial surfaces for sporting competitions?   *(7 marks)*

20 Practical coursework

In this chapter you will:

- understand what is required by candidates in terms of their coursework.

The coursework unit of the A2 part of the course (Unit 4) requires you to use the knowledge and understanding that you have gained from the whole course (AS and A2) to improve your own personal performance, either as a practical performer, a coach or leader, or as an official in one activity. This coursework is worth 40 per cent of the A2 marks.

In order to optimise your own performance, you will need to evaluate the quality and level of your own/others' performance. This is achieved through identifying your own weaknesses, suggesting a programme for improving these weaknesses and then working out whether the changes that you have made have enabled you to improve your performance.

There are three sections to the A2 coursework:

Section A – your ability to perform the relevant core skills/techniques as a performer, official or leader/coach within a fully competitive situation/equivalent scenario. (60 marks)

Section B – your ability to analyse and critically evaluate your own/others' weaknesses within a fully competitive/equivalent situation in relation to an elite-level performer. A performer should analyse their own performance; a leader/coach should analyse a named performer; an official should analyse their own performance. (30 marks)

Section C – your ability to identify theoretical causes for your weaknesses in performance and suggest appropriate corrective practices to optimise your performance. (30 marks)

Section A

For Section A, your performance must demonstrate the core skills of the activity (described in the specification) within a fully competitive game/performance situation in order to show that you have progressed from the demonstration situations experienced at AS and in order to allow you to perform to your full potential. Your performance must also allow you to demonstrate the application of rules, regulations and codes of practice of the activity, the purpose of the activity, winning/meeting targets or goals, and pressure from opposition at an appropriate level.

In order to do this, you must produce a movie of you performing your chosen role of performer, leader or official. The earlier this is completed, the longer you will have to analyse your own performance. Also note that you can produce as many movies as you wish. Your assessment should be based on your best performance.

For a performer, the assessment will be in three areas that vary across the different activities, but, for example, for games will involve attacking skills, defending skills and strategic skills. Each area is worth 20 marks.

An important aspect of the performance assessment is your personal physiological and psychological preparation and application during the performance. You must be fit enough for the activity and motivated to perform well and if necessary be able to maintain an optimal level of arousal.

If adopting the role of leader, you will be expected to plan, coordinate and lead others to demonstrate the core skills in a fully competitive setting. You must be aware of the strategies and tactics needed to maximise the strengths of the performers involved in the competitive event and be prepared to alter the tactics to help achieve a different outcome. You will also be required to justify your decisions both during and after the event.

The assessment of a leader will involve the same three areas as for a performer; for games players this is attacking skills, defending skills and strategies. Leaders will be assessed on their ability to communicate effectively with the performers and officials; their ability to prepare their performer/team immediately prior to the competition both physically and psychologically; the effectiveness of any modifications made to their performance and the timing and implementation of those decisions; and the carrying out of appropriate physical and psychological strategies to maximise future performances.

Fig. 20.1 *Performing a chosen activity may be a key part of your practical coursework*

If you have chosen to be assessed as an official, you must be able to officiate a fully competitive situation, and be able to demonstrate an understanding of the requirements and expectations of all the major roles before, during and after the event to ensure all participants are safe and the rules are consistently and accurately applied to maintain fair play. You should also make sure that you are suitably prepared and equipped to fulfil these roles. You need to show a clear understanding of the scoring systems, applying them as required, and have the ability to justify your decisions during and after the event.

For the official, the first and second areas of assessment are the same as those for the performer and leader, but the third area of assessment is concerned with your ability to communicate effectively with performers and other officials and maintain a safe playing environment. As in the other roles, your physical and psychological preparation and application during your performance will also be assessed.

There are two other main parts to the coursework assessment, but they may be looked at as parts of the same process. Sections B and C of the coursework look at your ability to analyse your own performance in comparison with an elite-level performer, and your ability to identify potential causes of weaknesses and suggest strategies to develop those areas. When attempting these sections many students make the mistake of simply outlining training drills and practices, but this will gain only a

Fig. 20.2 *You can choose to officiate in an activity as part of your practical coursework*

few marks. The main purpose of these sections is to assess your ability to apply the theoretical knowledge gained in physiology, psychology and socio-cultural lessons to a practical situation. To summarise what's required of you, you could say that you need to highlight your own faults, make comparisons with elite performers, suggest possible causes of these weaknesses and recommend ways of correcting your faults.

Section B

For Section B, you should try to show that you are able to analyse and critically evaluate either your own or another's physical performance (depending on choice of role) either through an oral discussion with supporting notes or through written notes. Often, the method of delivery is chosen by the centre. In general terms, much more is expected of you if you simply hand in a written document than if you provide information during an interview. Some centres even require their students to produce a PowerPoint presentation to highlight their own faults, comparisons, causes and corrections.

Fig. 20.3 *If you choose the role of a coach for your practical coursework, you will be asked to analyse the performance of others*

Section B is worth a maximum of 30 marks. Five marks are for the identification of weaknesses and comparison with an elite performer for each of the three areas of assessment listed in the specification. These vary depending on the activity but, as an example, for game activities they are split into the following sections:

- effectiveness of attacking skills
- effectiveness of defensive skills
- effective application of strategies and tactics.

Other activities have detailed criteria that are specific to the requirements of the activity and students should refer to the AQA specification for details.

Table 20.1 *Breakdown of marking for Section B*

Area of assessment	1	2	3	Total
Identification of weakness in own/ other performance	5	5	5	15
Comparison to elite performer	5	5	5	15
				30 marks

Section C

For Section C, you should be able to critically evaluate the factors affecting your own or another's performance (depending on role taken) and suggest strategies that will lead to optimisation of performance. Again, you can demonstrate your knowledge and understanding either through an oral discussion or in written notes.

The following criteria should apply:

- performer – analysis of their own performance
- leader/coach – analysis of a named performer
- official – analysis of their own performance.

When analysing your/others' performance across the three areas of assessment, you must identify the causes of the weaknesses and, using the knowledge and understanding you gained throughout the GCE course, suggest appropriate physiological, biomechanical and psychological corrective measures.

Section C is also worth a maximum of 30 marks. (Sections B and C together are 60 marks, which is the same as the personal performance in Section A.)

In Section C, five marks are available for identification of possible causes of weaknesses of each assessment area highlighted in Section B. Five marks are available for identifying potential corrective practices that could improve performance.

Table 20.2 *Breakdown of marking for Section C*

Area of assessment	1	2	3	Total
Causes of weaknesses/faults	5	5	5	15
Corrective measures	5	5	5	15
				30 marks

In order to perform well in these sections of coursework, try working through the following in logical order:

What are my main weaknesses in specific situations (for example, attacking play, defending play and strategies in games), and how do they affect my competitive performance? For each area of assessment, you should identify three weaknesses to analyse and evaluate.

- What does an elite player, official or leader do in the same situation and how does it affect their performance?
- What physiological, mechanical, psychological or socio-cultural factors might have caused my weaknesses?
- What strategies can I use to improve my performance?

A common mistake in Sections B and C is to simply focus on the technical weaknesses that you have when compared with an elite performer. Each weakness that you identify should have a theoretical cause, which you need to be able to explain in the same sort of detail as exists in A2 textbooks. Don't limit your weaknesses to ones covered in GCSE-level materials. People may identify lack of power as a weakness that causes them to be slow about the pitch. They may then go on to simply say that power is strength × speed and can be improved with training. These types of answer are just not good enough. More realistically, you need to analyse movements in terms of preparation, action, follow-through and result. Often skills break down because of bad limb positions and/or weak information processing. Look to talk about the harder areas of the subject to get higher marks; mention of muscle fibre types, sliding-filament hypothesis, energy systems, application of forces, schema theory, anxiety and arousal is much more likely to impress!

Possible causes of weakness can and should come from any area of the specification, including AS. You do not have to limit possible causes to one per weakness; there could be several possible causes of a weakness. But try not to keep repeating yourself; saying that a lack of power is the reason for several different weaknesses will not gain much credit! Always remember that nobody can genuinely say that your possible cause is not a valid reason for a weakness. If you say that a performer is over-aroused, that could be a possible explanation and therefore will gain credit.

What follows are lists of some potential contributing factors taken from the specification that could relate in some way to your weaknesses. The lists are not comprehensive and could easily be added to.

Physiological factors

Some contributing physiological factors are:

- inefficient use of levers, muscles and joints
- lack of specific (named) fitness components
- fast- and slow-twitch muscle fibres
- fatigue through lactate accumulation and/or glycogen/phosphocreatine depletion
- low maximal oxygen consumption
- lack of training/poor training methods/poor application of training principles
- weak/poor ineffective energy systems
- poor application of forces/Newton's laws of motion
- ineffectual application of angular motion
- incorrect projectile motion
- inefficient delivery of oxygen/removal of carbon dioxide

■ inefficient cardiovascular response to exercise

■ inefficient respiratory response to exercise.

Psychological factors

Some contributing psychological factors are:

■ personality types

■ plateaus of learning

■ theories of learning

■ types of practice

■ methods of teaching

■ forms of guidance

■ types of motivation

■ transfer of learning

■ weaknesses in perception

■ effectiveness of information-processing systems

■ lack of experience/memory

■ aggression

■ attitudes

■ anxiety

■ group dynamics

■ leadership

■ levels of and/or control of arousal

■ achievement motivation

■ self-efficacy and learned helplessness.

Socio-cultural factors

Some contributing socio-cultural factors are:

■ school physical education experiences

■ National Curriculum for Physical Education

■ experience of play sport, leisure and physical recreation

■ experience of outdoor and adventurous activities

■ historical factors and traditions

■ lack of equal opportunities

■ socio-economic groupings

■ lack of facility provision

■ National Lottery funding

■ role models

■ effectiveness of national and local organisations

■ media coverage and commercialisation.

■ Summary of achievement descriptors at A2 for PHED4 for Category 1 and Category 2 activities

Section A

Very high achievement

51–60 marks

A wide range of skills to a very high standard. Skills performed extremely accurately, even advanced skills within competitive situations. Accuracy and quality of skill remains high under pressure. Performance indicates advanced tactical and strategic awareness. Knowledge of the demands and requirements of the activity. Extremely high levels of commitment and motivation. Performance and progress are very high standards; very high levels of learning and understanding achieved.

High achievement

36–50 marks

High standards of core skills with consistent success in more advanced and technically demanding context. Able to introduce and use more developed tactics and strategies to achieve success in skills. High levels of commitment and motivation. Performance and progress very reliable. High levels of learning and understanding achieved.

Sound achievement

16–35 marks

Performs well with consistency all core skills. Improved success when extending skill to advanced levels. Under pressure, and in competition, demonstrates some success but not always consistently or accurately. Able to use tactics/strategies within performance to satisfactory level. Sound and developing perception of demands/requirements to perform the activity. Satisfactory performance and progress during course. Learning and understanding achieved.

Limited achievement

1–15 marks

Moderate mastery of the basic skills but lacks consistency. Limited signs of performing advanced skills. Under pressure quality and technical accuracy reduces. Rudimentary perception and ability to apply and adapt the skills. Little appreciation of quality of movements. Limited improvement in learning and understanding and level of performance.

No work offered = 0 marks

Section B

Very high achievement

26–30 marks

Excellent in-depth knowledge of activity. Can identify faults and weaknesses in both individual technique and performance of the activity. Logically able to suggest appropriate in-depth remedial strategies relating to individual techniques/performance/game situations. No supplementary help needed. Clear understanding of rules and technical terms and is able to apply them appropriately. Can recognise strengths and weaknesses in personal skills in team/competition performance and can analyse and evaluate accurately.

High achievement

16–25 marks

Good knowledge of major techniques and performance strategies. Can identify general and specific weaknesses in relation to individual techniques and performance strategies/tactics. With help, can identify causes and suggest appropriate remedial strategies/plans relating to both individual game techniques and performance. Good knowledge of rules and terminology and can use it when discussing and playing/competing without prompting. Recognises strengths and weaknesses in personal skills in team/competition performance and can analyse and evaluate accurately.

Sound achievement

6–15 marks

Sound knowledge of major aspects of technique and performance in either the activity or game situation. Able to identify major faults and weaknesses. With help, can identify causes and suggest appropriate simple strategies/plans to correct faults. Sound knowledge of rules and terminology and can use it without help, but falters on more technically demanding aspects. Recognises strengths and weaknesses in performance, but not the more complex skills/situations/tactics. Can give some feedback to optimise performance in skill and in planning training and practice, but needs some help.

Limited achievement

1–5 marks

Basic knowledge of major techniques in activity or game situation. Able to identify general/major weaknesses and faults in individual techniques, but has limited understanding of their effect/application within performance. With help is able to identify some major/simple faults and show a limited ability to suggest appropriate remedial strategies. Shows some knowledge of basic rules and terminology, but ability to identify strengths and weaknesses hampered by inability to break down skills/techniques and tactics into recognised aspects.

No work offered = 0 marks

Section C

Very high achievement

26–30 marks

Excellent knowledge of activity. Able to relate to theoretical areas of specification. Can analyse performance of individual techniques and strategies/tactics relating to appropriate strengths/weaknesses/faults identified. Can suggest appropriate in-depth remedial strategies/plans, relating these to relevant theoretical areas. Needs no extra questioning. Can plan practices to optimise performance, and fitness sessions to improve appropriate fitness levels. Has a good understanding of perfect model. Clear understanding of whole course, and can apply knowledge appropriately.

High achievement

16–25 marks

Good level of understanding within practical work. Able to apply many major areas/concepts of theoretical content through critical evaluation of performance being observed. Fault identification/corrections are well supported by application of appropriate theoretical knowledge. Needs occasional supplementary questions. Understands how to plan for optimisation of performance and fitness, and relates it to other aspects of course. Shows some understanding of the way that whole subject fits together.

Sound achievement

6–15 marks

Sound knowledge of major techniques and performance phases in performance situation. With questions to draw out knowledge and help its application, can identify major strengths and weaknesses of techniques. With help, causes and appropriate strategies to correct faults can be identified. Has some idea of how course fits together, but needs help to show basic knowledge of various elements of course and how to apply some of them.

Limited achievement

1–5 marks

Shows basic knowledge of techniques/performance and basic ability with continual help to apply knowledge and understanding of theoretical areas to practical activity being observed. Limited in ability to apply theoretical knowledge logically in order to develop understanding of corrections of faults and weaknesses. Weak ability to plan skill practices and training. Limited knowledge of what is required to perform the basic skills well. Has some knowledge of some parts of course, but finds it difficult to apply them.

No work offered = 0 marks

Summary of achievement descriptors at A2 for PHED4 for Category 3 activities

Section A

Very high achievement

51–60 marks

Able to perform/choreograph all the core skills/techniques in both isolation and the structured/choreographed sequence/routine to a very high standard. Possesses excellent body management skills. Is likely to be able to, or choose to, assimilate the core skills/techniques into more advanced demonstrations or routines/choreographed sequences. The sequence/routine shows excellent flow and continuity.

High achievement

36–50 marks

Can perform/choreograph all the basic core skills/techniques to a consistently high standard both in isolation and within the routine/ sequence. Has good levels of body management and is able to demonstrate a good appreciation of quality in a wide range of movements. The routine/choreographed sequence indicates a high-level appreciation of flow and continuity. As a result of their experience, the candidate demonstrates high levels of achievement and success.

Sound achievement

16–35 marks

Can perform/choreograph well and show consistency with all the basic skills/techniques. Shows some quality of movement in many, but not all, of the skills/techniques within the routine/sequence. The choreographed sequence/routine indicates an awareness of the flow and continuity. The performer experiences a sound level of achievement/success.

Limited achievement

1–15 marks

Can perform/choreograph the basic skills to a moderate level, but not always consistently. Finds difficulty in performing the skills/techniques consistently in the structured routine/choreographed sequence. Shows little appreciation of the quality of movements. Body tension is limited in some movements. The sequence/routine shows limited flow/continuity. The candidate experiences moderate but limited achievement.

No work offered = 0 marks

Section B

Very high achievement

26–30 marks

Excellent in-depth knowledge of activity. Can identify faults and weaknesses in individual technique and performance of activity linked to appropriate skills/techniques. Able to suggest in-depth remedial strategies/plans relating to individual techniques/performance/game situations. Needs little supplementary help. Has clear understanding of rules and correct technical terms and can apply them. Can recognise strengths and weaknesses in personal skills in team/competition performance and analyse and evaluate them accurately.

High achievement

16–25 marks

Good knowledge of major techniques and performance strategies/tactics. Able to identify general and specific faults and weaknesses in relation to individual techniques and performance strategies/tactics. With occasional help, is able to identify causes and suggest remedial strategies/plans relating to individual game techniques and performance. Shows good knowledge of rules and has very good knowledge of terminology of activity and uses it when discussing and playing/competing. Recognises strengths and weaknesses in personal skills in team/competition performance and can analyse and evaluate accurately.

Sound achievement

6–15 marks

Sound knowledge of major aspects of technique and performance in activity or game situation. Able to identify major faults and weaknesses. With some help, can identify causes and suggest simple strategies/plans to correct faults. Has sound knowledge of rules of competition and has knowledge of terminology and can use it in discussing situations/demonstrations and solving problems without help, but may falter on technically demanding aspects. Can recognise strengths and weaknesses in performance, but not of more complex skills/situations/tactics. Can give some feedback to optimise performance in skill and in planning training and practice, though needs some help.

Limited achievement

1–5 marks

Basic knowledge of major techniques in activity or game situation. Able to identify general/major weaknesses and faults in individual techniques, but has limited understanding of effect within performance. Needs help to identify some major/simple faults and shows limited ability to suggest any remedial strategies. Has some knowledge of basic rules and terminology, but ability to identify strengths and weaknesses is hampered by inability to break down the skills/techniques and tactics into recognised aspects.

No work offered = 0 marks

Section C

Very high achievement

26–30 marks

Excellent knowledge of activity. Able to relate to theoretical areas of specification. Can analyse performance in terms of individual technique and strategies/tactics relating to strengths/weaknesses/faults identified. Having identified the relevant strengths and weaknesses/faults, is able to suggest appropriate in-depth remedial strategies/plans, for all relevant theoretical areas, thereby demonstrating a full understanding of the application of these areas to performance. Needs little supplementary questioning. Can plan practices to optimise performance, and fitness sessions to improve fitness levels. Has good knowledge and understanding of perfect model and can discuss it. Shows clear understanding of whole course, and can apply knowledge appropriately.

High achievement

16–25 marks

Good level of understanding within practical work. Able to apply many major areas/concepts of theoretical content in logical and critical evaluation of activity performance being observed. Fault identification/corrections are well supported by application of theoretical knowledge. Needs occasional supplementary questions to help maintain logical approach. Has understanding of planning for optimisation of performance and fitness, and can relate it to other aspects of course and show some understanding of how whole subject fits together.

Sound achievement

6–15 marks

Sound knowledge of major techniques and performance phases in performance situation. With general questions in order to draw out knowledge and help in its application, can identify major strengths and weaknesses of techniques. With help, causes and appropriate strategies to correct faults can be identified. Has some idea of how course fits together, but needs help to show basic knowledge of various elements of course and how to apply some of them.

Limited achievement

1–5 marks

Basic knowledge of techniques/performance and basic ability with aid of continual help to apply knowledge and understanding of theoretical areas to practical activity being observed. Limited in ability to apply theoretical knowledge logically in order to develop understanding of corrections of faults and weaknesses. Ability to plan skill practices and training is weak. Has limited knowledge of what is required to perform basic skills well. Able to show some knowledge of some parts of course, but finds it difficult to apply them.

No work offered = 0 marks

Exam skills

The marks you achieved for the AS part of the Physical Education course are added to the marks you achieve for the A2 part. A2 Physical Education is assessed through both examination and coursework. Unit 3 content is assessed through the exam paper, known as PHED3.

The examination is worth 60 per cent of the A2 course and the exam is taken at the end of the course in June. The examination consists of a two-hour paper containing three questions, 1, 2 and 3, in three sections, A, B and C:

▓ Section A is on applied exercise physiology to optimise performance.

▓ Section B is on psychological factors that optimise performance.

▓ Section C is on evaluating contemporary issues.

In each section there is a compulsory 14-mark question, which is part (a), and three optional parts – (b), (c) and (d) – worth 7 marks each. You must answer part (a), which is the 14-mark question, and two out of the three optional parts (the 7-mark questions).

This means that each section is worth 28 marks (14 + 7 + 7), and the paper totals 84 marks (3 × 28).

The quality of written communication for this paper is assessed through each of the compulsory part (a) questions.

Each question is structured. That means that it is subdivided into different areas. A question in each section will ask you about different aspects of applied exercise physiology, psychology, and contemporary issues. The exam paper does provide you with the opportunity to choose topic areas and hence to specialise.

▓ Preparing for the examination

You need to revise. You need to revise every topic area because there are no question choices in the examination. Revision is at best time consuming and difficult to motivate yourself for. But it is necessary.

It might help if we look at an analogy. Exams could be seen as being just like involvment in a physical activity. You are out to show just how good you are. In activities this demonstration is for the opposition; in an exam it's for the examiner.

Most of you will accept the idea that preparing for a physical activity is important; so is preparing for an exam. Most of you will practise for a physical activity. This is what you must do for the exam. In physical activities the best form of practice is realistic – remember schema theory. So for exams the best form of practice is past examination papers. Initially this will obviously be difficult – there are no past papers. But this specification is very similar to the previous specification and so exam papers from the previous specification are quite appropriate.

Many schools and colleges will run revision classes for you – make sure you attend. Several private companies will offer Easter revision courses or intensive revision days. If possible go to these as well. Learning in a different way and in a different environment is always beneficial.

Link

For information on schema theory, see *AQA Physical Education AS*, Chapter 9 – Learning and Performance (page 108).

Revision is time consuming and difficult, but so is training outdoors on a cold November evening. What your coach will do on such occasions is to make it fun and have regular changes in what is being done to maintain interest. You must do the same when revising. Your coach should not let you simply play a game as a practice. You must not simply read your notes for revision. Remember what you learned about memory – there are limits to what can be stored in short-term memory and storing things in long-term memory involves rehearsal, meaningfulness and over-learning. Try some of the following:

- Get organised – find a base where you can work and even leave all your 'stuff' in place where it won't get disturbed.
- Set a time limit for revision – many and often is better than few and long. If you want to revise for longer than an hour then set yourself two clear periods for revision, with a good break between the revision sessions.
- Work to a plan – maybe revise a topic each day – and stick to the plan. Allow time for leisure/non-revision sessions.
- Get a copy of the specification – highlight (in red!) those areas that you are not sure about – revise these first.
- Provide yourself with rewards – breaks/biscuits/coffee/TV programme after completing some revision.
- If you prefer it then revise with headphones and music.
- Have a break after about 20 minutes; then return to the revision.
- Review what you have revised – after that break test yourself.
- Try to produce images from your notes – diagrams/flowcharts/mindmaps/tables – we remember pictures better than words.
- Reduce information down to key words and phrases – these are easier to remember.
- Produce revision cards – your own are better than any others.
- Don't leave it all to the last minute – there are three sections to revise and each one has many topics. Revision should begin soon after or even before Easter.
- There are some topics that tend to come up on nearly every examination – revise these the most and make sure you know the answers to likely questions.

On the day

- Get plenty of sleep – you perform best when you are refreshed.
- Don't revise the morning of the exam – you wouldn't train before a game – you'd get tired – so does your brain.
- It's a competition – arrive as you would for a match – with plenty of time to get ready and with the correct equipment – take spares if necessary.
- Don't talk to the opposition – your fellow pupils – get 'in the zone'.
- Stay calm – if you are too worked up you will be unable to perform at your best.
- Enter the examination room early and do all that you can before the start – write your name etc. on the answer booklet.
- When you are told to begin just simply read the questions – don't start writing straight away.
- Use a highlighter to identify the important words used in each question.
- If there are questions you are confident about then do these first, leaving those where you are uncertain until last.

- You haven't got to answer the questions in the order in which they have been set.
- Always remember that the examiner knows the question. Don't start your answer by stating the question.
- If you can't remember something, leave a space for the answer; it might come to you later.
- Keep checking the time – it's a two-hour exam – you have to answer seven questions – that's 17 minutes for each question. Call it 15 to allow for reading through the paper at the beginning and allowing time for a final read through.
- If you appear to be running out of time start to use bullet points, but don't do that for question 7 – that needs sentences for the answer.
- Question 7 requires you to show good use of technical terms – use them!
- At the end, read through your completed paper – have you answered every question; could you add something to one of the first questions you attempted?

Interpreting questions

One of the hardest parts about doing PE exams is trying to understand what the examiner wants as an answer. To understand this better you need to look at exam questions in more detail.

There are usually three parts to a question:

- a **command** word which tells you what the examiner wants you to do
- a **subject** word which tells you which area of the specification the question is about
- a **subject qualifier** which tells you in more detail what aspect of the subject you need to talk about.

For example, in the following question –

'Explain how the reaction time of a performer might be improved' –

- the command word is '**explain**'
- the subject word is '**reaction time**'
- the subject qualifier is '**improved**'.

In the following examples, the command word has been **circled**, the subject has a **rectangle** around it and the subject qualifier has been **underlined**.

Command words

1 (Identify some) possible causes of a |learning plateau|

2 (Explain how) |oxygen| is transported around the body

3 (List the) main forms of |guidance|

Examiners have a number of command words that they use regularly, and each has a different meaning – learn their meanings!

The more commonly used ones are listed below:

Account – Give reasons for.

Briefly – Be concise and straightforward, but do not make a list – use sentences.

Classify – Divide into groups or categories.

Comment on – Summarise the various points and give an opinion.

Compare – What is wanted is a point-by-point identification of the main similarities (when **contrast** is used as well look for differences). Use words like 'larger', 'quicker', 'more' in your answer, or start sentences with words like 'however', 'as compared to', 'whereas'.

Define – or **what do you understand by**, or **explain the meaning of** – Needs a short answer giving a precise meaning of the term.

Describe – Very commonly used – On its own it means 'what is the examined feature like?' Can be linked to other words – 'describe the characteristics of' or 'describe the differences between' or 'describe the effects of' or 'describe and explain'. 'Describe and comment on' requires more than just a description – also needs some judgements about the description.

Discuss – Needs you to argue both sides of the issue – produce a written debate with a conclusion.

Evaluate or **assess** – Weigh up the importance of the topic – similar to **discuss**.

Explain – Give reasons or causes – very popular. A description is not enough.

How – same as **describe**.

Identify – **State** or **name**. Point out and name – short answers.

Justify – Usually goes with questions where you have to make a decision about something and then justify your decision – explain why you arrived at your decision.

Outline – Note the main features.

Suggest – Put forward an idea or reason.

Glossary

A Band: the dark band in a myofibril.

acceleration (ms⁻²): the rate of change of velocity or the difference between final and initial velocities divided by the time taken, measured in metres per second squared.

achievement motivation theory: the theory that an individual's behaviour is determined by their interaction with the environment and their desire to succeed.

actin: thin protein filament.

active recovery: the use of light energy to aid recovery.

actual behaviour: the behaviour shown by the leader.

adenosine triphosphate (ATP): our energy currency, found in all cells; when broken down it releases its stored energy.

adipose tissue: special tissue made up of cells in which fats are stored; mainly found under the skin and surrounding major organs.

aerobic: with oxygen.

aerobic capacity: the maximum rate at which a person can consume oxygen.

aggression: in sport, behaviour intended to harm another person, physically or psychologically, outside the laws of the game.

air resistance: friction between a body and air particles.

all or nothing law: muscles fibres either contract or do not contract; there is no such thing as a partial contraction.

all-weather surface: a synthetic (artificial) playing surface, used instead of traditional grass.

amateur: a person who plays sport for fun and for no financial gain.

anabolic steroid: a hormone that increases protein use and muscle cell production.

anaerobic: a process that takes place without oxygen.

anaerobic energy system: a process that provides energy for the resynthesis of ATP without the use of oxygen.

angle of release: the angle at which an object is released, measured from the horizontal.

angular: a word used to describe the motion of a mass when it is rotating or spinning.

angular acceleration: the rate of change of velocity during angular movement.

angular momentum: the amount of motion that the body has during rotation – angular velocity × moment of inertia.

angular movement: the movement of a body or mass around an axis – spinning, rotating, turning.

angular velocity: the rate of movement in rotation.

anxiety: a negative aspect of feeling stress; worries over the possibility of failure.

arousal: the state of general preparedness of the body for action, involving physiological and psychological factors.

assertive behaviour: the use of physical force that is within the rules or ethics of a sport and is therefore legitimate.

athleticism: a fanatical devotion to sport that developed the physical, social and moral aspects of young men.

attentional control: maintaining concentration on appropriate cues.

attentional narrowing: focusing on too narrow a range of information or on the performance of a skill; this causes the performer to ignore important cues or information.

attitude: a complex mix of feelings, beliefs and values that predisposes somebody to behave towards something or some person in a consistent way.

attitude object: a person, event or behaviour towards which a person has an attitude.

attitude scale: a form of question design used in questionnaires to gauge an individual's attitudes; using a pre-set scale of measurement, the respondent is asked to agree or disagree with a set of statements.

attribution: the perceived cause of an event, e.g. a win or a loss, as given by a participant.

attribution retraining: methods of helping the performer to change the way that they explain the causes of success and failure; in the case of failure, they are encouraged to focus on factors that can be controlled.

autocratic style of leadership: in sport, a style that is usually win oriented, very structured and task oriented.

beta blocker: a drug that blocks the release of chemicals, such as adrenaline, thereby causing the heart rate to stay low and helping the performer to stay calm.

beta-oxidation: breakdown of fats into acetyl CoA within sarcoplasm.

bicarbonate of soda: a white soluble compound ($NaHCO_3$) used in effervescent drinks and as an antacid.

biofeedback: information about changes in physiological variables; the patient watches a monitor displaying changes in readings of a variable associated with somatic anxiety and tries to lower the reading by distracting their attention away from the cause of the anxiety.

body mass index (BMI): a statistical comparison of weight and height.

Bosman ruling: the ruling by the European Court of Justice, giving a professional player the right to a free transfer at the end of their contract.

breathing control: using diaphragmatic breathing as a means of focusing on relaxation.

buffering: the ability of the blood to compensate for additions of lactic acid or hydrogen ions and maintain the pH level.

C

caffeine: a naturally occurring stimulant. It is no longer listed as a banned substance by WADA or UK Sport.

catastrophe theory: a theory that predicts a rapid decline in performance resulting from the combination of high cognitive anxiety and increasing somatic anxiety.

catharsis: the release of pent-up emotions or feelings of aggression through harmless channels, such as the physical and emotional activity of sport.

centering: using deep breathing as a way of refocusing your concentration.

channelled aggression: feelings of aggression that are diverted into useful, positive actions.

codification: the gradual organisation and defining of rules, including rules for the actual playing of the sport and the conduct and behaviour of participants.

cognitive anxiety: thoughts, nervousness, apprehension or worry that a performer has about their lack of ability to complete a task successfully.

cognitive dissonance: tension resulting from having contradictory thoughts or beliefs about something or someone.

cohesion: the dynamic forces that cause a team to stick together.

commercialisation: the treating of sport as a commodity, involving the buying and selling of assets, with the market as the driving force behind sport.

conditioning: physical activities that prepare the body for intense exercise.

conservation of angular momentum: the principle that the angular momentum of an object remains constant as long as no external force (moment or torque) acts on that object.

contract to compete: an unwritten code governing how to strive to play fairly, within the rules.

core strength/core stability: the ability of the core muscles to maintain correct alignment of the spine and pelvis while the limbs are moving.

coupled reaction: a chemical reaction in which energy is transferred from one side of the reaction to the other.

creatine: substance formed by the body that stores energy and is used as an energy source for ATP resynthesis.

cryogenic: any process carried out at very low temperature, below $-50\,^{\circ}C$.

cryotherapy: the general or local use of cold temperatures in the treatment of injury.

D

deceleration: a negative change in velocity over time or negative acceleration.

dehydration: the condition that occurs when the amount of water in the body falls below normal, disrupting the balance of sugars and salts (electrolytes) in the body.

delayed onset of muscle soreness (DOMS): the pain felt in the muscles the day after intense exercise.

democratic style of leadership: in sport, a style that is athlete centred, cooperative and person oriented.

Department for Culture, Media and Sport (DCMS): the government department that oversees government policy for sport.

deviance: behaviour that falls outside the norms or outside what is deemed to be acceptable.

displacement: the shortest straight-line measurement between two points.

diuretic: a drug used to increase urine formation and output.

drive theory: a theory of arousal that proposes a linear relationship between arousal and performance; as arousal increases so does the quality of performance.

E

effort arm: the part of the lever system from where the effort is applied to the fulcrum.

ego oriented: interpreting success as a sign of superiority over others.

electrolytes: the scientific term for the ions of salts such as sodium. Ions are electrically charged particles.

electrolytic balance: the proportion or concentration of electrolytes within the fluids of the body.

electron transport chain: series of chemical reactions where hydrogen is oxidised to water and large amounts (34 molecules) of ATP are generated.

elite sport: sport participated in by international performers and/or professionals or by teams performing at national or international level.

emergent leader: a leader who comes from within the group through possession of some skills.

emotional arousal: perceiving physiological arousal as indicating emotion.

energy sources: the substrates (starting chemicals) used to provide the ATP that is used for muscle contractions.

English Institute of Sport: a distributed network of support centres providing facilities and services to develop elite performers in England.

ergogenic aid: a performance-enhancing aid or substance, legal or illegal.

erythropoietin: a hormone that controls red blood cell production.

evaluation apprehension: a sense of anxiety caused by a performer's thinking that their performance is being watched and judged by somebody.

excess post-exercise oxygen consumption (EPOC): the volume of oxygen consumed above resting levels following exercise/during recovery.

F

fair play: allowing all the performers an equal chance of success and treating other performers with respect.

fast (alactacid – i.e. without lactic acid) component: oxygen used for rapid resynthesis of phosphocreatine and resaturation of myoglobin.

fast-twitch type IIa (FOG): characteristics are fast contraction, large force, fatigues easily.

fast-twitch type IIb (FG): characteristics are very rapid contractions, very large forces, fatigues very easily.

footfall: the action of the foot making contact with the ground when walking, running or jumping.

force: something that tends to cause a change in motion, measured in metres per second squared (kg/ms^{-2}).

friction: a force that opposes movement between two surfaces.

G

gamesmanship: 'bending the rules' – often seen as time wasting in some sports.

gentleman amateur: a sportsman who, because of his social position and financial situation, had no need for monetary reward from participating in sport.

glucose: the main form of carbohydrate found in the body; dissolves in blood plasma; used as an energy source.

glycaemic index: a system for ranking carbohydrates according to how quickly they are converted to glucose and enter the bloodstream, raising blood sugar levels.

glycogen: a stored form of carbohydrate found in muscle and liver; used as an energy source.

glycogen loading: a technique used by long-distance athletes to alter the body's stores of glycogen to above normal levels through changes in diet and exercise, thereby artificially increasing the amount of glycogen available during an event; also known as carbo-loading.

glycolysis: the process of breaking down glycogen into pyruvic acid, producing some (four molecules) ATP.

goal setting: a technique used to control anxiety by directing attention away from stress and towards an achievable target.

golden triangle: the link between sports events, sponsorship by businesses and the media.

gravity: the force of attraction between two bodies; force pulls objects towards the centre of the earth.

ground reaction force: the equal and opposite force given to a performer who exerts a muscular force into the ground.

group: two or more individuals interacting with each other – or connected to each other via social relationships – often with a common objective.

group dynamics: the study of, and a general term for, the interactive processes that occur between people in a group.

H

height of release: the highest point above the ground that an object is released.

HGH: artificial human growth hormone; when produced using recombinant DNA, this looks identical to the natural hormone.

hooliganism: the behaviour of those who engage in unruly, destructive or violent acts, often linked to supporters of professional football.

horizontal component: the horizontal motion of an object in a parabolic flight curve.

hyperbaric chamber: an air-tight chamber that can simulate air pressure at altitude or at depth.

hyperthermia: a condition in which body temperature is elevated to a very high level.

hypohydration: a condition in which there are very low levels of fluid in the body.

hypothermia: a potentially fatal condition occurring when the core body temperature falls below 35°C.

hypoxic tent: a form of hyperbaric chamber that simulates low-pressure or altitude conditions.

H zone: the lighter region in the centre of the A band.

I band: the light band in a myofibril.

iceberg profile: the POMS profile (e.g. higher vigour) that is associated with successful athletes.

imagery: creating mental images to escape the immediate effects of stress.

immune system: the integrated system of organs, tissues, cells, and antibodies that protects us from illness and disease.

impulse: the effect of a force acting over a period of time.

industrialisation: (of the workplace) mechanisation of the manufacturing industry.

inertia: the reluctance to change the state of motion.

interactionist theory: an explanation of behaviour that assumes that our personality depends on our traits and on the environment.

inverted U theory: a theory of arousal that considers that optimal performance occurs when the performer reaches an optimal level of arousal.

kinetic chain: a system consisting of muscles, joints, and neural components that must work together to enable optimal movement.

Krebs cycle: a series of chemical reactions in the mitochondria that oxidises acetyl CoA to carbon dioxide and combines hydrogen with hydrogen carriers.

lactate anaerobic energy system: the system that produces energy for ATP resynthesis by breaking down glucose without oxygen and producing lactate as a by-product.

lactate threshold: the level of exercise intensity at which you are producing more lactate than can be removed or resynthesised; lactic acid starts to accumulate in the bloodstream and muscle, owing to excess hydrogen combining with pyruvate to form lactate.

lactate tolerance: the ability to withstand the effects of lactic acid accumulation.

laissez-faire style of leadership: the leader makes few decisions, provides little feedback and lets the group do as it wishes.

learned helplessness: the state that occurs when a performer believes that failure is inevitable and that they have no way of changing that outcome.

Likert scale: a method of attitude measurement involving a number of statements with which respondents are asked to agree or disagree by choosing one of five positions: 'strongly agree', 'agree', 'neither agree nor disagree', disagree' and 'strongly disagree'.

locus of causality: the internal/ external factors that a performer believes caused an event or an outcome.

locus of control: the extent to which a performer believes that the outcome was within their control (or not).

Long Term Athlete Development Programme (LTAD): a generic strategy for the development of performers from the nursery to the podium. Sport NGBs adapt it to their specific needs.

macrocycle: a long-term training plan with a long-term goal, often a single competition.

maximal oxygen consumption ($\dot{V}O_2$ max): the maximum amount of oxygen taken in, transported and used by the body per minute. Also known as aerobic capacity and measured in millilitres of oxygen,

for each kilogram body weight each minute (ml/kg/min).

media: the collective name for the means of mass communication of information, usually taken to mean television, newspapers and radio.

merchandising: the practice in which the brand or image from one product is used to sell another. The most common adult-oriented merchandising is that related to professional sports teams and their players.

mesocycle: a goal-based block of training sessions.

microcycle: a repeating group/ pattern of training sessions.

mitochondria: organelles (within the cell) where chemical reactions of aerobic production take place.

moment: the turning effect produced by a force, measured in newtonmetres (Nm); also known as torque.

moment arm: the perpendicular distance from the point of application of a force to the axis of rotation.

moment of inertia: the resistance of a body to a change of state when rotating.

momentum: the quantity of motion of a body; mass × velocity.

motor unit: a motor neurone and its muscle fibres.

muscle fatigue: the decline in muscle function as muscles are used intensively and repeatedly.

muscle spindles: receptors in muscle that supply information about the changes in length of muscle and also about the rate of change in muscle length.

myofibril: part of a muscle fibre, contains sarcomeres and the contractile proteins actin and myosin.

myosin: thick protein filament.

N

national governing body: an organisation responsible for the promotion, development and regulation of a sport in the UK.

National Lottery: a national form of gambling, regulated by the government, where the proceeds are divided between prize money and good causes such as sport.

need to achieve (nAch): the motivation to succeed or attain particular goals; people with nAch-type personalities show approach behaviours.

need to avoid failure (Naf): the motivation to avoid failure; people with Naf-type personalities show avoidance behaviours.

negative deviance: behaviour that goes against the norm and has a detrimental effect on individuals and on society in general.

negative impulse: a force generated when absorbing body motion – landing.

Newton's first law: (the law of inertia) a force is needed to change a body's state of motion.

Newton's second law: the magnitude and direction of applied force determines the magnitude and direction of acceleration given to a body.

Newton's third law: (the law of action/reaction) to every action there is an equal and opposite reaction.

O

Olympism: competing in the spirit of sportsmanship with the emphasis on taking part rather than winning.

onset of blood lactacid accumulation (OBLA): the point at which lactic acid (lactate) starts to accumulate within the blood; normally a rapid increase follows.

overtraining: the physical and mental state that is due to excessive training without adequate recovery.

oxygen consumption: the amount of oxygen used by the body.

oxygen deficit: when insufficient oxygen is available at the start of exercise to provide all the ATP needed aerobically.

P

parabolic curve: the flight path of a projectile in the absence of air resistance.

pay-per-view: a system by which the television viewer can pay for a private telecast to their home of an event.

peak flow: a state in which the performance is at its best, achieved without thought, effortlessly and with total confidence.

peaking: making sure that both mind and body are at their best for a competition.

performance accomplishments: previous successes at the task.

periodisation: dividing the overall training programme into parts or periods that are designed to achieve different goals.

perpendicular: at right angles to.

personality: an individual's predisposition to behave in a certain way.

person-oriented leader: a leader who concentrates on developing interpersonal relations within the group.

phosphocreatine: an energy-rich compound of creatine and phosphoric acid, found in muscle cells.

plyometrics: a type of training designed to improve power. Plyometric exercises involve bounding, jumping or hopping to make muscle groups work eccentrically before a powerful concentric contraction.

popular recreation: recreation for the masses, involving violent, unruly 'mob games'.

positive deviance: behaviour that is outside the norm but with no intention to harm or break the rules.

positive impulse: an impulse that moves the body.

positive self-talk: developing positive thoughts about one's actions.

preferred behaviour: behaviour of the leader that is demanded by the group members.

prejudice: a preformed opinion or judgement of someone, based on irrational, incomplete or inaccurate stereotypical views.

prescribed leader: a leader who is appointed by an external source.

principle of moments: for a body to be in equilibrium (balance), the sum of the clockwise moments is equal to the sum of the anticlockwise moments about the fulcrum (pivot).

professional: a sports performer who is paid to play their sport.

Profile of Mood States (POMS): a way of measuring the moods of those who participate in sport.

progressive muscular relaxation (PMR): learning to be aware of the tension present in muscles and removing it by relaxing.

proprioception: the body's awareness of position, posture, movement and changes in state of balance.

protein drink: a drink that is approximately 70 per cent protein; it is made from powdered substances mixed with milk, orange juice, etc.

pyruvic acid/pyruvate: the end product of glycolysis.

R

radian: one radian equals 57.3 degrees.

rational recreation: the development of rules and organisation of sport.

rehabilitation: treatments designed to support the process of recovery from injury or illness, enabling the performer to regain maximum self-sufficiency and function as soon as possible.

relative deviance: deviant behaviour that is not acceptable in wider society but may be deemed to be acceptable by those involved in a sub-culture.

required behaviour: behaviour of the leader that is demanded by the situation.

resistance arm: the mass and the lever system from the mass to the fulcrum.

respiratory exchange ratio: the ratio of carbon dioxide released to oxygen used by the body.

Rest, Ice, Compression, Elevation (RICE): an immediate treatment plan for acute soft-tissue injury; it limits inflammation and swelling.

resynthesise: to rebuild/remake/make again.

reversal theory: the proposal that whether a performer views arousal as pleasant (or unpleasant) is likely to have a positive (or negative) impact on performance.

Ringelmann effect: the diminishing contribution of each individual as group size increases.

S

sarcomere: the repeating unit of a myofibril, goes from one Z line to another.

sarcoplasm: the equivalent of cytoplasm – the liquid interior of a muscle fibre.

sarcoplasmic reticulum: equivalent to the endoplasmic reticulum of cells. It forms a network of channels that spread out over the surface of the myofibrils and acts as a store of calcium ions that when released initiate muscle contraction.

scalar: a quantity that has a single dimension, magnitude.

self-confidence: a person's belief in their ability to achieve success.

self-efficacy: situation-specific self-confidence.

self-serving bias: the tendency to attribute success to internal factors and losses or failures to external factors; protects our self-esteem.

sexism: discrimination on the basis of sex, especially the oppression of women by men.

skeletal muscle: the muscle that causes our bodies to move, also called striated muscle.

slow (lactacid – i.e. with lactic acid) component: oxygen used to remove lactic acid and maintain high heart rate, breathing rate and body temperature.

slow-twitch muscle fibres: contract up 10 times as slowly as fast-twitch fibres but have greater endurance.

social cohesion: found in a group that is bound together by social bonds, social attractiveness and relationships.

social facilitation: the beneficial influence of the presence of others on performance (the others can be in the audience or coactors who are doing the same activity).

social inhibition: decrease in performance due to the presence of others.

social loafing: loss of individual effort in a group due to a reduction in motivation.

social norm: a rule that is socially enforced, or a standard of behaviour; can apply to appropriate or inappropriate values, beliefs or attitudes.

socio-economic status: an individual's position in the social structure; it depends on a combination of occupation, education, income and where they live.

sociogram: a chart showing the inter-relationships within a group.

soda loading: ingesting sodium bicarbonate to improve the buffering of hydrogen ions during anaerobic exercise.

somatic anxiety: physiological responses to a situation where a performer feels that they may be unable to cope; symptoms include increased heart rate, sweaty palms, muscle tension and feelings of nausea.

spatial summation: changes in strength of contraction are brought about by altering the number and size of motor units involved.

speed of release: the velocity of the object when it is released from the hand.

sponsorship: provision of funds or other forms of support to an individual or event in return for some commercial return.

sport coach UK: the body responsible for developing a national coaching framework and for overseeing coach education and development in the UK.

Sport England: the non-governmental body responsible for developing participation and the standards of sport in England.

sport law: the body of legislation, case law, and precedence that applies to sport.

SportsAid: a charitable organisation that raises money to support talented young performers, or those with a disability not supported by national programmes such as the World Class Performance Programme.

sportsmanship: conforming to the rules, spirit and etiquette of a sport.

stability dimension: the stable/unstable factors that a performer believes caused an event or an outcome.

stakeholder: a person, group, or organisation that affects or can be affected by an organisation's actions.

state anxiety: (A-state) anxiety felt in a particular situation.

steady state: the period of exercise when oxygen consumption matches the energy being used.

stimulant: a drug that temporarily quickens some vital process such as in the central nervous system.

supercompensation: storing more glycogen than normal.

 T

talent-identification programme: a systematic method of identifying and selecting those who have the ability or qualities to progress further to a higher competitive level.

tapering: reducing the amount of training and/or the training intensity prior to competition day.

task cohesion: found in a group that is bound together in a drive to achieve a common objective, a focus on the task.

task oriented: interpreting success as playing well.

task-oriented leader: a leader who concentrates on setting goals and completing the task as quickly as possible.

television match official: (TMO/ video referee) a sports official called upon to help adjudicate a sports match by using television footage.

testosterone: a steroid hormone that develops muscle mass and is responsible for the development of male secondary sexual characteristics.

thought-stopping: conditioning the mind to think of alternatives to the anxiety-causing negative thought.

trait anxiety: (A-trait) an enduring personality trait, giving a tendency to view all situations as threatening.

traits: innate, enduring personality characteristics that allow behaviour to be predicted.

transverse tubules: a network of folds/tubes from the membrane of a myofibril that provide access for electrical activity to the inside of the myofibril.

triadic model: a hypothetical, testable proposition that holds that attitudes are made up of three components – cognitive (what we think), affective (what we feel), behavioural (how we behave).

triglycerides: main form of stored fat; used as an energy source.

tropomyosin: thread-like protein that winds around the surface of actin.

troponin: globular protein on actin.

 U

UK Sport: the UK-wide organisation responsible for delivering world-class sporting success in conjunction with a range of partner organisations.

urbanisation: development of cities caused by the movement of the working population from rural areas (where jobs were disappearing because of mechanisation) to towns (where new jobs were being created in factories).

 V

vector: a quantity that has two dimensions, magnitude and direction.

velocity (ms⁻¹): the rate of change of displacement or displacement

divided by time, measured in metres per second.

verbal persuasion: encouragement from significant others.

vertical component: the upward motion of an object in a parabolic flight curve.

vicarious experience: watching others of similar standard successfully perform a skill.

visualisation: the process of creating a mental image of what you want to happen or feel.

 W

Whole Sport Plan: a four-year plan produced by an NGB for the development of its sport; it determines the level of funding from Sport England.

World Anti-Doping Agency (WADA): established in 1999, the agency is responsible for promoting, coordinating, and monitoring at international level the fight against the use of drugs in sport.

World Class Performance Pathway: the template by which support is provided to elite performers, depending on how close they are to winning medals at international level.

World Games: sport competitions involving individuals, clubs or national teams in world, continental or regional championships.

 Z

Z line: the darker region in the centre of the I band.

zone of optimal functioning: the area between the upper and lower levels of arousal within which optimal performance takes place.

Index

Note: key terms are in **bold**

Gower College Swansea
Library
Coleg Gŵyr Abertawe
Llyrfgell